All the
POPE'S MEN

ALSO BY JOHN L. ALLEN, JR.

Conclave: The Politics, Personalities,
and Process of the Next Papal Election

Cardinal Ratzinger: The Vatican's Enforcer of the Faith

All the POPE'S MEN

THE INSIDE STORY OF HOW THE VATICAN REALLY THINKS

JOHN L. ALLEN, JR.

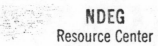

NDEG
Resource Center

Doubleday

New York   London   Toronto   Sydney   Auckland

PUBLISHED BY DOUBLEDAY
a division of Random House, Inc.

DOUBLEDAY and the portrayal of an anchor with a dolphin are
registered trademarks of Random House, Inc.

Book design by Donna Sinisgalli

Library of Congress Cataloging-in-Publication Data

Allen, John L., 1965–
All the Pope's men : the inside story of how the Vatican really thinks /
John L. Allen, Jr.
p.   cm.
Includes bibliographical references.
1. Catholic Church. Curia Romana.   2. Vatican City.   I. Title.

BX1818.A46 2003
282'.136—dc22
2003067484

ISBN 0-385-50966-9

PRINTED IN THE UNITED STATES OF AMERICA

July 2004

7 9 10 8 6

To Raymond and Laura Frazier, my grandparents, whose love made this book possible; to the Capuchin Franciscans in Hays, Kansas, whose wisdom helped to make the book intelligible; to my colleagues in Rome and at the National Catholic Reporter, *whose companionship made researching and writing the book enjoyable; and to my wife, Shannon, whose unfailing support made the book a reality.*

CONTENTS

INTRODUCTION

The aim of this book is to promote better informed, and hopefully less acrimonious, conversation between the Vatican and the English-speaking world by identifying the core values and experiences that underlie specific Vatican policy choices. In that way, discussion can be based on real, as opposed to presumed, motives, and thus can be more akin to genuine dialogue. The book is rooted in my experience of covering the Vatican on a daily basis in Rome, as well as following the Pope to scores of spots around the world, and then translating these experiences for English-speaking audiences. I approach this work both as a journalist and as a Catholic, and it's probably in order here to say a word about each.

As a journalist, my goal is to inform and to explain. I want to tell readers what's happening, but I also want to help them understand why it's happening and what importance it might have. This way of conceiving the task takes me beyond the strict objectivity of simply "recording the news," in the way that a wire service such as the Associated Press or Reuters approaches things, and into the more subjective realm of context, background, and consequences. I stop short, however, of offering my personal opinion on the news, such as whether a particular Vatican document or policy choice is right or wrong, good or bad, successful or not. First of all, I doubt most readers care what John Allen thinks (though I'm always surprised, based on my mail, how many people are convinced they *know* what I think, and how often these hypotheses contradict one another). In any event, my personal conclusion would be the least interesting aspect of any story. Far more intriguing is trying to ferret out where a particular Vatican choice came from, how it reflects the logic and psychology of the institution, and what implications it might have across a range of other issues. This work of analysis aids readers in forming their own judgments, and I hope my journalism is of equal interest to all parties—liberal and conservatives, Vatican critics and defenders, reformers and traditionalists. I do not intend to take sides. Of course, this describes my *intent*, and how well I pull it off is for others to judge.

Despite the fact that I'm Catholic, I do not view covering the Vatican as a religious mission. The principal danger with many Catholic journalists is that they tend to fall into one of two camps: either Catholics angry with the institution seeking to reform it or Catholics in love with the institution seeking to propagate it. Both can be noble instincts, and I believe they can coexist in the same soul. Neither, however, makes a good point of departure for analytical journalism, because both end up skewing one's judgment toward one side of arguments that are always complex. I do not see my role as promoting a particular set of theological or ecclesiastical conclusions. Truth to be told, in many cases I wouldn't have personal judgments to offer even if I thought someone wanted to hear them. One puzzling aspect of public discussion these days is the way that everyone is expected to have an opinion on everything, regardless of what they actually know about the subject. My experience is that the more shades of gray you perceive in a situation, the harder it usually is to be definitive about who's right and who's wrong. Personally, I'm not sure if celibacy should be made optional, or if the Pope should travel less, or whether celebrating Mass with both priest and people facing East would enhance the reverence of the liturgy. I can see good arguments on all sides. What I can talk about with authority, however, is what the main points of contention surrounding these issues are, what values motivate the various parties to the debate, and what consequences might flow from particular choices. That's the service I can offer as a journalist, and it is the spirit in which this book is written.

The suspicion that I *must* have a theological agenda is sometimes exacerbated by the fact that the newspaper I write for, the *National Catholic Reporter*, is widely identified as the leading voice of liberal Catholicism in the English-speaking world. Some readers assume I must be trying to push a liberal point of view, and if it's not obvious how I'm doing that, it's probably because I was especially crafty at concealing my premises. It's true that my paper does express a strong perspective on its editorial pages, but thankfully I'm left clear of all that. I don't write the paper's editorials, and am rarely consulted about them. In terms of my own work, I have never been pressured by *NCR* to pursue a particular story, or to take a particular line, in order to score an ideological point. I have always felt free to try to describe the reality of the Holy See as honestly and fairly as possible. When I have occasionally disappointed or angered some elements of the readership, the editors have always stood by me. The fact that I am paid by a newspaper with a strong editorial line does not, I hope, mean I am incapable of living up to the journalistic aims described above. All I ask is that readers judge my work on its merits. In the same way, it's true that I was raised, educated, and acquired most of my professional experience prior to Rome in moderate-to-liberal American Catholic environments. But everyone emerges from a particular context; that can't be helped. The question is how well one is able to bring other points of view into focus and to do them justice. That's a discipline the Thomist in me wants to believe everyone, at least in principle, is capable of exercising.

It would be disingenuous, however, to suggest that my work is value-neutral with respect to my religious affiliation. As a Catholic, I hope my journalism is of value to my Church. I see that contribution, however, not in terms of steering the Church in some specific direction, but in facilitating conversation among Catholics that is informed and respectful. After four years of covering the Vatican, my perception is that often people base their judgments about "Rome" on misconceptions and mythology, imputing motives or making assumptions that are either inaccurate or, at best, highly selective. Lacking context, people spin off into accusation and acrimony. By providing better information and context, I hope I can promote better understanding.

As an American Catholic, I see this work as especially crucial because quite often America and Rome are not on good speaking terms. I saw this repeatedly during both the sexual abuse crisis and the war in Iraq, both cases in which many American Catholics, though not necessarily the same ones on both issues, felt misunderstood, even sometimes betrayed, by the Vatican. Officials in the Holy See felt equally uncomfortable, dismayed, and even occasionally scandalized by what they saw coming from the American Catholic community. The emotion on both sides often reflected incomprehension. Communication between Rome and America was sometimes impossible, not because there was nothing to talk about, but because the two parties were talking past each other, making assumptions that were often flawed and then responding to those assumptions rather than to what was really motivating the other. Americans, for example, often assumed that the Vatican's "real" concern in both the sex abuse crisis and the war was maintaining its own power, while officials in the Holy See sometimes suspected that what was really motivating the Americans in both cases was money. In truth, neither factor explains very much, as we will see later on in chapters 6 (the sex abuse crisis) and 7 (the Iraq war).

My agenda in my work qua Catholic is to bring the local church from which I come, that of the United States and, more broadly, the English-speaking world, into more fruitful conversation with the center of the universal Church in Rome. Naturally, putting things this way glosses over much complexity; not every English-speaking Catholic and not every Vatican official thinks alike. These are ideal types, not real people. Still, there is a genuine communications problem between Rome and the world I write for, and it fuels an atmosphere of division that is not in anyone's interest. At the very least, I hope this book will help English-speaking Catholics see that in many cases the values Rome is striving to protect are dear to them too, even if they differ on specific applications, and that this shared set of values provides a basis for dialogue. If one wants to place a theological label on this, I suppose it would be *communion*. I hope to serve communion in the Church by helping Catholics speak the same language.

Striving to explain the Vatican is a slippery business, however, because it is easily confused with trying to justify the Vatican. This point was brought home for me one night in May 2002, during the peak of the sexual abuse crisis in the Catholic Church in the United States. CNN, the network for which I serve as a Vatican analyst, had asked me to appear on that night's segment of Q&A, which usually has two guests representing different points of view, plus a host who fires questions back and forth. This particular night, the lineup featured a victim of sexual abuse at the hands of a Catholic priest and me. Perhaps it was naivete on my part, but it never occurred to me that the producer for Q&A expected me to play the role of someone "opposed" to the victim. That didn't become clear until about three minutes into the show, which went out live, after the host had asked the victim to tell his terrifying story of being abused by a trusted priest when he was ten years old. This guest, a soft-spoken and articulate young man of perhaps twenty-five, described in heartbreaking terms the psychological fallout from that experience. He added that he was repeatedly ignored when he sought acknowledgment from Church officials, above all from the bishop whose job should have been to protect him, and failing that, to give him comfort when the Church had let him down.

The host took it all in, paused for dramatic effect, then flung the gauntlet down: "John Allen, how can you possibly justify that?"

After choking back a wave of panic, I tried calmly to explain that I had no way to justify this person's suffering, nor was I inclined to justify it, and what's more, it was not my role to do so. My job is to analyze and explain the Vatican, not defend it. I could, and did, explain the logic that might have led the Vatican to approve of bishops trying to keep struggling priests afloat, in part out of a sense of brotherhood within the clerical fraternity, in part out of a need to fill slots in a priest shortage. I could, and did, also try to explain why the Vatican does not step in and clean house when bishops fail, because the understanding of the bishop's office is quite different in Rome from the corporate model many Anglo-Saxon Catholics hold. But it's not my job to tell CNN's viewers, or my readers in the *National Catholic Reporter*, whether these Vatican perspectives are right or wrong, good or bad, adequate to the task of resolving the crisis or not.

The danger that journalists will be seen as apologists is compounded on my beat because the Vatican often does such a poor job of telling its own story. If this had been the White House, or the Pentagon, or IBM, CNN would have had no problem filling its slot with a smooth-talking spokesperson who could have articulated the institution's point of view. When there is a major news story breaking, American institutions deploy an army of spin doctors to get their message out. Look how many talking heads the Bush team provided every day during the Iraq war to make sure we got the news and perspective the White House and Pentagon wanted us to get. The Vatican simply does not respond this way. Reflecting the ethos of an age before 24/7 news cycles, the Vatican still believes in communicating only when it has something to say. Most of the time when colleagues in either the broadcast or print media are looking for someone to speak on behalf of the Vatican, they can't find anyone and are forced to resort to "expert commentators" to represent the Vatican's view. Ironically, therefore, on TV and radio I am often cast in the role of balancing out the Vatican critics. This is a precarious situation for a journalist, because it can easily lead to confusion about one's role.

A related problem is that English-language journalism generally does not take the Vatican seriously. This also fuels misunderstanding. The Rome correspondent for The *New York Times*, for example, is responsible not just for the Vatican, but for Italian politics, finance, and culture, as well as the Southern Mediterranean, plus some of Central and Eastern Europe. The current occupant of the post says that he devotes roughly 25 percent of his time to the Vatican. For the broadcast media, the situation is about the same. To take but one example,

CNN's Rome bureau chief missed every Vatican story from late February 2003 until early May because he was imbedded with the Marine Expeditionary Force in Iraq. Yet the *Times* and CNN are fortunate to even have people in town. Most American news outlets parachute someone into Rome to cover the Vatican when something breaks, expecting them to "figure it out as they go along." The irony is that the Vatican is perhaps the world's most singular institution, utterly unlike anything else an English-speaking journalist has ever encountered. It is not city hall or the White House. For one thing, most business here is conducted in Italian. Beyond that, there's the question of context. On the White House beat, a reference to something that happened in the Clinton administration is considered ancient history. Around the Vatican, it's nothing for officials to cite decisions made by regional church councils in the fourth century. If a reporter doesn't have at least some background in Church history and theology to make sense of such things, it's a prescription for misunderstanding. The result is that English-language reporters tend to rely on a stock set of great myths about the Vatican, recycling them endlessly in different combinations. This is not principally the fault of the reporters, most of whom are talented professionals doing the best they can. But bad judgments and sloppy conclusions are inevitable when news organizations don't invest the resources necessary for reporters to do their jobs. The bottom line is that English-language coverage of the Vatican often sheds more heat than light.

All the Pope's Men is thus an attempt to understand how the Vatican thinks, why it reacts in certain ways and not others, how it sees the world. The book's aim is to open up the psychology and culture of the Vatican, so that outsiders can understand what the institution values, what it fears, and what its instinctive patterns of behavior are. It will provide a few facts and a bit of history about the Vatican, but that is not its primary purpose. Many other books offer basic information about Vatican structures, personnel, history, scandals, and vicissitudes. The aim here is different. My intent is to sketch a psychological profile, to explain the Vatican from the inside out, not in terms of its structures, but of its mind. My hope is that after reading this book, a reader will be able to ponder the next Vatican appointment, policy choice, or document and say: "Ah yes, I see where that comes from. I see why they did that."

I come to this subject as one of a handful of journalists working in the English language whose full-time specialization is covering the Vatican from Rome. Day in and day out, I follow the liturgical disputes, theological controversies, makings of saints, comings and goings of bishops and diplomats, and all the rest of the flotsam and jetsam that make up the daily business of the headquarters of the Roman Catholic Church. A few times a year, I go up to the papal apartments to watch John Paul receive some head of state or other dignitary, and sometimes I get a chance to exchange a quick word with the Pope afterward. (The Pope, unlike presidents and prime ministers, does not give interviews.) Almost every day takes me into the Vatican on some bit of business. I've taken a seemingly endless string of curial officials to lunch and dinner, the two occasions of the Roman day when most real business seems to get done. I've been to hundreds of roundtable discussions, conferences, symposia, book presentations, and press conferences held by every imaginable group, movement, and force in the Catholic Church. I also move when the Pope moves, so I've followed John Paul II all over the globe—to Greece and Syria, Kazakhstan and Armenia, Bulgaria, Canada and Guatemala and Mexico, Poland, Croatia and Bosnia-Herzegovina. Over the years, I've probably interviewed at least two hundred people who work in the Roman Curia in one way, shape, or form and spent countless more hours in informal conversation about their lives and work.

My task is to make all this activity intelligible for an English-speaking audience, helping readers understand why the Vatican does what it does. Like Margaret Mead in *Coming of Age in Samoa*, I see my-self as engaged in a sort of cultural anthropology, trying to explain the way inhabitants of a remote island—in this case, a 108-acre walled compound in the middle of Rome—think, act, and live. I do this every week in the pages of the *National Catholic Reporter* and in my weekly Internet column on the *NCR* website called "The Word from Rome," as well as from time to time on CNN and National Public Radio. I also lecture in America and Canada, taking questions of the "everything you always wanted to know but were afraid to ask" variety about the Vatican, the Pope, and the Catholic Church. I've lived in Rome for four years, learning to negotiate the "cultural gap" that so often separates the people I write about from those I write for.

One final point about my aims and assumptions. I said above I want to foster informed and respectful conversation. Part of respect is taking others at their word about the logic for their decisions, and treating seriously the arguments they provide for particular actions and choices. Thus when I cover the Vatican, I do not start with the assumption that Church officials are guilty until proven innocent and that the Vatican's motives for any given decision can be assumed to revolve around power and self-interest unless shown otherwise. To tell the truth, my experience is that most of the time Vatican officials are trying to make the best calls they can for the common good of the Church, based on the information available to them and the political and theological convictions they hold. One can debate the wisdom of those judgment calls, and I hope this book will provide tools to do that, but the debate will suffer from fatal confusion unless the challengers appreciate the values Vatican officials are seeking to defend and the logic that led them to particular decisions.

What I have just written may come as a jolt to those of a certain mentality accustomed to thinking of Vatican officials as the heavies, casting the outsiders, prophets, and reformers as the heroes. I understand that view. In my career I've had the good fortune of knowing some of these prophets, and they can indeed be impressive people, pressing the Church to realize its best self. On the Catholic left, such figures might include Sr. Joan Chittister or Fr. Hans Küng; on the right, one thinks of Fr. Richard Neuhaus or Bishop Fabian Bruskewitz of Lincoln, Nebraska. Although all are quite different from one another, they share the courage to speak out about what they believe is wrong with the Church, to risk giving offense for the sake of speaking the truth that they see. Their relations with the institutional Church, or at least with certain elements of it, can sometimes be painful. This is true even of someone like Bruskewitz, who is himself a member of the hierarchy, but who is willing to challenge ecclesiastical structures or personnel if he sees them as compromised.

Yet there is a sometimes forgotten, but very powerful, compensation that comes with being a prophet: for those who share your point of view, you are a celebrity. I have attended conferences of the liberal Call to Action group, for example, at which popular reformers such as James Carroll and Eugene Kennedy are greeted with rapturous standing ovations. On the other side of the street, I have listened to young men at the North American College, where U.S. seminarians preparing for the priesthood in Rome live, swap stories about handshakes with papal biographer George Weigel like other young people might talk about meeting one of the Rolling Stones. Prophets may sometimes be struck down by the powerful, but they are also lifted up by their disciples. They have the opportunity, at least within a certain circle, to receive wide acclaim and affirmation.

Most of the men and women of the Roman Curia I know will never have this experience. Fr. Frans Thoolen, a plucky Dutch priest who works in the Pontifical Council for Migrants and Refugees, will probably never walk into a crowded ballroom and hear a packed room explode in applause for him. Long lines of people will probably never cue up to have Fr. Donald Bolen, a soft-spoken Canadian who works the Anglican/Methodist desk in the Pontifical Council for Promoting Christian Unity, sign a book. Catholics are not likely to tell their grandchildren about the time they met Sr. Sharon Holland, a quietly effective American, in the Congregation for Religious. Those who work in the Roman Curia are generally not public figures, and the occasional media darling such as Cardinal Joseph Ratzinger is the exception that proves the rule. Vatican officials are involved in the art of the possible, making compromises rather than waves, trying to get things done. By definition and necessity, most of their work is in the shadows. In most cases, the documents into which they pour their blood, sweat, and tears will never bear their names. Their role in forging steps forward in Catholic tradition will likely be known only to a small circle of experts. Such is the cost of progress in a bureaucracy that can only move so far, so fast. The Roman Catholic Church, as I am fond of saying, is not built for speed.

Any social institution needs both its prophets and its bureaucrats. It needs those who will create a clamor for reform from the outside, but it also needs those who will do the hard, patient work of making change happen from within. The person who chooses to labor on the inside, without adulation, exercises a different, but, to my way of thinking, equally real kind of courage. Many of these men and women have put their own desires on hold to do this work, because they think it's important. Some have sacrificed careers as academics, or pastors, or missionaries in order to answer the Church's call to serve at a desk in Rome. I have learned to respect their choice, and I hope this book bears the imprint of that respect.

Much of the research for this book arose from the daily experience of covering the Vatican over four years. I also wanted to test my own perceptions, however, against those of the men and women who serve in and around the Holy See. I therefore conducted thirty-five interviews specifically for *All the Pope's Men*, most with officials of the nine congregations, eleven councils, three tribunals, and other offices that make up the papal bureaucracy. I aimed for a representative sampling across different types of offices, as well as different nationalities and linguistic backgrounds. I also included a few heads of religious orders who have regular contact with the Vatican and a couple of diplomats accredited to the Holy See. In every case, the condition of the interview was that the individual would not be identified by name or even acknowledged in a general way in this introduction. This was both to ensure that people felt free to speak candidly, but also a concession to the requirement of the Vatican's employee handbook that officials below the level of undersecretary must have the authorization of their superiors before submitting to an interview. Thus I can only express a generalized note of deep thanks to these remarkable souls who move the levers of the institutional Catholic Church and who helped me understand their world.

A number of other people have been instrumental in making this book possible, often without realizing they were doing so. I want to acknowledge those who contributed to whatever virtues the book may possess. First a word of thanks to my colleagues in the Vatican press corps: Gerard O'Connell, Giancarlo Zizola, Gianni Cardinale, Phillip Pullella, Orazio Petrosillo, Marco Politi, Marco Tosatti, Luigi Accattoli, Victor Simpson, Sylvia Poggioli, Greg Burke, John Thavis, Cindy Wooden, John Norton, Robert Blair Kaiser, Robert Mickens, Jeff Israely, Jim Bitterman, Alessio Vinci, Hada Messia, Robert Moynihan, Delia Gallagher, Sandro Magister, Allen Pizzey, Bill Blakemore, Keith Miller, Bruno Bartoloni, Anna Matranga, Paddy Agnew, Frank Bruni, Melinda Henneberger, Alessandra Stanley, Richard Boudreaux, Tracy Wilkinson, Manuela Borraccino, Richard Owen, Dennis Redmont, Franca Giansoldati, David Willey, Ludwig Ring-Eifel, Andreas Englisch, Renzo Giacomelli, Giovanni Avena, Eletta Cucuzza, Ewout Kieckens, Philippa Hitchens, Charles Collins, Tracy McClure, and many others. They have offered me several lifetimes' worth of insight, expertise, and friendship.

I also want to acknowledge other friends and colleagues who have offered me valuable nuggets, even if they were not conscious that their contribution would help shape this book: George Weigel, Fr. Thomas Reese, Fr. Richard McBrien, Fr. Andrew Greeley, Fr. Richard Neuhaus, Fr. Timothy Radcliffe, Fr. Peter-Hans Kolvenbach, Fr. John Jay Hughes, Giovanni Ferro, James Nicholson, Brent Hardt, Alberto Melloni, Fr. Antoine Bodar, Fr. Antonio Pernia, Austin Ruse, Fr. Bernardo Cervellera, Bill Burrows, Fr. Borys Gudziak, Fr. Brian Johnstone, Fr. Bruce Harbert, Fr. Bruce Williams, Sr. Clare Pratt, Fr. Daniel Madigan, Fr. Dan McCarthy, Fr. Keith Pecklers, Fr. Mark Francis, Fr. David Fleming, Fr. David Jaeger, Fr. Dennis Billy, Fr. Donald Cozzens, Donna Orsuto, Fr. Drew Christiansen, Eugene Fisher, Rick McCord, Duncan MacLaren, Erich Leitenberger, Christa Pongratz, Ernesto Galli della Loggia, Sr. Filo Hirota, Fr. James Moroney, Francis Pimentel-Pinto, Fr. Franco Imoda, Fr. Michael Hilbert, Fr. James Puglisi, Hubert Feichtlbauer, Fr. Jacques Dupuis, Fr. James Hentges, James Walston, Fr. Jeremy Driscoll, Fr. John Baldovin, Fr. John Huels, John Page, Fr. John

Wauck, Fr. Robert Gahl, Marc Carroggio, Fr. Flavio Capucci, Fr. Jose de Vera, Julia O'Sullivan, Fr. Ken Nowakowski, Fr. Kieran O'Reilly, Robert Mickens, John Wilkins, Margaret Hebblethwaite, Austen Ivereigh, Sr. Marie MacDonald, Mario Marazziti, Francesco Dante, Claudio Mario Betti, Fr. Mark Morozowich, Markus Bakermans, Michael Novak, Michael Waldstein, Nelly Stienstra, Fr. Nikolaus Klein, Fr. Nokter Wolf, Otto Friedrich, Fr. Paul Robichaud, Fr. Greg Apparcel, Fr. Jim Moran, Fr. Peter Phan, Phillip Jenkins, Fr. Raymond de Souza, Fr. Robert Geisinger, Fr. Robert Taft, Fr. Joseph Tobin, Fr. Peter Jacobs, Fr. Ron Roberson, Russell Shaw, Fr. Sebastian Karotemprel, David Clohessy, Richard Gaillardetz, Salvador Miranda, Fabrizio Mastrofini, Fr. Stephen Privett, Fr. Ted Keating, Fr. Thomas Green, Fr. Thomas Michel, Fr. Thomas Rosica, Thomas Seiterich-Kreuzkamp, Fr. Thomas Splain, Fr. Thomas Williams, Fr. Anthony McSweeney, Fr. Virgil Funk, Fr. William Henn, Fr. Willy Ollevier, Fr. Gerald O'Collins, Fr. Michael Scully, Archbishop Charles Chaput, Bishop Howard Hubbard, Bishop William Skylstad, Cardinal Roger Mahony, Cardinal James Francis Stafford, and Archbishop Michael Fitzgerald.

To Trace Murphy at Doubleday goes my thanks for his interest and support, especially as the concept for *All the Pope's Men* took a few twists and turns along the way. To Tom Fox, Tom Roberts, and the rest of the team at the *National Catholic Reporter* go my thanks for their constant support, including allowing me to take three weeks in the summer of 2003 to work on this project. Cardinal James Francis Stafford, Archbishop Charles Chaput, Bishop Howard Hubbard, Gianni Cardinale, Sandro Magister, Fr. Tom Reese, Fr. Gerald O'Collins, Fr. Donald Cozzens, Phil Pullella, Greg Burke, Fr. John Huels, and Richard Gaillardetz were generous in reading portions of the manuscript and offering comments. Obviously, the book's defects remain my own. The staff of the Park Hotel ai Cappuccini in Gubbio, Italy, was magnificent. I cannot recommend the facility or the people highly enough.

Much of this book was written in Gubbio from July 10–31, 2003. Word reached us upon our arrival that on July 9, 2003, Gary MacEoin had died at the age of ninety-four. Gary was a reporter, author, editor, and human rights activist who specialized in the politics and poverty of the Third World, especially Latin America, and a longtime contributor to the *National Catholic Reporter*. He was also a friend. It was Gary who had suggested to Shannon and I years ago that we should visit Gubbio, saying it was his favorite spot in Italy. We filed the information away for a rainy day and finally got around to acting on it when I needed a place to write. I believe it's not an accident that I sat down to work on this book just as the lights finally went out in those magnificent Irish eyes, and that some of Gary's magic was meant to find me here. I hope at least a small part of his passion and his integrity finds an echo in these pages.

1

VATICAN 101

*I*f you mill about St. Peter's Square long enough, you will eventually see a black Mercedes sedan exiting from the Vatican, bearing a cardinal or a gentleman of His Holiness to some important engagement. (The "gentlemen" are Italian laymen, often from noble families linked to the papacy for centuries, who help the Pope greet visiting dignitaries and assist at other ceremonial occasions.) The passenger is usually seated in the rear, dressed to the nines, projecting an air of worldly power and importance. One can sometimes be forgiven for straining to see the connection between such affectation and the gospel of Jesus Christ. The world-weary Romans, who have seen it all over the centuries, have developed a kind of gallows humor for resolving the tension between the high ideals of the Church and its human realities. For example, those sedans from the Vatican bear license plates that read "SCV," which stands for *Stato della Città del Vaticano*, Vatican City State. The Romans, however, say that it really means *Se Cristo vedesse . . .* If only Christ could see.

Similar jokes at the expense of the human side of the Vatican are legendary. Monsignor Ronald Knox, an Anglican who joined the Catholic Church, once famously quipped: "On the barque of Peter, those with queasy stomachs should keep clear of the engine room." (*Barque* is an antiquated word for boat. Thus "barque of Peter" is an old, but still venerable, metaphor for the Catholic Church.) Here's another classic. Question: Why is Rome such a spiritual city? Answer: Because so many people have lost their faith in it. Even popes sometimes get in on the cynical act. Beloved roly-poly Pope John XXIII (1958–1963) was once asked how many people work in the Vatican, to which he is supposed to have replied: "About half."

Yet the Catholic Church, like any social movement, needs an institution with which it can organize its common life. Without an institution, a social phenomenon dies. It's not enough for Roman Catholics merely to have the Pope as a symbolic figurehead. The Church needs structures with teeth in order to make decisions, and to keep its 1-billion-strong worldwide membership in some kind of basic unity. Decisions have to be made about what the Church teaches, how it worships, and what position it's going to take on important issues. Thus the Catholic Church needs a central administrative system through which information can circulate, contacts can be maintained, and decisions can be communicated and enforced. If Roman Catholicism did not have the Vatican, it would have to invent it.

This was what Pope Innocent III meant when he wrote to the bishops of France in 1198: "Although the Lord has given us the fullness of power in the Church, a power that makes us owe something to all Christians, still we cannot stretch the limits of human nature. Since we cannot deal personally with every single concern—the law of human condition does not suffer it—we are sometimes constrained to use certain brothers of ours as extensions of our own body, to take care of things we would rather deal with in person if the convenience of the Church allowed it." Pope Sixtus V was equally candid in 1588 in *Immensa aeterni Dei*: "The Roman Pontiff, whom Christ the Lord constituted as visible head of his body, the Church, and appointed for the care of all the Churches, calls and rallies unto himself many collaborators for this immense responsibility . . . so that he, the holder of the key of all this power, may share the huge mass of business and responsibilities among them—i.e., the cardinals—and the other authorities of the Roman Curia, and by God's helping grace avoid breaking under the strain."

The aim of this book is to explain how the Vatican thinks, not to focus on its structures. Yet those structures influence the psychology and culture, so some understanding of terms such as *Vatican, Holy See, congregation, superior,* and so on is essential. This chapter covers that basic ground, laying out the vocabulary one needs to have and offering an organizational overview that will at least hint at who's who and what's what. Think of this as a basic survey course in college that lays the foundation for more advanced study, a kind of Vatican 101. This will be quick and, for experts, frustratingly schematic. Readers wishing a deeper treatment will want to consult the classic on the subject, *La Curia Romana: Lineamenti Storico-Giuridici* by Niccolò del Re, published by the Vatican Publishing House in 1998. It is a comprehensive work, truly the best resource for this material, and much of the highlights in this section are drawn from Re's book. For those who don't read Italian, the best resource in English is *Inside the Vatican: The Politics and Organization of the Catholic Church,* by Fr. Thomas J. Reese, editor of the Jesuit-run *America* magazine.

THE POPE

A properly theological understanding of the Pope as the successor of St. Peter and the instrument of unity for the Church is offered in chapter 5. Here we'll take a more functional approach, asking what does the Pope *do?* One good way of answering that question is to consult the *Code of Canon Law,* which is the supreme law of the Catholic Church. Its answer is clear: the Pope is the man on whose desk the buck stops. Canon 331 describes the papacy this way: "The office uniquely committed by the Lord to Peter, the first of the Apostles, and to be transmitted to his successors, abides in the Bishop of the Church of Rome. He is the head of the College of Bishops, the Vicar of Christ, and the Pastor of the universal Church here on earth. Consequently, by virtue of his office, he has supreme, full, immediate and universal ordinary power in the Church, and he can always freely exercise this power." To use the language of political science, the Pope holds full executive, legislative, and judicial power in the Catholic Church. There are no "checks and balances" as in a modern secular state. It's often said that the Catholic Church is not a democracy, and from a canonical point of view that's right on the money. (This leads to the old joke that the Catholic Church is an absolute monarchy tempered by selective disobedience!) That should not be understood, however, in the pejorative sense that the Church is not accountable to anyone. The Church has its own system of accountability, and we will say more about that later.

Yet to put the accent on the Pope's power is, in a sense, to put the cart before the horse. Many non-Catholics don't realize, for example, that the Catholic Church had popes for nineteen hundred years before it had a formal dogma of papal infallibility. The Church has clarified the powers of the papacy over a long historical process, which implies that the Church knew what the Pope's job was well before it could list all the tools popes need to do it. The papacy is in the first place an *idea*, the conviction that Christ commissioned Peter to be the head of his Church, and that this role is passed on through time to Peter's successors. As the successor of Peter, the Pope is the agent of unity who holds the Catholic Church together across space and through time. The powers of the office are the institutional expression of this spiritual and sacramental identity.

One traditional way to understand what the Pope does would be to list his titles: His Holiness; Bishop of Rome; Vicar of Jesus Christ; Successor of St. Peter; Prince of the Apostles; Supreme Pontiff of the Universal Church; Patriarch of the West; Servant of the Servants of God; Primate of Italy; Archbishop and Metropolitan of the Roman Province; Sovereign of the Vatican City State. Such language, however, doesn't mean a great deal to modern ears. A more illuminating way to proceed is to consider the papacy's various real-world functions, which will be discussed here in terms of concentric circles representing different zones of responsibility.

The first and tightest circle is constituted by Rome, because the Pope is the Bishop of Rome and hence responsible for the affairs of his local diocese. Historically, the Pope came to govern the universal Church largely because Rome was its most important point of reference. Rome today has 2.5 million Catholics, according to 2003 figures from the *Annuario Pontifico*, with 334 parishes and 5,331 priests. Rome is a complex urban archdiocese, with all the spiritual, pastoral, financial, and administrative challenges that entails. In fact, the Pope doesn't take the government of the diocese personally into his own hands. He appoints a vicar, currently the powerful Cardinal Camillo Ruini, to handle its daily business. At the same time, however, the Pope remains an unsurpassed moral authority in urban affairs. In the summer of 2000, for example, the Roman city council rescinded a $200,000 contribution and official backing for an international gay rights festival because the Pope disapproved. (The march went ahead, however, thus illustrating at the same time the limits of the Pope's influence.)

Moving to the next circle, the Pope is also the supreme governor and legislator of the Catholic Church. He is responsible for setting policy, such as what theological ideas are acceptable, what liturgical practices pass muster, which saints to canonize, which bishops to appoint, and how to use the Church's charitable resources. He makes decisions about finance and personnel, scholarship and service, morality and metaphysics. Further, just as in the ancient Roman empire every citizen had a right of appeal to the emperor, every Catholic has the right to take his or her case to the Pope. This does not mean that Mrs. Smith's complaint about her son's third-grade religion teacher is necessarily going to end up on the Pope's desk. Most appeals are handled much further down the chain of command. But a few of these matters do reach the Pope, because they raise questions of doctrine or discipline that his subordinates believe the Pope himself should resolve or because the Pope takes a personal interest.

Inside the next ring, the Pope is the most important leader within the broader Christian world, and thus the most important force, for good or ill, in ecumenism—the effort to reunify the badly fractured

Christian family. (The *World Christian Encyclopedia* identifies over 34,000 separate Christian groups, not counting the myriad storefront Christian churches all over the world that have no institutional affiliation.) John Paul II made the thrust for unity one of the cornerstones of his pontificate, beginning with his outreach to the 250-million strong Eastern Orthodox churches. The Roman Catholic Church carries on a formal dialogue with almost every organized Christian denomination, and there are desk officers in the Vatican whose job is to liaison with these other Christian groups. (The Vatican hesitates to call all these bodies "churches" for theological reasons. A "church" has to have valid ministers and sacraments, which, in the Catholic view, many Western Protestant bodies do not.)

In the next circle lies the Pope's function as the chief spokesperson for Christianity in dialogue with other religions. Roman Catholicism is the largest and most visible branch of Christianity and that makes the Pope the superstar par excellence of the Christian world. To put the matter crassly: If the Archbishop of Canterbury, or the president of the Lutheran World Federation, visits Madras or Jakarta, he has to catch cabs like everyone else. If the Pope visits, he's a celebrity. By virtue of his high profile, the Pope has overwhelming influence on Christianity's relationship with the other religions of the world. John Paul has made this aspect of his job a priority, especially with both Judaism and Islam, the other major Western faiths. He became the first Pope to visit a Jewish synagogue in Rome in 1986, and the first Pope to enter an Islamic mosque in Damascus in May 2001. Three times he has called the religious leaders of humanity to Assisi together to pray on behalf of peace, a choice that was not popular inside his own circle of advisors. Some worried that the image of the Pope standing in a circle with shamans and Native Americans, Jewish rabbis and Buddhist monks promoted relativism (the idea that one religion is as good as another) and syncretism (a blending of elements of different religions into a kind of New Age pastiche). Obviously, however, John Paul was not deterred.

Inside the next circle one finds the Pope as the most important voice for religious belief in a secularized, skeptical world. Contemporary Western culture is often allergic to authority and hostile to tradition, and finds religion, especially religious institutions, hard to accept. The Pope is the most visible representative of institutional religion on earth and the most important dialogue partner with this largely arelegious culture. A Pope seen as compassionate and humble, with a relevant moral and spiritual message, can reawaken religious sensibility in people for whom it may have been long dormant. A Pope perceived as arrogant and hypocritical can deaden spiritual receptivity.

Finally, the outermost circle represents the Pope's role as a moral teacher, a voice of conscience for humanity on social and political questions. As such, there is almost nothing under the sun about which a Pope is not expected to pronounce, whether it's global warming or land mines or whether the United States should send in peacekeeping troops to restore order in Liberia. This makes the Pope an important player in world politics, a role that has never been more clear than during the U.S.-led war in Iraq. In the weeks leading up to the war, diplomatic heavyweights shuttled in and out of the Vatican like clients at a popular deli: Tony Blair, Joschka Fischer, Silvio Berlusconi, José María Aznar, Mohammad Reza Khatami (speaker of the Iranian parliament and brother of the country's president), Kofi Annan, and even Tarik Aziz. John Paul dispatched emissaries to both Saddam Hussein and George Bush to try to pull them back from the brink. The initiative failed in terms of preventing the conflict, but it succeeded in convincing many Muslims that the war was not part of a broader Christian offensive against Islam.

The roles a Pope plays are various and complex: Fortune 500 CEO, media superstar, diplomat, politician, theologian, philosopher, pastor, and voice of conscience. It is an impossible job, and no human being can perfectly do every task a Pope is called upon to perform. Every Pope will emphasize some aspects of the job at the expense of others. Pius XII, who governed the Church during the tumultuous days of World War II, was a superb diplomat, but did not project the pastoral face of John XXIII. John Paul II is a deep thinker, a media phenomenon, and maybe the greatest apostolic traveler since St. Paul (129 countries visited so far in his twenty-six-year papacy, the equivalent of two years on the road), but there has been a price to pay. He has had to leave many aspects of the governance of the Church in the hands of his aides. Yet every Pope exercises all of these roles at some stage, and the men and women of the Vatican assist him in doing so. One will never understand the psychology of the Vatican without grasping their sense of the gravitas and the importance of the papal office. For them, this is not the Queen of England at Buckingham Palace, a largely symbolic relic of a bygone era without real-world clout or significance. This is, from the Vatican's point of view, the living presence of Peter in the Catholic Church and the most important voice of conscience in human affairs.

Finally, a quick word about nomenclature. In normal English-speaking usage, most people refer to the head of the Church as the Pope, as in: "When will the Pope leave Rome for his summer break at Castel Gandolfo?" But in formal situations, especially in Rome, it is common to refer to him as the Holy Father, as in, "Would it be possible to arrange to attend an audience with the Holy Father?" Both are correct, and there's no shade of theological meaning between them. Unfortunately, however, they have taken on a kind of political resonance in the English-speaking world. When a conservative Catholic wants to display loyalty, he or she will often insist on "Holy Father" even when it sounds egregious. A certain kind of liberal, on the other hand, avoids such phraseology like the plague, even when protocol really requires it. When moving in and around the Vatican, the question is less one of ideology than courtesy. It's advisable for those who have dealings in Rome to learn to use the language of respect and make it *Holy Father* when the situation calls for it. (Not everyone bothers; when President George Bush and Secretary of State Colin Powell visited the Pope, for example, both men simply referred to him as "Sir.") In this book, I'll stick to *Pope* for simplicity of expression, and I'll keep the capital letter to signal respect for the office.

VATICAN, HOLY SEE, AND ROMAN CURIA

Now we're ready for some more important terminological clarifications. In conversation about the Vatican there are three terms often tossed around as if they're interchangeable, but that in fact describe different realities. They are the *Holy See*, the *Vatican*, and the *Roman Curia*.

First, the Holy See. The term *see* in this sense means "center of authority, jurisdiction, or office," and it comes from the Latin word *sedes*, meaning seat. The idea is that the bishop's chair represents his power and authority. This is where the notion of an ex cathedra pronouncement comes from, since in Latin, *cathedra* means chair. The sense of the importance of the bishop's chair runs deep in the Catholic tradition. Directly behind the main altar in St. Peter's Basilica, one finds the chapel of the Chair of Peter, and there is literally a large seat affixed to the wall to represent the authority of Peter as it is passed down to the present Pope. The Church's liturgical calendar recognizes a Feast of the Chair of Peter, February 22, which is one of the two traditional dates during the year that the Pope might create new members of the College of Cardinals. The other is June 29, the Feast of Sts. Peter and Paul, the two great patrons of the Church in Rome.

The *Holy See* is thus the proper term for designating the authority of the papacy to govern the Church. It is a nonterritorial institution, an idea rather than a place. Sometimes the term *Apostolic See* is used to mean the same thing, as in canon law, but *Holy See* is more common. The Holy See is an institution rather than a person and continues to exist even when there is no Pope—as during the *sede vacante*, or period of the "vacant seat," after the Pope has died and before a new one is elected. Canon 113 of the *Code of Canon Law* states that the legal personality of the Holy See is a matter of divine law. In other words, from a canonical point of view, God gave the Holy See its authority. It is not something erected by human beings on the basis of a social contract. By way of contrast, the legal personality of the Vatican City-State is based on a 1929 treaty with Italy. More on that later.

As the central government of the Roman Catholic Church, it is the Holy See, not the Vatican, that enters into treaties as the juridical equal of a sovereign state and sends and receives diplomatic representatives. It is the Holy See that conducts full diplomatic relations with 174 nations, plus lesser ties with Russia and the Palestinian National Authority. Many of these countries are non-Catholic and even non-Christian. The Holy See also maintains a presence in all major international organizations. Historically, this diplomatic activity dates to the time when the Pope was also the secular ruler of much of central Italy. The sovereignty and legal personality of the Holy See endured, however, even after the fall of the Papal States in 1870. The Holy See is recognized by a wide variety of international treaties and agreements. Article 16 of the 1961 Vienna Convention on Diplomatic Relations, for example, codified the informal practice that the ambassadors of the Holy See are recognized as the dean of the diplomatic corps in many countries to which they are accredited.

The Holy See is not dependent upon any physical territory for its sovereignty. Between 1870 and 1929, no bilateral treaty or international convention recognized the Holy See as the ruler of a physically defined space. Yet the Holy See during this period negotiated a total of sixty-two concordats with governments around the world to regulate the affairs of the Catholic Church, and these concordats were considered international conventions, with fully recognized legal force. In the same period, the Holy See acted as a mediator in several international conflicts: Germany versus Spain (1885); Ecuador versus Peru (1893); Argentina versus Chile (1900–1903); Colombia versus Ecuador (1906); and Haiti versus San Domingo (1926).

The Vatican, on the other hand, refers to the 108-acre physical territory in Rome. Historically the term referred to the *mons vaticanus*, the hill sloping up from the Tiber River away from the heart of ancient Rome. Pliny the Elder records that the area was known for snakes and bad wine. It was a cherished spot for early Christians because tradition regarded it as the burial spot of St. Peter, whose tomb was located in a pagan cemetery. (Claims have been made that later archeological discoveries under the basilica have identified the very bones of St. Peter, but this is a complicated discussion for another time.) The basilica erected by Constantine on the spot was never intended to be the center of papal government, but a shrine to Peter. The Pope's personal basilica was always considered to be St. John Lateran, and the administrative activity of the papacy was centered in the nearby *cancelleria* and the *Quirinale*, the latter of which is now the symbol of Italy's secular republic. Even today, when a new Pope is elected, among his first ceremonial acts is taking possession of St. John Lateran. The Vatican only became the center of papal activity in 1870 when the Papal States were lost along with the Pope's temporal authority. As a concession to the papacy's moral prestige, King Vittorio Emmanuel allowed the Pope to retain St. Peter's Basilica and the Vatican Palace.

The Pope at the time, Pius IX, refused to reconcile himself to the loss and declined to recognize the new Italian republic, declaring himself a "prisoner of the Vatican." That state of affairs endured until February 11, 1929, when Pius XI and the Italian government under Benito Mussolini reached an agreement. Vatican City was born, recognized under the Lateran Treaty as an instrument of the Holy See in its spiritual mission to the world. The Vatican City-State (*Stato della Città del Vaticano*) is, like the Holy See, recognized under international law, and it is party to international treaties such as the International Telecommunications Union and the Universal Postal Union. Unlike the Holy See, however, it does not receive or send diplomatic representatives and has no diplomatic relations with states. Former Secretary General of the United Nations Dag Hammarskjöld expressed this distinction: "When I request an audience from the Vatican, I do not go to see the King of Vatican City but the head of the Catholic Church."

Cardinal Renato Martino, the president of the Pontifical Council for Justice and Peace and for sixteen years the Holy See's observer to the United Nations, has offered a metaphor for understanding this relationship: "Vatican City is the physical or territorial base of the Holy See, almost a pedestal upon which is posed a much larger and unique independent and sovereign power: that of the Universal Church, respected and esteemed by many, suspected and combated by others, yet always present by its stature, its history and its influence in the international forum."

The Pope, through the Holy See, is the supreme governor of Vatican City. He delegates its administration to the Pontifical Commission for the State of the Vatican City. The legal system is based on the November 2000 Fundamental Law of the Vatican City-State, promulgated by John Paul II. Beyond that, canon law rules; if canon law is not applicable, the laws of the city of Rome apply. The Vatican City maintains the Swiss Guards, a voluntary military force, as well as a modern security corps. It has its own post office, commissary, bank, railway station, electrical generating plant, and publishing house. The Vatican also issues its own coins, stamps, and passports. Today the Vatican City-State has its own legal system for traffic control, customs duty, and telegraphic services, a nine-hundred-foot railway that connects with the main Italian line, electric power and water services from Rome supplemented by a local water supply, and a small electric power plant. Beyond St. Peter's Basilica, there is a parish church inside the Vatican, St. Anne of the Palafrieneri, for permanent residents and employees. It is staffed by the Augustinian friars.

The Vatican City-State also has its own penal system and tribunals, along with two jail cells. For the first time, in 2003, the Vatican issued a report on crimes committed on its territory. Presented by the city-state's chief prosecutor, Nicola Picardi, the report said there had been 397 civil offenses and 608 penal offenses in 2002, the vast majority petty crimes such as purse snatching, pickpocketing and shoplifting in the Vatican museums. If one uses the traditional measure of dividing the number of crimes by the number of citizens, the Vatican City-State would appear to have one of the highest crime rates in the world, since it has only 455 permanent residents. The museums, however, draw over 3 million visitors a year, so 608 minor crimes are far less dramatic. The perpetrators—like the victims, tourists to the Vatican—were rarely caught, with 90 percent of complaints never leading to a prosecution. There is a backlog of cases before Vatican courts, which had to deal with a record 239 cases in 2002, with 110 still unresolved into 2003.

Anyone sentenced to a prison term by the Vatican's civil court is transferred to an Italian prison, with the Vatican paying the tab.

The total number of employees of the Vatican city-state in 2003 was 1,511, which includes 4 top directors, 75 men and women religious, and 1,432 laity. Also on the books are 566 retired employees drawing a pension. Salaries for Vatican employees are shockingly low by American standards; a mid-level official working in the Vatican travel agency, for example, might earn the equivalent of $18,000 a year. Among Italians, however, Vatican jobs are highly coveted, because they bring access to the Vatican supermarket, clothing store, electronics store, and gas station, whose products are untaxed and therefore significantly cheaper than anywhere else in Rome. The Vatican also offers access to quality health care and a well-stocked pharmacy. In addition, salaries are not taxed, and the Vatican has a generous pension system and severance plan. (An employee of Vatican Radio who left in 2001 after thirteen years of service received the equivalent of one month's pay for every year he had put in, so he left with a check in hand for more than a year's salary.) Most importantly for a country where instability is chronic, the Vatican offers a secure source of employment—it is never going out of business. Under the Vatican's labor laws, which basically parallel those of Italy, it is also virtually impossible to fire someone. For example, one pontifical commission has a laywoman who does secretarial work and who became pregnant some years ago. Under the rules she was entitled to nine months of maternity leave, but by craftily navigating the system, she actually took more than eighteen months. The number two official of this small office tried to replace her, but gave up after a battle that stretched over four years.

To be precise, it is the Holy See that governs the Catholic Church on behalf of the Pope, not the Vatican. In this book I will slip back and forth between these two terms, because it is simply too repetitive to use only *Holy See,* and because the word *Vatican* is far more familiar to most English-speakers. Readers with a penchant for detail, however, will want to recall that the Holy See is the government of the Church, the Vatican is a place in Rome where the Holy See is currently located.

THE ROMAN CURIA

Finally we come to the *Roman Curia*, which is the bureaucratic instrument through which the Pope administers the Holy See and carries out his function both as supreme governor of the Catholic Church and as a sovereign diplomatic actor. The term *Curia* is borrowed from ancient Rome, where it referred to the seat of the Roman Senate. The Pope isn't the only figure in the Church with a Curia. The head of the Jesuits, for example, has his own Curia that helps him administer the affairs of that religious order. Though the Roman Curia has taken different forms over the centuries, it currently consists of the Secretariat of State, nine congregations, three tribunals, eleven councils, and a complex of offices that administer church affairs. There is a catchall term for these various departments in the Vatican, which is *dicastery*. The term comes from the Greek *dikasterion*, a court of law in Athens, with 501 jurors over thirty years of age, picked by lot. All deliberations had to conclude by nightfall. Applied to the Holy See, the word *dicastery* refers to the offices that assist the Pope in the government of the Church.

(Technically, the term *dicastery* refers only to the Secretariat of State, congregations, tribunals, councils, and certain offices—namely the Apostolic Camera, the Administration of the Patrimony of the Apostolic See, and the Prefecture for the Economic Affairs of the Holy See. It would not, therefore, include the Prefecture of the Papal Household or the Office for the Liturgical Celebrations of the Supreme Pontiff. Most Vatican-watchers use the word loosely, however, to refer to just about every department within the institution.)

Examined on a flow chart, the structure of the Roman Curia would seem rather straightforward, with lots of different offices reporting more or less independently to the Pope. There is some reality to this, as the dicasteries do operate in relative isolation from one another (and sometimes at cross-purposes; more on that later). Yet what the flow chart would fail to reveal is that some dicasteries are more equal than others. The Secretariat of State is sometimes called the "super-dicastery" because of the way it oversees and coordinates the work of the others. The Congregation for the Doctrine of the Faith was traditionally known as *la suprema*, "the supreme" congregation, prior to Pope Paul VI's reform in 1967, and in some ways it retains a kind of preeminence because of the gatekeeper role it plays on doctrinal questions. Any document or decision with doctrinal implications, which covers a great deal of what the Roman Curia does, has to be cleared with this congregation. These realities make the secretary of state and the prefect of the Congregation for the Doctrine of the Faith arguably the two most important men in the power structure of the Roman Catholic Church after the Pope.

Secretariat of State

The secretariat of state directs and coordinates the other dicasteries of the Curia. The incumbent secretary of state, Cardinal Angelo Sodano, is the Holy See's equivalent of a prime minister. The office dates back to 1644, with the appointment of Cardinal Giovanni Giacomo Panciroli by Pope Innocent X. Archbishop Giovanni Lajolo, secretary of the Section for Relations with States, is the Vatican's foreign minister, while Archbishop Leonardo Sandri, the *Sostituto*, is the man who runs the day-to-day operations of the Catholic Church.

The secretariat is divided into two sections.

• The First Section deals with internal Church affairs and is organized into language desks. The English desk, for example, at full strength has seven or eight priests handling all the correspondence into and out of the Secretariat of State in the English language. There's a history of heads of the English section moving on to higher office. Cardinal Justin Rigali, the current archbishop of Philadelphia, once held the job, as did Archbishop James Harvey, the American who now serves as prefect of the Papal Household. More recently, Bishop Brian Farrell was given the post of secretary of the Council for Promoting Christian Unity after heading the English desk. The overall head of the First Section is the *sostituto*, or "substitute," regarded as the figure with the most direct control over the day-to-day affairs of the Church. The *sostituto* is able to see the Pope without an appointment, a privilege not even the secretary of state himself enjoys. Giovanni Battista Montini was the *sostituto* under Pius XII before becoming archbishop of Milan and later Pope Paul VI. Cardinal Giovanni Battista Re, currently prefect of the powerful Congregation for Bishops, was John Paul's *sostituto* for eleven years. The number three official in the structure is known as the *assessore*, or "assessor," and this person too is usually someone who is going places.

• The Second Section handles the Vatican's relations with foreign governments and is organized into regional desks. One official handles the Balkans, for example, another deals with Central and Eastern Europe, and so on. The official tracking the United States is currently an Italian, Monsignor Paolo Gualtieri. The section is headed by the secretary for Relations with the States, currently an Italian, Archbishop Giovanni Lajolo. This position is known informally by the world press as the Pope's foreign minister. Below him is the undersecretary, currently an Italian named Pietro Parolin. This post too is often a launching pad for Church careers. One former occupant, for example, is now the Holy See's permanent observer to the United Nations, an Italian named Archbishop Celestino Migliore.

Compared to other bureaucratic structures with a comparable scope of responsibility, the Secretariat of State is either remarkably efficient or remarkably understaffed, depending on one's point of view. The United States Department of State, for example, has a workforce of eleven thousand, according to the Bureau of Labor Statistics, some nine thousand of whom are in Washington, and with roughly half that number representing policy and analysis positions. The Second Section of the Vatican's Secretariat of State, by way of comparison, has thirty people trying to do a comparable job. Under these conditions, it is a miracle that the Vatican's bilateral relations and its diplomatic activity are as professional and successful as they are. Management expert Peter Drucker once classified the Holy See as one of history's most efficient organizations, along with General Motors and the Prussian army. If the ratio of government employees to Americans were the same as Catholics to curial officials, Drucker found, the U.S. government would have a workforce of 588. It is also no secret, however, why some things slip through the cracks, and why analysis of world events or local situations can sometimes seem superficial or half-baked. Vatican legend records a quip along these lines from Cardinal Domenico Tardini, a close aide of Pope Pius XII and secretary of state under John XXIII. Someone once said to Tardini that the Holy See's diplomacy was the best in the world. "God help whoever's number two," Tardini is said to have replied.

Congregations

The congregations are the most important offices in the Curia because they have what canon lawyers call "the power of governance," meaning the power to issue binding documents, judgments, decrees, and dispensations. They deal with the most important issues: theology, clerical discipline, bishops, saints, the Eastern churches, evangelization, and so on. Technically speaking, each congregation is composed of a body of cardinals, bishops, and prelates of Eastern churches who are its full members. These groups are analogous to boards of directors in the United States, with a lower-level staff then responsible for the actual day-to-day work. While the staff has an extraordinary influence on what the dicastery does, it's also true that many important decisions—who gets a particular bishop's appointment, for example—are usually made around the table when the full body of cardinals and bishops that governs the congregations meets.

The congregations conduct their business in three types of meetings. A *plenary session* brings together all the cardinals and bishops who are members, which also includes the prefect and the secretary as voting members. The plenary generally meets once a year because of the difficulty of coordinating travel schedules and handles the most important questions. An *ordinary session* includes those members of the congregation who are resident in Rome, though any member who wishes to participate has the right to do so. Such meetings will be held a few times a year, outside "down" periods such as the August holidays, and handle more routine matters. The internal work of the congregation's staff, especially decisions about which matters to refer to the full body of members, is done at the *congress*, which is a meeting of the prefect, secretary, undersecretary, and other key personnel. (Some offices may have more than one undersecretary.) The congresses may happen once a month.

The congregations are:

• The Congregation for the Doctrine of the Faith, formerly known as the Holy Office, which determines the official teaching of the Church and investigates theologians who deviate from it. As mentioned above, it also screens the documents and decisions of other dicasteries to the extent that they have doctrinal implications, and much of the work moving through the Vatican does touch upon matters of doctrine. When the Pontifical Council for Interreligious Dialogue wanted to put out a document on the spirituality of interreligious dialogue, it had to be cleared with the congregation, and its consultors asked for significant revisions in the proposed text. This congregation also has legal responsibility for handling cases of particularly grave offenses by priests, including the sexual abuse of minors.

• The Congregation for Eastern Churches, which applies the role of the papacy as supreme governor to the twenty-one Eastern Rite churches that are in full communion with the Roman Catholic Church.

• The Congregation for Divine Worship and the Discipline of the Sacraments, which oversees the liturgical life of the Catholic Church, deciding which rites and texts are acceptable for Catholic worship.

• The Congregation for the Causes of Saints, which handles cases for beatifications, declaring someone "blessed," and canonizations, declaring someone a saint.

• The Congregation for Bishops, which handles the appointment of new bishops and the supervision of current bishops. It should be noted, however, that at least a third of the dioceses of the world are considered to be in "mission territory" and depend upon the Congregation for the Evangelization of Peoples for their bishops. Similarly, the bishops of the Eastern churches are elected by their synods and "confirmed" by the Congregation for Eastern Churches. The nominations of bishops for Eastern Europe are prepared by the Secretariat of State. For historical reasons, the congregation also has responsibility for the Pontifical Commission for Latin America.

• The Congregation for the Evangelization of Peoples, formerly known as Propaganda Fidei, which applies the role of the papacy as supreme governor to all the "mission churches," mostly in the Third World. This congregation administers perhaps the largest and most complex bureaucratic structure of all the curial offices. It is in effect a sort of "mini-Vatican" for the mission territories.

• The Congregation for Clergy, which has responsibility for overseeing clerical discipline, as well as the ongoing formation of clergy. The congregation has three sections: (1) life and ministry of the clergy; (2) preaching and catechetics; (3) temporal administration, including alienation of property above a certain value, pious foundations, and support of the clergy.

• The Congregation for the Institutes of Consecrated Life and the Societies of Apostolic Life (generally known as the Congregation for Religious), which deals with the creation and suppression of religious orders, any changes in their constitutions, questions of government, and property and privileges. The congregation works with councils of major superiors for both men and women.

• The Congregation for Catholic Education, which oversees Catholic schools, universities, and seminaries.

Tribunals

The Roman Curia is also the judicial branch of government. The Church has its own law code, the *Code of Canon Law*, which canon lawyers say is the oldest continually functioning system of law in the Western world, even if the first time the system was formally codified was in 1917. There is also a separate code of canon law for the Eastern churches. The 1983 Latin Rite code consists of 1,752 canons or rules, divided into seven topics, or books. Within the Curia are three tribunals whose function it is to apply this code to cases that arrive in Rome. They are:

• The Apostolic Penitentiary, which deals with what canon lawyers call the internal forum, meaning things that pertain to the sphere of individual conscience and can only be judged secretly, perhaps in the sacrament of confession. The Apostolic Penitentiary also handles a number of other delicate situations: sins and censures reserved to the Holy See; dispensations from hidden impediments to marriage and from irregularities (for example, someone who wishes to marry within the forbidden range of kinship); release from oaths; commutations of religious vows; release from duties derived from pious foundations and of every other kind of obligation; the regularization of invalid religious professions, of invalid divisions of ecclesiastical offices and goods, or of invalid marriages caused by some unsuspected impediment; and releasing possessors of usurped ecclesiastical goods from their obligations. Such cases are rare, but when they arise they can be extremely urgent. It's for this reason that the head of the Penitentiary keeps his job even during the interregnum between popes and is allowed to receive messages from his office even during the conclave, or election of the new Pope, when the cardinals are sealed off in the Sistine Chapel.

• The Roman Rota, which is the main judicial organ of the Holy See. It is an appeals court from decisions made by local tribunals around the world, and in the vast majority of instances these cases concern requests for annulment of marriages. The number of requests for annulments has been increasing for years. On December 31, 1991, there were 591 marriage cases pending, while on December 31, 2001, the total was 1,055. The Rota is also a court of first instance for cases that local tribunals cannot handle. For example, any case involving an appeal against a decision by a bishop has to go to the Rota, or, depending on the nature of the case, to a congregation, rather than the bishop's tribunal. Certain types of marriage cases also have to come directly to the Rota, such as annulment requests from royalty; Caroline of Monaco had to appeal to the Rota rather than the marriage tribunal of the Archdiocese of Monaco. She also had to wait ten years for a favorable decision. The court is called the *rota* because of the circular room in which judges at one time met to hear cases. In 2003 there were twenty-eight judges (technically called prelate auditors) who meet in panels of three to hear cases. The Rota pronounces between 150 and 200 sentences each year. Not just anyone can bring a case. The Rota has a list of lawyers, usually around seventy-five, that can bring business before the court.

• The Supreme Tribunal of the Apostolic Signatura, which is the highest court of appeal in the Roman Catholic system of justice. It has three sections: the first handles appeals against sentences of the Roman Rota and settles conflicts of competence among the various tribunals; the second handles appeals from the decisions of other dicasteries of the Roman Curia and settles conflicts over competence among the dicasteries; and the third section, which is analogous to a ministry of justice, is responsible for overseeing the work of courts, lawyers, and judges, including decisions on erecting or suppressing lower tribunals.

Councils

Councils are the heart of what is known as the "new Curia" that developed after Vatican II, and in general they are distinguished from congregations by the fact they have no power of governance. The two exceptions are the Council for Laity, which has the legal authority to recognize the statues of lay movements, and the Council for the Interpretation of Legislative Texts, which can issue binding clarifications about the scope, meaning, and force of legal decrees. Councils are instruments of persuasion rather than coercion—their function is to study issues and promote causes within the Church and the broader culture. That the councils are further down the pecking order is reflected in manifold ways: several councils are headed by archbishops, whereas a congregation is always headed by a cardinal; there are more lay officials, a sign that the council does not draw on the authority of holy orders; physically, many councils are located in the Piazza San Calisto in Trastevere, farther away from St. Peter's and the Pope.

The eleven councils are:

• The Pontifical Council for Laity, which is responsible for matters relating to the coordination and promotion of the apostolic activity and Christian life of the laity. This mission includes overseeing the so-called "new movements" in the Catholic Church, such as the Neocatechumenate and Communion and Liberation.

• The Pontifical Council for Promoting Christian Unity, which is responsible for ecumenical dialogue and relations with other Christian churches. This council also houses the Commission for Religious Relations with Judaism.

• The Pontifical Council for the Family, which is responsible for protecting and promoting the Church's vision of the family. This involves the council in sometimes fierce battles against divorce, birth control, gay liberation movements, de facto partnerships, and a host of other social trends in the Western world.

• The Pontifical Council for Justice and Peace, which is responsible for promoting the social doctrine of the Catholic Church as it applies to issues of war, economic development, the environment, and a host of other issues. Since Justice and Peace is often called upon to comment on many of the same international crises as the Secretariat of State, some curialists worry about the council pursuing a kind of "parallel diplomacy."

On the other hand, the council can sometimes be a useful instrument for saying things or pushing issues that the Secretariat of State or the Pope, for various diplomatic reasons, can't or won't take up.

• The Pontifical Council "Cor Unum," which is responsible for expressing the care of the Church toward those in need. It fosters charitable works by the faithful and assists those in urgent or calamitous situations and those in special need.

• The Pontifical Council for the Pastoral Care of Migrants and Itinerant Peoples, which is responsible for the care of people who are transient, such as the Roma people (commonly called gypsies) in Europe, and who are not readily cared for within traditional diocesan structures. It is also responsible for the Apostleship of the Sea dealing with pastoral care to sailors.

• The Pontifical Council for the Pastoral Care of Health Care Workers, which is responsible for assisting health care workers, addressing their spiritual needs and those of their patients, as well as assisting local churches to train and regulate the activities of hospital chaplains. The council is popularly known as the Vatican's Ministry of Health, and also exercises a sort of vigilance over Catholic hospitals around the world.

• The Pontifical Council for the Interpretation of Legislative Texts, which is responsible for determining the meaning of the canons in the *Code of Canon Law* or of legally binding decisions of various dicasteries when questions arise. In July 2000, for example, the council issued a document clarifying that remarried divorced persons who have not received an annulment fall under canon 915, which says that people "who obstinately persist in manifest grave sin" cannot receive the Eucharist.

• The Pontifical Council for Interreligious Dialogue, which is responsible for managing the Catholic Church's relationships with non-Christian religions, except for Judaism, which is handled by the Council for Promoting Christian Unity. The council was heavily involved, for example, in organizing the three gatherings of world religious leaders called for by Pope John Paul II in Assisi (1986, 1993, and 2002).

• The Pontifical Council for Culture, which is responsible for the Catholic Church's dialogue with the world of culture—the visual arts, literature, music, the various currents in intellectual life, science, and so forth. It was the Council for Culture, for example, that carried out a lengthy study culminating in Pope John Paul's 1992 statement expressing regret for the way the Church responded to Galileo's scientific theses.

• The Pontifical Council for Social Communications, which is responsible for promoting a Christian vision of the world of mass communications. The council has recently put out documents on advertising and the Internet. As a practical matter, the council also handles all requests from broadcast media for access to the Holy See. The council takes special interest in Catholic newspapers and periodicals, as well as radio and television stations, to ensure that they faithfully represent the teaching of the Church and spread religious news accurately.

Other Offices

The Roman Curia also features a number of other offices for handling tasks not subsumed under any other dicastery. They include:

• The Apostolic Camera, which is a department of the Curia created in the eleventh century to deal with the financial and administrative affairs of the Papal States. According to a 1967 constitution of Paul VI, the Apostolic Camera manages the financial holdings of the papacy during the interregnum. It is headed by the *camerlengo*, or chancellor, who governs the Church during the interregnum, although rules call for him to make no decisions that can await the next Pope.

• The Administration of the Patrimony of the Holy See, the office responsible for administering the property and goods of the Holy

See. According to 2003 Vatican figures, that patrimony was worth almost $800 million, representing largely real estate holdings and investment portfolios. This does not include, however, what most people conventionally think of as the patrimony of the Vatican, meaning masterpieces of Western art such as Michelangelo's *Pietà*, or the Basilica of St. Peter itself. These treasures, which can never be sold or borrowed against and hence have no practical value, are listed on the Vatican books at 1 Euro each.

• The Prefecture of the Economic Affairs of the Holy See, which is responsible for overseeing the annual operating budget of the Vatican, which in 2003 was $260 million.

• The Prefecture of the Papal Household, which is responsible for audiences with the Pope and administering the Papal apartments. The prefect, currently American Archbishop James Harvey, receives visiting heads of state and escorts them to the papal apartments. He is also generally seated next to the Pope during public functions. The papal household also includes those who are on most intimate terms with the Pope, including his butler, Angelo Gugel, and the Polish nuns who prepare his meals and take care of his clothes.

• The Office of the Liturgical Celebrations of the Supreme Pontiff, which is responsible for organizing all papal liturgies and assisting the Pope at those liturgies, including all the ceremonies on papal trips. As such, the office has the capacity to set the liturgical tone for the Catholic Church, since the way the Pope celebrates Mass and the other rites of the Church is widely studied and imitated.

PAST AND PRESENT

Very briefly, it's worth noting where these structures came from, because the Roman Curia has not always had its current configuration.

The first mention of the phrase "Roman Curia" to describe the civil service around the Bishop of Rome came in a document of Pope Urban II in 1089, though popes had already drawn upon the services of aides and advisors for centuries. Niccolò del Re distinguishes five stages in the growth and development of the Roman Curia.

Presbyters and Synods Up to the eleventh century, the papal bureaucracy consisted of secretaries who handled correspondence and registered decrees. The decision-making functions associated with the Roman Curia were performed by the presbyterate, or clergy, of the Rome diocese, and by occasional synods of bishops. Ignatius of Antioch, for example, mentions the body of clergy in Rome that assists the Pope as early as the second century. By the third century the Roman presbyterate was sufficiently conscious of its authority that it issued decisions even during the interregnum, when there was no pope. It intervened in 250, for example, after the death of Pope Fabian, in support of Cyprian of Carthage in a dispute over the *lapsi,* those who had been baptized but then renounced their faith during a persecution. Meanwhile a synod, or gathering of bishops in and around Rome, was held periodically (in certain eras, once a year) to deal with major questions, usually heresies. Many of their decisions found their way into a famous document called the *Decretals of Gratian,* which laid the basis for canon law.

Consistories From the eleventh through sixteenth centuries, popes relied increasingly on *consistories,* or gatherings of all the cardinals, to advise and assist them in the work of administration. The term *cardinal* at the time referred to clergy who had been "incardinated," or transferred, into a new position. Generally when a cleric was incardinated, it meant he had been promoted. These clergy were responsible for running important Roman parishes, administering diocesan programs, or advising the Pope in special capacities. By the eleventh century, they had become the most direct and important collaborators of the Pope. St. Bernard of Clairvaux (1090–1153) referred to the cardinals as the *judices orbis,* or judges of the world, in 1145. As the importance of the consistory grew, so did the frequency of its meetings. When Bernard wrote, the consistory met once a month; by the pontificate of Innocent III (1198–1216), it met three times a week, on Monday, Wednesday, and Friday. Also during this era, four organs took shape to assist the cardinals: the Cancelleria for managing correspondence and documents, the Camera Apostolica for governance and finance, and the Roman Rota and Apostolic Penitentiary for legal matters. These are therefore the most antique dicasteries.

Reform of Sixtus V In the wake of the Protestant Reformation, Pope Sixtus was convinced of the need to create a more professional, streamlined bureaucracy to help administer the Church. Pope Sixtus can rightly be considered the father of the Roman Curia. In 1588 he distinguished between congregations for executive matters, of which he authorized fifteen, and tribunals for judicial questions. Just prior to the Sistine reform, in 1542, Pope Paul III had instituted the first permanent congregation of the Roman Curia: the Holy Roman and Universal Inquisition, which would become the Holy Office and then today's Congregation for the Doctrine of the Faith. Its original purpose was to hold back the Protestant invasion and to combat heresies as they arose. Of those congregations recognized by Pope Sixtus, some are still in existence today, such as the Congregation for Bishops and the Congregation for Rites. Others, however, outlived their usefulness with the collapse of the Papal States: for example, the Congregation for the Naval Fleet, the Congregation for the Abundance of Food in the Ecclesiastical State, and the Congregation for Streets, Bridges, and Waters. (The papal navy, by the way, consisted of ten ships whose mission was to fight pirates along the coasts of the Tyrrenian Sea.) At one stage there were no fewer than forty congregations, and the result was often confusion: one congregation would condemn something, another would uphold it. Other dicasteries fell into disuse over time because nobody bothered consulting them.

1917 Code The reorganization of the Roman Curia carried out by the 1917 *Code of Canon Law* suppressed a number of offices that had been in disuse and generally streamlined the internal organization. The Congregation for Indulgences and Relics and the Congregation for the Index, for example, were abolished and their functions transferred to the Holy Office. Eventually relics would become the business of the Congregation for Rites and Indulgences of the Apostolic Penitentiary. The result was a Roman Curia composed of eleven congregations, three tribunals, and six offices—basically the same physiognomy today.

Paul VI/John Paul II Pope Paul VI, who had served as a key figure in the Roman Curia under Pope Pius XII, felt enormous respect for the Curia, as well as a keen awareness of the need for reform in light of the Second Vatican Council. His 1967 document, *Regimini Ecclesiae universale,* was the most significant reordering of the Roman Curia since Pope Sixtus V. Key points of the Pauline reform:

- The inclusion of diocesan bishops as full members of the congregations, in order to ensure that men with pastoral experience who lived outside Rome were involved in crafting policy.
- The "internationalization" of the Curia, whose members and officials had been almost exclusively Italian, but who now were to come from a wide variety of national and linguistic backgrounds.
- A time limit of five years for heads of dicasteries, their secretaries, and their consultors, to ensure a regular rotation in these important agencies. Paul also specified that the same people automatically step down when the Pope dies.
- The introduction of mixed commissions at various levels to deal with mixed questions, in an effort to resolve turf battles and promote consistency.

- Periodic meetings of the heads of all the dicasteries under the presidency of the Secretariat of State.
- Placing the Secretariat of State above all the other dicasteries and removing the title "*suprema*" from the former Holy Office.
- Removing the title "sacred" from the formal name of the various congregations.
- Requiring cardinals and secretaries to submit their resignations at seventy-five, undersecretaries at seventy. It is up to the Pope to decide whether to accept those resignations. At the age of eighty cardinals automatically lose their membership in all dicasteries.

John Paul II built on Paul VI's approach in his own 1988 document, *Pastor Bonus*, which is the constitution of the Roman Curia currently in force.

Today, 2,659 people work for the Roman Curia, of whom 744 are diocesan priests, bishops, archbishops, or cardinals, while there are 351 men and women religious and 1,564 laity. Also on the books are 892 retired employees drawing a pension. Those numbers could make it sound like laity are well-represented, but in fact the vast majority of these lay employees are engaged in work that is essentially secretarial. For example, every dicastery in the Roman Curia has someone, and sometimes several people, whose job it is to sit in the main reception room to answer the phone and receive visitors. These posts are almost entirely held by laity. If one considers the level of the *superiori*, the decision-making posts in the Curia consisting of the heads of dicasteries and their secretaries and undersecretaries, there are perhaps five hundred such positions and a mere handful of laity. In 2003, four laypeople had the rank of superior, all at the level of undersecretary or its equivalent: Uruguayan Guzmán Carriquiry, in the Pontifical Council for the Laity; Italian Angelo Scelzo, in the Pontifical Council for Social Communications; Italian Ivan Ruggiero, general accountant for the Prefecture of the Economic Affairs of the Holy See; and Spaniard Joaquin Navarro-Valls, head of the Holy See Press Office. There is only one case in the Roman Curia of a priest being under the authority of a layperson, and that's in the Press Office, where Navarro-Valls is the director and Italian Passionist Fr. Ciro Benedettini is the vice-director. Women are underrepresented in senior positions. The highest-ranking laywoman in the Roman Curia is an Italian, Paola Fabrizi, who is a *capo ufficio*, or head of a section, in the Pontifical Council for Promoting Christian Unity. Immaculate Heart Sr. Sharon Holland is also a *capo ufficio* in the Congregation for the Institutes of Consecrated Life and the Societies of Apostolic Life. Another prominent laywoman is Belgian theologian Marie Hendrickx in the Congregation for the Doctrine of the Faith, who presented the Pope's Apostolic exhortation "On the Dignity of Women" to the press in 1988 and who supervises the theological preparation of some of the Pope's letters. Hendrickx gained a fleeting fame in January 2001 when she published an article in *L'Osservatore Romano* criticizing unnecessary cruelty to animals, citing specifically the modern food industry. She also questioned the moral legitimacy of bullfighting.

Perhaps the best expression of the ideals to which the Roman Curia aspires came from the modern Pope who understood it best, and precisely because he loved it, wanted to make it truer to its noblest self—Paul VI. In a speech on September 21, 1963, here's what he had to say about the Roman Curia:

> A most worthy instrument, to whom it is no source of wonder that so much is demanded, so much is required, by everyone, and first of all by us ourselves! Its work demands supreme capacities and virtues, exactly because the office itself is supreme. It is a most delicate work, which is that of being the custodian or the echo of divine truth and to make of this a language for dialogue with the human spirit; it is an enormous work, which has as its borders the entire world; it is a most noble work, which is that of hearing and interpret-

ing the voice of the Pope and at the same time of ensuring that no piece of useful and objective information is denied him, no filial and thoughtful piece of advice. For this reason, how learned and expert must be the Roman Curia for being equal to its duty.

THE VATICAN DIPLOMATIC SERVICE

The Pope's diplomatic arm consists first and foremost of his *nuncios*, or ambassadors, who currently represent the pontiff to the 211 different countries, territories, and international bodies or agencies with which the Holy See has some diplomatic exchange. This list includes the European Community, the United Nations, the Organization of American States, the UN Food and Agriculture Organization, and so on. The nuncios report to the Second Section of the Secretariat of State. In most cases the Holy See possesses a physical embassy accredited to the country or international body and employs a nuncio and a small staff. In the Catholic nations of Europe and in Latin America, the nuncio is considered the dean of that country's diplomatic corps, since the Holy See has been sending out ambassadors longer than any other government on earth. Practically the only nations that do not currently have relations with the Holy See are China and Vietnam, both cases of ideological conflict between the Church and a communist regime, and Saudi Arabia.

Why is it important to the Holy See to have diplomatic relations? In part, in order to regulate the juridical and financial situation of the Catholic Church in the various nations. Questions about public funding, for example, or of property rights of the Church have to be resolved. The nuncio is also in a position to speak authoritatively in defense of local believers if there is a threat to their religious freedom. Moreover, the Pope's ambassadors have the capacity to promote the Church's foreign policy objectives. Usually these aims are pitched at a fairly lofty level, such as peace, justice, environmental protection, and sustainable development. But sometimes Vatican diplomacy takes on a more immediate and realpolitik aspect, such as efforts during the Iraq war to convince Muslims that the U.S.-led offensive was not a "clash of civilizations" between Christianity and Islam. In areas of the world where there is persistent conflict, such as the Holy Land, the nuncio represents the voice of the Pope in peace initiatives. Thus Archbishop Pietro Sambi, for example, as the nuncio to both Israel and a territory the Vatican identifies as "Jerusalem and Palestine," carries the moral authority of the Pope in negotiations aimed at finding a peaceful settlement, especially as concerns the status of holy sites in Jerusalem and elsewhere.

There is no other example in international diplomacy of a religious body acting as a sovereign state, and every now and then someone will object to the privileged status enjoyed by the Catholic Church. In 2000, for example, the liberal group Catholics for a Free Choice led a push, cleverly called the See Change Campaign, to try to revoke the Holy See's diplomatic status. While the campaign garnered a fair bit of media interest, it did not go anywhere politically. The United States Congress, for example, voted 416–1 to support maintaining the Holy See's sovereign status. The lone contrary vote came from California Democrat Rep. Pete Stark.

The diplomatic corps is highly prestigious in terms of the internal culture of the Vatican. Most nuncios are graduates of the Pontificia Accademia Ecclesiastica, the elite institution in Rome that since 1700 has trained future priests for careers in the diplomatic service. Five popes have been graduates of the Accademia and several more had been professors. Entering the diplomatic service of the Holy See is generally considered a very promising start to a clerical career. Often these men will end up back in Rome in some capacity, in part because they have already mastered the language skills necessary to function in an international environment.

Given the small size of the Secretariat of State, as well as the small staffs most nuncios have, the Holy See's diplomats might seem out of their depth compared to the resources that many other ambassadors and foreign ministries can deploy. Yet the nuncios possess some unique advantages. For one thing, the Holy See is not part of any power block or trade system that creates rivalries, so its working relationships are not limited primarily to those nations "on its side." While the U.S. ambassador to Germany, for example, has little chance of phoning his opposite number in the Iranian embassy and getting access to confidential intelligence, the papal nuncio is in a much better position to swap news and views with all parties.

Further, the nuncio in every country on earth has access to a network of intelligence and perspective that any spy agency would envy: the local church, meaning the local clergy and bishops, who know the situation, the people, and the language from the inside out. When the Vatican wanted to understand the impact of the UN sanctions regime in Iraq during the 1990s, for example, it did not have to send observers or commission studies. It could simply phone the head of the 1-million-strong Chaldean Catholic Church in Baghdad, or the archbishop of the Latin Rite, and ask for impressions. The nuncio and the Secretariat of State also have access to the vast network of missionary communities in the Catholic Church, who have missionary priests, brothers, and sisters in every nook and cranny of the planet. Nuncios who know how to deploy these assets can be among the best-informed members of any diplomatic corps.

In addition to handling affairs of state, the nuncio is also the Pope's eyes and ears for oversight of the local church. When Catholics in a given country have complaints about the bishop, it is the nuncio to whom they are addressed. The nuncio can decide how to process those concerns—whether to ignore them, to handle the matter himself, or to refer it on to Rome for review. These decisions are often fateful in terms of determining impressions in the Holy See. The nuncio also has the responsibility for preparing the *terna*, or list of three names of candidates for the appointment of new bishops. Of course, the Congregation for Bishops when it meets in its plenary session in Rome can change the order of the *terna* or add or subtract names, and the Pope has complete liberty to disregard the *terna* altogether and appoint someone of his own choosing. This is rare but not unprecedented; John Paul disregarded the set of three names presented to him in May 2000, for example, in order to name Edward Egan to succeed John O'Connor as the archbishop of New York. Yet according to Cardinal Jorge Mejia, former secretary of the Congregation for Bishops, between 80 and 90 percent of the time the first candidate on the *terna* prepared by the nuncio ends up getting the job. This makes the nuncio's role often a decisive one.

VATICAN COMMUNICATIONS

Like any major international organization, the Holy See has a variety of communications tools for getting its message out. These include a semi-official daily newspaper, *L'Osservatore Romano*, which some wags jokingly compare to the old *Pravda* in the Soviet Union because it is filled with pictures and speeches by the Great Leader and because it muffles criticism. (On August 19, 1914, *L'Osservatore* published a stinging editorial denoucing unnamed commentators who had suggested the previous day that Pope Pius X had a cold. Less than twenty-four hours later, Pius was dead.) *L'Osservatore Romano* is published daily in Italian, and weekly in English, Spanish, Portuguese, German, and French, with a monthly edition in Polish.

The Jesuit order puts out a twice-monthly journal whose pages are reviewed by the Secretariat of State prior to publication, called *La Civiltà Cattolica*. Vatican Radio is the largest single employer within the Holy See, boasting a workforce of more than four hundred people, including two hundred journalists from sixty-one different countries, producing programs every day in forty languages—including, quixotically enough, Esperanto. It is also a major drain on Vatican finances, since it sells no advertising and accepts no corporate sponsorship as other forms of "commercial-free" radio have learned to do. The Vatican TV Center produces a weekly news program in several languages and provides live television feed of papal events to the world's networks. The Vatican website has gone from a simple one-page Christmas greeting in 1995 to one of the most-visited sites on the Internet, with offerings from the Vatican museums and access to the full texts of papal documents as well as documents of most dicasteries. Archbishop Claudio Maria Celli, the Vatican official who oversees the site, said in a June 2003 press conference that it makes an attractive target for hackers and is subject to some thirty attacks a week, mostly from the United States. But to date, he said, none have succeeded. The culprits are not always teenage War Games–style prodigies: Celli said using sophisticated cyber-tracking software, the Vatican was once able to establish that a particular would-be hacker was a member of the Franciscan order. They elected not to prosecute: "We thought maybe he was just bored by the heat," Celli said, a joking reference to the torridly hot European summer of 2003.

The Press Office of the Holy See produces a daily bulletin, along with other documentation for journalists, and holds periodic press conferences in conjunction with the issuance of documents or in anticipation of major Vatican events. The director and vice-director of the press office are frequently called upon to make statements for journalists when stories about the Vatican arise, and Navarro-Valls has thus been easily one of the most visible of all Vatican officials during the pontificate of John Paul II. When the Pope travels, it is Navarro-Valls who speaks on his behalf to the world's press corps accompanying John Paul on the papal plane. Finally, the Pontifical Council for Social Communications provides a moral and theological perspective on the world of mass communications, as well as coordinating the activities of broadcast media in covering the Vatican.

The Holy See's media operation provides it with an impressive range of tools to communicate with the outside world. The trouble is making sure that all these outlets are on the same page, a challenge that will only grow as twenty-four-hours-a-day, seven-days-a-week, or 24/7, instantaneous news cycles become ever more voracious in their appetite for information, comment, and analysis.

THE SYNOD OF BISHOPS

Paul VI created the synod in 1965 as a means of providing the Pope with regular access to the voice of the world's bishops to assist him in governing the universal Church. The synod is not, as some analysts have dubbed it, a kind of "parliament for the Church," because it has no decision-making authority. All of its conclusions are merely suggestions to the Pope, and it is up to him to decide what to do. It is the Pope who issues the concluding document from the synod, in his own name. Nevertheless, Paul VI envisioned the synod as a sort of continuation of the Second Vatican Council in miniature, an experiment in collegial governance of the Church. An *ordinary* meeting of the synod is designed to deal with some question of universal relevance for the entire Church. An *extraordinary* meeting deals with some situation of urgent relevance for the universal Church. A *special assembly* considers a subject of relevance for one region, either a specific nation or an entire continent. To date, there have been twenty meetings of the synod.

Regardless of the type of meeting, the process is the same. Before the synod a working paper is drafted by the Synod Secretariat called the *lineamenta*, from a Latin word meaning outline, and sent out to participants for comment. After feedback is received, this document is revised into the *instrumentum laboris*, which is to be the guide for discussions during the meeting. In theory, speeches in the assembly should be phrased as comments on the *instrumentum laboris*, though in reality people are free to raise pretty much any subject under the sun.

The bishops, usually some 225 or so, along with a handful of other clergy, such as the head of religious orders, and occasionally a few lay members, spend the first week or so of each synod giving speeches. The format calls for each participant to signal when he or she wishes to speak. Names are put on a list each day, and each speaker reads his or her speech from a seated position in the auditorium. There is an eight-minute time limit, which is more or less enforced depending on who the speaker is. Cardinals and other celebrities, such as Kiko Arguello, founder of the Neocatechumenate, get more leeway. In theory, the speeches are the property of the Synod Secretariat and are supposed to be kept secret, with only short and typically anodyne summaries distributed to the press. In fact, however, there is always a flourishing black market for the full texts of these addresses, and journalists from the different language groups often arrange swap meets. In some cases, bishops themselves hand out their texts, which they want to see quoted in the world's press.

In the second phase of the synod, which usually lasts a week, participants divide up into small groups, called *circuli minores*, organized by language to discuss the ideas that have surfaced. Each puts together a list of suggestions for the Pope, which are then submitted to two facilitators called the special secretary and the general rapporteur, both positions appointed by the Pope. The two combine the proposals into a general list of propositions. In the third phase, the groups discuss the list of propositions. They can suggest amendments, but the ultimate decision as to what goes on the list belongs to the special secretary and the general rapporteur. Then the full synod votes up or down on the propositions, which are considered secret and go to the Pope. After some months, and in the case of the second assembly for Europe after three years, the Pope issues an apostolic exhortation offering the fruits of the synod to the world.

John Paul II obviously believes in this process, because he has sat through almost every day of each of the twenty meetings of the synod to date—a record that no one else can claim. At the same time, the Pope's faith is not universally shared. Critics complain that the synod amounts to sound and fury signifying nothing, since the process from start to finish is under tight Vatican control. The Synod Secretariat sets the agenda and prepares the working documents, and papal appointees determine what ideas survive in the propositions. In the end, the synod's conclusions are up to the Pope anyway. This reality has led to a sort of cynicism. For example, most days John Paul sits in front of the synod hall and is often seen praying his breviary, the book that contains the daily prayers of the Church. An old joke, however, has it that the Pope is not really reading the breviary, but the synod's conclusions while the event is still going on!

In the end, however, this may be a case of whether the glass is half-empty or half-full. It's true that synods do not produce the immediate, decisive action that many Catholics would like to see. But the Catholic Church, with its two-thousand-year history and 1-billion-strong global membership, is not designed to turn on a dime. It needs time for ideas to mature and for a wide base of support to build in order to accommodate change without rupturing communion. What the synod perhaps provides is a chance for ideas to get a first hearing, to be injected into the Catholic bloodstream in order to see how the body reacts. During those eight-minute speeches in the first week, participants have the liberty to raise whatever concerns they like, and the world's press is listening. The Asian bishops did just this in 1997, making a case for inculturation and an approach to "mission" based on dialogue and witness. At the most recent synod, more than fifty speakers raised the need for greater collegiality in the Church, despite specific instructions to avoid the topic. It was an unmistakable signal that this issue is "on the table" and will have to be confronted, even if the synod itself brought no closure. One could argue that the synod offers a valuable sounding board for the Church, even if its bark is, at present, worse than its bite.

2

TOP FIVE MYTHS
ABOUT THE VATICAN

*P*ilgrims who arrived at the famed cathedral in Siena, Italy, during the fifteenth and sixteenth centuries would have come across a series of busts of popes, including one bearing a rather remarkable inscription: "John VIII, a woman from England." The statue, placed in the cathedral around 1400, reflects the widely held conviction in Europe for more than three hundred years that a woman had once been Pope of the Roman Catholic Church. She was known as "Pope Joan," and there are more than five hundred textual references to her story during the late Middle Ages and early Renaissance. Even today some Catholic feminists take Pope Joan as a point of reference, even while, in most cases, recognizing that she's fable rather than fact.

Although there are different versions of the Pope Joan legend, the most common form goes like this. In the ninth century, a woman of English origin, but born in the German city of Mainz, begins to dress like a man and heads off to Athens, where she becomes a learned theologian. Later she moves to Rome, still dressed like a male, now in clerical garb. She begins to ascend the career ladder in the Curia, gaining a reputation for learning and virtue. Upon the death of Pope Leo IV in

855, she is elected Pope and takes the name of John. She rules for two and a half years before her secret is discovered, in the most shocking fashion possible. She becomes pregnant and gives birth to a child in the middle of a papal procession from St. Peter's Basilica to St. John Lateran. (The site is usually thought to have been between the Colosseum and the Church of St. Clement.) Some versions of the story say she was immediately stoned to death, others that she went into exile. Those who believe she survived often added that her child grew up to be the Bishop of Ostia.

Despite a complete lack of historical plausibility, Renaissance writers such as Boccaccio and Belli regarded the Pope Joan story as literally true. The Czech reformer Jan Hus, hauled before the Council of Constance in 1414 to defend ideas that would later help fuel the Protestant Reformation, cited the story of Pope Joan in his own defense, and no one challenged its veracity. It wasn't until the awakening of the science of historical criticism that people began to realize how wildly improbable the story actually was. There is very good evidence, for example, that Benedict III was elected Pope immediately after the death of Leo IV in 855, with no room for another Pope, female or otherwise, in between. None of the other time frames that have been suggested over the years work any better. The reality is, there never was a Pope Joan. Even so, the story continued to be recycled down the centuries, especially in Protestant and Masonic circles. What better evidence of the fallibility of the papacy than that it failed to detect a woman Pope for two and a half years, until she gave birth in the streets of Rome?

How did such a story get started? For one thing, when medieval popes took possession of the Cathedral of St. John Lateran, they apparently would seat themselves upon a marble throne in front of the cathedral that had come from the nearby Roman baths. It seems to have been, in fact, an ancient toilet, and hence was open in the middle. That fact gave rise to the rather vulgar fantasy that when the newly elected Pope was seated upon this throne, someone reached up from beneath to verify his manhood. The reason for such an inspection, as the legend went, was to avoid another Pope Joan fiasco. It's also true that medieval popes generally avoided the street between St. Clement's and the Colosseum when in a processional to St. John Lateran, ostensibly because it was too narrow, although many believed it was because of the memory of the illicit birth that had taken place on the spot. More basically, however, most historians believe the story reflects the female domination of the papacy in the tenth and eleventh centuries. While there was no Pope Joan, there were a number of female powers behind the throne effectively calling the shots. Pope John X, elected in 914, owed his elevation to his mistress, Theodora, whose beauty, talents, and intrigues had made her the unofficial queen of Rome. Theodora's daughter, Marozia, wielded a similar influence over Sergius III and helped engineer the election of her son by Sergius to the papacy with the title of John XI. At a still later period, John XII was so enthralled by one of his concubines, Rainera, that he entrusted her with much of the administration of the Holy See.

Over the centuries, the Vatican has acted as a magnet for legends, myths, and conspiracy theories such as that of Pope Joan. In part, this is because the odd dress, ritual, and language of the Holy See invite speculation, just like the Skull and Bones Society at Yale. In part, it's because the Roman Catholic Church tends to excite strong passions, among supporters and detractors, and all sorts of wild allegations that would not be taken seriously if attached to other institutions manage to get a hearing. The modern equivalents of the Pope Joan legend take different forms. Since popes are constantly on the public stage, it's no longer credible to believe that a cross-dresser could somehow go unnoticed. Our Vatican mythology is of a twenty-first century, *X-Files* sort: occult financial wheeling and dealing, vast political conspiracies, high-tech secrecy and treachery. Like the legend of Pope Joan in its day, however, these myths have a wide following. A surprising number of otherwise intelligent people, including many Catholics, regard the Vatican as an ultrasecretive, Stepford wives–type environment with a maniacal focus on wealth and power.

From a certain point of view, one could argue that these myths are basically harmless. It can be amusing to contemplate in a "what if?"

fashion the possibilities of something like the Pope Joan story. The problem, however, is that mythology gets in the way of understanding. Especially in the English-speaking world, people who want to talk about the Vatican usually start out with a bundle of stereotypes, rooted in movies and cheap novels and yellow journalism, that collectively make it difficult for them to see the institution for what it really is. Getting past these popular myths represents the biggest obstacle facing anyone seeking to explain what the Vatican is actually like.

To take just one example, every year during the Peter's Pence collection, an annual worldwide fund-raising drive in support of the Pope's charities, people will demand to know why the Vatican is asking for money. The obvious answer—it doesn't have any—is one that most people simply can't, or won't, accept. Their perceptions are shaped by the myth of vast Vatican wealth, fueled by sensationalistic media accounts of Vatican Bank scandals, plus movies and TV shows that showcase the glittering magnificence of the Apostolic Palace. My own family is no exception to such perceptions. One year my grandfather announced to his local pastor in Hill City, Kansas, that if the Pope really wanted to help the poor, he could sell "one of those hats" and give the proceeds away. Grandpa was referring to the papal tiara, a jewel-encrusted crown popes once wore, and he didn't realize that Paul VI had done just that in 1964. Unfortunately, there are more poor people than papal crowns to go around, and if the Pope wants to help them, he's got to get the money from somewhere. In reality, the Vatican is less well-heeled than most mid-sized American colleges, and all that artistic splendor people usually think of as "Vatican treasure" has no cash value because it can never be sold or borrowed against.

Before we can get down to the main business of this book, therefore, we have to clear away some of this intellectual clutter. This chapter is designed to make it possible to talk honestly and in a clear-eyed fashion about the realities of the Vatican. It will be difficult, and in some cases impossible, for readers to let go of these myths, either because they feed their prejudices or because they're simply too much fun. Once you puncture the myth of Vatican secrecy, for example, what's to become of legends about the elite Opus Dei movement acting in cahoots with rogue elements in the CIA, or some other secret agency, to advance a global plot? (Think of the success of the recent potboiler novel *The Da Vinci Code*.) Others will cling to the illusion that the Vatican is an idealized spiritual preserve, where no one ever thinks a political thought or acts for any motive other than perfect obedience to the Holy Father. Being willing to think past such mythology is, alas, the price that must be paid for seeing the Vatican as it really is.

MYTH ONE: "THE" VATICAN

This first bit of news, which will be surprising to many readers, is that there is no such thing as "the Vatican." At least, there is no "the Vatican" in the sense that most English-speaking journalists, commentators, and activists use the phrase. In the pages of the *New York Times*, or in press releases from activist groups such as Catholics United for the Faith or Call to Action, or in the comments of TV pundits, one finds phrases such as "The Vatican wants," or "The Vatican announced today," or "The Vatican is afraid that . . ." In reality, such formulae are built on an image of the Vatican that is more mythic than real.

The implicit assumption in such language is that there is a living creature somewhere called "the Vatican" with a single mind and a single will capable of wanting or fearing, capable of acting in a unified fashion. In fact, a moment's reflection should expose the falsehood of this notion. The Vatican is not an organism, it is a bureaucracy. It is staffed by human beings, each of whom has his or her own wants, fears, intentions, visions, hopes, and dreams. Anyone who knows a bureaucracy from the inside can spot where the fault lines lie, who's in which camp, and where the major disagreements are. Spend some time around the Holy See, and it will become clear that in some ways, though certainly not all, it reflects the diversity of the wider Catholic world. There are progressives and traditionalists, sticklers for liturgical fine points and social justice activists who couldn't care less when one kneels and when one stands, ecumenical dreamers but also hardheaded realists who think dialogue with Protestants is a waste of time. Only from a distance can the Vatican seem like an indistinct gray mass in which everyone looks alike, acts alike, and thinks alike. Seen from up close, it is far more polychromatic.

Two examples make the point.

The two most powerful Germans in the Holy See are Cardinal Joseph Ratzinger, who runs the Congregation for the Doctrine of the Faith, and Cardinal Walter Kasper, who heads the Pontifical Council for Promoting Christian Unity. Both are eminent theologians, both once taught at Germany's premier theological institute in Tübingen, and both have crossed swords over the years with the premier enfant terrible of twentieth-century German Catholic theology, Hans Küng. On different occasions, Küng has accused both of "scarlet fever," that is, a desire to move up the ecclesiastical ladder. Both were among the key figures in the launch of the theological journal *Communio*, founded as an alternative to the more liberal post–Vatican II publication *Concilium* dominated by Küng and his progressive allies. One might think, therefore, that Ratzinger and Kasper would be like two peas in a pod. In fact, the two men have serious theological differences and have explored them in a series of public exchanges.

The heart of the disagreement is over the relationship between the local church and the universal Church. Ratzinger believes that the Church was universal before it was local, that the Church was intended for all of humanity before it began to take on local forms in Jerusalem, Antioch, Damascus, Corinth, and so on. In a November 2000 address in Rome, Ratzinger said: "This ontological precedence of the universal Church, the one Church, the one body, the one bride, over the concrete empirical realizations in the particular Churches seems to me so obvious that I find it hard to understand the objections to it." Kasper, on the other hand, argues that the local and universal churches are intrinsically related—just as the local church cannot be fully itself apart from its reference to the universal, so the universal Church has no reality apart from its incarnation in a local setting. For Kasper it makes no sense to talk about which "came first."

The dispute may sound technical, but it has wide-ranging consequences. Ratzinger's accent on the universal Church tends to promote a top-down ecclesiology, emphasizing the authority of Rome. Kasper's view lends itself to a more decentralized vision. Here's how Kasper put it in his response to Ratzinger's Rome lecture: "A local church is not a province or a department of the universal Church: it is rather the Church in that particular place. The bishop is not a delegate of the Pope but rather a representative of Jesus Christ: he enjoys his own sacramentally-based individual responsibility." The article in which Kasper unfolds this argument was published first in a German theological journal, then in both the U.S. journal *America* and the English Catholic weekly *The Tablet* in separate English translations.

The editors of *America* invited Ratzinger to respond, which he did in the November 19, 2001, issue. The disagreement, Ratzinger wrote, should be clarified by reference to the "Letter to the Bishops of the Catholic Church on Some Aspects of the Church as *Communio*," published by his congregation on June 28, 1992. That letter contains the principle "that the universal Church (*ecclesia universalis*) is in its essential mystery a reality that takes precedence, ontologically and temporally, over the individual local churches." Ratzinger understands the concerns for authority that underlie Kasper's critique. He writes: "Why does this same association keep coming up everywhere, even with so great a theologian as Walter Kasper? What makes people suspect that the thesis of the internal priority of the one divine idea of the Church over the individual churches might be a ploy of Roman centralism?" He answers his own question by noting that the term "universal Church" is often understood to refer to the Pope and the Curia, while its deeper theological meaning is dismissed as a pure abstraction.

Kasper replied in a German essay: "The formula becomes thoroughly problematic if the universal Church is being covertly identified with the church of Rome, and de facto with the Pope and the Curia," Kasper wrote. "If that happens, the letter from the Congregation for the Doctrine of the Faith cannot be read as an aid in clarifying *communio*-ecclesiology, but as a dismissal of it and as an attempt to restore Roman centralism."

To close observers of the Vatican, the fact that two cardinals disagree on a theological question is hardly news. During the era of the Second Vatican Council, for example, clashes between Cardinals Alfredo Ottaviani, Ratzinger's predecessor, and Augustine Bea, Kasper's predecessor, were the stuff of legend. The subject was actually not all that different. Usually, however, an effort is made to contain these disputes behind closed doors, on the theory that it could be destabilizing to expose disagreements. In the case of Ratzinger and Kasper, they opted to go public, and many observers believe the Church is healthier for their example of reasoned and civil, but still very sharp, debate.

Let's take another classic case of Vatican officials not singing from the same hymnbook. There are two critical jobs in the Holy See when it comes to liturgy, meaning the ritual and worship of the Church. The first is prefect for the Congregation for Divine Worship and the Discipline of the Sacraments. This congregation approves liturgical texts such as the Roman Missal (the book of prayers for the Mass), translations of these texts into the various languages, and adaptations of liturgical practices on the local level. If a Catholic in Peoria doesn't like the way his local parish is celebrating the Mass, and if he can't get satisfaction from the bishop, it's the Congregation for Divine Worship with which he can lodge an appeal.

The second office with impact on the liturgy is the Office of the Liturgical Celebrations of the Supreme Pontiff. Its job is to organize the liturgies celebrated by the Pope, which include canonization and beatifications, the Holy Week and Christmas liturgies that are broadcast around the world, and all the Masses and prayer services when the Pope travels. The Master of Ceremonies, who is the head of the office, exercises tremendous influence because whatever people see the Pope doing will be widely imitated. "If it's good enough for the Pope, it's good enough for me" is a bit of Catholic wisdom that has resonated down through the ages.

From February 1998 to September 2002, the prefect of the Congregation for Divine Worship was Cardinal Jorge Medina Estévez, a Chilean who had been a *peritus*, or theological expert, at Vatican II. Along with Ratzinger, another former *peritus* from the council, Medina represented a current of opinion that the reforms unleashed by the council were going too far. That view had deep roots. On October 11, 1972, Medina, Ratzinger, and six other members of the International Theological Commission wrote to Paul VI to express urgent concern that the "unity and purity of the Catholic faith" was being compromised by inaccurate and theologically suspect translations of liturgical texts from Latin into the vernacular languages. They complained that the Congregation for Divine Worship was relying on local bishops' conferences to judge the quality of translated texts rather than examining them carefully in Rome. Thus twenty-five years later, when Medina was appointed to head this office, it was with a clear sense of what had to be done: break the structures that had engineered the liturgical reform.

In just under five years, Medina managed to push through sweeping changes in the rules according to which liturgical texts are translated into the vernacular languages, insisting upon a more literal and "Roman" approach. He also took a wrecking ball to the International Commission on English in the Liturgy, a translation body that had become a favorite target of conservative liturgical activists. Key ICEL personnel resigned under pressure, a stern new set of rules on translation was promulgated in the May 2001 document *Liturgiam Authenticam*, and a new set of statutes for ICEL was prepared to give Rome more control. Rome now has indirect power to approve ICEL staff, plus a clear acknowledgment that it is the Congregation for Worship, not the bishops' conferences, which erects the commission.

At the same time all this was happening, the papal Master of Ceremonies, Italian Archbishop Piero Marini, was an unabashed supporter of the very reforms Medina was intent on reversing. As a young cleric, Marini, now sixty-one, served as personal secretary to Archbishop Annibale Bugnini, head of the special Vatican commission that oversaw

liturgical reform. Bugnini became the lightning rod for what some regarded as unacceptably radical changes, and his fall from power in July
1975 was the beginning of a backlash that eventually culminated in
Medina's campaign. Marini worked in the Vatican on liturgical issues
until 1987, when John Paul II named him Master of Ceremonies. More
people have watched Masses planned by Marini than by any other litur-
gist in the world.

Marini clearly believes in the progressive liturgical vision of worship that is dynamic, participatory, and shaped by the local culture. In a
June 2003 interview with the *National Catholic Reporter*, he talked about
the tunnel vision before Vatican II: "It was the liturgical expression of
the countries of the Mediterranean Basin," he said. "With the separa-
tion of the Protestants, also in France, what remained was Spain, Italy,
Austria . . . the Church had been reduced to something relatively small.
But with the New World, Latin America, and the various missions in
Africa and Asia, it was necessary to open this liturgy that had been
closed to the new peoples. That happened with the Second Vatican
Council and with the trips of the Pope."

Hence for five years, the Vatican's top two officials on liturgy
were at loggerheads. One symptomatic flashpoint was liturgical dance.
The Congregation for Divine Worship, even before Medina, had
frowned on the idea of dance in the liturgy. In 1975 it issued a document titled *Dance in the Liturgy*, which concluded, "[Dance] cannot
be introduced into liturgical celebrations of any kind whatever. That
would be to inject into the liturgy one of the most desacralized and de-
sacralizing elements; and so it would be equivalent to creating an atmosphere of profaneness which would easily recall to those present and
to the participants in the celebration worldly places and situations."
Medina aggressively enforced this policy. In 1998, for example, he
wrote to the bishop of Honolulu to ban the use of hula dancing in any
liturgical context, a custom that had become common among Catholics
in Hawaii.

Yet when John Paul visited Brussels in 1995 for the beatification
of Fr. Damien DeVeuster, the famous saint of the Hawaiian lepers, a

hula dance was performed smack in the middle of the ceremony. For those who know Marini's style, it was hardly a surprise. Anyone who has ever attended a major papal liturgy, such as a World Youth Day Mass or a major canonization Mass, has seen enough dance to remind them of Broadway production numbers. During the World Youth Day Mass in Rome in the summer of 2000, for example, a troupe of young dancers bearing flags with different colors representing different countries was one of the highlights of the event. In Mexico, when John Paul II canonized Juan Diego, the indigenous visionary at the heart of the cult surrounding Our Lady of Guadalupe, native Aztec dancers gyrated down a walkway toward the Pope as native music blared forth. The next day, when the Pope beatified a pair of Mayan martyrs in the same spot, another native dance was performed. This time there was the further twist of a *limpia*, or purification, ceremony. The Indian blessing is believed to cure spiritual and physical ailments by driving off evil spirits. Indian women bearing smoking pots of incense brushed herbs on the pontiff, Mexico City Cardinal Norberto Rivera Carrera, and other prelates as the dancing unfolded.

Some people will be disillusioned to find this sort of clash within the Vatican. In fact, however, that reaction reflects a rather idealized vision of how the Church works. The Church may be protected by angels, but it is still staffed by human beings. Moreover, diversity is healthy. Any organization stagnates without internal tension to keep it creative. The Vatican is full of men and women who care passionately about the Catholic Church, and who bring their intelligence and vision to the task of serving it. Inevitably there will be disagreements, even serious ones. The result is a far greater degree of pluralism within the Holy See than most outsiders realize.

There is not, and never has been, a "Vatican" in the mythic sense. The Vatican is Joseph Ratzinger, but it's also Walter Kasper; it's Jorge Medina Estévez, but it's also Piero Marini. The next time someone tries to tell you what the Vatican is afraid of, what it wants, or what it thinks, the only proper response is: "Who are you talking about?" Not only does this make for clearer analysis, it's also good politics. Catholics of left, right, or center often assume that "the Vatican" is their enemy. The truth is, there are probably people within the Holy See who share their ideas, and identifying and supporting them could create powerful allies for those who can think beyond the mythology.

MYTH TWO: WHO'S IN CHARGE?

When I lecture on the Vatican, the single most frequent question I draw from audiences is, "Who's really in charge?" On one level, the question reflects the perfectly accurate observation that as Pope John Paul II becomes more frail, his capacity to keep track of issues and personnel diminishes. This reality means that a greater share of decisions fall to aides, and it's certainly legitimate to ask who they are. Yet also lurking behind the "who's in charge" question is a mythological assumption that somebody has to be "in charge" of everything. People accustomed to thinking of the Vatican as "the world's last absolute monarchy" assume that means the Pope makes all the decisions for global Catholicism, and if it isn't the Pope pulling the strings, somebody else, or a small cabal, must be doing it for him. The implied image is that there is a computer terminal somewhere deep within the Apostolic Palace and whoever's at the keyboard is running the Church.

Some people propose Ratzinger for this Rasputin role, others Archbishop Stanislaw Dziwisz, the Pope's private secretary. Others would nominate a small group of senior cardinals. Again, there is reality to such perceptions. Ratzinger is one of the most powerful men in the Vatican, and Dziwisz, like all papal secretaries, enjoys tremendous influence as the man who can speak authoritatively as to the mind of the Pope. It is also true that in the real world of the Vatican, some cardinals are more equal than others. Cardinal Giovanni Battista Re, who today runs the Congregation for Bishops, was *sosituto* in the Secretariat of State for eleven years and knows how to work the curial levers of power. That makes him a more formidable figure than, say, Spanish

Cardinal Eduardo Martínez Somalo, now retired from the Congregation for Religious.

Yet the basic reality is this: no one person or group of persons, including the Pope, makes all the key decisions for the Roman Catholic Church. Despite its image as an ultrahierarchical, rigidly controlled organization, the Church is actually remarkably decentralized. No one in the Vatican decides how much St. Anne's Parish in Arlington, Virginia, can spend on pencils. Even within the Holy See, offices operate quite independently of one another. Often the left hand really does not know, or in some cases does not approve of, what the right hand is doing. The result can appear to the outside world like incoherence. In theory and in canon law, the Pope has "supreme, full, immediate and universal ordinary power" in the Church. In reality, things are not as tightly controlled as the "Who's in charge?" myth suggests.

Consider, for example, the brouhaha that broke out in 2001 over the $10 million renovation of St. John the Evangelist Cathedral in Milwaukee, Wisconsin. Then-Archbishop Rembert Weakland, widely viewed as among the more liberal American bishops, is also a former abbot primate of the worldwide Benedictine order and a man with strong views on liturgical matters. Broadly speaking, Weakland subscribes to the Marini approach. Under his guidance, plans were made to reshape Milwaukee's historic downtown cathedral, which had been built in 1853 and then rebuilt after a fire in 1935. Controversial steps included moving the altar out of the sanctuary, placing the tabernacle in a Blessed Sacrament Chapel and an organ in the former sanctuary. This plan did not sit well with some conservative Milwaukee-area Catholics. "We had a beautiful cathedral," said Al Szews, head of the St. Gregory VII chapter of the conservative activist group Catholics United for the Faith (CUF). "The art and environment of that cathedral was very conducive to Catholic worship. A little refurbishing certainly was in order, but we became alarmed when we learned what the archbishop wanted to do."

The CUF members contacted the St. Joseph Foundation, an advocacy organization in the United States that tries to help Catholics assert their rights under canon law. The foundation filed a canonical appeal with Medina's Congregation for Divine Worship. On May 26, 2001, Medina faxed Weakland, asking that work be suspended until certain questions were resolved. The archbishop replied to Medina's questions in writing, flew to Rome to answer more questions on June 13, and then resumed the project when he returned. On June 30, Medina sent another fax citing concerns about moving the main altar, the organ in the apse, and the Blessed Sacrament chapel. The letter also noted "regrettable instances" of inaccurate statements in a pamphlet put out by the archdiocese that claimed the changes were sanctioned by liturgical law. On July 3, Bishop Joseph Fiorenza of Galveston-Houston, president of the U.S. Conference of Catholic Bishops, issued a statement of support for Weakland and expressed regret over the controversy.

Weakland then sent a letter to all his priests, stating that:

- *Liturgical documents give the local bishop authority to make "the ultimate decision on the disposition of the spaces."*
- *He and Medina differ on the priority to be given in adapting older churches to current liturgical practices.*
- *The Vatican congregation did not follow correct legal procedures in dealing with the complaint.*

Weakland also charged that a small group of people wanted to humiliate him before his retirement the following year and that others were simply resisting change or misunderstanding the role of a cathedral. In the end, Weakland was the one who signed the checks for the work, and it proceeded according to his specifications. Just to show that he had not lost his sense of humor over the episode, Weakland commissioned a marble plaque for the back of the cathedral to commemorate the renovation. Its tongue-in-cheek Latin inscription reads that the cathedral was redesigned "in accordance with the principles of the Second Vatican Council . . . notwithstanding certain difficulties."

The point of the story is that there are clear limits to how far the

Vatican can go toward throwing its weight around and that when lower levels of authority are determined to assert their prerogatives, they can often do so with surprising resilience. In fact, the Catholic Church is not designed such that the details like the fine points of cathedral design need to be worked out in Rome. On a wide range of matters, from finance to personnel to positions on specific public policy questions, most decisions in the Catholic Church are made on the regional, national, and local levels. When the Holy See intervenes on one issue, it makes news; when it refrains on ninety-nine others, no one notices. In response to the question of "Who's in charge?" as people normally intend it, that is, "Who controls everything that happens in global Catholicism?" the only honest answer is, "Nobody."

In a parallel way, it's fruitless to ask "Who's in charge?" in the sense of one person or force calling all the shots, of the Holy See itself. To be true to the reality of the Vatican, the question has to be rephrased as, "Who's in charge *of what?*"

The first reason is structural. The Vatican is highly compartmentalized, so that each dicastery works in relative isolation, without much communication, at least formally, with the others. There is a strong emphasis on respecting the juridical competence of each office, so that cardinals and their lower-level aides are often hesitant to intervene outside their specific area of authority. Documents and policy decisions can be in the works in one dicastery for months, in some cases for years, before anyone else knows about them. A classic example came with a February 2002 decision to create four new Roman Catholic dioceses in Moscow, a move that angered the Russian Orthodox Church who took it as a sign of Catholic plans to expand in Russia. Cardinal Walter Kasper was scheduled to travel to Moscow just days after the announcement, but given the sharply negative reaction, the trip had to be canceled. It emerged that Kasper had not been informed of the move and had no chance to alert his opposite numbers on the Orthodox side.

Why didn't someone working the Russia desk in the Secretariat of State pick up the phone and give Kasper what Americans call a "heads-up"? One reason that such informal communication is hit and miss is because the Holy See strives to respect official channels of information. An official in one dicastery is not supposed to call his friend in another to get the scoop as to what's going on, because that creates a kind of favoritism. Requests for information are directed to the secretary or undersecretary, who has consistent policies about what is said to whom. In that way, no one can complain about being cut out of the loop because they don't know the right people.

There's also a historical logic for the independence of each dicastery. The reform of the Curia carried out by Pope Pius X in 1908 specified that the congregations would be supreme and autonomous in their own area. An issue brought to the attention of the Holy See was to be dealt with by one and only one dicastery, and not by several at the same time. The idea was to solve the problem of overlapping jurisdiction that had plagued the Vatican in the nineteenth century, when appellants who didn't like the answer they got from one tribunal or congregation simply sought out another, with the result being a riot of often conflicting rulings. By putting up high fences around the work of each dicastery, Pius hoped for greater consistency. In fact, while his reform did result in greater consistency on an issue-by-issue basis, it also created the possibility for greater inconsistency at the big-picture level of overall institutional policy, with different dicasteries pulling in different directions. While the Roman Rota gives consistent responses on annulment cases, whether the Rota's response is also consistent with the theology of marriage being presented by the Congregation for the Doctrine of the Faith is another matter.

The 1967 reform of Paul VI in *Regimini Ecclesiae universae* attempted to tackle this problem by instituting periodic interdicasterial meetings of all the prefects and presidents of the various dicasteries to consider common problems, but to date those sessions have been episodic and of limited effectiveness. One problem is that the meetings try to cover too much ground, from routine administration to major philosophical questions. At one such gathering in 2003, for example, the assembled cardinals and archbishops were asked to discuss the possibility of creating an Eastern Rite patriarchate in Ukraine, and at the same time to consider how to solve the problem of employees clocking in late to work.

There is also a more realpolitik consideration as to why dicasteries often don't communicate well. Prefects and presidents sometimes don't want their employees building networks of information throughout the Vatican that could give them, in effect, an independent power base. One official told me that when he started out in the 1980s, his prefect told him that he would never put two speakers of the same language in the same office—too much possibility they might "gang up on me," the prefect said. As in every bureaucracy, in the Vatican information is power, and no one wants to share too much of it.

The relative autonomy of discasteries has been exacerbated in the pontificate of John Paul II by his own personal style. Those who know the Pope best say that when he came into office in October 1978, he felt that God had a logic for his election. It included addressing the Cold War split between the Soviet empire and the West, persuading Europe that it needs to "breathe with both lungs," East and West, reawakening the pastoral and evangelic dimensions of the papal office through travel, and pursuing a dialogue with the broader culture through his encyclicals and other writings. The price of pursuing these objectives was leaving much ordinary Church business in the hands of his aides. To some extent, John Paul II opted to work around, rather than through, the Roman Curia. The result is that heads of dicasteries have enjoyed a remarkable degree of freedom. That freedom can ebb and flow depending upon the strength and personal interests of the secretary of state, but with Cardinal Angelo Sodano, the incumbent since 1991, there has not been a strong push toward uniformity on most fronts.

Finally, there is a historical reason why, increasingly, no one is "in charge" at the Vatican in the mythic sense. As a papacy nears its end, there are always two camps within the Roman Curia. There are those who realize their service will end with this pope and are anxious to complete its unfinished business. This camp will seem increasingly hard-line in its policies. At the same time, there is another camp that would like to continue in curial service under a future pontificate.

Since it is impossible to anticipate what the next pope will be like, it is safer not to burn bridges. This camp will seem increasingly open to compromises. The nomination of German Bishop Karl Lehmann as a cardinal in February 2001, despite his famous clashes with the Vatican over the years as president of the German bishops conference, is an illustration.

Of course, the buck does still stop on the Pope's desk, and when he wants to bend the institution to his will, he can. John Paul II has ridden roughshod over internal Vatican opposition three times in order to call leaders of the world's religions together with him to pray for peace in Assisi. Yet the point is that for reasons both personal and structural, the Catholic Church is for the most part not directed from the Vatican, and even the departments of the Vatican work independently. If a Pope tried to call all the shots himself, he would do nothing other than make detailed policy decisions dicastery by dicastery, and that's an invitation to miss the forest for the trees.

MYTH THREE: VATICAN SECRECY

No myth about the Vatican is more enduring or widespread than the belief that it is an ultrasecret closed world, impermeable to the outsider. A cluster of adjectives expresses the idea: *Byzantine, mysterious, occult.* Here's how one major American daily newspaper packaged the image in the lead paragraph of a feature splashed across page A1, just ahead of Cardinal Bernard Law's December 13, 2002, resignation:

> *The sense of impenetrability begins at the Vatican gate just beyond St. Peter's Square. Swiss Guards . . . lift their pikes to allow passage only after receiving orders. Farther inside, a gatekeeper checks his list before giving a reluctant nod for a visitor to enter a 12-foot door reinforced with steel and iron spikes to repel invaders. . . . Inside the fortress-like building, an air of secrecy and monarchical*

power wafts through elegant, marble halls like a thick plume of incense.

It's a classic version of what most people believe the Vatican is like. It is also enormously misleading. For one thing, there are far more security checks to enter the White House than to enter the Vatican, despite the absence of iron spikes and Swiss Guards at 1600 Pennsylvania Avenue.

Let's unpack the mythology. Does the Vatican have secrets? Yes, as every government, corporation, NGO, and other institution does. Moreover, for those things it really wants to keep under wraps—such as the files of theologians under investigation or correspondence from American bishops about sexually abusive priests—the Vatican is far more insulated from pressures for disclosure than secular democracies. There are no sunshine laws that compel the Vatican to release case files, no civil judges who can order the institution to turn over records. After the Swiss Guard murders of 1998, for example, the Vatican judiciary conducted its own investigation, the results of which have never been released even to the families of those who died. Unlike corporations, the Vatican does not have to file audited financial statements or release environmental impact studies. Further, the internal culture of the Vatican often resists putting materials in the public realm, for reasons to be discussed later. At an individual level, Vatican officials can range from dismissive to unhelpful when pressed for information. Every journalist I know in Rome has a story of being told, more or less gently, to "buzz off" by a Vatican official when they asked for some insight or data.

The relevant question, however, is this: Granted all the above, is the Vatican more successful than anyone else at keeping things quiet? Not from anything I can tell. To put the point as clearly as possible: the Vatican may try to be secretive, but for the most part, it doesn't succeed. If you are determined and capable, there's very little about the Vatican you can't discover.

For example, each time the Synod of Bishops concludes its business, it produces a set of propositions for the Pope. These proposals, designed to reflect the consensus of the synod, are supposed to be for the Pope's eyes only, so that he won't be influenced by public pressure either for or against particular propositions. The final set of propositions is distributed to participants only on the date of the vote itself, in a stamped and numbered copy, and then collected in an attempt to prevent its circulation. Yet an Italian news agency called Adista obtains the propositions and publishes them within a matter of days after the close of the synod every time. How? They do what reporters do—they gather news from their sources, without getting an engraved invitation from officialdom to do so.

Another example. Roughly a year into my stint as a Vatican correspondent, my newspaper, the *National Catholic Reporter*, broke a story regarding the sexual abuse of nuns, often by priests, in Africa and elsewhere. In some cases the priests looked to these nuns, who were often very young, as safe targets of sexual activity in the midst of the HIV/AIDS epidemic. In at least one case, a priest had actually arranged to abort the child he had fathered with a nun. The disclosures, as shocking as they were in the court of public opinion, were nothing new to the Vatican. In fact, our story was based on five documents that had been submitted to the Vatican as early as 1994. We had been working on the story over a number of months and decided to go forward when I managed to obtain the fifth and final document from a Roman source. The story became a blockbuster, and pushed the Congregation for Religious, working in combination with the major umbrella groups for men and women's religious communities, to take steps to be sure that religious women in Africa, especially in communities that depend entirely on the local bishop, are less vulnerable. At no stage in the reporting of this story did we have any official assistance from the Vatican. In fact, I provided the Vatican press office with a one-page summary of the story several days in advance of publication, seeking comment. There was no response until after we published, when Vatican spokesman Joaquin Navarro-Valls indicated the Holy See was aware of what he called a "geographically limited" problem.

The point of the episode is that "Vatican secrecy" did not prevent the *National Catholic Reporter* from doing this story, any more than "corporate secrecy" allowed Enron to block stories about the financial scandals that eventually made that company a symbol of fiscal meltdown in the United States. The lack of sunshine laws and court orders to unseal documents did not, in the end, stop reporters from getting their hands on the incriminating materials. Is the Vatican going to bend over backward to help out when a news agency wishes to do a story that will not paint it in a flattering light? Probably not anymore than Tony Blair's 10 Downing Street rushed to open its files to British journalists investigating the death of David Kelly or than the Clinton White House made its files available to reporters working the Whitewater investments story. But the bottom line is that, in my experience, the Vatican is no more successful than other major bureaucracies in controlling the information flow.

Comparing it to other centers of global power, the Vatican is actually a great deal less secretive, because it has no off-the-books budgets for spy agencies, no classified weapons programs, no "eyes only" intelligence from satellite intercepts and wiretaps. It has, in short, no secrets of state. Moreover, despite the ominous-sounding names of some of the Vatican's official storehouses of information, such as the Secret Archives, most documentary records are open to any researcher who is willing to buy a *tessera*, the equivalent of a library card. The Vatican policy of unsealing records by pontificate, usually seventy years after the death of the Pope, compares favorably with similar policies for releasing official government records in the United States and Great Britain. Indeed, some historians say the Holy See has been more forthcoming with critical records from World War II, for example, than either British or American intelligence agencies. Moreover, part of the reason that the Vatican can't just throw open its archives is not a penchant for secrecy, but simply logistics: documents have to be sorted, stamped, registered, and bound. That's expert work requiring a specialized knowledge of languages, church history, and Vatican systems, and at one stage the Holy See had only two full-time archivists on the job. Today that number is larger, but there are still under ten, because this kind of specialization doesn't grow on trees.

It certainly is true that the Holy See imposes an official obligation of secrecy upon employees. The *Regolamento generale*, or employee handbook, distinguishes in article 38 between two types of secrecy. The first is the *segreto d'ufficio*, or secret of the office. It stipulates that no employee may give information about decisions or other news that they may know because of their work to anyone who does not have a right to that information. It might be called routine secrecy, a more acceptable-sounding word for which to Western ears would be "confidentiality." The second is the *segreto pontificio*, or pontifical secret, which is more rigorous, historically replacing the old "secret of the Holy Office." It calls for swearing an oath to protect the confidentiality of major decisions that concern the life of the Church. Matters that fall under pontifical secrecy are listed below. Violations can be punished with excommunication.

Every employee, from the moment he or she assumes an office in the Roman Curia, is expected to observe the rules on secrecy in both the general *Regolamento* as well as in the specific handbook for their dicastery. Personnel are also obliged to swear a profession of faith, an oath of fidelity, and a pledge to observe the *segreto d'ufficio* before the head of the dicastery or another superior, according to a formula set out in article 16 and appendix 1 of the *Regolamento*. The rules of pontifical secrecy are further spelled out in an instruction of February 4, 1974, *Secreta continere*. Falling under pontifical secrecy are: 1) the preparation and redaction of pontifical documents for which pontifical secrecy is expressly anticipated; 2) affairs that have to be dealt with by the Secretariat of State under pontifical secrecy; 3) doctrinal denunciations and publications of the Congregation for the Doctrine of the Faith, as well as the investigations leading up to these acts; 4) extrajudicial denunciations of crimes *contra fidem* or *contra mores*, meaning against the faith or against morals, and crimes against the sacrament of penance, as well as the procedures leading to these denunciations; 5) acts of representatives of the Holy See relative to matters covered by the pontifical secret; 6) the creation of cardinals; 7) the nomination of bishops, apostolic administrators, and other ordinaries with episcopal power, including vicars,

apostolic prefects, and pontifical legates, and all the informational procedures related to these appointments; 8) the nomination of superiors
and other major officials of the Roman Curia; 9) anything that refers to
codes and coded correspondence; 10) the affairs and practices of the
Supreme Pontiff, of the chief cardinal or archbishop of a dicastery, and
of pontifical representatives of sufficient importance to be covered by
the pontifical secret.

These obligations may sound sweeping, but for the most part they
boil down to, "Don't give out the office's business before it's finished."
It's an expectation that most bureaucratic systems impose. It should also
be noted that the Holy See sometimes has good reasons for insisting
upon confidentiality. In canon law cases involving allegations against
priests or lay employees, for example, secrecy is designed to allow witnesses and other parties to speak freely, the accused party to protect his
good name until guilt is established, and victims to come forward without exposing themselves to unwanted publicity. Absolute transparency
would not necessarily serve the interests of justice.

Three other values have traditionally supported secrecy in the
Church. First is a certain view of law. Law, from a Roman point of
view, is the expression of a human ideal, a descriptor of a perfect state of
affairs. This view carries with it a realism that most people, most of the
time, will fall short of the law's ideal. It is important to uphold that
ideal, however, to point people beyond themselves. Too much focus on
violations could lead people to question the wisdom, or the feasibility,
of the law. The public forum is for discussion of the ideal; the private
forum, behind closed doors, is where individual failures are addressed.
Second, there is a respect for authority. If the working assumption of
democracies is that power corrupts, within the ecclesiastical system it's
precisely the opposite—power ennobles, because it flows from Holy
Orders and draws on the grace of the sacrament. Secrecy thus carves
out a space in which Church authorities can use discretion, finding a
solution that best fits a particular set of circumstances, without fear that
it will become swept up in broader public debates. The third value is
objectivity. It drives some people crazy that the Vatican will not hand

over its case files even to interested parties. The logic, however, is to protect the independence of the one giving judgment by not making public the input he or she has received, thus subjecting it to "spin." (This point will be further developed in chapter 3.)

There is also a spiritual logic for a certain parsimony when it comes to public disclosure. Fr. Timothy Radcliffe, former master general of the Dominican order, puts it this way: "At the heart of Catholicism and indeed of the Jewish and Christian tradition, is a belief in the immense power of words. Creation is the fruit of God's word, and the Incarnation is a Word made flesh. The sacraments are also an instance of the transformative power of words in our faith. So it follows that one cannot bandy words around irresponsibly. They can give life, but they can also kill. St. Thomas Aquinas believed that one of the most serious sins was to destroy another person's reputation by what one says. This is something that the press does frequently. I believe that this reverence for words is at least implicitly there in the traditional concern for secrecy."

While it's true that the Vatican is hard for outsiders to grasp, this is less because it's secretive than because it's unique. It takes time to become familiar with the system and its personnel. Once that's accomplished, however, there's very little an enterprising observer can't ferret out. For a reporter to understand the Vatican, one must master three "languages": Italian; the specialized language of the Catholic Church, meaning a knowledge of church history, scripture, theology, liturgy, and canon law; and the language of the Roman Curia, meaning its systems and culture. One doesn't have to be a genius to crack these codes, but it requires time. One has to take Vatican officials to lunch and dinner, to attend the sometimes tedious symposia and book presentations and embassy parties where contacts are made and impressions formed, to read the theological journals and news services in several languages where intelligence on the Vatican is found. One has to have the phone numbers and e-mail addresses of theologians and church historians and diplomats handy, with the understanding that these folks are disposed to be helpful. It's a beat where personal contacts outside official channels make an enormous difference, and all that takes time to cultivate. It is essential, however, if journalists wish to accurately open up this world to the public.

Finally, the Vatican is becoming steadily less secretive under the impact of a generational transition. For Vatican officials today in their fifties and sixties, whose formative experiences of the Curia came in the 1960s and 1970s, their mentors were products of the Italian-dominated, pre–Vatican II Roman culture, which was considerably more insular, more suspicious of the outside world, more clannish in its approach to working relationships, more clericalist and elitist. Curial officials who started out in the 1990s have been shaped instead by men who came of age in the Curia after the reforms of Paul VI. The internal culture under these officials is more professional and modern, with greater tolerance for diversity and open conversation. This tolerance may still be less than in most white-collar workplaces in the Western world, but it's a striking change. Curial officials in their thirties today are generally less threatened by the press and less intimidated by their superiors.

An official in a congregation told the following story: "When I first arrived, I was asked to prepare a response to a letter we had received asking the reasons for a particular decision. I worked hard on it, hitting the books to explain the mind of the congregation on this particular point. What I came up with was two pages long. When I finished, I submitted the draft to the secretary. He called me into his office to tell me I had to learn the style of the Roman Curia, which, he said, is *secco, formale, e non dice niente* . . . dry, formal, and doesn't say anything. He handed back the draft with everything crossed out except one line where I acknowledged receipt of the person's correspondence." The official says things are different today. "There's been a definite change of style. We're much more open, more forthcoming, even though I wouldn't say we're effusive."

Let's be very clear: Would it be healthier for the Catholic Church if the Vatican were more transparent? Unquestionably. The heart of this book is the conviction that the Vatican's unique psychology and culture are difficult for people, including most Catholics, to grasp, which generates miscommunication and animosity. Some of this could be avoided if the Holy See were to make a greater effort to bridge the cultural gap. The Vatican is still a long way from what John Paul said he wanted it to be in January 1984, speaking to one thousand journalists: "A 'house of glass' where all can see what is happening and how it carries out its mission in faithfulness to Christ and the evangelical message."

At the same time, it is a serious error—in fact, a myth—to believe that by virtue of its alleged secrecy the Vatican is impossible to penetrate or understand. For anyone willing to take the institution seriously on its own terms, and to spend the time to learn its rhythms, it is quite comprehensible.

MYTH FOUR: VATICAN WEALTH

One can't always blame outside forces for certain myths. Sometimes the Vatican leads with its chin, as it often has on its alleged "fantastic wealth." Consider the Vatican Bank scandals of the 1970s and 1980s, which combined shady business tactics with spectacular ineptitude on the part of key Vatican officials and their banker friends. The affair fired the imaginations of journalists (in his book, *In God's Name*, David Yallop speculated that Pope John Paul I was murdered because he was getting too close to the truth) and filmmakers (Francis Ford Coppola, *Godfather III*). The affair solidified popular suspicion that Vatican officials spend as much time with spreadsheets as with prayer books and that the Vatican must be swimming in untold billions.

Of course, you don't need conspiracy theories to be dazzled by alleged Vatican wealth. The Vatican museums groan with some of the greatest artistic treasures known to humanity, and at least some Vatican officials live and work in exquisite Baroque structures whose cash value defies reckoning. I once took a tour of the Basilica of St. Peter offered by the Fabbrica di San Pietro, the Vatican agency that administers the facility. The layman who runs the office said they had recently asked a well-known Italian contractor to make an estimate as to what it would cost in today's dollars to build the basilica, exactly as it is, from the ground up. He started to work it out, then called off the assignment. There's no point, he reported back to the Fabbrica; the resources required would be so astronomical that no government or corporate entity would ever contemplate such a project today, and the costs are literally incalculable. For German-speakers the Basilica of St. Peter is an especially bittersweet sight, because it was the sale of indulgences to pay for its construction that helped trigger the Protestant Reformation.

Over the years these riches have scandalized and disillusioned many Christians who fail to see the connection between playing international currency markets and following Jesus of Nazareth. Here's a rather typical sentiment, from a guest opinion piece written by Marguerite Lilly of Mesa, Arizona, and published in the *Scottsdale Tribune* of August 13, 2003: "Imagine Jesus walking into the Vatican today. What would he say to those exalted priests dressed in elaborate robes and surrounded by unbelievable wealth? Would he feel he was once again in the temple, face to face with the Pharisees and moneychangers? Sadly I believe so." Or, to take another instance, in August 2003 I published a column about the brutal summer heat in Europe. William McGrane of Easton, Massachusetts, wrote me to ask rhetorically, "How about selling off a few Vatican treasures, buying some air conditioners and opening up cooling centers, i.e., schools, auditoriums, concert halls, etc., and providing genuine relief? Surely Rome could afford it."

Reality is more prosaic. To put it bluntly, the Vatican is not rich. It has an annual operating budget of $260 million, which would not place it on any top 500 list of major social institutions. To draw a comparison in the nonprofit sector, Harvard University has an annual operating budget of a little over $1.3 billion, which means it could run the equivalent of five Vaticans every year. This is to say nothing of the corporate world. The Microsoft Corporation in 2002 spent $4.7 billion on research and development alone, meaning that its R&D budget could fund the Vatican eighteen times over and still take clients out to lunch. That number, by the way, represents a mere 16 percent of Microsoft's annual sales of $293 billion. The point should be clear: on the scale of the world's mammoth enterprises, the Vatican doesn't rate. Its budget would qualify it as a mid-sized American Catholic college. It's bigger than Loyola-Marymount in Los Angeles (annual budget of $150 million) or Saint Louis University ($174 million), but substantially less than the University of Notre Dame ($500 million).

Where does the money come from? Three principal sources: investments and financial activity; earnings from real estate holdings; and contributions from Catholic dioceses, groups, and individuals. The Holy See had about $100 million in investments in 2002, with losses outstripping earnings by $18.4 million. Real estate holdings brought in roughly $50 million. This means the largest source of support came from contributions. Canon 1271 of the *Code of Canon Law* obligates bishops to provide funds to support the Holy See, just as parishes support their diocese: "By reason of their bond of unity and charity, and according to the resources of their dioceses, bishops are to join together to produce those means which the Apostolic See may from time to time need to exercise properly its service of the universal Church."

Each year the largest givers, in terms of nationality, are the Catholics of the United States, Germany, and Italy. The Vatican went through twenty-three money-losing years until 1993. The situation turned around after bishops from around the world agreed to directly assist the Vatican, with prodding from an American, Cardinal Edmund Szoka of Detroit, who was brought to Rome to help turn the economic crisis around.

But is the Vatican sitting on a large pile of wealth that doesn't show up in its annual budget? The total patrimony of the Holy See, meaning its property holdings (including some thirty buildings and seventeen hundred apartments in Rome), its investments, its stock portfolios and capital funds, and whatever it has stored up in a piggy bank for a rainy day, comes to roughly $770 million. This is substantial, but once again one has to apply a sense of scale. What the Holy See calls patrimony is roughly what American universities mean by an endowment—in other words, funds and other assets designated to support the institution if operating funds fall short. The University of Notre Dame has an endowment of $3.5 billion, a total 4.5 times as great as the Vatican's. Once again, when it comes to Vatican wealth, there is less "there" there than most people believe.

A word about the "Vatican Bank," technically known as the Institute for the Works of Religion, or IOR from its Italian acronym. According to an April 2002 report in the *Independent*, the bank manages approximately $3.5 billion in annual assets. It should be noted, however, that the IOR does not belong to the Holy See, and neither do those assets. They belong, as in any bank, to the depositors—in the case of the IOR, these include religious orders, Catholic organizations, Vatican employees, and other private individuals. Profits and dividends from the bank go to the Holy See, but they do not generate mammoth amounts of money (presuming a 10 percent rate of return, the bank might produce $3.5 million each year). The Pope cannot simply spend the Vatican Bank's $3.5 billion in assets as if it were his own money, and the bank is precious little help in offsetting annual operating costs.

But what of the some eighteen thousand artistic treasures in the Holy See? No one's ever done an accounting of their potential cash value, but certainly it would run into the billions. Yet the artworks are nowhere included in official Vatican figures. From the Holy See's point of view, they are part of the artistic heritage of the world, and may never be sold or borrowed against. In 1986, facing a $56 million budget deficit, the Vatican put out a statement saying the artworks and cultural artifacts owned by the Roman Catholic Church constitute "a treasure for all humanity" and cannot be sold. In February 2002 a rumor made the rounds that Pope Paul VI had flirted with the idea of selling Michelangelo's *Pietà* and donating the proceeds to the poor. A French book about Daniel Wildenstein, one of the world's most famous art merchants, claimed that Paul had asked him about the logistics of arranging the sale. Vatican spokesman Navarro-Valls, however, denied the report, stating: "This news has absolutely no foundation. Indeed, it was Paul VI who, following the exposition of the *Pietà* in the United States, gave specific indications that Michelangelo's marble sculpture should not leave the Vatican again without special permission from the Holy Father, through the Secretariat of State."

Michelangelo's famous *Pietà* statue, the Sistine Chapel, or Raphael's famous frescoes in the Apostolic Palace are all listed on the Vatican books at a value of 1 Euro each. In fact, those artistic treasures amount to a net drain on the Holy See's budget, because millions of Euros have to be allocated every year for maintenance and restoration. In some cases, the Vatican wouldn't be able to afford this work without outside support. The Nippon Television Network Corporation of Japan, for example, funded the restoration of Michelangelo's Sistine Chapel to the tune of some $3 million, in exchange for the exclusive right to film sections of the frescoes in the late 1980s. One could argue that the personnel of the Holy See profit because they live and work in the midst of all this gorgeous art, but that doesn't pay the rent or build up retirement savings. Moreover, only the lucky personnel of the Secretariat of State have offices with ceilings etched by Raphael. If you work in the Congregation for Worship, for example, or in the Council for the Laity, you're stuck in an anonymous bureaucratic space that might as well be in the Pentagon or General Motors.

There is one other bit of mythology connected to Vatican finances. This is the notion that Catholics around the world who are dissatisfied should put pressure on the Holy See where it hurts—in the pocketbook. By withholding contributions, this line of reasoning goes, angry Catholics will get the kind of attention that keen theological argument cannot generate. This tends to be an especially common refrain in the United States, since American Catholics are the number-one contributors to the Vatican's annual budget and because Americans are disposed to believe the credo "money talks" more than other peoples.

Again, however, reality paints a different picture. First, it does not seem that American Catholics are inclined to withhold support from the Holy See in times of discontent; in 2002, at the peak of the sex abuse scandals, American giving to the Vatican registered an increase. More to the point, even a successful boycott would seem to have limited potential. Even if we assume that the U.S. share of the Vatican's annual budget is one-quarter, and even if we assume that every Catholic in the United States were to refuse to give a cent, that would mean a shortfall of $61.25 million. In 2002, global contributions to the Holy See went up by $55 million, so that continued increases in annual giving elsewhere might offset a boycott. If not, there are certainly enough rich Catholics in various parts of the world, fiercely loyal to the Holy See, that an emergency appeal could probably raise the difference. It would be especially likely to succeed if it were phrased as a campaign to save the Holy See from pushy Americans. If American Catholics are going to bring pressure for change onto the Holy See, they will have to find a way other than their wallets.

Any number of times I have sat down with intrepid journalists and researchers mesmerized by tales of Vatican wealth, who are without fail enormously disappointed when I lay out the reality. Sometimes a form of denial sets in. "But," they insist, "you haven't actually seen the Vatican's books, have you? You can't say for sure that the Vatican doesn't have a horde of gold stashed away somewhere, or a secret stock portfolio worth billions?" No, I can't. I also can't prove there's no invisible monster under your bed. What I can say is that if the Vatican is sitting on a secret stash of riches, there's little evidence of it in the way the institution functions. While there are a few black Mercedes limousines to ferry VIPs to and fro, and some cardinals do have fairly nice apartments, for the most part Vatican personnel do not live especially large. Most offices are sparsely furnished and rather low-tech, living quarters are plain, and salaries for most officials are strikingly low by First World standards. Hence stereotypes about the opulence of the Vatican would remain largely false, even if it could be shown that the official ledgers have somehow managed to disguise certain assets.

MYTH FIVE: CLIMBING THE CAREER LADDER

An entire corpus of popular entertainment, from Otto Preminger's *The Cardinal* to the Colleen McCullough classic *The Thorn Birds*, have taught outsiders to regard the conflict between career and personal integrity as the essential drama of the clerical life. Ambition in the clerical world tends to create a special sense of scandal, since priests are supposed to be, in a famous phrase of the former Jesuit General Fr. Pedro Arrupe, "men for others." The idea of a priest calculating his climb up the career ladder—first to monsignor, then bishop, then archbishop, then a cardinal's red hat, finally the papacy itself—rankles, since it appears contradictory to Christ's injunction that "the last among you shall be first."

Given that context, it's understandable why some Catholics approach Vatican personnel with suspicion. These are, after all, clerics who by most standards have "moved up" and may be destined for even higher office. The Villa Stritch, where American diocesan priests working in curial service live, is something of an incubator for bishops. Three current American archbishops are former residents: Edward Egan of New York, Justin Rigali of Philadelphia, and William Levada of San Francisco. Moreover, whenever there is a bishop's opening in their diocese, men who serve in the Roman Curia from that diocese will generally be considered candidates.

In the popular mind there's often a de facto assumption that a priest in the Roman Curia is probably a careerist, unless it's proven otherwise. Frequently bundled with that assumption is the suspicion that the priest is capable of doing some shady things—undercutting rivals, for example, or taking positions based on convenience and popularity rather than conscience—if necessary in order to secure his own advancement. This explains the popular belief that the Vatican is a hornet's nest of cutthroat competition. St. Augustine once cautioned that, "Whoever looks in the Church for something other than Christ is a mercenary," and by that standard, popular mythology seems convinced that there are an awful lot of mercenaries in the Holy See.

To call this perception a myth is not to deny that it possesses elements of truth. Are there clerics in the Roman Curia who want to move up the ladder and organize their lives and work accordingly? Yes. Most people who work in the Vatican, in fact, can point them out. Are there episodes, sometimes quite infamous, in which personnel inside the Vatican have engaged in outrageous conduct in order to smear the reputation of a rival or otherwise enhance their own prospects for a promotion? Again, yes. One doesn't have to resort to Monsignor Luigi Marinelli's *Gone With the Wind in the Vatican*, a kiss-and-tell classic by a former Vatican official, to find such tales. Sit down over coffee with anyone who works in the Holy See, and they'll be able to tell terrific anecdotes to illustrate the point.

However, careerism is a case in which reality has become mythologized in terms of quantity rather than quality.

First, it would contravene the laws of human nature were there not some careerism in the Vatican. This is a hierarchical system, and promotion is the primary way the system expresses approval of someone's work. To complain that curial personnel like to be rewarded for a job well done is a bit like complaining that they're human beings. Moreover, some degree of ambition is no bad thing, because it usually means that the person is willing to work hard. This double standard, in fact, offers a classic example of how the Roman Curia can't win. One bank of critics calls them lazy, pointing out how long it takes to get things done; another faction faults them for possessing any drive at all. In other walks of life, we applaud ambition, since it is often the motor fuel of success. Only in the Roman Catholic priesthood do we expect people to turn in consistently excellent work with no thought of personal affirmation. That's a noble ideal, but it is also to some extent unrealistic.

Second, simply as a matter of accurate observation, it is not true that ambition and careerism are the dominant psychological traits of the men and women in the Holy See. Most officials who clock in each morning do not spend the rest of the day trying to figure out how to move up. In many cases, in fact, officials in the Roman Curia never even applied for their job, and after several years have only vague suspicions of how they got there. Dicasteries of the Roman Curia do not placed classified ads in a help wanted column in *L'Osservatore Romano*. When there is an opening, a superior of the dicastery will usually ask around, quietly, among friends and colleagues, looking for qualified personnel. Sometimes the dicastery will reach out to a trusted bishop or the head of a religious order to suggest someone. In some cases a potential Vatican official is not aware he or she is under consideration until the decision has already been made. In almost no case does the official apply for the job. There are no applications to fill out, no curriculum vitae to send in. It is, literally, a case of "don't call us, we'll call you."

In some cases when a candidate is approached, the first response (and sometimes the second and third) is no. The person may have a promising academic career, may prefer not to live in Rome or may want a pastoral assignment rather than working behind a desk. Some want to be free to write and publish under their own name. Most have no desire to be in the Curia forever, or even very long. One of the untold stories of curial hiring, in fact, is how difficult it can be to fill certain slots because people with the proper training and professional experience don't want the job. I could fill a small dicastery with friends who have been approached about working in the Roman Curia and turned it down. It's not that these friends are less career-oriented than the officials who eventually said yes. In some cases, in fact, they rejected the curial job precisely because they knew they would find more prestige, more affirmation, greater personal satisfaction, and even more money with other pursuits.

It will be useful at this stage to allow three curial officials to speak for themselves, as a window onto what the real attitudes within the Holy See are on the careerism issue. The first is a North American priest in his fifties, who has worked in the same dicastery since the 1980s; the second is an Italian in his forties who is considered a rising star in the Secretariat of State; and the third is a young Northern European who works in a congregation and who is at the same time trying to complete a doctoral degree at a Roman university.

The North American never wanted to work in the Roman Curia, and in fact did everything he could to avoid the assignment. He was first approached in the mid-1980s, after he had finished a doctorate in Rome and had returned to his home diocese to teach in the seminary, which had been his dream. One of the cardinals of the Roman Curia was looking for someone whose first language was English and had asked around town for suggestions. This man's name came up, and so the curial cardinal sent him a letter. The priest went to his vicar general in his home diocese, saying he didn't want the job, but the vicar encouraged him to go to Rome and to hear what the curial cardinal had to say. The priest did so and was offered the job. After consultation with his spiritual director back home, he turned it down. After a few weeks, he got a phone call from his own cardinal's secretary, saying the cardinal wanted to see him. When the priest showed up for the appointment, the cardinal asked if he had made a firm decision. The priest said yes, he was happy teaching in the seminary and had also just been accepted for another doctoral program in the States that he wanted to pursue on a part-time basis. The cardinal advised him to think again, and asked, "Why not just go over for a year or two?" In the end, the priest realized that the curial cardinal had enlisted his own cardinal's blessing, and that no was not an acceptable response. He agreed to go to Rome for two years, and has been in the dicastery ever since, some twenty years now. For him, the idea that he came to Rome to make his career is absurd— he came kicking and screaming, and being here for almost two decades has not shot him up the ladder. He is in the same job he was when he arrived.

The Italian had completed his studies at the Pontificia Accademia, the training ground for future diplomats in the Church, when he was approached by the rector of the college where he was living, the Capranica. (In the European system, a college is a residence, not a place of study.) Anyone who knows Italy realizes that a young cleric who is selected to study at the Accademia and to live at the Capranica is going places, and it was no great shock when the rector said there was interest in this man's services at the Secretariat of State. "Before the rector proposed it, I had never sought it," the priest insists. "But it was not unusual." Like many Italians, he takes a very realistic view of clerical ambition. "We are human beings, sensible to all the gratification that conditions a normal human life," he said. "People do have ambitions and desires. I believe that you have to be honest with yourself. The goal of your work is not to become first, but to render service. If it's possible to do this with gratification of being recognized, all the better. We're not called to become martyrs." The priest added that in his job he is often asked to liaison with secular governments, where he said the drive for career advancement is far more palpable than in the Roman Curia. "Yes, some of us hope to be bishops, in the same way that a vice-pastor wants to be pastor, a pastor wants to be the vicar general or president of the tribunal, and the vicar wants to be bishop. Maybe those of us of the Roman Curia feel this a little more, because we spend so much of our time with high-profile contacts. But on the other hand, I know of two cases where a curial official turned down a bishop's appointment, arguing that they were better suited for other work."

The Northern European priest, a soft-spoken and short man who looks much younger than his forty-one years, was training to teach Scripture in his diocesan seminary when a friend in Rome approached him about working in one of the Vatican congregations. He said he had already promised himself that he would never seek an assignment in his priestly career, and he would never exclude an assignment, in order to be open to what God might want. He told his friend that if the congregation was serious, they should contact his cardinal. Later that fall he saw the cardinal and asked if he should send in his curriculum vitae. The cardinal said no, let the congregation deal with me. The priest had the impression that the cardinal was not inclined to let him go, and so he forgot about the prospect. Next spring, however, the cardinal told him to go to the dicastery for an interview, which happened over the summer. At that time it seemed clear they had already settled on him for the job. By September he began work, having received the obligatory *nulla osta*, or "all clear," from the Secretariat of State. He's been in his congregation now five years, and says that if the call came to come home tomorrow, he'd be ready to go. "I don't want to be here just to be here. I don't want that awful kind of possessiveness," he said.

Bottom line: none of these three men sought their assignments, and none would be crushed to let their job go. The Italian priest in the Secretariat of State, reflecting the general tendency of Italian clerical culture, is more frank about his career ambitions, but does not seem consumed by them. In each case, they appear to have balanced, sober attitudes toward life and work that do not resemble the preening lust for power that the careerism myth suggests. Each man concedes that he knows colleagues who seem overly anxious for the next step up the ladder; each reports, however, that they are exceptions. As the Northern European puts it: "That kind of person will rise, but not too far, and certainly not far enough or fast enough for their own taste. They'll be miserable and make other people miserable. Thank God, they're not the majority."

Finally, there is a special variant of the careerism myth, which is that every cardinal dreams of being Pope. Certainly this kind of ambition does happen. Italian journalist Benny Lai's 1993 biography *The Pope Never Elected*, about Cardinal Giuseppe Siri of Genova, made clear that Siri unabashedly felt he would have been a good choice for the Church's top job. Frankly, however, the number of cardinals who entertain such dreams is probably much lower than, say, the number of United States senators who fantasize about becoming president. There are two reasons why. First, the gap between being a senator and being the president is comparatively small. It's easy enough for a senator to imagine himself in the Oval Office. The psychological and theological distance between being a cardinal and being the Pope, on the other hand, is enormous. Most cardinals genuinely have a difficult time believing themselves worthy of such an enormous responsibility. Second, one can have a life after being president. Bill Clinton was only fifty-four upon leaving office after two terms, meaning he could look forward to perhaps as many as twenty-five productive years to do something else. There is no such thing as an ex-Pope. (This is not the place to pursue the point, but canon 332 of the *Code of Canon Law* does provide for a papal resignation. The last time this happened without outside pressure, however, was 1294. The reality is that popes don't resign.) There is no lecture circuit to hit, no memoirs to write, no papal library to open. One carries the burden of office until death. Contrast that with the relatively plush life of a retired cardinal, and it's clear why most members of the College of Cardinals pray that "this cup may pass."

3

VATICAN PSYCHOLOGY

*V*atican officials realize that no one likes being told no. Every time Rome silences a theologian, or tells a priest to get out of politics, or turns down a document from a bishops' conference, or orders a Catholic seminary to pull a textbook, Vatican officials know somebody's going to be unhappy. They also know such crackdowns are likely to generate bad press—sometimes just a rumble, sometimes an avalanche. They realize that these moves can divide the Church internally and blacken its eye externally. While some in the Holy See may pride themselves on displaying nerves of steel in the teeth of such controversy, the vast majority do not seek opportunities to knock heads simply to get a few notches in their belt. The stakes have to be fairly high before most Vatican officials will be willing to intervene.

That said, perceptions as to just what the stakes are, and when they're high enough to justify action, can be very different in Rome than in other places. To outsiders, Vatican choices can occasionally seem not just debatable, but almost inexplicable. Such was the case in mid-November 1997, for example, when the Holy See released a document titled *Instruction on the Collaboration of the Non-ordained Faithful in the Sacred Ministry of Priests*. The prefects of eight congregations signed the letter (technically known as an interdicasterial document) and the Pope approved it. Among its other provisions, the document stipulated that:

- Only a priest can direct, coordinate, moderate, or govern a parish.
- Laity may not assume titles such as pastor, chaplain, coordinator, moderator, which can confuse their role with that of the pastor, who is always a bishop or priest.
- The homily during Mass must be reserved to the priest or deacon, even if laypeople act as pastoral assistants or catechists.
- In Eucharistic celebrations, deacons or laity may not pronounce prayers or any other parts of the liturgy.
- Laity may not wear sacred vestments (stoles, chasubles, or dalmatics).
- Laity may distribute Communion only when there are no ordained ministers, or when those ordained ministers are unable to distribute Communion.

Reaction was, for the most part, predictably hostile. The document was widely seen as a naked attempt to keep the laity "in their place." In some instances, its edicts also seemed completely impractical. To take one example, some 80 percent of hospital chaplains in the United States are laity. Trying to fill those positions with clergy in an era of priest shortages would be an exercise in futility. Many commentators were amused that the Vatican considered the use of the title "chaplain" by lay people a serious enough crisis that it required the heads of eight dicasteries to handle it. It seemed almost a self-parodying variant of, "How many Vatican officials does it take to screw in a lightbulb?" The same incredulity surrounded the document's apparent fear that the sky would fall in if a layperson donned a stole at Mass or distributed Communion on a regular basis. Reflecting this climate of opinion, most reporters presented the document almost entirely as an assertion of Vatican power. The story was one of those cases where journalists fell back on what they knew, power politics, to explain a Vatican move that otherwise seemed irrational.

This sort of incomprehension greets many documents or disciplinary moves from Rome. It's almost axiomatic in some circles that everything the Vatican does is motivated by either power or fear, if not both. Yet when one understands the value system of the Holy See, the *Instruction* made all the sense in the world. Consider:

- Historically, periods when the Church has been fuzzy about the identity of its clergy have tended to coincide with deep crises. The corruption that paved the way for the Protestant Reformation, for example, was made possible by absentee bishops who let their priests go to seed. Ensuring that priests are clear as to their powers and responsibilities is thus considered a service to the health of the Church. This historical perspective is known as "thinking in centuries."

- While theologically sophisticated communities in the First World may scoff at the notion that a layperson wearing a cassock or preaching a homily or being called "chaplain" could confuse anyone as to the identity of the ordained priest, the Vatican has to make policy for the whole world. In mission territories, especially young churches in Africa and Asia, this sort of mixed symbolism can indeed be a real problem for catechists. It's typical Western arrogance, some Vatican officials quietly say, to assume that because something's not a problem in New York or Cologne, it's not a problem for anybody.

- The sacrament of holy orders, and the distinction it implies between the ordained and laity, is rooted in the will of Christ. From the Vatican's point of view, protecting the identity of the priesthood is not just about being a stick in the mud, or running an exclusive club, but about being faithful and accountable to Catholic tradition.

- Laypeople who insist upon wearing chasubles and giving homilies sometimes end up just as clericalized as the clerical caste they set out to dislodge. In some respects, therefore, this document was intended as a defense of the lay role of the average Catholic, out in the world, against an elite that seeks quasiclerical privileges inside the Church.

- Finally, Vatican officials are realistic enough to realize that universal prescriptions such as these may not make sense in every context on the planet, and they are generally willing to turn a prudent blind eye when the situation calls for it. The point of this document was to defend the principle behind the law. Indeed, laity in the United States are still using the title of chaplain seven years after this decree was issued, and no one from the Holy See has brought down a hammer. (Bishop Thomas Doran of Rockford, Illinois, an astute canon lawyer, noticed that the document said laity may not "assume" the title, which left open the possibility that bishops could delegate it to them.)

The point here is not to defend the *Instruction*. It may well be that the document was ill timed or that it should have been more generous. The point is rather to observe that seen from within the mindset of the Holy See, the document was eminently rational and premised on more than simply the maintenance of clerical power. If one wishes to challenge the *Instruction*, that challenge will be more effective if one can show how an alternative strategy could better serve the legitimate values the Holy See was trying to uphold, rather than just scolding the Vatican for arrogance.

This angle of vision is the difference between analysis and judgment. One has to understand why a choice was made, what historical and psychological factors were at work, before a judgment can be based on anything more than one's own biases. This means having the intellectual self-discipline to set aside one's assumptions and to take the perspective of the other seriously. The purpose of this chapter is thus to "get inside the head" of the Roman Curia, to present its worldview in an accurate and sympathetic way, so that decisions of the Holy See can be located within the value system that actually shapes them.

I have elected to make this presentation through the device of a list of Top Ten Vatican Values. By values, I mean the basic principles that form the building blocks of Vatican policy, the ends that Vatican personnel generally strive to protect and defend. This is my list, not the Vatican's. These values are not printed in the employee's handbook of the Holy See or posted in curial hallways. At the same time, however, I didn't pull them out of the air. When I've asked Vatican personnel to explain the subtext to particular issues, whether it was the beatification of Pius IX or the Holy See's stance on the Iraq war, certain core values kept surfacing. Usually we wouldn't start out talking about these values, but in order for officials to explain what the Vatican was trying to accomplish, they fell back on one or more, and usually some combination, of the values listed below. By the way, I am aware that some Catholic moralists shun the term "values" because of its association with Nietzsche and moral relativism. That is obviously not the sense in which I use the term here.

While individual Vatican officials might quibble with one or another choice, overall I believe most people in the Holy See would recognize this set of principles as a fair expression of their institutional culture. I asked several Vatican officials to go through the list with me, item by item. Collectively, I hope these values add up to a profile of what is sometimes called *Romanità*—the unique atmosphere of "Romanness" that permeates the Holy See. Taken in themselves, each value describes a genuine good. As with most things, it is when the value is pushed too far in a particular direction that virtue can turn into vice. Bear in mind, of course, what we said in chapter 2 about the myth of a single-minded creature called "the Vatican." Not everyone who works in the Holy See thinks alike, and no one is going to perfectly identify with this or any other list. Some Vatican personnel actually chafe, occasionally ferociously, against one or more of these values. Nevertheless, as a working guide to the psychology of the Holy See, I believe they amount to a pretty good introduction. The values are listed alphabetically.

Finally, offering this list of values is more than a descriptive exercise. It is also an invitation to more fruitful conversation between the Holy See and Catholics around the world, especially in the English-speaking realm. Since all these values are positive in themselves, or at least have positive dimensions if properly understood, they should be the basis for dialogue in the Church. That is, presumably all Catholics, not merely Vatican officials, strive to uphold these values, even if they may differ on their application in a given set of circumstances. Hence the next time the Vatican is contemplating a policy measure of concern to English-speaking Catholics, it would be useful to phrase arguments not in terms of imputed Vatican motives such as power or fear, but rather to show how an alternative course might better satisfy these common values. Then all parties to the discussion would at least be speaking the same language, and it might lead to surprising areas of common ground.

TOP TEN VATICAN VALUES

Authority

Cardinal Godfried Daneels of Belgium observed during the October 1999 Synod on Europe that the developed West is allergic to the concept of authority, and nowhere is this more true than in English-speaking countries, where Enlightenment-inspired individualism has made self-assertion the heart of what it means to be free. Most English-speakers, certainly most Americans, regard the idea of doing something because they were told to do so as suspect. Obedience is often seen as a kind of cowardice or moral surrender, associated, for example, with German soldiers mindlessly carrying out the orders of their Nazi superiors. It is regarded as something unworthy of educated, emancipated adults. Cultural critics would note that Americans are a nation of "rugged individualists" who drive the same cars, wear the same clothes, drink the same colas, and see the same movies. Nevertheless, it cuts against the grain to accept something solely on the basis that it comes from a superior level of authority. We are in that sense children of Nietzsche, regarding the exercise of our own wills as the *summum bonum* of the moral life.

This is not how things look within the Holy See. Like most bureaucracies with a clear chain of command, such as the Army or General Motors, there's an emphasis on following orders. Yet the roots of the attitude toward authority in the Vatican run much deeper. Its internal culture is closer to the ancient Greco-Roman view of learning, which takes submission to a teacher and a particular tradition of inquiry as its point of departure. Think of Plato's descriptions of the disciples of Socrates gathered around the master, or of the disciples of Jesus pondering the Sermon on the Mount. From this point of view, authority is not opposed to reason, but a prerequisite to it. To put the point in slightly more complex terms, Roman Catholicism is a kind of "narrative tradition" as described by philosopher Alasdair MacIntyre, in which reasoning makes sense only from inside a tradition and under the guidance of those who have mastered it. Taking something on authority is not the sacrifice of one's own conscience, but a decision to shape one's conscience in accord with the tradition, on the theory that doing so will lead to greater clarity and insight. Here's the basic difference: for most Westerners, doing something because they are told to do so by an authority would be irrational. For someone who accepts the claim of a tradition, however, submitting to the decisions of authority, even when its logic is not clear, is an affirmation of faith in that tradition. It's a way of saying, "I'm not an isolated atom but a member of this community of inquiry, and I trust its wisdom."

That philosophical conviction is bolstered by the Church's theology of authority. Power within the Church, according to the perspective widely held in the Vatican, comes from the risen Christ and is entrusted to the apostles and to their successors in the apostolic college, first and foremost to the successor of Peter, the Pope. In a 1995 address to the Congregation for the Doctrine of the Faith, John Paul II described his authority as "a means of guaranteeing, safeguarding and guiding the Christian community in fidelity to and continuity with tradition, to make it possible for believers to be in contact with the preaching of the Apostles and with the source of the Christian reality itself." Obviously, the culture of the Holy See puts a premium on the authority of the Holy Father. Beyond that, there is a strong emphasis on accepting the authority of one's superiors, especially the prefects and secretaries of the various dicasteries, who draw on both the Pope's authority and their own as bishops. As we saw in chapter 2, the working assumption of modern democracies may be that power corrupts, but within the ecclesiastical system it's precisely the opposite—power ennobles, because it flows from Holy Orders and draws on the grace of the sacrament. The bias is always in favor of authority.

That said, few Vatican officials are under the illusion that ordination inoculates their superiors, including the Pope himself, against sometimes being ill-informed, naïve, stubborn, or just plain wrong. Indeed, some of the Pope's fiercest critics are just down the hall from him, or across St. Peter's Square. One *monsignore* who works in the Vatican, for example, told me the Pope has made a serious doctrinal error with his interreligious gatherings in Assisi, and huffs that, "The man has never apologized!" We were looking out his office window toward the papal apartments as he spoke. Other Vatican insiders complain that the Pope was careless in allowing his appeals for peace in Iraq to be seen as an endorsement of the antiwar movement, which lumped together socialists, communists, eco-radicals, and a host of others not always congenial to a Catholic worldview. It's not just the Pope who is the subject of this sort of griping. I've known mid-level officials in dicasteries who, at various times, were convinced that their superior was an idiot or mentally unhinged or simply too weird to be believed. This is all par for the course in any organization full of intelligent, passionate people with their own strong visions about how things ought to be done.

The key point is that for most of the men and women of the Curia, and for others formed in the same intellectual tradition, their respect for authority is not dependent upon any particular exercise of it. It rests instead on the philosophical pillar that the tradition is usually wiser, that it sees further, than the individual. This is coupled with the theological conviction that ultimately authority in the Church comes from God. Submission to authority, even when one can't in the moment see the logic for its choice, is usually a higher value than assertion of one's own vision. Ironically, while Vatican officials are often accused of arrogance, on this point at least their institutional culture enforces a certain epistemological humility. They are shaped to believe there is a wisdom higher than their own. While many Westerners might wonder why that *monsignore* who disagrees with the Pope about Assisi doesn't just walk out, from his point of view, the call of authority trumps his private feelings.

The Vatican's respect for authority rests on two other foundations, one moral, the other historical. The moral element is rooted in Thomism, and the conviction that authority is intended to foster virtue, leading to the practice of a moral life and, ultimately, to salvation. The hierarchically structured Christian Church is thus, by definition, a virtuous community. While allowing that individual bishops may screw up, the assumption is that most bishops, most of the time, use their authority for good ends. Note that this is an assumption about the Church, not about any given official. It does not mean that people in the Curia are naïve about abuses of power. In my experience, Vatican officials usually have no problem believing that Bishop X may have committed mistakes, ridden roughshod over people's rights, or been too weak to assert the interests of the Church. In that sense, they are terrific realists. They see this sort of thing all the time, and, in fact, can site chapter and verse on episodes of episcopal incompetence that would make one's toes curl. But they do not move from such episodes to a systematic criticism of authority in the Church, because they perceive a value in authority that transcends particular acts of poor judgment. It is the value of moral uplift—that by trusting the authority of the Church, over time, despite the potential for disappointments and setbacks, the overall affect will be growth in the moral life pointing toward eventual union with God.

The historical component comes from a recognition that for better or worse, the Catholic Church tends to rise and fall in tandem with how the authority of its bishops and other clergy has waxed and waned. As early as the end of the first century, Ignatius of Antioch urged the local church to be subject to the bishop. In the third century, Cyprian of Carthage wrote, "The bishop is in the church, and the church is in the bishop." For nearly two thousand years, communion with the bishop has been the hallmark of Christian identity. Weak bishops have often been the cause of serious ecclesiastical crises. In the sixth to the ninth centuries, for example, when the bishops in Europe were often subservient to kings and local nobles, the moral standards of the clergy were in disarray and the management of church affairs was shoddy. All one has to do is to read the edicts of the regional synods and councils of the day, which vainly attempted to rein in embarrassing clerical comportment. The Council of Vaison, for example, in 529, complained of drunkenness, incontinence, scandals from the renewal of married life after ordination, theft, and murder. All this was possible in part because weak and compromised bishops, hobbled by lay lords, weren't capable of putting a stop to it.

Similarly in the late Middle Ages, as abbeys and religious orders sliced off progressively bigger chunks of the bishop's authority, and more and more decisions were reserved to the authority of the Holy See, bishops drifted into idleness and the Church suffered. Some became "absentee bishops," holding the title to a see and collecting its revenues but living, often in luxury, someplace else. This meant nobody was supervising the clergy, monitoring what was being taught in schools, and so on. By the time of the Council of Trent in the mid-sixteenth century, a bishop had not lived in Milan for one hundred years. This neglect allowed all sorts of anomalies to flourish, including outlandish requests for indulgences, which was part of the landscape that led to the Protestant Reformation. Trent revivified the bishop's office, reestablishing the bishop's authority and insisting that he live in his diocese to exercise it. Bishops were now obligated to personally ordain all the clergy destined to work in their diocese. What followed was the Counter-Reformation, one of the most glorious and productive periods of Catholic history. Similarly, many observers in the Holy See read the American sex abuse scandals of 2002 in terms of the failure of bishops to exercise their authority.

Policy measures or theological proposals that seem to undercut ecclesiastical authority will thus almost always trigger suspicion in the Holy See. This is not merely a matter of defending clerical power, but about making sure the people of God have the tools they need to form future generations in the faith and to defend the Church when it is under threat. The central tool in that toolbox, from the Vatican's point of view, and rooted in its sense of history, is a strong bishop capable of teaching, sanctifying, and governing the faithful. To take an example of how this plays out, there was considerable negative reaction within the Holy See in May 2003 when Bishop Thomas O'Brien of Phoenix renounced certain powers to oversee his clergy as part of a deal to avoid criminal prosecution related to sex abuse scandals. "It's not so much the details of the agreement that bother me," said one senior Vatican canonist. "He delegated certain responsibilities to a priest, which is envisioned by canon law. It's the idea that the civil authority compelled a bishop to renounce his authority—that's a dangerous precedent." The canonist saw it as dangerous not because it implied the loss of clerical privilege (at least not primarily), but because by weakening the bishop, the long-term well-being of the community could be put at risk.

Bella Figura

This value is drawn from Italian culture: the cult of the *bella figura*, meaning literally "beautiful figure," and translated loosely as the importance of always looking good. Its prevalence in Italy is one reason why Milan is the capital of the world's fashion industry. It's why Italians will spend lavishly to repaint the outside of their houses every year even when the plumbing and electricity don't work. The neighbors don't see the plumbing! Even today, when an Italian is leaving to spend time overseas, a relative is almost sure to issue a reminder: *Si deve fare una bella figura all'estero*, meaning, "You have to make a good impression when you're away!" The bottom line is that no matter what happens, one has to keep up appearances.

This can sound like a rather vain and superficial principle, and at its worst it becomes an excuse for not confronting inner rot as long as the surface looks good. Many Catholics would say that this value played a role in the failure of some bishops to react vigorously when priests were guilty of sexual abuse, contenting themselves with negotiating secret payouts that prevented public scandal. It was in this sense that then-Bishop Sean O'Malley, now the Archbishop of Boston, invoked the term during floor debate at the November 2002 meeting of the U.S. bishops in Washington, D.C. "Church leaders dealt with sexual abuse by clergy in a *modus operandi* that was suggested by a theology of sin and grace, redemption, permanence of the priesthood, but also a great concern about scandal, the *bella figura*, and the financial patrimony of the Church," O'Malley said. "We know now that not enough attention was given to the reporting of crimes, the protection of children, and the spiritual and psychological damage done to victims." The potential for hypocrisy latent in this value is bluntly expressed by the *Economist* magazine, in its guide to business customs in Italy: "When doing business, maintain your *bella figura*—the Italian expression for showing your best face," the magazine counsels. "This means never admitting you are wrong."

The *bella figura* in this sense is undeniably influential in Vatican psychology. Public discussion of problems can sometimes be discouraged simply out of reluctance to air one's dirty laundry in public, an instinct sometimes rationalized as a desire to protect the faithful from shock or hurt. Aside from the rather patronizing nature of such concerns, experience shows they almost always backfire, as the stonewalling generates far more hurt than disclosure would have in the first place.

(This is perhaps the place for a quick footnote about scandal. Sometimes people charge that Church officials try to sweep problems under the rug in order to "avoid scandal," using the term in its generic sense as a publicized incident that causes outrage or disgrace, like the

"Enron scandal." This is not the sense in which Church documents, however, generally use the word. For example, a May 1999 document from the Vatican, defrocking an American priest named Robert Burns, made a brief flurry in the media because it stipulated that Burns "ought to live away from the places where his previous condition is known," unless his presence "will cause no scandal." Some took this as evidence that Rome had ordered a cover-up of Burns's abuse in order to avoid bad press. In Catholic parlance, however, *scandal* has a more technical definition. It means inducing someone to sin against the faith or morals of the Church. The Church has always taught that certain things should be kept quiet if making them public might lead people into serious sin. For example, if a priest committed a heinous act and his bishop felt it was possible that public disclosure would lead people to conclude it was okay for them to do the same thing, that might be a good reason to keep it quiet. Obviously, it's a principle open to abuse. The point is that when the Church says it wants to "avoid scandal," it doesn't mean bad publicity. It means leading people to endanger their souls.)

The *bella figura* can sometimes be an impediment to dealing honestly with disagreements or problems. No one wishes to embarrass a colleague or create negativity within a dicastery, and sometimes this means that errors, poorly reasoned decisions, and even rank incompetence go without challenge. Officials not up to their jobs can survive much longer than in corporate environments, in part because it is considered discourteous to criticize someone's job performance. Curial officials all have stories about meetings dominated by a sort of "emperor's new clothes" dynamic, where there was an obvious personnel problem no one had the courage to point out, and so the entire session was spent pretending not to notice it was there. Sometimes the price of progress is a momentary bit of ugliness, but this can be a very difficult thing to do in a culture that teaches people to avoid confrontation. This doesn't mean that Vatican officials do not get angry as often as everyone else, simply that dealing openly with such emotion can be frustrated by the cult of appearances.

Let's take another example of this sense of the *bella figura*. Cardinal

Giovanni Battista Re, currently the prefect of the Congregation for Bishops, was for eleven years the *sostituto*, or number two official in the Secretariat of State in charge of day-to-day Church affairs. In that position, he earned a reputation as the ultimate curial powerbroker, because, in the words of one Vatican official, "You never left his office without a solution." His genius was finding face-saving compromises that allowed all sides to feel like they had prevailed. Fans of Re's approach, and there are many, hailed it as the best of the Italian diplomatic art. Detractors, however, complained that Re seemed more concerned about maintaining the Church's *bella figura* than resolving underlying problems or making a stand on matters of principle. Christianity, these critics insist, has to be about more than conflict resolution.

All this is the pejorative sense in which the *bella figura* is often invoked. There is a more positive dimension, however, to the *bella figura*. At its best, it draws upon a deep conviction that life is a form of art, and it should reflect the Thomistic insight that truth, beauty, and goodness are different names for the same reality. In that sense, it can function as an antidote to the hypercapitalist belief that the only thing that really matters is efficiency, or "getting things done." At the bottom of the *bella figura* is the recognition that *being* is more important than *doing*. Catholic writer Hillaire Belloc once expressed this distinctively Roman emphasis on the good life a bit more colorfully: "Where e'er the Catholic sun doth shine / There's music and laughter and good red wine. / At least I've always found it so, / *Benedicamus Domino!*" This aspect of the *bella figura* shows up in all areas of Italian life. For example, when one pops into a *pasticceria*, or pastry shop, to grab a couple of cookies, time will be consumed waiting for the clerk to carefully place the items on a tray and wrap it with colored paper and twine. No brown paper bags are worthy of holding these treasures. The result will look great, even if meanwhile five people have lined up awaiting their turn.

In the world of the Roman Curia, one runs up against this sense of *bella figura* in several different forms. Perhaps the most obvious is the *pasticceria* principle: if there's a choice between doing something quickly and doing it beautifully, beauty is going to beat speed every time. One of the reasons that it can take long periods of time to elicit a response from a dicastery is that officials want to craft something "for the ages," meaning a result that is satisfying not merely from the point of view of systems management, but also aesthetically. This is especially the case since, from the curial point of view, much of their work participates in the magisterium of the Pope, and it has to be perfect not just as to content but as to form. It is, in a word, worth doing well. One should not romanticize curial production in this sense—Vatican offices are just as capable of putting out sloppy or incomplete work as anyone else. Yet there is an emphasis on going slow, taking one's time, and sweating the details that does often lead to results that reflect a touch of art. Even routine correspondence sometimes is crafted with a rhetorical attentiveness that can be striking.

Another reflection of the *bella figura* is the frequent insistence on maintaining a degree of formality in working relationships that would be curious by conventional American standards. In many American companies, for instance, employees call the boss by his or her first name, even when this becomes almost self-parodying, as in twenty-two-year-old junior programmers at Microsoft referring to their CEO as Bill. Even in the absence of such informality, they certainly don't address him or her as "Mister President" every time he or she walks into the office. In the Vatican, however, it's customary for subordinates to refer to the head of their dicastery as *Eminenza*, "Your Eminence," even after working for the same official for a number of years. It would also be extremely unusual for a subordinate to use the informal *tu* (you) in direct address to a superior. Far more common is the formal *lei*, which implies a certain social distance between the two people speaking. Customarily one has to be invited to use the *tu*. This is in part to ensure that the boss doesn't play favorites, allowing some subordinates to be informal and keeping others at a distance. In part, however, it's simply the linguistic equivalent of dressing up—a way of keeping up appearances. It's meant to ensure that the seriousness, the gravitas, of the work being performed does not slip from view.

A classic instance where the *bella figura* has a profound impact on curial psychology is in attitudes toward law. Once again, this reflects the surrounding Italian culture, where law is regarded as the expression of a human ideal, a descriptor of a perfect state of affairs, and everyone realizes that most people will fall short. This is very different from a typical Anglo-Saxon approach, which expects the law to reflect what people actually do. Thomists believe the purpose of law is to promote virtue; in the social contract theory underlying Anglo-Saxon jurisprudence, the law represents the minimum infringements on personal liberty necessary to regulate social life. In this sense, Italians might best be described as "Thomistic realists"—they think the law should indeed promote higher standards of morality, but they don't really expect it to work. While they grumble about lawlessness, fundamentally they are believers in subjectivity. No law, they believe, can ever capture the infinite complexity of human situations, and it's more important for the law to describe a vision of the ideal community than for it to be a lowest common denominator of civic morality. Italians have tough laws, but they're also enormously forgiving. Not for nothing is their equivalent of John Ashcroft known as the "Minister of Justice *and Grace*."

One place where the difference between Italian and Anglo-Saxon cultures on this point becomes clear is sports. Anglo-Saxons like games that are complex and laden with rules, such as American football or cricket. Italians prefer free-flowing *calcio* (soccer), with a few simple, clear rules, and lots of room for subjective judgment about how they apply. In American football, league officials meet at the end of every season to discuss rules changes based on last year's experience. When new problems arise, they are met with a new rule. In *calcio*, the rules almost never change, even if they're forever arguing about how to interpret them (especially offsides). The rules are considered lapidary, literally carved in stone, gilded. You adjust on the ground, as it were, in the crucible of real human experience, not in the realm of theory and principle. In this sense, Anglo-Saxons are Aristotelian, crafting rules based on experience and observation; Italians are Platonic, regarding rules as an unchanging ideal existing in a world of pure form.

The *bella figura* idea that the reach of the law should exceed the grasp of most human beings reflects what writer Christopher Dawson has described as the "erotic" spirit of cultures shaped by Roman Catholicism. Dawson says Catholic cultures are based on the passionate quest for spiritual perfection, and he opposes this "erotic" spirit to the "bourgeoise" culture of the United States, shaped by Protestantism and based on practical reason and the priority of economic concerns. In erotic cultures, the law is premised on the aspirations of the spiritual athlete, not the capacity of the spiritual couch potato. Curial officials shaped by this understanding accept that laws will be broken. That, in their view, is what the sacramental system of repentance and reconciliation is for.

This value system means that while Vatican officials often project a stern moral image on the public stage, in more pastoral settings they can be quite patient and understanding. For example, in May 2003 Archbishop Angelo Amato, a Salesian and Cardinal Joseph Ratzinger's deputy at the Congregation for the Doctrine of the Faith, gave a lecture in Rome on John Paul's encyclical *Ecclesia de Eucharistia*. Amato's talk was fairly conventional, largely summing up the contents of the encyclical. He did so with a sense of humor; while explaining that group confession is reserved for exceptional circumstances, such as a lack of priests, he wryly noted that in Rome there's no such excuse: "Here we've got more confessors than faithful." The key moment relative to the curial understanding of law came when a man asked if he had to make a confession before taking Communion. He had a sin on his conscience he didn't feel he was ready to confess, but at the same time he wanted to receive the Body and Blood of Christ. "I repeat, you should go to confession," Amato responded. "But now let me talk to you person-to-person. As a priest, I can't substitute my conscience for yours. I can't tell you to go or not to go. You have to make that choice in conscience, always bearing in mind that it must be a well-formed conscience." That's the *bella figura* for you: the law's ideal must be upheld, but individuals have to make the choices that correspond to their own unique situation. Whether that's hypocrisy or humanism will depend upon your point of view.

Cosmopolitanism

Critics of the Vatican often complain that curial officials are too far removed from local situations to really understand the issues. "Those guys over there," the standard gripe goes, "just don't get it." But if closeness to the local scene is a virtue, its corresponding vice would be provincialism, an incapacity to see the forest for the trees. From the Vatican point of view, provincialism is often the most besetting vice they have to confront in their contacts with bishops, clergy, and lay Catholics from different parts of the world. People see issues through the lens of their own experience, often without considering how it might cohere with policies developed elsewhere or with the problems faced by other groups within the Church. Yet the idea that in the age of the Internet you can isolate issues in a local church is naïve. Inevitably, decisions made one place have immediate repercussions elsewhere. One example would be the case of Oblate Fr. Tissa Balasuriya of Sri Lanka, a previously obscure theologian whose 1997 excommunication by the Congregation for the Doctrine of the Faith made him a global celebrity overnight. This tendency for local matters to "go global" in a hurry is especially exaggerated in the United States, because of its wealth and influence. Whatever choices the U.S. Catholic Church makes, therefore, inevitably have global consequences, and the Holy See feels obliged to pay careful attention.

Vatican officials are inevitably thrust into the position of contemplating how policies will resonate not just in one part of the world, but everywhere. The complexity can be staggering, and an anecdote illustrates the point. In the fall of 2001, I attended an international conference of seminary rectors in Rome. One of the workshops was devoted to *Dominus Iesus*, a controversial Vatican document which concerns the relationship between Christianity and other religions. The session was offered by well-known German Jesuit theologian Hans Waldenfels. He provided an overview of the document, then invited participants to respond. One rector, from Bangalore in India, shot up and said, "This document is a disaster because it has destroyed our dialogue with the religions of Asia. They are offended by this kind of exclusivist language." Another rector, from St. Petersburg in Russia, then took the floor and said, "This document is a Godsend because it has saved our dialogue with the Orthodox. Their Christology is even higher than ours, and this is the only Vatican document in recent memory that's really excited them." The same text, filtered through two different cultures, produced exactly opposite effects. The experience drove home this point: Vatican officials have to be in the habit of thinking not just about how something will play in Peoria, but in Pretoria and Peking and São Paulo. This need to think through policy implications in global terms generates a very cosmopolitan sense of things in the Vatican.

Rome, and the Holy See itself, is also a remarkable crossroads of humanity. In an average day, an official of the Council for Migrants and Refugees might read newspapers in Italian, French, and English first thing in the morning; have breakfast in his religious community with brethren from Holland, the Philippines, and Germany; meet with a group of Indonesian bishops in Rome on their *ad limina* visit; have a talk with his English superior; lunch with colleagues from Colombia and Brazil; spend the afternoon reading case files on the latest refugee crisis in the Congo; and then dine with American friends, followed by a concert by a visiting choir from Russia. That's just when the official is actually at his desk in Rome. He probably also spends a fair bit of his time traveling, visiting Catholic facilities for refugees around the world, staying with the nuncio or local bishops, and taking part in international conferences. Such experiences, repeated day after day and year after year, inevitably cut through a person's psychology, teaching him instinctively to think in global terms, as a citizen of the planet, as opposed to framing issues solely in terms of his national or regional dimensions.

In the Roman Curia, there is deep awareness that Roman Catholicism is a worldwide communion of 1 billion people, representing every culture, language, and worldview on earth. Inevitably, to be part of this global family of faith means sacrificing a bit of one's own personal vision for the sake of maintaining the bonds of communion. For example, some Western reformers and activists are passionately convinced that the ordination of women to the Catholic priesthood is a matter of justice. Setting aside the theological merit of that view, what if large majorities of Catholics across the developing world think differently? African Catholics, for example, tend to be conservative on matters of sexual morality and gender roles. Are the activists willing to be patient, bracketing their own visions, in order to remain in communion? This question can pose a special challenge for American Catholics, who can be somewhat jingoistic when it comes to ecclesiastical matters. Americans often want to do things their own way, and if Rome puts on the brakes, it's a form of oppression. From Rome's point of view, however, sometimes it's precisely the reverse—they're saving the rest of the Church from being involuntarily "Americanized."

One danger inherent in this cosmopolitan approach is that it can end up in paralysis, since the simplest way not to "rock the boat" in a complex global system is not to do anything. Moreover, sometimes cosmopolitanism is more honored in the breach than in the observance. I have often spoken to Third World bishops, for example, who complain about curial officials who either know nothing about their local situations, or who treat them like children because they assume that a bishop from the developing world can't handle theological and political complexity. In fact, when the *National Catholic Reporter* broke the story in 2001 about the sexual abuse of nuns by priests in Africa and elsewhere, one African bishop said: "This is all we need, since a black bishop already has to work twice as hard to be taken seriously by Rome."

The Vatican's cosmopolitanism can also breed a kind of arrogance, a sense that "we here in Rome" always see farther and deeper than anyone else. This is sometimes especially pronounced among the Italians in the Curia, who tend to believe that they have a "vocation" for governance born of Rome's long centuries as *caput mundi*, "head of the world." One Italian *monsignore* in the Secretariat of State put it to me this way: "Italians by nature tend to have a more universal vision. It's part of our psychological structure. The unity of Italy happened just one hundred years ago, and our national identity is still not very strong. We tend not to be confined by nationalism as much. . . . I worked for

Cardinal X, and he's a great man, but very American. I also worked for Cardinal Y, another great man, but extremely French. I think what we Italians bring is a more intuitively international approach." At its best, this Italian sense of cultural openness can be enriching and broadening; yet it's also true that career Italian Curialists can sometimes be condescending toward other nationalities they consider narrow and juvenile.

At bottom, however, this cosmopolitan perspective, kept in the proper balance, is valuable for the Holy See because it reflects a real justice issue. The Vatican is the only agent in the Church in a position to ensure a kind of rough global equilibrium, seeing to it that the sensibilities of all parties, all local churches and all cultures, are taken into consideration when decisions are made. Inside the Church it shouldn't be the case that "money talks," that those national churches with the most resources and the biggest media megaphones always get their way. The culture of "thinking globally" that characterizes the Roman Curia, when it works the way it's supposed to, is a guarantee of "Catholicity" critical in a Church becoming steadily more global.

Loyalty

Italians in curial service have a shorthand way of referring to someone they trust. They say that he or she is *della famiglia*, "of the family." What they mean is that this person can be counted upon to be loyal, not to betray the institution or its members, to stand by them in times of trouble. The saying reflects the deep emphasis on loyalty within the institutional culture. The Vatican is a small, 108-acre island surrounded by what is sometimes perceived as a secularized, postreligious, uncomprehending world, and it's easy to imbibe a "We few, we happy few, we band of brothers" sort of attitude. In such a context, loyalty becomes critical. One archbishop put the point to me this way: "The only real currency in the Church, besides faith, is loyalty." In part, loyalty in ecclesiastical life can be a noble instinct of gratitude, trust, and common purpose; in part, it can also become an insistence on muzzling legitimate criticism. Where one ends and the other begins is often difficult to distinguish.

For certain offices in the Church, this bond of loyalty is formalized in what is known as an "Oath of Fidelity." Canon 833 of the *Code of Canon Law* obliges vicars general, episcopal vicars, judicial vicars, pastors, rectors, and professors of theology and philosophy at seminaries, rectors of universities, and anyone who teaches subjects dealing with faith and morals, and superiors in religious orders to take this oath, along with a Profession of Faith. The Oath of Fidelity is as follows:

> *I, _____, on assuming the office _____ promise that I shall always preserve communion with the Catholic Church whether in the words I speak or in the way I act.*
>
> *With great care and fidelity I shall carry out the responsibilities by which I am bound in relation both to the universal church and to the particular church in which I am called to exercise my service according to the requirements of the law.*
>
> *In carrying out my charge, which is committed to me in the name of the church, I shall preserve the deposit of faith in its entirety, hand it on faithfully and make it shine forth. As a result, whatsoever teachings are contrary I shall shun.*
>
> *I shall follow and foster the common discipline of the whole church and shall look after the observance of all ecclesiastical laws, especially those which are contained in the* Code of Canon Law.
>
> *With Christian obedience I shall associate myself with what is expressed by the holy shepherds as authentic doctors and teachers of the faith or established by them as the church's rulers. And I shall faithfully assist diocesan bishops so that apostolic activity, to be exercised by the mandate and in the name of the church, is carried out in the communion of the same church.*
>
> *May God help me in this way and the holy Gospels of God which I touch with my hands.*

For the men and women of the Vatican, the primary object of loyalty is first of all the Pope. For most, it is a very personal sensation. Vatican officials feel a tie to the office of the papacy and to the particular Pope they serve. In the culture of the Holy See, it is usually considered fair game to gripe about one's superiors and about the Church in general, but belittling remarks about the Pope, even in private, are out of bounds. I was once in the office of a Vatican undersecretary when an American prelate known to be somewhat liberal arrived for an appointment. "He doesn't like the Pope," the undersecretary said to me quietly with respect to the American, and it was understood that this was a very negative thing.

While Vatican officials and senior Church leaders may have private disagreements with the Pope's policies, they will rarely air them in public. The Catholic world was startled, for example, when Cardinal Joseph Ratzinger publicly expressed reservations about the 1986 Assisi interreligious prayer gathering, saying that, "This cannot be the model." (In fairness, Ratzinger may well have been referring to the execution and atmospherics of the Assisi gathering, not the Pope's idea in itself.) The shock was not so much that a thoughtful intellectual such as Ratzinger might have doubts about Assisi, since no group of people who think deeply and care passionately about something can be expected to be in perfect agreement all the time. The shock was rather that Ratzinger gave public voice to his doubts. Typically, Vatican officials praise the Pope's statements and initiatives in public, referring to every speech as "important," every trip as "timely" and "historic," every liturgy as "moving." Among themselves, such uncritical language is sometimes an object of humor, but it is considered one of the obligations of office.

This is a special struggle for Vatican officials from more rambunctious parts of the Catholic world, such as Northern Europe or North America, when they go home and friends draw them out on "what's really going on." On the one hand, officials want to be able to talk openly about the latest scuttlebutt, and in some cases are anxious to demonstrate that they still understand why Catholics in the trenches sometimes become frustrated with the hierarchy. On the other hand, the tug of loyalty is deep, and officials don't want to seem ungrateful or flippant about the trust the Pope has placed in them. They sometimes find themselves walking through a minefield, not wanting to seem like anything less than a "team player."

This emphasis on public solidarity is one of the most oft-criticized aspects of Vatican culture. American theologian Fr. Richard McBrien of the University of Notre Dame put it this way in a May 11, 2003, interview with the *Boston Globe* about the appointment of bishops: "The Vatican looks for complete, utter, uncritical loyalty to the Holy See, especially as it pertains to hot-button issues like the ordination of women, celibacy for priests, and the whole spectrum of sexual and reproductive issues. They are not going to appoint anyone who has ever expressed a doubt, much less a criticism, about these issues." On the other hand, defenders of the Holy See question whether a United States president or a corporate CEO would appoint subordinates who are disloyal to key policies of the government or the company. Would George Bush appoint a secretary of defense who disagreed with his policies on Iraq? Would the head of Ford Motors appoint a regional manager who went on record saying he thought GM sold a better product? Moreover, they insist, this is not simply a matter of loyalty. The Church's positions on the issues McBrien lists are *true*, they argue, and officials should be expected to defend them.

Some would also question the extent to which the Holy See "suffocates" debate in the name of loyalty. Professor Mary Ann Glendon of Harvard University, a frequent papal delegate to United Nations conferences and other events, put this point in perspective in a June 1, 2002, interview with the *Sydney Morning Herald:* "Compared with my experiences in a big law firm and in a big university, there is more open and robust discussion of everything within the Catholic Church than there is within a university, where there are many taboos." Glendon argued that law schools, like other academic departments, tend to have an internal culture that fairly rigidly screens out other points of view. "Let me just take my own law school," she said. "We don't have many Republicans. And we don't have many openly avowed Christians."

Loyalty in the Curia applies to a lesser degree to one's circle of friends and colleagues, including those with whom one studied, those with whom one entered curial service, and those with whom one has a special bond. Such a bond may be due to the fact that both parties come from the same region of Italy, for example, or because they both were promoted by the same cardinal-patron. Inside the Vatican, these various networks of informal support and protection are called a *parish*. When a Vatican official is promoted Italians will often ask, "*Di quale parrocchia è?*," What parish is he from? The presumption is that the appointment can be explained, at least in part, by whose patronage the individual is under. There is something to this. For example, in 2003 Monsignor Josef Clemens was named the new undersecretary of the Congregation for Religious. One would look in vain in Clemens's curriculum vitae for any special qualifications he held for the post, but the fact that he was Cardinal Joseph Ratzinger's longtime private secretary goes much further toward explaining the appointment. Within a matter of months, Clemens moved on to yet a higher post in the Pontifical Council for the Laity. Similarly, when Justin Rigali was named archbishop of Philadelphia after nine years in St. Louis, many Vatican observers attributed the move to the fact that Rigali's longtime friend, Cardinal Giovanni Battista Re, had taken over at the Congregation for Bishops. Rigali and Re both entered curial service under Cardinal Giovanni Benelli, the right-hand man of Pope Paul VI. Rigali had been the only former secretary of the Congregation for Bishops not yet made a cardinal.

The impact of curial loyalty, however, should not be pressed too far. For one thing, many men and women in the Vatican are not conscious of having a special patron or protector, and frankly don't want one if it means being evaluated on the basis of personal connections rather than the quality of their work. This is especially true for the non-Italians. Moreover, it would be a mistake to believe that Vatican appointments are driven for the most part by clannish personal loyalties. In fact, most of the personnel in the Holy See got their jobs because of perceptions about their potential contributions, often without having ever sought the position. Loyalty, in the end, will not save someone who is morally compromised or professionally disastrous, although the emphasis on maintaining a *bella figura* may mean that nonpublic means are sought to ease such officials out of the way.

Nor is it the case that publicly challenging the Pope or key Vatican officials is necessarily the kiss of death to one's career, despite the premium on loyalty. When Walter Kasper was still bishop of Rottenburg-Stuttgart in Germany, for example, he signed a letter urging a reconsideration of the ban on divorced and civilly remarried Catholics receiving the sacraments. The letter's argument was rejected by Cardinal Joseph Ratzinger, and many thought it was the end of Kasper's forward momentum. Today, however, he is a member of the College of Cardinals and head of the Pontifical Council for Promoting Christianity Unity. Karl Lehmann, another German bishop, was also a signatory to that 1993 letter. Moreover, as president of the German bishops' conference, Lehmann led a two-year effort, ultimately unsuccessful, to fend off attempts from Ratzinger and the Pope to force the German Church to withdraw from a state-sponsored abortion counseling service. Many people felt Lehmann would never win the "red hat" because of his insubordination. Today, however, he is Cardinal Karl Lehmann. Hence it is possible to fight city hall in the Catholic Church and live to tell the tale.

Objectivity

Tensions are generated in any bureaucratic system when a higher level of authority intervenes with a lower one. When the United States federal government issues a new regulation, for example, legislators and agency personnel at the state level frequently grouse that "the feds don't understand our situation." The same lament will come from branch managers in a corporation, local commanders in the army, and anybody else who ever finds himself or herself in the position of taking orders from on high. Thus it is also in the Catholic world whenever the Holy See issues a directive, or responds in the negative to some request from a local church. Then, too, voices will be heard complaining that "the Vatican is out of touch," that it is absurd that officials thousands of miles away in Rome, living in a different culture and speaking a different language, should make decisions about a local church.

Seen from Rome, on the other hand, local officials sometimes seem too close to the local scene to think straight. Every professional knows the dangers of getting too close. One reason editors at newspapers read stories before they're published is because sometimes journalists get sucked into the drama they're covering, losing their objectivity and taking sides. Editors may have to pull them back, remind them of their obligations to balance. Similarly, pastors and even bishops can sometimes be overwhelmed by political pressures or personal sympathies into fudging the teaching or discipline of the Church. Naturally, some degree of pastoral flexibility is appropriate in trying to resolve complicated human situations. How much is too much, however, is in the eye of the beholder, and it's probably true that the closer one is to the situation, the greater the danger of losing perspective.

Moreover, Vatican officials are generally not out of touch, ignorant of local situations, in the sense critics often mean. Actually, the officials of the Holy See tend to be quite well informed about affairs in local churches, especially the larger ones. Every dicastery of the Roman Curia has at least one American on the staff, for example, and often that individual has responsibility for tracking issues in the English-speaking world within that dicastery's area of competence—liturgy, doctrine, clerical discipline, or whatever the case may be. The official usually also has the informal responsibility of explaining American situations to colleagues who may from time to time be called upon to deal with them or simply when conversations come up around the water cooler. With the Internet they're able to read the American press each morning, at least the *New York Times* and often their local paper as well, and they see U.S. bishops when they happen to be in Rome, thus keeping up to date on the latest developments. With 377 American bishops, someone is always in town. At the Villa Stritch, a residence funded by the U.S. bishops' conference for Americans in the Curia, dinner conversation is often about the latest news back home, so these men probably discuss American church affairs far more than the vast majority of priests who actually live in the United States. They also may from time to time participate in meetings and conferences in the States on their issues.

All this means that Vatican officials usually have an acute sense of the issues, the players, and the trends in the local church. The same point, to greater or lesser degrees, could be made about the Germans, the Indians, the Argentinians, and the other nationalities represented in the Curia. One *monsignore* who works in a congregation of the Roman Curia put it this way: "It's a chronic misunderstanding that the Roman Curia is a monolithic institution that has trouble understanding local cultures. They don't realize how many different cultures are present here to bring about a truly Catholic perspective. We're usually very well informed about their situation, but we may just have a different perspective on it."

What might that different perspective be? In a word, objectivity. Seen from a Vatican point of view, the passions surrounding a particular issue sometimes have the effect of overwhelming rational judgment. It is precisely the benefit of having some distance from the "rattle and hum" that allows the Holy See, its defenders argue, to bring a more objective, a more serene, judgment to the matter. Thus Vatican officials would insist that they are not isolated in the negative sense that critics intend, that is, ignorant of local realities. There is, however, a positive kind of isolation they believe comes with their office, which is being insulated from the political and cultural pressures that tend to intrude on sober reflection when one stands too close to the flame. In other words, sometimes seeing and acting on the truth requires distance. That's why they believe the Holy See is often capable of an objectivity that eludes local pastors.

One classic example of how this works was offered by the American sexual abuse crisis. In Dallas in June 2002, the American bishops adopted a set of norms that relied on a bishop's exercise of administrative authority to remove accused priests from ministry. In part, the bishops opted for this route because their experience of canon law courts in Rome had been that procedures tended to drag out for long periods, and in some cases, procedural strictness had led to orders of reinstatement for at least a few accused abusers. The bishops wanted to be able to promise the American public swift and sure justice, and adopted a program that relied on their stroke of a pen to impose final judgment. At the time a small knot of bishops voiced concern that this amounted to "hanging priests out to dry," treating them as guilty until proven innocent, but in the pressure-cooker atmosphere of Dallas this argument cut little ice. After the norms were issued, priests' groups and canon lawyers voiced fears that the bishops had in effect tried to resolve one injustice, which was sluggishness in responding to accusations of sexual abuse, with another injustice, which was a rush to judgment against priests.

In fact, the fierce debate over Dallas was in one sense unnecessary, because it was abundantly clear that the Holy See never had any intention of approving the norms as written. They did not wish to embarrass the American bishops (recall the *bella figura*), so instead of saying a flat no, they invited the bishops into a mixed commission made up of four officials from the Holy See and four U.S. bishops to produce a set of norms. What resulted was a streamlined canonical procedure that sped up the administration of justice but also preserved the priest's due process rights. Most observers, even those normally cynical about the motives for Vatican interventions, tend to grant that in this case the system worked. In Vatican circles, the evolution of the American norms has now become a *locus classicus* for why review of local policy at the level of the universal Church is so important.

Rumors in June 2002 had it, in fact, that some American bishops voted for the Dallas norms in order to satisfy public demands for dramatic action with the expectation that Rome would intervene. Whether that's true or not, it does illustrate a point familiar to anyone who works inside an institution: sometimes it's easier to let a higher level of authority make an unpopular decision. Teachers rely on principals to run interference with complaining parents, reporters sometimes fall back on editors to explain why certain stories turned out the way they did, and soldiers explain to disgruntled citizens that they're only following orders. Likewise, in some cases bishops will submit a case to Rome when they know full well how it will shake out, but they'd rather have people blame the Vatican for bringing the hammer down. It is a tendency that irritates some Vatican officials, who feel that bishops ought to have the courage of their convictions, but everyone recognizes that it happens. Distance, the theory goes, buys the Vatican precious insulation from local reaction.

There are two other senses in which the value of objectivity is a key that unlocks Vatican behavior. The first concerns Vatican documents. Whether a particular text is issued by the Pope or by one or more of the dicasteries, it is almost always treated as a document of the Holy See rather than the product of individual authors. Journalists and Church insiders enjoy speculating about who actually wrote them, and in some cases authorship becomes an open secret. The Pope's September 1998 encyclical, *Fides et Ratio*, for example, is known around Rome as "Fisichella et Ratzinger" because two of the most important contributors were Bishop Salvatore Fisichella and Cardinal Joseph Ratzinger. When *Dominus Iesus* appeared in September 2000, its primary authors, Monsignor Fernando Ocáriz and Salesian Fr. Angelo Amato, joined Ratzinger at the press conference presenting the document. (Ocáriz is the vicar general of Opus Dei, while Amato has since become archbishop and secretary of the Congregation for the Doctrine of the Faith.) Even in these instances, however, the Holy See never officially acknowledges individual authorship, because it does not want the authority of the document to depend upon the personal qualities of its authors. Its authority depends upon the fact that it has been duly promulgated. Its authority, in other words, is objective rather than subjective. This is the same reason that documents from dicasteries are usually signed by both the prefect and the secretary. The idea is that its authority is dependent upon its due issuance, not the personality of any one figure. (The prefect and secretary are expected to sign the document, by the way, even if they voted against it in the plenary assembly.)

The second way in which objectivity is relevant to understanding Vatican behavior has to do with secrecy. Many times the Vatican comes under fire because it will not release the case files that have given rise to controversial judgments. For example, censured theologians such as

Hans Küng and Charles Curran have long complained that despite the fact the Vatican monitored their work for decades, launching investigations that ended in disciplinary action, they have never been allowed to see their own files. Küng, in an interview with me, compared the Congregation for the Doctrine of the Faith to the KGB on this basis. Or to consider another instance, the Vatican has never released the results of its eight-month investigation into a 1998 Swiss Guard murder-suicide, despite repeated appeals from the mother of the corporal who, according to the Vatican reconstruction, shot his commander and his wife, then himself. To observers outside the Vatican's world, denying people the right to see information that concerns them directly seems arrogant and almost incomprehensible.

Aside from privacy concerns, the primary logic of nondisclosure is to protect the objectivity of those who must make judgments based on this information. If case files were a matter of public record, then pressure could be brought to bear to try to sway those judgments one way or the other. Lobbying and spin would be the result. The classic example, which still looms large in the Vatican's collective imagination, is the 1967 publication by the *National Catholic Reporter* and *Le Monde* of the majority report from Paul VI's birth control commission, which had supported a change in Church teaching. Pope Paul decided against this proposal, and the publication of the commission's report subjected the pontiff to withering public criticism for "ignoring" his own advisors. The culture of the Holy See resists exposing its decisions to the pressures of public relations or interest group politics, neither of which are viewed as reliable means for arriving at truth. The refusal to turn over files, even to people directly concerned, is thus to the Vatican's mind not about covering up the truth, but, on the contrary, about a different concept of how best to foster fair and impartial judgments. From the Vatican point of view, parliamentary inquiries in which conservatives treat liberals as guilty until proven innocent and vice-versa, with the outcome hinging on who has the most votes, may be more transparent than procedures in the Holy See, but that's hardly any assurance they're more equitable.

Populism

Of all the values listed in this chapter, this one may be the most difficult for many outside observers of the Vatican to understand or accept. People are accustomed to thinking of the Holy See as "the world's last absolute monarchy," a place where a tiny ecclesiastical aristocracy makes decisions based on their own vision of how the Church and the world ought to be run. Whether this is considered a good or a bad thing will vary with the observer, but there is a measure of truth to such perceptions. Vatican officials are not subject to the same democratic scrutiny as personnel in other governments, nor to the commercial pressures of the bottom line faced by the corporate sector. At the same time, however, Vatican personnel by and large do not see themselves as imperialists imposing their will on the rest of the Catholic Church. In many instances, the exact reverse is the case: they see themselves defending the people against elites running roughshod over their rights. Vatican officials perceive themselves to be the last line of defense for the "simple faithful" against avant-garde theologians who would betray the faith, against experimental liturgists who risk transforming the Mass into something profane or banal, or against ecclesiastical bureaucrats, including bishops, who fancy themselves above the law. They see themselves, in other words, as populists.

One sometimes hears diocesan bishops complain about being pushed around by junior curial officials when they come to Rome on their *ad limina* visits, about being treated like altar boys. Part of this is a generational dynamic. No man in his sixties who is a senior leader of a major international organization enjoys coming to headquarters and being questioned by someone in his twenties or thirties. Part of this, undeniably, is the fact that certain curial officials are a bit drunk on their own power and enjoy asserting themselves, often in ways that exceed their actual authority. Yet in most cases curial officials are loathe to confront bishops (recall what was said above about reverence for authority), and will do so only in order to vindicate the rights of lower clergy or laity when there has been what seems to them a clear abuse of power. In other words, it is sometimes not a bureaucratic power play, but a

rather idealistic insistence upon equality before the law, that leads a curial official to push around a bishop. In such a case, the bishop's complaint about process may ignore the deeper question of whether the
Vatican was right on content.

No one has articulated this view more forcefully over the years
than Cardinal Ratzinger, even well before he arrived in the Vatican in
1981. In 1970, for example, Ratzinger and his Bavarian friend and colleague Hans Meier put out a volume called *Democracy in the Church*. In
it, Ratzinger accuses advocates of democracy in the church of posing as
populists, but in reality harboring a snobbish disdain for the simple faith
of the great mass of believers. "Those circles which talk especially loud
about democratization of the Church," Ratzinger wrote, "manifest the
least respect for the faith shared by the community." To those who
claim that he has strained the relationship between the Vatican and theologians, Ratzinger replies that keeping theologians happy is not his
main concern. Above all, he must protect the right of simple believers
to have the faith preserved in each generation. "Those who can't fight
back intellectually have to be defended against intellectual assault on
what sustains their life," he said in 1998's *Salt of the Earth*, a book-length
interview with German journalist Peter Seewald. Elsewhere in that
book: "This is His Church [meaning Christ's], and not a laboratory for
theologians." In a 1988 interview with the Austrian daily *Die Presse*,
Ratzinger said his role was to defend those Catholics "who do not
write books or learned articles." The point is clear: Ratzinger sees himself not as an inquisitor but as a tribune, protecting ordinary Catholics
from intellectual abuse by self-appointed elites. To varying degrees, this
attitude, perhaps expressed in different language, would characterize
many officials in Vatican service.

One way this concern for the little guy shows up is that few institutions on earth take their mail more seriously than the Holy See. Every
letter that comes into the Vatican is registered and processed, even if the
decision is eventually made not to respond, because it would be a waste
of time, because no one's quite sure what to say, or because the writer
is too wacky. As one American Vatican official put it in an interview:

"Letters do make a difference. People underestimate the capacity of the Holy See to evaluate these things. The mail gets taken seriously." Curial officials describe heartbreaking letters from mothers whose children lost their faith because of what was being taught in the local Catholic school, or grown men who say they will never darken the door of a church again because of a sacrilege they saw during the Sunday Mass. Some of these accounts are of course exaggerated, or overly sensitive. It is also true that letters complaining about various abuses or difficult pastoral situations will elicit more sympathy from Vatican officials when those letters express a point of view that coincides with their own. Since in general most Vatican officials tend to be theological conservatives, the populism of the Holy See tilts to the right.

Still, one will misunderstand the psychology of the Roman Curia by believing that they send faxes around the world dictating details for liturgical celebrations, or ordering a halt to the publication of theological journals, simply for the thrill of issuing orders. We should be under no illusions, of course, that sometimes people do act out of arrogance. One curial veteran puts it this way: "Narcissism in this world is a real danger. We have a certain power and influence, and there's an absence of foils to a strong will." At the same time, even granting these issues of power and control, it's not true to the psychological reality to believe that many people in the Holy See consciously make decisions simply on this basis. Far more often, they perceive themselves to be defending the rights of Catholics around the world to have the faith transmitted in its integrity, to have the Mass celebrated according to the rules, to be sure that Catholic schools are in synch with the Church, and so on.

In that sense, and despite the incredulity such language is bound to provoke, one could say that from a Roman point of view, the men and women of the Holy See regard themselves as the real "Voice of the Faithful" in the Catholic Church.

Realism

Though Vatican officials may have a high-minded sense of service to the Holy Father, they also believe in having their feet on the ground when it comes to how things work in the real world. This realism applies first of all to the Church, and the very human qualities of the men and women who serve it. Vatican officials generally have spent most of their lives inside the institutional Catholic Church, and are under no illusions that the mere fact of ordination or having taken religious vows makes people more generous, or honest, or patient, or forgiving. They know that people in the Church can be petty and mean-spirited, and sometimes can fail in spectacular ways. If the official works in a congregation with responsibility for discipline in some area of Church life such as liturgy, doctrine, clerical life, or education, he or she may spend a good part of each day dealing with case files documenting just such instances of moral or theological corruption. Indeed, one could probably make the argument that no one is in a better position to understand and appreciate the imperfect character of the Catholic Church than the personnel of the Holy See. Italians tend to be especially realistic in this sense about the Church, having seen it all over the centuries.

This ecclesiastical realism was clear during the American sex abuse crisis, when many Vatican officials initially had a hard time grasping just what it was that American Catholics were so upset about. That a Catholic priest might break his vows of celibacy is disappointing, of course, and that he might do it through the sexual abuse of a minor is horrifying. Yet two thousand years of Church history teaches that priests are capable even of the most despicable acts. Being human, some of them will fail. What, many Vatican officials wondered, is the revelation? Are Americans just discovering in 2002 that priests too are marred by Original Sin? They wondered if the outrage in the American press related to the Catholic sex abuse scandal was a reflection of the same Calvinist hysteria about sex that was on display during the Bill Clinton/Monica Lewinsky farce. It took time for many Vatican officials to grasp that the real source of American anger was not so much the sexual misconduct of a small percentage of priests, but the moral (and perhaps criminal) failure of the bishops to intervene when they should have known better.

This realism also applies to the way the institutional Church relates to the world, and it's in contrast with a kind of ecclesiastical docetism that would like to see the Church move through history uncontaminated by contact with sin. An episode from the fall of 2001 illustrates the difference. Pope John Paul II had called Christians to a day of fasting on December 14, the last day of Ramadan, as a post–September 11 gesture of solidarity with Islam. He suggested that people donate the money they would have spent on food that day to the poor. The Vatican's charitable arm, called Cor Unum, opened a special account with the Bank of Rome to collect contributions for this purpose. The idea was sufficiently important to Vatican officials that they installed a special pop-up window on the Vatican website explaining how to transfer money into this account. The respected Italian Catholic missionary journal *Missione Oggi*, however, swiftly called for a boycott of the Vatican account, on the grounds that the Bank of Rome is a major player in the global arms market. The journal, published by the Xaverian Missionaries, charged that the Bank of Rome financed $106 million worth of arms deals in 2000, earning $8 million in transaction fees. When I called an official at Cor Unum for comment, I was rather wearily told that the Xaverian stance, while laudable, was also unrealistic, given that most banks are engaged in some kind of ethically debatable commerce. "If you want to get anything done, sooner or later you will find yourself doing business with someone who's got dirty hands in one way or another," the official said. "But our account is certainly not an endorsement of the arms trade." This was not intended as surrender in the face of evil, but a realistic appraisal of what it means for the Church to be in history.

Vatican realism also applies to international relations. When John Paul II visited Chile in 1988, for example, he administered communion to then-president Augusto Pinochet, and appeared with him on the balcony of Moneda Palace to the cheers of Pinochet supporters. The imagery scandalized some human rights activists, given that 3,191 people were confirmed either killed or disappeared under Pinochet's regime, while unofficial estimates put the total at several times that number. Yet Vatican officials argued that the Pope cannot nominate the rulers of the countries he visits, and the price of bringing his message to the world is sometimes "doing business" with unsavory regimes. It was the same logic, for example, that justified the visit of Cardinal Roger Etchegaray to Saddam Hussein in the lead-up to the American-led war in Iraq, and the visit of Tarik Aziz to the Vatican and to Assisi during the same period. The argument is that this philosophy of "doing business" bears more fruit in the real world than a morally satisfying, but largely ineffective, disengagement. Defenders of this approach say that Chile offers a prime example: John Paul made it clear on the papal plane that he saw the Pinochet regime as "transitory by definition," and in fact a plebiscite marking the transition to civilian rule took place a few months after the papal trip.

When President George Bush succeeded Bill Clinton in the United States, many analysts believed the Holy See would welcome the transition, since the Church had more in common with the Bush administration on issues such as abortion, cloning, and the role of religion in public life than with Clinton. Toward the end of Bush's first year in office, before 9/11 or the war in Iraq, I interviewed a senior Vatican diplomat on what seemed the warm rapport between Bush and the Holy See. His response was illuminating: "Yes, we like this man better. He at least seems to be a genuine religious believer, a sincere person of faith. But at the end of the day, business is business. We'll be able to work with him on some things, like cloning, but on other issues that are important to us, such as the International Criminal Court and globalization, it may be that Clinton was actually better. Diplomacy is the art of the possible, and you have to see what you can do together case by case. The attitudes of individuals only get you so far." When the Holy See and the Bush administration found themselves at loggerheads over Iraq, few in the Vatican were surprised by the standoff.

Finally, Vatican realism also applies to the internal management of the Church, especially how far and how fast one can move at any given time. Many Vatican officials, when pressed for their own ideas about how things in the Church ought to work, will offer a vision that is quite different from current realities. When pressed as to why they don't do more to try to shake things up, they will smile and patiently explain a few of the thousand and one political, sociological, and institutional reasons why doing so, for now, is impossible. It's a bit like Michelan-gelo's analysis, as Irving Stone described it in *The Agony and the Ecstasy*: In any given hunk of marble, there's only one statue inside. The trick is to find out which is "the statue in the stone," and remove everything that is superfluous. Try to force that block of stone to produce a statue that's not inside it and, however beautiful the idea, the result will be dis-aster. Vatican officials have been taught by their experience to be realis-tic about utopian ecclesiastical proposals that sound great, but whose actual impact is anyone's guess.

Rule of Law

At first glance this value may seem in contradiction with the *bella figura* understanding of law described above. To some extent that may be right, since nowhere is it written that a culture's value system has to be per-fectly consistent. Yet the seeming contradiction is more like two sides of the same coin. The *bella figura* means that Vatican officials can have a sur-prising tolerance for human failure, but they will defend the law tena-ciously at the level of principle. That's the essence of their insistence on the "rule of law"—however difficult application of the principles of the *Code of Canon Law* may be in practice, it must always remain the norm and goal of Church life. In that sense, Vatican officials often come across as "sticklers" for the law, with a strong by-the-book approach.

Law is, from this point of view, the translation of the Church's principles of justice into the practical realm. A high percentage of Vati-can officials are by training canon lawyers, rather than theologians, philosophers, or biblical scholars. Even personnel whose background is in other fields will usually have a working knowledge of the *Code of Canon Law*, because much of what the Holy See does is the application of the *Code* to specific situations in local churches. From the Vatican's point of view, the *Code of Canon Law* and its parallel *Code of Canons of the Eastern Churches*, governing the twenty-one Eastern Rite churches in communion with Rome, are foundational texts for understanding how the Church is supposed to work.

Vatican officials become annoyed when critics oppose canon law to "pastoral" instincts, as if the law isn't itself pastoral. In a February 2003 address to Brazilian bishops in Rome on an *ad limina* visit, John Paul made this point. "It is necessary to remember that pastoral action cannot be reduced to a certain 'pastoralism,' understood in the sense of ignoring or attenuating other essential dimensions of the Christian mystery, among these the juridical," the Pope said. "The pastoral truth can never be contrary to the truth of the Law of the Church."

It is frustrating to curial personnel that many Catholics have never bothered to so much as crack a copy of the code. Even many of the world's 4,563 Catholic bishops have, at best, a rudimentary understanding. This was a frequent complaint inside the Roman Curia at the peak of the American sex abuse crisis. For many Vatican officials it has become an article of faith that the American bishops were wasting their time by drafting a new set of norms and procedures for the removal of abuser-priests. The existing *Code of Canon Law*, these officials said, already gave the bishops all the tools they needed, had they been serious about applying them. The problem, from their point of view, was never the absence of law, but the absence of nerve.

Vatican officials thus tend to be protective of the code. In September 2002, the Congregation for Catholic Education issued a decree extending the period of time required to obtain a *licentiate*, or basic degree, in canon law from two years to three, and mandating that a detailed knowledge of Latin be part of the program. This same spirit of protectiveness sometimes means Vatican officials are sticklers for the fine print of the code. In some cases, reverence for episcopal authority gives way to irritation with bishops for neglect of the requirements of the law. Few places on earth probably witness more "bishop-bashing," in this sense, than the chambers of the Roman Rota and the Apostolic Signatura, or the offices of the Congregation for Clergy and the Council for the Interpretation of Legislative Texts. One of the great untold stories of the Vatican is how often in this allegedly ultrahierarchical institution bishops find their decisions challenged by lower clergy or laity, and, in a surprising number of cases, overturned. The philosophy one often hears invoked in such circumstances is that "no one is above the law." Granted, this sort of judicial intervention happens less often with archbishops, and very rarely with cardinals, but in neither case is it unprecedented.

This passion for law must be understood in its proper psychological context. It is not merely, or even primarily, a matter of busybodies insisting that everyone follow the rules. It is a matter of defending a uniform standard of justice. The philosophy is that the hearing one gets from the Church should not depend on accidents such as how a bishop is feeling that day, or whether the tribunal in a particular area is liberal or conservative. Beyond this emphasis on consistency lies an even more fundamental concern for the just ordering of relationships in the Church. The *mens*, or mind, of canon law has as its prime directive a balance between the rights of the individual and the well-being of the entire community. When bishops or anyone else become cavalier about the code or succumb to the illusion that "the rules don't apply to me," Vatican officials believe, both individuals and the community suffer. Insistence on the letter of the law is, seen through their eyes, a protection of the common good, as well as of the little guy in the Church whose only defense against the abuse of power is the *Code*.

A classic illustration of this bias in favor of proper legal procedures came in 2002, when the Apostolic Signatura, the Catholic Church's Supreme Court, overturned a suspension issued by then-Archbishop George Pell of Melbourne, against a priest named Barry Whelan, who has since resigned. Pell, now the cardinal of Sydney, had removed Whelan from ministry in 1996 based on allegations of sexual abuse, but the Signatura found procedural defects in Pell's action and ordered Whelan reinstated to Sacred Heart Parish in West St. Kilda. He remained there until the new Archbishop of Melbourne, Denis Hart, had to intercede again in 2002, once again on the basis of sex abuse allegations. Whelan's story is revealing, because Pell is well-liked and respected in Rome, where there is great sympathy for what is perceived to be the difficult cultural situation facing him in Australia. If the system were always stacked in favor of bishops with the right connections, Pell would have prevailed. In this case, however, the Holy See's judgment was that Pell could not use administrative means to impose a permanent removal from ministry—precisely the same concern for due process that would later inform the Holy See's response to the sex abuse norms adopted by the American bishops in Dallas. This must be clearly understood: It's not that anyone in the Vatican wants to use legal niceties to shield priests who engage in sexual abuse. It's rather that they insist even priests guilty of the most horrific offenses are entitled to a just process of law.

Americans will recall a similar case from the early 1990s involving Bishop Donald Wuerl of Pittsburgh and a priest named Anthony Cipolla, whom Wuerl had removed and the Vatican ordered reinstated. Wuerl eventually prevailed, but only following a long and complex battle. The case is discussed in chapter 6.

Time

To listen to some wags talk about the slow pace in the Vatican, one would think it's a Mexican village from a Sergio Leone movie—men taking siestas with sombreros pulled over their eyes, dogs listlessly wandering in search of shade, an air of stupor about the entire scene. The amount of time it takes for the Vatican to produce certain decisions is the stuff of legend. At one stage, the Catholic Biblical Association in the United States actually had an on-line clock tracking how long it was taking the Vatican to approve a new *lectionary*, or collection of readings for the Sunday Mass. The final period, from the two-thirds vote in favor of the text from the U.S. bishops to formal approval by Rome, was 1,954 days, or five and one-half years! Frustration with such delays is widespread. One longtime observer of the Vatican, Jesuit Fr. Robert Taft, a leading expert on Eastern liturgy and a consultor to the Congregation for Eastern Churches, told me that the length of time it takes to get a response from the system is, in his view, its single least attractive feature.

None of this means, however, that curial personnel lack a work ethic. Although some observers complain that they work only half days, in fact the workday runs from 8:30 A.M. to 1:30 P.M., Monday through Saturday. Twice a week, usually Tuesday and Fridays, officials return to the office from 4:00 to 7:00 P.M. That amounts to a thirty-six-hour workweek, which is perhaps less than the customary American forty hours, but hardly half-time. Rumor has it that not everyone goes back in the evenings, but a majority certainly does. Moreover, many curial personnel take mountains of work home in their off-hours. Of course this is not universally true, and as in any bureaucracy, there are some Vatican officials who are on autopilot. Most, however, are reasonably earnest, some incredibly so. Diplomats say that when Cardinal Giovanni Battista Re was the *sostituto*, or number two official in the Secretariat of State, he would sometimes return phone calls at 2:00 A.M. because that was when he had the time. Re's predecessor and patron, Giovanni Benelli, had two secretaries so one could go home after a ten-hour shift, allowing the other to be on hand for whatever Benelli needed, since he would routinely work twenty-hour days.

A large part of the reason that things can take such a long time is not because Vatican personnel are lazy, but because, relative to the work it's trying to do, the Roman Curia is understaffed. The second section of the Secretariat of State does the work of a fully functional foreign ministry, but with a staff of thirty. That means that one officer is responsible for the entire Balkans region and another for all of Central Europe. Simply trying to keep up with the daily press from those places, let alone monitoring the ecclesiastical situation and knowing local dynamics well enough to make intelligent policy recommendations, is beyond any one person's capacity, however polished their linguistic skills and however spongelike their reading facility. The Congregation for Worship has roughly twenty-five officials whose job is to try to monitor, and shape, liturgical texts and rituals in every language on the surface of the earth. It is, once again, an almost comical mismatch of resources to the size of the challenge. All told, the Roman Curia is trying to administer the affairs of a church with 1 billion members, in addition to participating as a sovereign state in global affairs, with a staff of twenty-five hundred. It should be no mystery why, despite the greatest dedication imaginable, things get bogged down.

Yet the time lag is not simply structural, but psychological. There is a built-in bias in favor of delay when facing virtually any decision in the Vatican. This is expressed in words such as *opportune* and *mature,* as in: "I'm not sure that an intervention at this time would be opportune," or "Perhaps it would be best to allow the problem to mature for a few months and then see where we are." There is a resistance to being rushed that is part of the genetic code. In part, of course, this is a standard bureaucratic device to buy time and hope that a problem will solve itself. In part, however, it is also a wise appreciation that sometimes problems, like wine, do get better with time. Sometimes the heat of the battle is not the best moment to make a judgment, because emotions are too inflamed and passions too raw. In some cases only time can allow one to grasp the true dimensions of an issue. When I've taken colleagues from the secular press along with me to visit curial offices, one of the first things they usually notice is how much more quiet it seems inside, as compared to the noisy Roman streets and public spaces. There is a kind of calm that is palpable, and I think it's in part to promote an unrushed, steady approach to work.

Obviously, the rhythms of the liturgical calendar and the Roman year also have an impact on the pace inside the Vatican. Liturgically, the chunks of time around Advent, Christmas, Epiphany, Lent, and Holy Week tend to be dead periods in the Vatican, so that work comes to more or less a standstill while the liturgical celebrations of the season unfold. In Rome, moreover, the annual custom is that summer is basically down time with the annual *Ferragosto* break meaning that from late July to early September, the Vatican is in effect idled. There's a sense in which most of the action in a year in Rome is crammed into seven months: late September through late November, and late February through mid-May. During other periods, liturgical observances, vacation schedules, closings of pontifical universities and institutes all mean that it is difficult to arrange meetings and to make work schedules coincide, so things slip into a lower gear. In the world of the Vatican, it's nothing for someone to say in early November, "We'll deal with this after the holidays," meaning we'll get back to it in late January or so.

Moreover, the respect for authority that was described above also influences the sense of how long it ought to take to resolve a problem.

Despite public perceptions to the contrary, Vatican officials are usually loathe to force a confrontation, especially if it involves bishops. For one thing, they want to avoid an open display of disunity, which they often believe would compromise the Church's public image. But it's also the case that psychologically, many curial officials cringe at the idea of attacking or undercutting the authority of a member of the hierarchy. Therefore, if it's possible to wait out a problem with a bishop, maybe until the bishop retires, if he happens to be near the mandatory age of seventy-five, that will often be the preferred solution. In this way, face can be saved all around.

Finally, there's the impact of history on the way that curial personnel tend to think in centuries. Many Vatican officials work in buildings that are five hundred years old. Some, such as members of religious communities, may live in churches that date back fifteen hundred years. Italians have historical memories not just of the Church, but of political and cultural accomplishments that are some twenty-five hundred years old. Walking down the Via dei Fori Imperiali, from the Piazza Venezia to the Colosseum, one sees the maps of ancient conquests that Mussolini had erected to remind Romans of past glories. In Vatican conversation, it's a routine matter to invoke Church fathers who wrote seventeen hundred years ago. Of course, all this secular and ecclesiastical history has to be set against the even more sweeping background of salvation history, the record of God's dialogue with humanity from Creation through Redemption to Final Judgment. There's a famous remark of Pope St. Pius X (1903–1914) that makes the point. During squabbles with the French government over Church property, some critics felt the Pope was too slow to defend the rights of the Church. Pius responded: "God could have sent us a Redeemer immediately after the Fall. And He made the world wait thousands of years!" All of this shapes a perspective in which one's horizons are much broader than yesterday and tomorrow. Policy choices have to be understood in terms of a very long history, and projected into a potentially equally long future. Perspective, not efficiency, is the most admired quality in this culture.

An anecdote illustrates how the Curia's conception of time can affect policy choices. On October 1, 2000, John Paul II canonized 120 Chinese martyrs, including 87 native converts and 33 foreign missionaries, most of whom had been killed during the anti-Western Boxer movement of the early twentieth century. The Communist government in China complained bitterly about the canonizations, in part because they see most of these martyrs as having in fact been agents of Western imperialism. In part, however, the complaints were also based on the fact that October 1 is National Day in China, marking the day the Communist Party came to power. To stage the canonizations on October 1, according to the Chinese government, thus amounted to a deliberate provocation. The truth was that the Congregation for Saints simply didn't bother consulting a Chinese calendar to explore potential conflicts. Once the conflict was pointed out, however, the Vatican took no steps to resolve it. As it happened, I ran into Archbishop Edward Nowak, secretary of the Congregation for the Causes of Saints, at a party at the American Embassy that week. Kathleen Drexel, the second American-born saint, had been canonized at the same time. I asked Nowak his point of view on the controversy. He said: "You know, in one thousand years the Communist Party will be a footnote in Chinese history, but we will still be celebrating a holy day on October 1 in the memory of these martyrs." It was a classic instance of taking the long view.

Yet none of this means the Vatican is incapable of change, sometimes surprisingly swift change. To take just one example, John Paul II is today numbered among the strongest anti-death penalty campaigners in the world. During his January 1999 trip to St. Louis, his personal plea to Missouri's then-governor Mel Carnahan saved the life of convicted murderer Darrell Mease. The Vatican's diplomatic corps around the world is under instruction to deliver papal requests for clemency every time an execution is scheduled. Various Catholic organizations, such as the Sant'Egidio Community, are leaders in grassroots activism against the death penalty, and this activity is blessed and celebrated from the Apostolic Palace. Yet just over one hundred years ago, popes not only supported capital punishment, they practiced it. In Rome's Museum of Criminology, one can still see the official twelve-foot-tall papal guillotine, last used in 1868, just before the fall of the Papal States. More than a hundred people were beheaded by papal edict on the guillotine, introduced in Rome by Napoleon. As is well-known, Catholic catechisms presented the death penalty as not merely acceptable, but indeed obligatory, well into the post–Vatican II period. Indeed, a provision for capital punishment remained part of the fundamental law of the Vatican City-State until Paul VI declared it null in 1969. It was not actually removed from the books until February 2001. The theological, liturgical, and political nexus surrounding capital punishment developed in the Catholic church over centuries, yet it needed only one determined papacy to dissolve. Rapid movement on seemingly intractable issues is, therefore, possible.

Moreover, the Holy See is capable of rapid response when the situation calls for it. This was clear in the American sex abuse crisis of 2002. Perhaps it's a fair criticism that the Holy See was slow to grasp the depth of the crisis, but once that message was received, it moved beyond business as usual. When the U.S. bishops took their first stab at adopting a new set of sex abuse norms in Dallas in June, the Vatican had its response ready by mid-October—which may not seem remarkable by conventional business standards, but is certainly an accelerated reaction in ecclesiastical terms. Even more remarkable, however, was the Vatican's offer to create a mixed commission, four officials from the Holy See and four bishops from the United States, that would produce a revised set of norms in advance of the November meeting of the U.S. bishops in Washington, D.C. The commission met over just two days in Rome, October 28 and 29, and was ready to present its results to the public November 4. Before the meeting, I had been asked for comment by several broadcast media outlets in the United States, and I expressed skepticism that the commission could really accomplish anything in such a short period. "Around the Vatican, it takes two days to open the mail," I joked. In fact, however, the commission was equal to the task. The norms it produced were then adopted by the U.S. bishops and formally approved by the Vatican. The point is that when the chips are down, and, perhaps equally important, are understood to be down, the Holy See can move fast.

Tradition

The Vatican is one of the few places remaining on earth where the argument "we've always done it this way" is vigorously defended from a philosophical point of view. If one accepts Christ's promise that the Holy Spirit would always be with his Church, this means the Spirit has been guiding the growth and development of the Roman Catholic Church over two thousand years of history, and its structures and practices are not the product of chance or human invention. They represent where the Spirit was calling the Church in a particular moment in its history. Of course, it's always possible that the Church misread the Spirit's intentions, or that in changed times the Spirit may be eliciting a new response. But an extra degree of caution comes into play in evaluating any proposal for reform, because there is a presumption in favor of the wisdom of tradition that is difficult to override.

Can this insistence on tradition be stifling? Yes, especially to Western sensibilities accustomed to the constant arrival of new and improved versions of everything. Sometimes the presumption in favor of how things have always been done sits in the Curia like a lead weight, making even the simplest and most obvious changes in customs difficult to execute. When John Paul II received twenty-three thousand e-mails for his eighty-third birthday in May 2003, for example, every one of them had to be printed out on paper and boxed for shipping up to the Secretariat of State, where they were distributed to the language desks, considered, and given a response. Obviously, the purpose of e-mail is precisely to avoid the need for paper in such a situation. The Secretariat of State has a computer system, and the e-mails could easily have been forwarded with a tap of a keyboard button. But tradition dictated that incoming correspondence to the Holy Father be processed on paper. So it was written, and so it was done.

The Vatican's emphasis on tradition is not, however, merely an excuse for sloughing off new ideas out of laziness or indifference. It is also a recognition that an institution with two thousand years of history has its reasons for doing things a certain way, and caution is in order before one starts cutting through all that to solve today's particular problem. In a sense, it is rather a democratic instinct, a belief that the preferences and insights of all those who have come before ought to have weight in the deliberations.

G. K. Chesterton expressed this view in his book *Orthodoxy*, and it's worth quoting him at length.

> *But there is one thing that I have never from my youth up been able to understand. I have never been able to understand where people got the idea that democracy was in some way opposed to tradition. It is obvious that tradition is only democracy extended through time. It is trusting to a consensus of common human voices rather than to some isolated or arbitrary record. The man who quotes some German historian against the tradition of the Catholic Church, for instance, is strictly appealing to aristocracy. He is appealing to the superiority of one expert against the awful authority of a mob. It is quite easy to see why a legend is treated, and ought to be treated, more respectfully than a book of history. The legend is generally made by the majority of people in the village, who are sane. The book is generally written by the one man in the village who is mad. Those who urge against tradition that men in the past were ignorant may go and urge it at the Carlton Club, along with the statement that voters in the slums are ignorant. It will not do for us. If we attach great importance to the opinion of ordinary men in great unanimity when we are dealing with daily matters, there is no reason why we should disregard it when we are dealing with history or fable. Tradition may be defined as an extension of the franchise. Tradition means giving votes to the most obscure of all classes, our ancestors. It is the democracy of the dead. Tradition refuses to submit to the small and arrogant oligarchy of those who merely happen to be walking about. All democrats object to men being disqualified*

by the accident of birth; tradition objects to their being disqualified by the accident of death. Democracy tells us not to neglect a good man's opinion, even if he is our groom; tradition asks us not to neglect a good man's opinion, even if he is our father. I, at any rate, cannot separate the two ideas of democracy and tradition; it seems evident to me that they are the same idea. We will have the dead at our councils. The ancient Greeks voted by stones; these shall vote by tombstones. It is all quite regular and official, for most tombstones, like most ballot papers, are marked with a cross.

This emphasis on tradition also informs the Vatican's sense of accountability. Critics sometimes complain that the Vatican does not regard itself as accountable to the people of the Church, and there's a sense in which this is true. Leadership in the Church, from the Vatican point of view, is accountable primarily to the tradition, and ultimately to God, who is its author. Policy is based on theological and philosophical principles derived from the tradition, the deposit of faith, entrusted by Christ to the apostles. Vatican officials believe the defense and transmission of the tradition is the highest service Church leaders can offer to their people. In that sense, they do not perceive themselves to be unconcerned or unaccountable to the people. Indeed, as discussed above, there is a sense in which they actually see themselves as populists. At the same time, it is certainly true that opinion polls, ballot boxes, and the other instruments of democratic government are not part of the accountability mechanisms within the curial world.

Truth to be told, most people who work in the Curia have a pet reform they'd like to push through, some area where they sincerely believe tradition has become dysfunctional or oppressive or simply outdated. An official I know in the Congregation for Saints, for example, thinks the time has come to do away with the penultimate step of beatification before canonization. Originally, beatification was designed to approve local veneration of a holy person, while canonization approved that person's cult for the universal Church. In a globalized world in which the distinction between local and universal is increasingly relative, however, this official believes beatification no longer makes sense. Yet he's not rattling cages to put this issue on the fast track. Why not? In part, because most Vatican officials also have a story of a time when they challenged a tradition only later to appreciate its wisdom. A German priest, for example, began working some years ago in a dicastery and was assigned an office whose window faced in the direction of St. Peter's Square. When he moved in, he found the window had been painted shut. He inquired with his superior why this was so, and was informed, "It was like that when I got here." This German, a moderate-to-progressive who grew up on the Second Vatican Council, regarded this restriction not merely as silly, but a metaphor for everything that was wrong with the contemporary Church and its failure to live up to Pope John XXIII's spirit of "throwing open the windows" of the Church. One day he brought a chisel and a small knife and knocked out the paint, opening up his window. He regarded this as a small but symbolic victory for the postconciliar church. Business called him out of the office for several hours, and when he returned he discovered the logic for the tradition—a gaggle of pigeons had settled down on his desk, his filing cabinet, and everywhere else in the office. After spending a clumsy, and messy, afternoon getting rid of the pigeons, the paint went back on the window. The priest has not stopped pressing gently for reform, but he also moves with a more modest appreciation that sometimes there are reasons things are the way they are.

This core belief in the wisdom of tradition also means that most Vatican officials would be considered, by the standards of the total spectrum of opinion in the Catholic Church, conservatives. By no means should this suggest that the men and women of the Roman Curia are narrow-minded traditionalists. A surprising number of curial officials might vote in favor of married priests in a secret ballot and some would support a relaxation in the teaching on birth control. A handful might be open to the eventual ordination of women as priests. Yet even those leaning toward the reform position on these issues typically also see the wisdom in contrary views, since the benefit of the doubt would go to the tradition, and they would regard compromise and patience as the best strategy. In classifying Vatican personnel, in fact, I have found it relatively unhelpful to think in terms of liberal and conservative, since most people in the Curia would be by conventional standards moderate-to-conservative. The more illuminating category is open and closed, that is, those whose regard for tradition does not inhibit them from entertaining criticism, and those inaccessible to any critique.

Finally, it should be noted that at times the Holy See's reverence for tradition can shade off into arrogance toward those who are not comparably grounded in the fine points of Roman Catholic history, theology, spirituality, and law. Vatican officials rightfully insist that the Catholic Church is the product of a two-thousand-year history, which has given it a rich and multifaceted culture. They can become impatient with reformers demanding that this culture be stood on its head in response to a challenge that, in the context of two thousand years, just arose yesterday. They have every reason to demand that people who want to make proposals for change in the tradition at least master it first, so they'll know what they're taking about. At the same time, it is unreasonable to expect that average lay Catholics must become professional theologians or canon lawyers before their experience and insight counts. Vatican officials thus face the challenge of fostering an appreciation for tradition, so that proposals for change can be evaluated in the proper ecclesiological context, and yet not setting the bar so high that they rule out of bounds all views but their own.

4

VATICAN SOCIOLOGY

By the standard of contemporary best practices in the corporate world, the Holy See's top level of management doesn't make a great deal of sense. Quite often, there is no discernible relationship between the work performed by a given division of the Vatican and the qualifications of the person tapped to lead it. As of the fall of 2003, the Catholic Church's chief liturgical officer had no background in liturgy, its top official on missions had never been on a mission, its education czar was a canon lawyer, and the man who ran its ministry of health had no medical training. Indeed, it was hailed as a major breakthrough in 2000 when the Pope appointed as prefect of the Congregation for Eastern Churches a man who was at least a member of one of the twenty-one Eastern Rite churches. The previous occupant of the job had been an Italian, Cardinal Achille Silvestrini. Likewise, Cardinal Joseph Ratzinger is the first qualified theologian to run the Church's doctrinal office since Cardinal Robert Bellarmine in the seventeenth century.

Why does the Holy See place seemingly unprepared and ill-suited officials in such sensitive posts? The answer is that the Vatican's personnel policy, which is informal and largely unspoken, arose well before MIT or Harvard Business School began to contemplate the science of hiring. Content-area knowledge is not the highest value in this system. Traditionally, churchmen have been assigned Vatican jobs not so much on the basis of their training or professional expertise, but their loyalty, their ecclesiastical pedigree, and the compatibility of their vision with that of the Pope or of other top officials such as the secretary of state. Expertise can be developed or brought in at lower levels of management; the most important quality the top official must possess is not competence, but commitment.

This way of doing business reflects centuries of cultural history, shaped not by the ethos of corporate efficiency but by dynastic politics, in which family loyalties were usually a far more important criterion for holding a leadership post than academic credentials. Luigi Barzini, in his famous book *The Italians*, offered the example of Napoleon Bonaparte (who was born into an Italian family on Corsica in 1769, and narrowly missed being an Italian citizen since the French had occupied the island just two years before):

> *As soon as he was able to, he made adequate arrangements for his brothers, sisters, in-laws, and stepsons. His older brother Joseph was made King of Naples for a time and later promoted to King of Spain; his younger brother Lucien, who mistrusted Napoleon, was made Prince of Canino, a rich fief north of Rome, in the Maremma; his sister Elisa was married to Prince Felice Bacciocchi and was first given the Duchy of Lucca and later the Grand Duchy of Tuscany; his brother Louis became King of Holland; his sister Pauline married Prince Camillo Borghese; his sister Caroline married Joachim Murat, who was appointed King of Naples; his brother Jerome, who had married the American beauty Elizabeth Patterson of Baltimore, had to divorce her and marry the not very pretty Catherine of Württemberg to become King of Westphalia; his stepson Eugene de Beauharnais was an excellent viceroy of Italy.*

As Barzini went on to note, this tradition survived in Italy well into the twentieth century. "Brothers, brothers-in-law, sons, sons-in-law or cousins of prominent politicians in the Christian Democrat party are ensconced in comfortable and rewarding positions in state-controlled or nationalized organizations, industries and holding companies, posts for which they seldom hold a particular training." In the Holy See today, this belief in putting family members in key jobs is more figurative than literal; trustworthy individuals are sometimes said to be *della famiglia*, in the family. In past centuries, however, popes would appoint blood relatives as the equivalent of their secretary of state, a position that came to be known as the cardinal-nephew. That office was suppressed in 1692 with the bull *Romanum decet Pontificem*.

This will seem irrational, or corrupt, behavior only by post–Industrial Revolution standards of efficiency, where it is assumed that the most important criterion of leadership is specialized expertise. But in precapitalist cultures, there was less bureaucratic emphasis on experts; it was assumed that a general education would suffice to make big-picture decisions and that the details could be delegated to others. What was more important was placing someone in a leadership post who would be in lockstep with the overall philosophy of the ruling regime, who would not betray his patron for a better offer, and who would be a team player when the time came to make sacrifices. The efficiency sought was not that of maximizing profit and minimizing cost, but of ensuring that all the component parts of the operation were serving the same ultimate end.

The Holy See in many ways still lives in this precapitalist world. This is more than mere stick-in-the-mud unwillingness to modernize. Philosopher Alasdair MacIntyre has explained that every institution operates out of a particular "narrative tradition," and in the Aristotelian-Thomistic framework of the Catholic Church, there is an instinctive distrust of claims to specialized expertise from people who don't share the moral and metaphysical worldview of Catholicism. They may indeed know how to build a better mousetrap, but in the process they could be asphyxiating the soul. For this reason, the Church has preferred to put people in leadership roles who may or may not have a technical command of the issues involved, but who can be relied upon to grasp the larger theological and spiritual aims the work is intended to serve.

When one tries to understand how senior Vatican officials get their jobs, therefore, it simply can't be done through the prism of twentieth-century Anglo-Saxon corporate psychology. This is a classic instance in which the European and Italian roots of the Holy See shape its culture. That insight suggests the subject of this chapter: How does the surrounding environment influence the thinking, the experience, and the frame of reference of the men and women who serve in the Vatican?

What does it mean, for example, that the Catholic Church is governed by the *Roman* Curia, and not by a group of people working in New York or New Delhi? Those 2,659 curial employees, according to the 2003 count, find themselves living in multiple cultural worlds, and each exerts its own special kind of gravitational pull. There is first of all the world of the Vatican itself—its rather unique approach to labor and to compensation. Then there's the context of Rome. The Roman newspapers, the Roman streets, Roman virtues and vices all influence the Vatican officials who spend their working hours inside their 108-acre enclave, but pass most of their afternoons, evenings, and weekends in the Eternal City. Next there's the Italian layer, the unique features of Italian politics, entertainment, sports, and fashion that exercise a special influence. Finally, there's the fact of being in Europe, which ushers in all the cultural and psychological differences between Europeans and Americans that became the object of reams of amateur anthropology during the war in Iraq. All these layers of sociological reality affect and shape the worldview of those who work in the Roman Curia.

In the end, as much as the Holy See is an international institution serving a universal Church, its personnel cannot help but be shaped by the particular cultural contexts they inhabit. For people who work in this environment, all this is second nature, but it's a revealing exercise to peal back the layers and consider what each contributes to the whole. Being human means being shaped by place, time, and experience. To understand the Vatican, therefore, we need to understand the various elements that contribute to shaping its world.

THREE VATICAN OFFICIALS

The relationship between officials of the Roman Curia and their environment is even more complex than sketched above, because the layers of environment are not the only variables. Each person in the Holy See is also unique, bringing a distinctive background and point of view to his or her encounter with the Vatican, Rome, Italy, and Europe. Recall what was said in chapter 2 about the myth that there is such a creature as "the Vatican." It is just as much a piece of mythology that there is a typical Vatican official. Few bureaucracies gather under one roof a group of people whose interests and work assignments are so strikingly different. Before we can consider what Vatican officials have in common, we first need to record how diversified their personal situations actually are. To make this point, we'll consider the following three officials in three different offices: the Pontifical Council for Promoting Christian Unity, the Congregation for Divine Worship and the Discipline of the Sacraments, and the Pontifical Council for Migrants and Refugees. These three positions are fairly representative of the various kinds of jobs officials in the different dicasteries hold. There are real individuals who hold the jobs described below, but the details of their work offered here are not based on their personal experiences; they are the product of my own imagination.

The Council for Promoting Christian Unity is divided into desks covering the different branches of Christianity with which the Catholic Church has an official dialogue. The dicastery also has responsibility for the dialogue with Judaism, so there is also a full-time official assigned to this relationship. There is someone responsible for the Lutherans, for example, someone for the Baptists, and so on. Let's take as an example the official responsible for relations with the Anglicans, who also covers the Methodists, since historically Methodism is a reform out of the Anglican tradition. Each day he reads the press from traditionally Anglican regions, above all England, scanning for news or commentary about the Anglican Communion. He also reads carefully the sermons, pronouncements, and interviews given by the Archbishop of Canterbury. If there is a major story breaking in the Anglican world, such as the crisis in 2003 concerning homosexual bishops and the blessing of same-sex unions, he will spend long hours tracking it—reading position papers, talking to friends and contacts, keeping his superiors informed. He studies the resolutions adopted by Anglican synods around the world, as well as all the documents produced by official Catholic/Anglican dialogues. He might be involved in helping prepare the next round of talks for the official Anglican/Roman Catholic International Commission (ARCIC). Whenever officials from the Anglican world come to Rome, he is a primary point of contact, helping to arrange meetings with other Vatican officials, and taking his Anglican counterparts to lunch or dinner in order to swap information and talk about the future of the relationship. Whenever the cardinal who heads his dicastery is invited to speak to a group of Anglicans or Methodists, this official helps prepare his remarks and briefs the cardinal on what he should expect.

Given the nature of his work, it's likely that this official may be more plugged into the politics of Canterbury than those of Rome. On at least some issues he may be able to speak more knowledgeably about the positions of the last Lambeth Conference, the once-a-decade gathering of all the Anglican bishops of the world, than he could of the acts of some Roman Catholic ecumenical councils. He may have almost as many friends in the ranks of Anglican clergy as he does on the Catholic side. The same thing goes for his relations with Methodism and Methodist clergy. Despite the fact that this person is a Vatican official, he does not pass most days thinking about the internal dynamics of the Vatican. Due to the nature of his job, he is far more directed at the world outside the walls of the Holy See.

The official at the Congregation for Worship has a more intra-Catholic frame of reference, but not necessarily more intra-Vatican.

This dicastery is divided into two sections, one dealing with liturgical principles, the other with sacramental discipline, especially valid marriages and the sacrament of Holy Orders. The liturgical side is further divided by language, so if our official is a German, he's working on questions of liturgical practice and texts that arise in the German language. He spends a great deal of time reading proposed liturgical translations from Latin into German—the order for funerals, the rite of baptism, the lectionary (a collection of readings for the Mass), and all the other liturgical books necessary to carry out the approved rites of the Catholic Church. In the process as currently envisioned in Rome, the German bishops have the responsibility for arranging for translations of these texts, which since the Second Vatican Council has largely been entrusted to the Internationale Arbeitsgemeinschaft der Liturgischen Kommissionen im deutschen Sprachgebiet (IAG), housed at the Deutsches Liturgisches Institut in Trier. Member countries include Germany, Austria, Switzerland, Luxembourg, and Liechtenstein, along with a handful of other German-speaking dioceses. After IAG completes its work, the German bishops must review and approve it, and then it must go to the Vatican for final promulgation.

One primary task of this Vatican official is to coordinate this Vatican review, bringing in consultors and experts as needed to ensure that the text is consistent with the principles of the May 2001 Vatican document, *Liturgiam Authenticam*, which calls for the most faithful translation possible to the original Latin. Given the nature of his work, our official likely has some background in Scripture and ancient languages. By its nature, this kind of analysis is slow and painstaking, and the devil is always in the details. The official would thus spend much of his time in conversation with experts in linguistics, languages, and liturgical history. When liturgical officials from German-speaking regions come to Rome, he would be their primary contact. He would be in contact with colleagues in the German, Austrian, and Swiss bishops' conferences, and professors of liturgy on Catholic theological faculties in those countries. When German-speaking bishops arrive in Rome, he quite often would go out to lunch or dinner with them or at least meet with them in the office to chat about the current state of affairs. This official will brief the rest of the staff in the dicastery, and especially his superiors, about what's happening in the German-speaking liturgical world.

Finally, consider an official in the Pontifical Council for Migrants and Refugees. This dicastery is organized based on the particular set of issues handled: migrants, the apostolate of the sea, airports, refugees, and so on. Our official has the desk for refugees, and his responsibility is to track the global situation, to monitor the Catholic response to refugee issues, and to be ready to intervene in moments of crisis. He spends a great deal of time each day reading reports from various United Nations agencies and humanitarian groups on the refugee situation in Africa, or in Asia, or Latin America, or wherever war or natural disaster has produced a significant flow of people. In 2002, the United Nations High Commission for Refugees reported that there were 19.8 million people "of concern" to the agency, roughly one out of every three hundred people on earth. He also monitors reports from Catholic aid agencies, especially Caritas and Catholic Relief Services, about their contact with refugees and the services these agencies offer. When officials of various humanitarian groups looking for support from the Catholic Church come through Rome, he is a primary contact, often trying to arrange hearings for them with Vatican officials higher up the chain of command. He sometimes attends international meetings on refugee issues to represent the position of the Holy See, which is generally an uncontroversial stance in favor of human dignity, but can involve controversial debates over whether birth control devices ought to be distributed along with food and medicine in refugee camps. On these trips, the official will sometimes visit refugee camps in particularly afflicted parts of the world, which cannot help but form a visceral emotional attachment to these suffering people. When bishops from various parts of the world come to Rome, he will brief them on the refugee situation, help them develop response strategies, and ask them about what the Catholic Church in their diocese or country is already doing. This official's horizons are focused well beyond Vatican walls, to one of the great humanitarian concerns of the day.

All three of the above are Vatican officials. All three have offices in Rome, two just off St. Peter's Square and the third in the nearby neighborhood of Trastevere, in the Piazza San Calisto. All three go to work wearing a clerical shirt and Roman collar and carrying a briefcase. To see them in a lineup, one could easily assume they're almost interchangeable. Yet they have radically different backgrounds, interests, and areas of professional competence. They could go years in curial service without ever meeting one another. If they do happen to rub shoulders, they would probably have no idea the other worked in the Vatican. As a journalist, I am more likely to know people in different dicasteries than most curial personnel, even after many years of service. Such is the nature of the Vatican, where each dicastery tends to be highly compartmentalized and where many officials spend most of their time dealing with people on the outside. Someone who works in the Council for Justice and Peace rarely has occasion to meet people who work in the Congregation for Bishops, who in turn spend little time with staffers of the Apostolic Signatura. These officials all work in the Roman Curia, but their experience of what that means differs radically. This point must be borne in mind as we examine the layers of culture that encircle the Holy See. Each Vatican official interacts with these layers, and is affected by them, but the nature of the impact will vary. We'll be using formulae such as "Vatican officials" and "the men and women of the Roman Curia," but this is a shorthand device that glosses over enormous diversity.

Layer One: The Vatican

One thing all Vatican employees share is the bureaucratic system that shapes their work environment. Every curial employee, no matter what they do, is assigned a number on the Vatican's scale of employee status, everyone is subject to the Vatican's salary and pension system, everyone faces challenges with housing and personal finance. Since how an organization handles such matters says a great deal about its values, the experience of navigating this system cannot help but shape the attitudes of curial personnel to their work and the institution they serve.

According to the *Regolamento generale*, or employee handbook of the Holy See, issued June 7, 1992, every dicastery is led by a cardinal prefect or president, or by an archbishop president, nominated directly by the Pope. This top official is assisted by a prelate superior, also nominated by the Pope. This is normally the secretary of the dicastery, but several other officials are also considered to be at the prelate superior level: the *sostituto* and the secretary for Relations with States, both in the Secretariat of State; the regent of the Apostolic Penitentiary; the secretary of the Apostolic Signatura; the dean of the Roman Rota; the prefect of the papal household; and the papal Master of Ceremonies. Prelate superiors are also appointed directly by the Pope, and although it's understood that they are to work in close cooperation with the prefect, the *Regolamento* recognizes a kind of independent responsibility. Depending on the relationship between these two figures, in some dicasteries the secretary may be the real authority, or even at times a rival authority. A prefect does not always get the man he wants as his secretary. Cardinal Joseph Ratzinger, for example, succeeded in picking his own replacement as secretary of the Congregation for the Doctrine of the Faith when Archbishop Tarcisio Bertone was transferred in December 2002 to Genoa. The person who took over, Salesian theologian Angelo Amato, was a longtime consultor for the congregation who shares Ratzinger's theological concerns. Cardinal Walter Kasper in the Council for Promoting Christian Unity, on the other hand, did not have such a role in picking his new secretary when the man who had held the job, Marc Ouellet, became archbishop of Quebec. In January 2003 Kasper was assigned Bishop Brian Farrell, a longtime official of the Secretariat of State. Many felt this was a stratagem on the part of the Secretariat of State to plant a spy in Kasper's office, but if so, things do not seem to have worked out that way. Kasper and Farrell seem to have developed a good working relationship.

The number-three officials in most dicasteries are the undersecretaries, who likewise are also "superiors." Also considered to be at undersecretary level are: the promoter of justice in the Congregation for the Doctrine of the Faith; the prelate-theologian and the relators in the Congregation for the Causes of Saints; the promoter of justice and the defender of the bond in the Apostolic Signatura; the promoter of justice and the defender of the bond of the Roman Rota; the general accountant of the Prefecture of the Economic Affairs of the Holy See; the regent of the papal household; and the director of the Press Office of the Holy See. Below the level of superiors come the mid-level officials in each dicastery. The most significant would be the *capi uffici*, who direct the work of a section or department within a dicastery. Only the larger dicasteries with multiple sections have a *capo ufficio*. Then come the *aiutanti di studio* and the *addetti di segreteria*, the desk officers who do most of the day-to-day work of handling correspondence, processing case files, preparing meetings. Each office will also have a support staff of receptionists, people to do the typing and filing, and so on.

Under the Holy See's salary system, every employee is assigned a number from one to ten, representing the lowest to the highest grade on the pay scale. Which number a particular employee holds, and why, can be among the great mysteries of Vatican life. Roughly speaking, the numbers correspond to competence, but in Vatican-speak this does not mean one's ability. It refers instead to the nature of the job one holds—the more complex and the more authority it entails, the higher up the scale. In terms of paychecks, the Vatican is definitely not a meritocracy. The numbers to some extent reflect seniority, so it's possible for an official to be at level nine, yet doing the same job he began with twenty years ago at level six. Certain jobs cap out at a given number because of the nature of the position. An *addetto tecnico*, for example, is classified at a lower level, usually referring to people who type and file, and the maximum pay grade is typically six. A *monsignore* in one dicastery is regarded as among the world's leading experts in his field, he lectures widely and is quoted as the voice of the Holy See, and yet for quirky reasons is classified as an *addetto tecnico* and is stuck at level five. Several times over the years he has tried to get cardinals to intervene on his behalf, but to no avail.

Functionally speaking, the level someone holds is not terribly important in terms of relations with other personnel, since employees generally do not know what number their colleagues hold. Often when two lay Vatican employees are introduced to one another, especially the

Italians, this is among the first questions they ask: What's your number? It's considered a bit uncouth among the clerical ranks to express curiosity on the point, and usually officials have to know one another fairly well before it comes up. They know one another's job classification—*addetto*, undersecretary, and so on—because it is published in the Vatican's *Annuario*, its yearbook. As a rule, a priest who is a new hire for a mid-level position in a dicastery will begin at level six for a probationary period and will automatically move up to level seven within a few months. Movement up the scale depends upon time, promotion, and the goodwill of one's superiors.

Outsiders are generally shocked at the low salaries drawn by Vatican officials, many of whom hold advanced degrees, in some cases doctorates, and who would be considered the equivalent of white-collar middle managers in any other major multinational organization. Here is a representative set of monthly pay stubs denominated in Euro from a real Vatican official, a priest who entered curial service as an *addetto di segreteria* in February 2001:

FEBRUARY 2001   (Level 6)
Salary   1,291.48
Special addition   68.13
Preliminary Total: 1,359.61 (Annual salary: € 16,315.22)
(minus)
Health Insurance   26.39
Severance   19.79
Net Earnings: 1,313.43 (Annual net: € 15,761.16)

Note: The "special addition" is an additional payment intended to offset increases in the cost of living. Twice a year a special Vatican commission meets, and, on the basis of figures generated by the Italian government regarding the rate of inflation, determines if an additional contribution to salary should be provided. The mechanism for determining the amount is complex, and the formula is based not on one's total salary, but only a portion. Hence the addition tends to be relatively small.

Health Insurance refers to a fund, called the Fondo Assistenza Sanitaria, which covers medical services, ambulance costs and pharmacy expenses for employees, retirees, and family members who live with or are otherwise dependent upon employees or pensioners.

Severance refers to a payment made by the Vatican to an employee when he or she resigns, retires, is fired, or leaves at the end of a temporary contract. Generally the amount, to which both employee and employer contribute, is equivalent to one month of pay for every year of service. Someone who leaves the Vatican after twelve years will be paid a full year's salary.

JULY 2001

Salary	1,313.25
Special addition	82.04
Preliminary Total:	1,395.29 (Annual salary: € 16,743.48)
(minus)	
Health Insurance	29.63
Severance	22.21
Net Earnings:	1,343.45 (Annual net: € 16,121.40)

JANUARY 2002

Salary	1,313.33
Special addition	81.58
Preliminary Total:	1,394.91 (Annual salary: € 16,738.92)
(minus)	
Health Insurance	27.90
Severance	20.92
Net Earnings:	1,346.09 (Annual net: € 16,153.08)

APRIL 2002   (Promoted to Level 7)

Salary	1,372.11
Special addition	85.34
Overdue gross	58.78
Overdue special addition	3.76
Preliminary Total:	1,519.99 (Annual salary: € 18,239.88)

(minus)

Health Insurance	30.40
Severance	22.80
Net earnings:	1,466.79 (Annual net: € 17,601.48)

Note: The overdue category refers to a back payment owed to an employee that is now being paid. For example, if one is promoted in July but with an effective date of the preceding March 1, an overdue gross will be paid for the salary differential for those three months, along with the overdue addition to compensate for increases in the cost of living.

MAY 2002

Salary	1,372.11
Special addition	85.34
Preliminary Total:	1,457.45 (Annual salary: € 17,489.40)

(minus)

Health Insurance	29.15
Severance	21.86
Net earnings:	1,406.44 (Annual net: € 16,877.28)

JUNE 2002   (Qualified for Pension)

Salary	1,372.11
Special addition	85.34
Preliminary Total:	1,457.45 (Annual salary: € 17,489.40)

(minus)

Pension 5%	72.87
Health Insurance	29.15
Severance	21.86
Net Earnings:	1,333.57 (Annual net: € 16,002.84)

JULY 2002

Salary	1,372.11
Special addition	106.67
Preliminary Total:	1,478.78 (Annual salary: € 17,745.36)

(minus)

Pension 5%	73.94
Health Insurance	29.58
Severance	22.18
Net earnings:	1,353.08 (Annual net: € 16,236.96)

JANUARY 2003

Salary	1,478.78
Special addition	18.72
Preliminary Total:	1,497.50 (Annual salary: € 17,970.00)

(minus)

Pension 5%	74.88
Health Insurance	29.95
Severance	22.46
Net earnings:	1,370.21 (Annual net: € 16,442.52)

FEBRUARY 2003

Salary	1,478.78
Special addition	18.72
Bienni	32.25
Preliminary Total:	1,529.75 (Annual salary: € 18,357.00)

(minus)

Pension 5%	76.49
Health Insurance	30.60
Severance	22.95
Net earnings:	1,399.71 (Annual net: € 16,796.52)

Note: The *bienni* is an additional monthly payment awarded after every two years of service, so someone with sixteen years in the Curia will receive a *bienni* payment that has been increased eight times. The amount is calculated on the basis of the number of years at each level of service, so if the employee was at level seven for six years, then at eight for five, then at nine for five, the *bienni* will be calculated on the basis of three different figures reflecting each of those periods of service.

After two years of service and a promotion up the pay grade, this official makes less than US $20,000 a year—an amount that most lawyers, doctors, architects, and other white-collar professionals would consider an insult as a starting salary fresh out of college. To be fair, Vatican employees receive an extra month's pay during the second ten-day period in December of each year, which takes the place of a Christmas bonus. Still, compensation is anything but profligate. This Vatican official, by the way, travels the world representing the Holy See at international meetings, prepares speeches that are pronounced by the Pope, and is called upon to negotiate complex treaty agreements with NGOs and United Nations agencies. Yet when he travels to New York or Geneva on business, most of the time he can't afford to go out for dinner at night unless someone else offers to pick up the tab. It goes without saying that Vatican officials are not issued company credit cards and do not have expense accounts.

A few other observations are in order. First, these earnings are untaxed. A mid-level white-collar official in the U.S. government might make $65,000 a year, but one-third is eaten up in taxes, so the official only sees $43,333 in net pay. That is, obviously, still much higher than the $18,842.72 our Vatican official nets, given Euro/U.S. dollar exchange rates as of this writing. Second, the Vatican official in question is a priest, so he does not have a family to support. By the same token, he does not have the possibility of marriage to someone bringing in a second paycheck. Whether the curial official has to pay for housing or not depends on the particular circumstances. For superiors, housing is generally provided. Cardinals are generally expected to maintain at least a minimum household staff. Lower-level officials are more on their own. American diocesan priests in curial service typically live in the Villa Stritch, a facility subsidized by the United States Conference of Catholic Bishops. They pay $250 a month, which includes meals. Priests of other nationalities may have to pay an amount closer to the typical costs of apartment rental in urban Rome, which can be 1,000 Euro a month. In some cases, they get lucky and find housing at a reduced cost. One Maltese official, for example, lives in an apartment owned by the English College and pays a nominal rent. Curial officials generally travel home for vacation at their own expense at least once a year, and many are required by the nature of their job to maintain a car in Rome—an expensive proposition given the demands of gas, parking, and insurance, to say nothing of routine repairs.

One big variable in how officials are able to live lies in whether or not their home diocese pays them a salary while they are in Rome. Among the Americans, some priests continue to draw full diocesan salary while working in the Vatican, which can be $25,000 or more annually. Others get a partial supplement. Still others draw nothing, which tends to be a sore point for officials in that situation. To some extent, these differences are a matter of divergent diocesan policies, but they may also sometimes come down to the personal interest a bishop takes in supporting personnel on loan to the Curia. One official in a dicastery told me that he had been working in the Vatican for two years when, on a visit to Rome, his bishop finally got around to asking him, "So, how do you get paid over here?" When he explained the salary system, the bishop immediately promised to begin sending a supplement, which has allowed this official to go back to the United States twice a year instead of once to visit his family, including his mother, who is in a nursing home.

John Paul addressed the issue of curial salaries in a November 20, 1982, letter about working in the Holy See: "Among those who collaborate with the Holy See, many are ecclesiastics, who, living a vow of celibacy, do not have within their sphere of responsibility the care of a family. Hence they merit a remuneration proportional to the duties they carry out, sufficient to assure a decorous support and to allow them to fulfill the obligations of their state in life, including those responsibilities they can have in certain cases to come to the aid of their own parents or other relatives who may depend on them. Neither should the exigencies of their particular social relations be obscured, especially the obligation to aid the needy; an obligation that, on account of their evangelical vocation, is for ecclesiastics and religious more compelling than for the laity." The Pope seems to imply that because ecclesiastics do not have wives and children (except for clergy from one of the twenty-one Eastern Rite churches), they do not need large paychecks, though he acknowledges that in some cases family members may depend upon the official for support. The Pope also seems to argue that the compensation of curial officials should not be so substantial that it distances or alienates them from the poor.

In the same letter, John Paul II notes that the Catholic Church has, since the birth of its modern social doctrine in the nineteenth century, supported the right of workers to organize. Yet when it comes to the Holy See, the Pope writes, account must be taken of its "specific nature." It is not a corporate or a political reality, such as a state. The Holy See exists to perform a pastoral service to the human family, the Pope writes, and as such calls for a special sort of collaboration on the part of those who are in its service. The implication is that a traditional union would be out of place. In fact, most priests and religious who work in the Vatican do not have any sort of collective bargaining, since the vast majority would be considered management. Lay employees do have such an association: the Associazione Dipendenti Laici Vaticani, created in 1980. It is sometimes referred to as the "Vatican union," and it is affiliated with CISL, the Confederazione Italiana Sindacati Lavoratori, one of the chief Italian federations of labor unions. Yet it is not a union in the traditional sense, because it is prohibited by statute from calling a strike or from utilizing any other means of "class struggle." Its spirit is supposed to be one of cooperation. Its last major campaign came in 2000, when it pushed the Vatican to make its pension system compatible with that of the Italian government so that if employees leave Vatican service their pension is not lost.

The bottom line is that Vatican officials cannot expect their work to draw the conventional rewards of other professions: high pay, large homes, fancy cars, fat stock portfolios, and the like. Nor can most of them expect fame instead of fortune, since most Vatican work is performed anonymously. As human beings, since money and glory are denied to them, many Vatican officials will seek their rewards elsewhere. This perhaps helps explain the fact that some in the Vatican are so attentive to who is promoted, how fast, and into how important a position. It helps explain why the question of who becomes a bishop, for example, can be so staggeringly important. In the rarified world of curial service, these are among the few ways people have of "keeping score." It also helps explain why Vatican officials sometimes preen, or comport themselves in ways that come off as arrogant or self-inflated. In other walks of life, big paychecks or a public following are the ways that professionals satisfy their egos, but those channels are closed in the Holy See. If Vatican officials sometimes seem keen on power and career, therefore, this context should be borne in mind. That's not to excuse the behavior, which is by no means universal. But perhaps it will at least seem less shocking if one understands how the curial system is, from a twenty-first-century corporate point of view, in almost willful denial of the normal laws of human motivation. This is another instance of the *bella figura* view of law: set the expectations high, as a way of fostering virtue, and accept that many will fall short.

Layer Two: Rome

Outside the walls of the Vatican, the men and women of the Curia live and move in the city of Rome, with all its chaos and magnificence, all its modern woes and ancient glories. Just as journalists often develop story ideas based on the things they trip across on their way to work, Vatican officials cannot help but be influenced in their conception of what's going on in the world by their experience of the streets and public squares of Rome. This influence shows up in ways large and small. One example: real insiders say the true fault line in the Holy See is not between liberals and conservatives, or between Italians and non-Italians, but between *Romanisti* and *Laziali*—fans of Rome's two professional soccer clubs, Roma and Lazio, whose bitter rivalry divides families, neighborhoods, and workplaces. (In one potential sign of divine favor, Roma won the Italian championship that began during the Holy Year of 2000.)

In most ways the experience of this urban milieu is a healthy one, because it puts curial personnel in contact with the live reality of ordinary people. On the other hand, it means that if Romans have a skewed view of things, that skew tends to be reproduced in curial attitudes. In either case, one can establish this basic rule of thumb about Vatican sociology: If something is important in Rome, it's also likely to be considered important in the Vatican; if something is invisible in Rome, it's probably invisible in the Vatican as well. In this section, we'll consider two examples from ecclesiastical Rome and two examples from secular Rome of how the realities of Roman life help shape the worldview of the men and women in the Vatican.

ECCLESIASTICAL ROME

One of the burning questions Catholics from around the world typically ask about the Vatican is, "What are they planning to do about the priest shortage?" This for the obvious reason that the priest shortage is a serious problem in many parts of the world. In the rural United States, for example, a typical diocesan priest in his late sixties may struggle to cover four or five parish Masses on a given Sunday, sometimes spread over hundreds of miles. Since 1975, the number of priests in the United States has dropped nearly 24 percent, from 58,900 to 44,900 in 2002. The number of diocesan priests, who do the majority of parish work, fell from 36,000 to 30,000 during the same period. At the same time, the Catholic population jumped from 48.7 million to 62.2 million. One quarter of diocesan priests are seventy or older. In 1965, 994 priests were ordained in the United States; less than half that number, or 450, were ordained in 2002. Already 2,000 parishes in the United States are without a resident pastor. All this means that American Catholics can touch, smell, and taste the priest shortage.

Vatican officials are well aware of these trends, and the situation is a matter of deep, and sincere, pastoral alarm. Yet if one asks if officials of the Roman Curia go to bed at night worrying about the priest shortage, the answer is generally no. In part this is because they are consoled by worldwide statistics that suggest a small upturn in priestly vocations, fueled by dramatic growth in the Third World. They also are cheered by the success of the new ecclesial movements and religious communities in generating vocations, such as the Legionaries of Christ, with some 2,500 seminarians worldwide. Yet there is another, more socio- logical factor: Curial officials are not reminded of the crisis by their daily experience, because there simply is no priest shortage in Rome.

According to the latest Catholic directory for the Rome archdio- cese, there are more than 5,000 priests currently working in Rome— nearly 15 for each of the 334 parishes. Of course, not every priest in the Eternal City is involved in parish work. Many work in the Vatican, or teach in one of the 24 ecclesiastical universities, or work in schools, re- treat centers or office jobs. In such a milieu, it's difficult to be personally anxious about a shortage of clergy. For example, when the pastor of Santa Susanna, the official American parish in Rome, needs to be out of town on a weekend, there are literally dozens of American priests he can call upon to cover for him. Few pastors in the United States have a similar wealth of options.

Many of the priests in Rome are not official members of the local church. Some 832 are on temporary loan from other dioceses, while more than 3,100 belong to religious orders. Another 115 are priests who belong juridically to the Church's lone personal prelature, Opus Dei. But that's only the beginning of the story. When students and others who have no apparent job or ministry are added to the equation, the 5,000 priests burgeon to at least three times that number. That means there are 15,000 priests in Rome, giving an impression of sur- plus rather than shortage. That's not even to speak about the thousands of not-yet-ordained seminarians, many of whom are dressed in Roman collar and black clerical dress. With such a visible presence of clerics, it's no wonder that Vatican officials can have a difficult time appreciating just how urgent the lack of priests can seem in other places. It's one thing to ponder shoddy construction practices when one's own house is safe and sound. If water is filling the basement, on the other hand, one feels a whole different level of urgency.

A second example of the impact of ecclesiastical Rome upon Vat- ican psychology concerns attitudes toward the new ecclesial move- ments, such as Opus Dei and the Legionaries of Christ. (Technically, neither one of these groups is a movement; one is a personal prelature, the other a community of priests. But this is fine print we can ignore for now.) In the English-speaking Catholic world, these new ecclesial movements have become a lightning rod for controversy, symbols of the cultural wars in the Church between liberals and conservatives. In part this is because in the English-speaking Catholic mind, the movements are associated with the conservative wing of the Church. Those movements that are best known among English-speakers, such as the Legionaries of Christ, Opus Dei, and the Neocatechumenate, tend to be the most conservative, both politically and theologically. English-language Catholic literature contains a number of critical books about the growing power of the movements, such as *The Pope's Armada: Unlocking the Secrets of Mysterious and Powerful New Sects in the Church* by Gordon Urquhart and *Their Kingdom Come: Inside the Secret World of Opus Dei* by Robert Hutchinson. Liberal Catholics in the English-speaking world consider it almost obligatory to be alarmed about the movements, while conservatives champion them, often in both cases without any personal experience. Few subjects get English-speaking Catholics as worked up as Opus Dei; in my years covering the Vatican, the topic that has consistently generated the most reader mail is Opus.

There is little such climate of alarm in Rome. In part, this is because Vatican officials tend to be doctrinal conservatives and appreciative of the stands taken by the groups mentioned above. In part, this is because Vatican officials are more likely to have personal experience of some of the movements. Several lay employees in the Congregation for the Doctrine of the Faith, for example, belong to the Focolare movement. The Communion and Liberation movement has many admirers in the Holy See. When one has friends and colleagues who belong to a particular group, that tends to put a human face on it and reduce apprehension.

But an even more decisive factor is that, seen from the Roman perspective, the movements are not predominantly conservative. Historically, the most visible movement throughout Italy has been Catholic

Action, whose guiding spirit has always been centrist, which politically allied it with the old Christian Democratic party, placing it equidistant from the extreme right (neofascism or monarchism) and from the extreme left (communism). Today the complex world of lay Catholic movements in Italy, such as Pax Christi, Beati i Costruttori di Pace, Tempi di fraternità, Cipax, ACLI, and the Federazione Universitaria Cattolica Italiana, tend to be identified with the political left. The more moderate are considered by political analysts as a reliable base of support for center-left candidates such as Romano Prodi, who governed Italy as prime minister in the mid-1990s and then became president of the European Commission. Those further to the left may have links to the no-global movement and Italy's Refounded Communist Party.

In recent times, the highest profile movement in Rome itself has been the Community of Sant'Egidio, the only one of the new movements born in the Eternal City. It was founded in 1968 by a group of young Catholic leftists who did not want to drift off into secular radicalism, but wanted to stay anchored to the gospel. Initially they set up schools for the poor around Rome's periphery. Eventually they needed a meeting place in the middle of town, and took up residence in the Piazza di Sant'Egidio in Trastevere, from where the community takes its name. Today Sant'Egidio is active across a wide range of issues, from conflict resolution in Mozambique to abolition of the death penalty to ecumenism and interreligious dialogue. Sociologically and politically, the center of gravity in Sant'Egidio is on the left, yet it has terrific contacts in the Vatican. Founder Andrea Riccardi is sometimes dubbed *un cardinale laico* by the Italian press, because despite being a layman, he has the Pope's ear and moves in all the right ecclesiastical company. Rarely is there a high-profile conference or symposium in Rome that Riccardi is not on the panel. Occasionally Riccardi publishes an essay on some cultural debate on the front page of *Corriere della Sera*, Italy's most respected daily newspaper. This is not to say that Sant'Egidio lacks detractors—respected Italian journalist Sandro Magister, for example, has published critical commentaries about their recruiting tactics and the cult of personality around Riccardi. Even that sort of negative public commentary, however, has increased Sant'Egidio's profile on the Roman scene.

Hence when officials in the Vatican think about the "new movements," they are not thinking of a cluster of right-wing groups. They do not have the impression that the movements are an ideologically identifiable phenomenon, and therefore tend not to think of them as divisive or polarizing. In short, the negative images that some English-speaking Catholics have of the movements simply are not in the air in Rome. Of course, this does not mean that Vatican officials are unaware of the debate surrounding the movements in other parts of the world. They realize that some have developed a reputation as being elitist, secretive, and hard to reconcile with the pastoral agenda of local parishes and dioceses. But their sense of the urgency of these problems, and what context to put such complaints in versus the good that the movements do, is likely to be quite different when one sees the issue from the Roman vantage point.

SECULAR ROME

Rome, like many urban centers in Europe, tilts to the left politically. In most elections, the city will reliably come in for the center-left coalition, with a good chunk of votes for the Refounded Communist party, while the wealthier communities in the hills outside vote center-right. This means that living and working in urban Rome, as most Vatican officials do, one's sense of "popular opinion" may sometimes be distorted. For example, hanging out in Roman cafes one would be astonished that conservative Prime Minister Silvio Berlusconi was ever elected in Italy, because you'd struggle to find anyone who admits voting for him. Polls at the time of this writing show, however, that Berlusconi has the support of some 60 percent of Italians. It's not that those people are figments of pollsters' imaginations, but they simply don't spend much time in wine bars in the capital city. Thus when Vatican officials take stock of what's going on by opening their eyes in the middle of Rome, what they see is real, but not always representative.

One example came in late 2002 and 2003, during the long and diplomatically fractious buildup to the U.S.-led war in Iraq. John Paul II and the Holy See emerged as a leading global center of opposition to the war. This opposition was in the first place a principled moral stand that the proposed action did not meet the tests of a just war, and furthermore that it risked damaging the rule of international law and triggering a "clash of civilizations." It was also a realpolitik calculation that a war would not be in the interests of the 14 million Christians living in the Arab world, and that by visibly opposing the war, the Pope could help the Islamic street distinguish between the Bush administration and "the West." As the diplomatic wrangling became more intense, the Vatican took comfort from what officials perceived as near-unanimous public support for the Pope's antiwar stance. This perception was easy to understand if one took as the barometer of public opinion what was visible in the streets of Rome, where antiwar sentiment was nearly unanimous. Virtually every building in town had at least one, and often dozens, of the rainbow-colored peace flags that became the symbol of the antiwar movement hanging out its windows. Newspapers were full of antiwar commentary, alarmist analyses about the growing isolation of the Bush White House, and warm praise for the Pope's stance. On February 17, 2003, organizers claimed some 3 million people clogged the center of Rome for an antiwar rally. Even though police estimates knocked the number down to roughly 1 million, it was still an enormous turnout. For weeks, smaller groups of young protestors disrupted crosstown traffic by sitting or lying down in the middle of roads in the center of the city.

In such a climate, it was indeed tempting for Vatican officials to conclude that virtually everyone was with the Pope. In an interview with the *National Catholic Reporter* on February 4, then-Archbishop Renato Martino, now a cardinal, an Italian who serves as president of the Pontifical Council for Justice and Peace, said as much: "Everybody is against the war." Several Vatican commentators referred to the massive social movements in favor of peace as one of the great positives of the Iraq crisis, reflecting this sense that the world was almost speaking as one, with only the Bush administration holding out against it. John Paul himself, on March 24, 2003, referred to the "vast contemporary movement in favor of peace." In fact, that perception was exaggerated, even if it is true that the solid majority of Western European opinion was antiwar. Polls showed that the proposed action had the support of a majority of Americans. In much of Eastern Europe there was widespread agreement with the Bush position. After the fact, of course, the world discovered that the Iraqis themselves were divided, but many seemed grateful for the American intervention. The notion that "everybody is against the war" was not fully correct, but it was an understandable surmise given the Roman vantage point.

Another instance in which the streets of Rome became a window onto the world for Vatican officials came in the summer of 2000, with the two great mass events of that year: the World Gay Pride festival in July and the Catholic Church's World Youth Day in August. The first event brought some 1 million people to Rome for a march in favor of gay liberation; the second brought some 2 million Catholic youth to the streets of the city center, and eventually to the Mass site of Tor Vergata, for an encounter with the Pope.

While Vatican officials were preoccupied with the growing social acceptance of homosexuality prior to 2000, there's little question that the Gay Pride festival of that summer, especially landing in the middle of a papally decreed Jubilee Year, brought the concern home. As things turned out, it could have been much worse. Sensationalist news reports before the event predicted that gays would copulate in the streets of Rome, storm St. Peter's Basilica, or accost several thousand Polish pilgrims who were in town at the same moment. Far-right forces had threatened a showdown; in the days leading up to the march, they paraded through the streets with banners reading, "Gays at the Colosseum? With lions inside!" None of this came to pass. At the same time, however, pictures in local papers and on TV of scantily clad homosexuals bumping and grinding as they moved down the streets of the Eternal City created an alarm over the homosexual issue in Vatican offices that had previously not existed. It is one thing to read about Act-Up demonstrators in St. Patrick's Cathedral in New York. It's another to witness in person the familiar flamboyant touches of Gay Pride events—men dressed up as women, men and women hardly dressed at all, and enough spiked collars, feathers, leather, and bizarre mascara to cast a *Rocky Horror Picture Show* remake. Given the proximity of the Vatican, there were also a few special twists—a Swiss man sporting a Roman collar and ultratight shorts blowing kisses and an overweight Italian in a tight T-shirt wearing a bishop's mitre reading "God loves me too." Some of the alarm in the Holy See over homosexuality, which led in summer 2003 to the issuance of a document from the Congregation for the Doctrine of the Faith on gay marriage, can perhaps be traced to lingering sense-memories of the 2000 march.

World Youth Day, on the other hand, made converts of a number of Vatican officials who had previously not been sold on youth ministry. For a solid week, Catholic youth from every part of the globe filled the city of Rome. At times the crowds were so thick one literally could not cross the Piazza Navonna or the Piazza della Rotonda in front of the Pantheon. The *papa-boys*, as the Italian press dubbed them, stuffed themselves into buses and trams, filled *pizzerie* and *trattorie*, and otherwise occupied the city. Italian television carried the culminating events live, including an evening prayer vigil with the Pope and the Mass the next morning. It was a massive logistical operation, but it filled Rome with life during the traditional *ferragosto* break. Vatican officials who were in Rome, and who had only seen a World Youth Day on television or read about it in the papers, were dazed at the vitality of these young people and by their love for the Church and for the Pope. To be sure, journalists reported that many of the *papa-boys* did not necessarily agree with the moral stands of the Church on a range of issues. It caused a brief flurry when some newspapers claimed that used condoms were found among the garbage collected afterward. This is probably an urban myth, but in any event it misses the point. The young people were not coming to make a political statement in favor or against a particular set of Church teachings, but for something much deeper—a sense of connection to the divine, and to a person, the Pope, who calls forward the best in themselves. They wanted to be affirmed in their quest to be spiritual and moral persons, regardless of what specific conclusions they might draw about what that means. Many Vatican officials afterward said they had once entertained doubts about the value of these papal megaevents, but not anymore.

The point is that if you want to get the attention of the Roman Curia, for good or ill, the best way to do it is to come to Rome. Books can be in circulation for years, but until they are translated into Italian and presented at a launch in Rome, many people in the Curia will be unaware of their existence. If something is in the streets in Rome, if it's in the papers and on the TV, you can be sure it will penetrate the consciousness of most of the men and women who serve in the Vatican. That can at times produce an idiosyncratic way of construing the world, but then every location comes with its own perspective. If the Vatican were in Manhattan, there would be a similar skew, though with its own peculiar characteristics. One cannot lift the Vatican out of space and time and give it a purely objective view of reality. The next best thing is to understand what being in Rome means for the way the Vatican sees things, and translate accordingly.

Layer Three: Italy

Despite the internationalization of the Roman Curia launched by Pope Paul VI and extended under John Paul II, the Italian influence in the Vatican remains enormously consequential. Taking into consideration the Secretariat of State and the all-important nine congregations, as of September 2003 there were three Italians in a top-level prefect's job (including Cardinal Angelo Sodano, the secretary of state), but seven Italians at the level of secretary and nine Italians at the level of undersecretary. Even allowing for the fact that a few congregations have two secretaries, and others have two or more undersecretaries, that remains an overwhelming Italian presence in the key decision-making positions. No other national group could claim more than one official at each of these three superior levels. The result is that the rhythms and assumptions of Italian culture tend to be crucial in shaping the worldview of those who set Vatican policy.

We have already noted in chapter 3, discussing the value of the *bella figura* in Vatican psychology, the difference between an Italian-Mediterranean view of law and the Anglo-Saxon concept. If one took a poll of Anglo-Saxon Catholic clergy who have spent time in Italy, that conceptual gap might well emerge as the most important way in which Italian culture conditions the mind of the Holy See. But it is the tip of the iceberg. The Vatican is an institution that has been rooted in Italian culture for two thousand years, and cannot help but bear its imprint in manifold ways. Here we'll take two examples from Italian ecclesiastical life and two from the secular realm to illustrate this impact.

ECCLESIASTICAL ITALY

When American Catholic intellectual Michael Novak came to Rome during the buildup to the Iraq conflict in spring 2003, one of the points he made was that according to the *Catechism of the Catholic Church*, it is the role of the civil authority to make prudential judgments about war. Gently implied was that it is *not* the role of the clergy. Some in the Vatican felt Novak was deliberately missing the point, since one of their differences with the Bush administration was precisely over *which* civil authority had that authority. The Vatican felt that only the United Nations could authorize a preventive use of force, not the White House. But setting that dispute aside, Novak had indeed struck a nerve. Many critics in the United States and elsewhere were puzzled by what they saw as the explicitly political line coming from Rome, and the fact that organs of the Holy See such as the Jesuit-run journal *Civiltà Cattolica* and Vatican Radio seemed to be issuing weekly jeremiads against U.S. policy. This was especially galling for some American Catholic families whose sons and daughters were risking their lives in Iraq, and who wanted to turn to the Church for comfort, not scolding. To hear what sounded like partisan political commentary in such a moment was, for these Catholics, discouraging and painful.

In truth, however, for anyone who lives in Italy, there was nothing new to the daily drumbeat of political commentary from the Vatican. The only novelty was that this time the whole world was listening. In overwhelmingly Catholic Italy, clergy are by definition also politicians. The Vatican is a critical point of reference not just on religious questions, but on everything. If a proposal for a new highway were to arise, journalists would beat a path to the Vatican's door for an opinion. Every year when the annual Italian budget moves through the system, observers wait for *L'Osservatore Romano* to deliver a judgment. Every Thursday, the director of Vatican Radio goes on the air to deliver observations about current political, social, and diplomatic events that are often surprising for the sharpness of his judgments.

Of course, this does not mean the Vatican's view always prevails. As early as May 1974, when 59.3 percent of Italians voted against the Church in order to uphold the country's divorce law, it was clear that the Church could no longer single-handedly impose its will. Some political analysts believe the Church remains in a position to move votes, and even if it's only 5 percent, in a tight election that could make the difference. Others say the Church has no political impact in this sense, but that does not stop politicians from eagerly seeking to cultivate the impression that the Church supports them, or at least does not oppose them. There isn't a candidate in Italy who would say no to a picture with the Pope.

Beyond the Church's capacity to tip the electoral balance, however, there is a deeper reality at work. Italy, despite proud assertions of its identity as *uno stato laico*, a lay Republic, has really never separated Church and State. During the Holy Year of 2000, the Vatican sponsored a "jubilee of politicians" and virtually every political figure of note in the country's power structure attended. When John Paul II spoke at the Italian parliament in November 2002, leaders of all parties fell over themselves to applaud his leadership. The site itself was a symbol of the inevitable intertwining of Church and State here: Montecitorio, the site where the parliament meets, once housed the ecclesiastical tribunals of the Papal States. This is a country where Cardinal Giacomo Biffi of

Bologna could propose in 2000 that Catholics, such as Filipinos and Latin Americans, be given preference in immigration because they are more compatible with the national identity, and the proposal was taken seriously. Newspapers spent days dissecting it, and the idea sparked wide national debate.

For every issue that comes up in Italian national life, one of the first things journalists will do is seek out the opinion of a member of the College of Cardinals. That opinion will often get more prominent play than any other views except those of the prime minister and top opposition figures. As I write these words, Italy is debating whether Adrian Sofri, a leftist radical convicted and sentenced to life in prison for conspiring to kill an Italian policeman in May 1972, but who has become a widely respected author who no longer espouses violence, should be given a pardon. As soon as the debate broke out, *Corriere della Sera*, the country's leading daily newspaper, prominently featured an interview with eighty-nine-year-old Cardinal Ersilio Tonini, who is sort of the David Brinkley of Italian culture, a man whose distinctive voice and opinions help set the tone for public discussion. Tonini favored the pardon. Anytime the public debate is over a matter of sexual morality, Bishop Elio Sgreccia, the vice-president of the Pontifical Academy of the Family, is a staple of Italian talk shows. A small, pudgy, balding figure, Sgreccia looks a bit like Yoda from *Star Wars*, and on Italian TV his wisdom is sought out just about as often.

Everything in Italian culture, therefore, teaches clergy to regard themselves as omnicompetent. Their opinions on every conceivable issue, from cloning to tomorrow's soccer matches, are solicited and weighed with great seriousness. In such a context, it requires an act of self-discipline to say, "That's outside my competence." Italian culture gives clerics every reason to conclude that nothing is outside their purview and that the world is anxious to hear what they have to say. This can be frustrating for lay observers of the Italian political scene. Prominent political scientist and editorialist for *Corriere della Sera*, Ernesto Galli della Loggia, told me in a 2003 interview that he finds it absurd that Italian clergy are expected to provide judgments on matters of politics and economics when Italian seminaries provide no training in these subjects whatsoever. "They recycle the same banalities, which often hurt more than they help in terms of trying to really penetrate issues," Galli della Loggia said. "Either they should stay out of these matters or have something to say." Yet one can hardly blame clergy for responding in this way, when the broader culture gives them every reason to believe this is their role. If Italy is willing to offer the Church the front page of its newspapers and leading spots on its public affairs programs, why should its representatives say no? At the same time, this aspect of Italian culture does produce a certain fuzziness about the distinction between lay and clerical roles that can frustrate Catholics around the world.

Another way in which the unique situation of the Italian Catholic Church has an influence on Vatican thought patterns is in their appreciation for the nature of the challenge facing the Church today. In Italy, like anywhere else, the Church has its problems. While 97 percent of the population of 57 million is baptized, many Italians are effectively uncatechized, and only 25 percent go to Mass on a weekly basis. That figure disguises regional variations; in the more developed north, the figure can in some places fall below 10 percent, paralleling the situation in Northern Europe. (Italian analysts note, however, that declining participation in the life of the Church is not necessarily linked to modernization. The strongest Catholic organizations in Italy are in Lombardia and the Veneto, the most developed regions of the country.) In the diocese of Rome, the Pope's own backyard, a recent study commissioned by the Church found that 90 percent of males ages sixteen to twenty-two held hostile attitudes to the institutional church and had shockingly little knowledge of essential points of the Catholic faith. To offer a personal example, my private Italian tutor, a well-educated young woman in her thirties who lives in Rome, once told me she had never seen the papal flag, or known that such a thing existed, until she visited my office.

All that said, the Italian Catholic church still has a vitality and a social profile that reflects two resources few other national churches enjoy: the culture and the state. On the cultural front, Italy is in many ways still an intact Catholic society in which the church's liturgical seasons still shape the annual calendar and in which Catholic customs and vocabulary are part of the ordinary public consciousness. People in Italy know when it's Lent, they know when it's Advent, and they certainly know when it's Christmas. Cab drivers can explain the difference between Franciscans and Dominicans, and hotel clerks can describe the fine points of major Roman basilicas. There's a sense in which Catholicism is in the marrow of the place, which gives clergy an enormous pastoral advantage. There are certain concepts they don't have to explain, certain social manifestations of the faith they don't have to justify. It can be hard for Italian clergy to appreciate sometimes the reality of ministering to cultures that are not traditionally Catholic, in which this support system doesn't exist. I have a friend, for example, who is a Dutch priest, and who today serves as pastor of the cathedral parish in a Dutch diocese. For years, however, he split time between Rome and Holland, wearing his Roman collar both in Rome and back home in Amsterdam. In Rome, he was a face in the crowd; in Amsterdam, he's a curiosity and a conversation piece. Those who know only the cultural world of Rome are thus missing what it's like to represent the Church outside this peculiar cultural milieu.

That sensibility is also affected by the way the Italian government supports the church, above all through the so-called *otto per mille* system. In essence, the Italian government allows taxpayers to elect to assign a percentage of their taxes intended for social services to one of the country's religious organizations or to the state. When Italy's currency was still the lire, the amount was eight lire for every thousand paid in taxes, thus the phrase *otto per mille*. The Catholic Church and five other religious bodies, including the Waldensians and the Seventh Day Adventists, are included in the distribution. Since many Italians don't really trust the government, many choose to assign their *otto per mille* contributions to the religious groups, and some 87 percent choose the Catholic Church. But the support doesn't end there. Under the formula applied by the Italian government, the *otto per mille* contributions of all those taxpayers who leave this section blank, which is the vast majority, 22 out of 36 million in 2002, are apportioned based on the percentages of those who do make a choice. This means the Catholic Church in Italy gets 87 percent of all the unassigned contributions as well. The result is a windfall. In 2002, for the first time, the Italian church received more than 1 billion Euro through the *otto per mille* system.

That money supports clerical salaries, pastoral expenses, as well as administration costs for the Italian bishops' conference. These resources allow the Catholic Church in Italy to operate a vast network of endeavors, including a well-respected daily newspaper, *L'Avvenire*, its own television channel, Sat2000, and a lineup of symposia and congresses and continuing education offerings that would put many Ivy League universities to shame. Ironically, only 18 percent of the *otto per mille* funds assigned to the Catholic Church are directly spent on charitable purposes, which was the original intent of the law. As a spokesperson for the Italian bishops put it, however: "Charity walks on the legs of human beings, whom the church has to form and sustain, also economically." The result is that the Catholic Church in Italy operates a massive bureaucratic operation that is sustained largely through public funds.

Italian clergy, and especially Italian bishops, can therefore at times be cavalier about the challenges in other parts of the world when it comes to formation of culture or financial support. At times, one hears a rather preemptory attitude of "God will provide" when dismissing proposals brought by clergy from other parts of the world for adaptations that might make their own circumstances more manageable. Of course, that's an easy thing to say when one realizes that even if God doesn't come through, the *otto per mille* will. Even beyond the question of finance, there is an assumption in the Italian clerical world that the state can, and should, support the institutional dimensions of the Church. During the American sexual abuse crisis, for example, Italian clergy more than once expressed puzzlement at why American bishops couldn't simply "work something out" in quiet with the judges or the police. This was not necessarily a matter of wishing to evade justice, but it reflects a culture in which Church and state are assumed to be partners and collaborators. Clergy formed in the Italian ecclesiastical milieu, in other words, can sometimes be a bit insulated psychologically from the real challenges of running the Catholic Church in places where it does not enjoy the same safety net of cultural and political support.

SECULAR ITALY

Among the first things an ex-patriate notices about life in Italy is the suffocating bureaucracy, which makes everything more complicated than it ought to be. Obtaining one's *permesso di soggiorno*, a living permit, is a rite of passage for new arrivals. Many an innocent foreigner has waited hours in line at the *questura*, the Italian police station, only to be informed that they needed two state-issued stamps to complete their application rather than one. These cannot be obtained at the *questura*, but must be purchased at a tobacco shop, and the hapless applicant must start the process all over again. So it goes. Getting a phone line installed, arranging auto insurance, and subscribing to the satellite TV service are equally infamous quagmires. (It should be noted, however, that true veterans say that all these systems are better than they once were. The last time my wife and I renewed our *permessi di soggiorno*, for example, it took us an hour. We were seated next to a British woman who works for the United Nations Food and Agriculture Organization, who told us that "this used to be a day's business.")

Italians, and people shaped by Italian culture, are used to bureaucracies not making a lot of sense. They're used to things not working, to even simple matters taking far longer than they should. One American veteran of Rome said this was revealed to him the first time he went back to the United States after a couple of years abroad. He had set a full day aside to run errands, got in his car at 9:00 A.M., and was done by 10:30. Paying a couple of bills and renewing his driver's license, which would have taken all day in Rome, had required all of ninety minutes in his mid-sized California city. People who live in Italy are accustomed to strikes suddenly leading to canceled flights or demonstrations in the middle of town meaning that it takes an hour to cover a route that should take fifteen minutes. Tell an American that it will take two weeks to fix a problem in their bathroom, and he'll call another plumber; tell an Italian, and he'll shrug. All this shapes the cultural context of the Roman Curia. The men and women of the Curia learn from life experience not to become impatient when things take longer than they would like. They more easily accept irrational and burdensome bureaucratic requirements, because that is part of the world in which they live. Life teaches them that fulminating and complaining are of limited value, and not to expect that any of the proposed solutions are really going to make things better.

The flip side of bureaucratic indifference, however, is the importance of human contact. Italians may struggle to make their bureaucratic systems work, but they shine at interpersonal relationships. One sees this reality in every social context. Everything changes in Roman restaurants, for example, when one becomes a regular. Menus become irrelevant because waiters know what you like, and the service becomes an occasion for catching up among old friends. In banks, in post offices, in grocery stores and barbershops, the quality of service one gets is heavily dependent upon what level of personal connection the person delivering the service feels. A quick anecdote makes the point. I once went to the Gregorian University to look up a doctoral dissertation by a man who had just been named to an important curial post. I presented myself and was told I needed to wait for authorization from the rector of the library, who was busy. A half-hour went by, and no one seemed the least bit concerned. Finally I got out my cell phone and dialed Jesuit Fr. Gerry O'Collins, an eminent Australian theologian who teaches at the Gregorian, and who is a friend. He happened to be in his office, and I asked him if he could come down and wave me through. O'Collins arrived within seconds, and instead of simply getting me past the door, he took me down to the library offices and introduced me to the rector. He told her I was "an eminent Vatican writer." Thus I entered her realm of personal contacts, and she was effusive—insisting, for example, that if I needed to make photocopies that I use her personal machine. She thrust her card into my hands and told me to return any time. That, in a nutshell, is the importance of connections in Italian culture.

This ethos of personal contacts is replicated inside the Vatican. Officials might be unresponsive, even hostile, to strangers in a way that Americans would find rude. But once you have met the person in a social context—an embassy party, perhaps, or a book presentation—they feel an obligation that goes beyond what Americans would feel toward a casual acquaintance. In such a context, even when Vatican officials may not be able to satisfy your particular request or to respond directly to the question you have asked, they will search for some other way to be helpful. One curial undersecretary put it this way: "Even something as simple as getting a book printed by the Vatican printers can be a very different experience depending upon whether they know you or not. When I first started taking things over there, they would just give me a standard answer of 'two months,' and I could tell they were thinking, 'Who is this guy? Is he going to stick around?' Now they know me, and if I need something in a hurry, they'll make it happen." For Americans, building an adequate network of personal contacts can be a special challenge, because the typical American in the Curia will rotate back to the United States after five years. In the Vatican, five years can feel like the blink of an eye. Having forged those ties, however, it is often remarkable what people can accomplish, regardless of their job title or official level of importance.

Another sense in which the Italian sociological reality has consequences for the Vatican is the impact of Italian journalism. Because the Vatican is in their backyard, Italian news organizations invest tremendous resources on the beat. Each of the major Italian newspapers—*Corriere della Sera, La Repubblica, La Stampa, Il Messagero, Il Giornale, Il Manifesto*—has a full-time Vatican correspondent, what the Italians call a *Vaticanista*, and it is among the more prestigious and high-profile assignments. Their coverage of the Vatican thus reflects the best and worst characteristics of Italian journalism. The best is that Italian media encourage subjectivity, they allow journalists to bring their passions and their convictions to their work, so that each correspondent develops a unique perspective. When one reads Orazio Petrosillo in *Il Messagero*, one gets a very different point of view than Marco Politi in *La Repub-*

blica. Petrosillo is generally Vatican-friendly, while Politi is often more critical. Reading the major *Vaticanisti* is always a fascinating, thought-provoking exercise. The disadvantage of this approach, however, is that concern for factual accuracy is not the highest value. Sometimes journalists will publish rumors or hypotheses—perhaps flagged as such by use of the conditional tense, perhaps not—without much effort to determine if they're true. In part, this is because Italian journalism is often seen as an extension of politics. Papers allied with the center-left parties publish articles hostile to the center-right government of Prime Minister Silvio Berlusconi, for example, often without great concern for the details. This is all considered more or less fair game.

This reality has two consequences. First, it means the coverage of the Vatican in the entire world press is often dreadful, because it is heavily dependent upon the Italians. Reporters in Rome for the *London Times*, or German television, or *O Globo* in Brazil, who are not full-time Vatican specialists, tend to take their cues from what's in the Italian press. Even when they realize that it's not always reliable, under the pressure of deadlines they will simply take an account from *Il Messagero* or *La Stampa*, rewrite it with a couple of fresh quotes, and file it for their own news outlet. In May 2003, for example, *Il Messagero* published an article claiming, falsely as it turned out, that the major schismatic movement of Latin Mass traditionalists was about to be reconciled with Rome. The *London Times* rewrote the story the next day, propelling it into the English-speaking realm. The result is that poor reporting is multiplied around the world. How many times have you seen stories about Pope John Paul's alleged retirement, for example, or his alleged use of some new miracle drug like papaya extract, only to have the story fall apart? That's the "Italian effect." To be fair, many Italian reporters are careful, serious professionals who are themselves mortified by this sort of sloppiness or indifference to the facts.

Second, the nature of Italian journalism exacerbates the reluctance of many in the Vatican to deal with the press. "They're just going to make it up anyway" is the attitude one often hears from curial officials who feel that there's little to be gained from greater openness. Understandably, Vatican officials who have had bad experiences of being mis-represented, or being the objects of unfounded speculation, will be re-luctant to engage the media. In truth, most Vatican officials just laugh when they see the more outlandish instances of this sort of thing and are capable of distinguishing between journalists who are serious and those who are not. Yet the cumulative effect of the way the Italian press cov-ers the Vatican is to deepen a sense that the media is unreliable, which is the last thing likely to be helpful for an institution struggling to emerge from its historical shell.

A final example of the impact of Italian culture on the Vatican concerns attitudes toward criminal justice. This point played an impor-tant role in Vatican reactions to the American sexual abuse crisis, espe-cially in the way curial officials reacted to proposals to require bishops to report allegations of sexual abuse against priests to the police. Most Americans regard this as a "no-brainer." Sexual abuse of a minor is a crime, so when a bishop receives an accusation against a priest, he should turn it over. Yet some in the Vatican blink at such a require-ment. In part, the concern is to protect a zone of intimacy in a bishop's relationship with his priests, so a priest does not have to worry that every time he discusses a problem with his bishop, the police will be in-volved. This reflects the traditional theology of the bishop's office, in which a bishop is understood as a paterfamilias, a head of the family, and his priests are both his brothers and his sons. But there's another factor, more sociological than theological, which is Italian skepticism about the impartiality of secular justice.

An episode from 2002 makes the point. On November 17, a bombshell verdict was delivered against seven-time former Prime Min-ister Giulio Andreotti, who was sentenced to twenty-four years in prison by an appeals court for allegedly instigating the murder of a muckraking journalist in 1979. Andreotti was first charged in the slaying in 1995 on the basis of testimony from a turncoat mob member and, after a long le-gal process, was exonerated in September 1999. Under Italian law, how-ever, prosecutors as well as the defense can appeal a verdict, so the case went before an appeals court. Against all expectations, that panel found

Andreotti guilty, even though it acquitted the men who were supposed to have actually done the killing. Andreotti is an avatar of the old Christian Democratic political order linked to the Church. He directs the influential Catholic journal *30 Giorni* and is a daily communicant at the church of San Giovanni Battista dei Fiorentini. His supporters believed that leftist magistrates were engaged in a campaign of political persecution using trumped-up allegations.

This view was widespread in Vatican circles. Cardinal Achille Silvestrini, a key player in the Roman Curia in the years that Andreotti was in power, called the lower court ruling "incredible." Cardinal Fiorenzo Angelini compared Andreotti to Jesus Christ, another victim of an unjust verdict, and hoped for a "resurrection" from the Supreme Court. *L'Osservatore Romano*, the official Vatican newspaper, expressed "full solidarity" with Andreotti, saying the verdict "can only be rejected by good sense." Cardinal Camillo Ruini, head of the Italian bishops conference and a key advisor to the Pope, took the occasion of an address to the Italian bishops to express his "intact personal esteem" for Andreotti. Conservative Prime Minister Silvio Berlusconi minced no words, charging that Andreotti was the victim of "politicized sectors of the magistrates that have tried to change the course of democratic politics." Berlusconi, who has made attacking the alleged bias of the judicial system a staple of his rhetoric, was elected in a landslide to the prime minister's job on May 13, 2001, despite the fact that he faces several rather serious criminal indictments himself. Many Italian voters simply assumed the charges were politically motivated and looked past them.

The point is not whether Andreotti is guilty or innocent. (In the end, the case was heard by Italy's highest court, which reversed the appeals court and absolved Andreotti on all charges.) Most Italians assumed the courts didn't really care about guilt or innocence. The episode confirmed for them how criminal trials are often an extention of politics by other means. Liberal judges will convict conservative defendants, and vice-versa. As one writer in *La Repubblica*, a major Roman daily, put it November 20, 2002, "Practically every high-profile case in Italy is 'instrumentalized' and transformed into a new Dreyfus affair."

The result is deep ambivalence inside the Vatican about automatic referral of accusations against priests to the police. What about situations, Vatican officials wonder, in which the civil authorities are out to get us? It is a question that strikes many Americans as paranoid, but not so in Rome. Americans will insist that this is not our experience, that by and large our district attorneys and judges are fair and independent, and their involvement is needed to correct the Church's tendency to protect its own. Why can't the Vatican trust the American church to craft policy that makes sense for its situation? There's merit to that question, and in the end the Vatican did not block U.S. policies requiring credible allegations to be relayed to civil authorities. Yet in a globalized world, nothing remains local for very long. The Vatican is keenly aware that the United States is the world's leading culture and that whatever American Catholics do will be watched and imitated. The Vatican was convinced that the American bishops were setting a global precedent, and they worried about what that precedent might mean in cultures with different experiences of the trustworthiness of the legal system.

Layer Four: Europe

During the diplomatic wrangling over the war in Iraq, U.S. Secretary of Defense Donald Rumsfeld made his infamous distinction between "old" and "new" Europe, suggesting that opposition to the U.S. position was coming from a superannuated old guard. Whatever the merits of Rumsfeld's analysis, there is no place that's more "old Europe" than the Holy See, since it is both Europe's oldest state and its oldest continually functioning institution of any sort. On many contemporary issues, from Church/state relations to gay marriage, the Holy See embodies a sort of antique European tradition that stands over against the present secularized European consensus. At the same time, many of the officials who call the shots in the Holy See have grown up in the same prominent families, attended the same schools, and move in the same cultural circles as Europe's political, industrial, and intellectual leaders. They cannot help but be, in many ways, cut from the same cloth.

When I arrived in Rome in July 2000, one of the first things I did was to make the rounds of English-speaking ambassadors accredited to the Holy See. The ambassadors can be good sources of insight on the Vatican, because in some ways they have an insider's knowledge, but at the same time they are not part of the Holy See and can maintain a critical distance. One of the ambassadors gave me the following advice in trying to make sense of Vatican diplomacy: "Never forget that the Holy See is located in Europe, and most of its key decision-makers are European. If all else fails, ask yourself how European governments see a particular issue, and nine times out of ten that will end up being the stand of the Holy See."

Not everyone, it should be said, buys this bit of analysis. I once asked Cardinal Francis Stafford, an American who heads the Pontifical Council for the Laity, if he believed the Vatican thinks like other European governments. He laughed, asking: "European governments of what century?" Stafford has a point—the Holy See and, say, the post-revolutionary government of France have some deep philosophical differences. Yet the ambassador's comment also reflects a genuine insight, which is that the sociological reality of European upbringing and a primarily European circle of discourse cannot help but exercise a tug on the way the personnel in the Vatican think. Here we'll take two examples of the point: Vatican attitudes toward the Middle East and toward the United Nations.

MIDDLE EAST

European governments tilt toward the Palestinians on the Israeli/Palestinian problem, driven in part by a widespread European sympathy for the suffering of the Palestinian people, in part (at least in Britain and France) by the legacy of colonial pro-Arab policies. The European left, for whom colonialism is akin to original sin, has watched as the Israeli government repeats what they regard as the classic oppressive behavior of a colonial power, and it has fueled a severe political reaction. This tendency has been especially pronounced since the 1982 Israeli incursion into Lebanon, and the massacres at the Sabra and Shatila refugee camps carried out by Israel's Lebanese allies. The election of Ariel Sharon, widely regarded as the author of that atrocity, as Israel's prime minister brought European sympathy for the Palestinians to a new level. For those in search of a more crass explanation, there is also a long history of trade relations between Europe and Arab nations.

Whatever the reason, the Palestinians generally see Europe and the EU as a major beachhead of international support. For much of the 1990s, the European Union was a principal source of financial backing for the Palestinian National Authority. In March 1999, the European Council affirmed the Palestinians' "unqualified" right to self-determination, "including the option of a state." Some observers sympathetic to the Israelis say that at times European governments have veered dangerously close to tacitly endorsing terrorism. On April 15, 2002, Austria, Belgium, France, Portugal, Spain, and Sweden supported a UN Human Rights Commission resolution that approved the use of "all available means, including armed struggle" to establish a Palestinian state. It is difficult to imagine the United States, especially in the post-9/11 era, voting to accept such language.

These policy choices reflect popular sentiment. A May 2002 survey conducted by First International Resources for the Anti-Defamation League found that by a two-to-one margin Europeans are more sympathetic to the Palestinians than the Israelis on the conflict in the Middle East. The survey also found that the more closely Europeans follow their media, the more likely they are to support the Palestinians, which reflects the pro-Palestinian tilt of much of the European press. In 2003, for example, Israel's Foreign Ministry briefly refused to speak with the BBC after it aired a documentary comparing Israel to Iraq, implying that Israel is not a democracy and suggesting that Israel had used nerve gas against the Palestinians. The film employed concentration camp imagery, drawing jailed nuclear spy Mordechai Vanunu clutching at and peering through a barbed wire fence. It also juxtaposed America's refusal to discuss Israel's nuclear capability with Bush saying "the greatest danger facing America and the world is outlaw regimes that seek and possess nuclear, chemical and biological weapons."

This wide European sympathy for the Palestinians has long been reflected in the Holy See. The Vatican has vocally supported the Palestinian right to self-determination. John Paul II repeated the point in March 2003, when he received the credentials of Oded Ben-Hur as Israel's ambassador to the Holy See. "The Holy See is convinced that the present conflict will be resolved only when there are two independent and sovereign states," the Pope said. Sometimes the rhetoric can be much sharper. In April 2002, Vatican spokesperson Joaquin Navarro-Valls issued a statement saying that the Pope "rejects the unjust and humiliating conditions imposed on the Palestinian people as well as reprisals and revenge attacks which do nothing but feed the sense of frustration and hatred." During the 2002 crisis at the Church of the Nativity in Bethlehem, when Palestinian gunmen forcibly entered the basilica and refused to leave, *L'Osservatore Romano*, the Vatican newspaper, regularly referred to the standoff as an Israeli "siege," even accusing the Israelis of trying to "exterminate" the Palestinian people.

In terms of specific policy proposals, the Vatican has long supported the deployment of international observers, meaning some kind of peacekeeping force, to the region and a special international status for Jerusalem—both proposals anathema to Israel's conception of its own sovereignty. The Vatican's affection for the Palestinians is visible in ways large and small. In the chapel just off the main hall used for meetings of the Synod of Bishops, for example, the walls are lined with a set of pearl-white Stations of the Cross, a gift to John Paul from Yasser Arafat. The Pope personally instructed that Arafat's gift be placed in this high-profile spot.

The European cultural matrix of the Holy See is, of course, only one factor shaping this stance. Vatican diplomats are genuinely convinced that the current state of affairs amounts to a serious injustice against the Palestinians. Beyond that, there is also the realpolitik concern for the fate of the 300,000 Christians in Israel, Palestine, and Jordan, of whom a little under half are Catholic. These Christians are almost entirely Palestinian Arabs, and their welfare is linked to the general situation of the Palestinian community. Under the weight of the second Intifadah, the occupation, and the general economic malaise, Christians have been abandoning the "Holy Land" in large numbers. In the town of Bethlehem, for example, the proportion of the population which is Christian has dropped from 80 percent before 1948 to less than 33 percent today. The Holy See's nightmare scenario is that the holy sites in Jerusalem, Bethlehem, Nazareth, and elsewhere will become museums without living Christian populations. More broadly, the Holy See is concerned about its dialogue with Islam, especially given post-9/11 concerns about a clash of civilizations. The Holy See's perceived support for the Palestinian cause is obviously of value in fostering good relations with Islam, at both the global and local levels.

In this mix, the European contribution is one factor that produces a foreign policy tilted toward the Palestinian cause. In extreme form, this tendency can lead the Church into embarrassing situations. Witness the case of Auxiliary Bishop Hilarion Cappucci, a member of the Syrian Greek–Melkite rite who served in Jerusalem in the 1960s and 1970s and who holds the personal title of patriarch. He was arrested by Israeli security forces in 1974 on his way back from a trip to Lebanon, after his Mercedes sedan was found loaded with TNT and rifles headed for the Palestinian Liberation Organization. At the time Cappucci belonged to Fatah, the Palestine Liberation Organization's main faction, and was a member of the PLO's parliament-in-exile. He was sentenced to twelve years in prison, but released in 1977 after a personal appeal from Pope Paul VI. Now in his eighties, Cappucci has lived since 1977 in a private apartment in Rome. He was supposed to keep away from the limelight, but that did not stop him from being at the right hand of Tarik Aziz, Saddam Hussein's deputy, when Aziz visited Assisi in February 2003.

Within the internal debates in the Holy See, there are relatively few voices that challenge the pro-Palestinian consensus, because virtually all the senior officials who are at the table when decisions are made come from a European cultural milieu in which this orientation is conventional wisdom.

UNITED NATIONS

Those aware of the titanic battles the Holy See waged at United Nations conferences in Cairo and Beijing in the 1990s, or the criticism the Vatican directs at United Nations agencies on issues of family planning, sometimes find the Holy See's strong pro-UN bias on most other matters puzzling. In 2000, for example, the Holy See accused the United Nations system of "utilitarian" and "Malthusian" values in connection with a manual on birth control in refugee camps. The fact is, however, that in concert with other European governments, the Holy See has been among the leading supporters of a strong role for the United Nations in international affairs. As papal nuncio to France, Angelo Roncalli—later to become John XXIII—was active in behind-the-scenes work on the drafting of the UN's Universal Declaration of Human Rights. When the General Assembly took up the declaration in 1948, observers from the Holy See were present. In later years, the Vatican was the fifth nation to ratify the UN convention on the rights of the child and was among the first to ratify the anti–land mine treaty that won for its supporters a Nobel Peace Prize.

This stance was clearly on display during the buildup to the Iraq war, as one of the grounds upon which the Vatican criticized the proposed U.S. action was precisely the lack of an international warrant. "A single member of the international community cannot decide: 'I'm doing this and you others can either help me or stay home.' If that were the case, the entire system of international rules would collapse. We'd risk the jungle," said French Archbishop Jean-Louis Tauran, at the time the Vatican's top diplomat. Then-Archbishop Renato Martino, an Italian who heads the Pontifical Council for Justice and Peace and who is now a cardinal, made a similar point January 4, 2003. "Evidently, unilateralism is unacceptable," Martino said. We cannot think that there is a universal policeman who takes it upon himself to punish those who act badly. . . . The United States, being part of the international assembly, has to adapt to the exigencies of others."

The Holy See is uniquely positioned to speak about the need for global governance, since it has been exercising a kind of planetary responsibility for the Catholic Church for two millennia. The Catholic worldview is by definition supranational, which is what has always made the Church dangerous to totalitarian states. In part, this concern for a meaningful international order is born of the sense that in a globalized world, only an international body will be able to ensure that economic, social, and political transformations are channeled in directions that promote the common good. Without an international political entity in which citizens can exert influence over their own destiny, the global stage is left to commercial and military actors that do not have the same motivations to pursue the welfare of all.

Yet the European cultural subtext to the Vatican is also part of this picture. Europeans tend to be among the most enthusiastic supporters of the United Nations system based on their own twentieth-century history, which painfully illustrated the bankruptcy of nationalism. This is an especially telling point for John Paul II, who was nineteen when the Nazis invaded Poland and spent much of his adult life under the Soviet system imposed on Poland after the Second World War. The same instinct that led Europeans to be willing to surrender chunks of sovereignty in order to make the European Union work is also behind the push for a beefed-up UN. For most Europeans, support for the United Nations falls into the category of common sense, outside the bounds of most political debate. It's a policy upheld by both left and right. Inside the Vatican, therefore, with the exception of personnel concerned most directly with issues of family and sexual morality, the bias in favor of the United Nations, and other international bodies such as the International Criminal Court, is strong. We'll return to this point in chapter 7, in the context of flashpoints in the relationship between the Holy See and the United States.

5

VATICAN THEOLOGY

One night during the October 1999 Synod of Bishops, *National Catholic Reporter* publisher Tom Fox and I had been out for dinner with colleagues, and afterward, shortly before 11:00 P.M., we began to make our way across St. Peter's Square. It was a cold autumn evening, after the peak of tourist season, and the square was virtually deserted. From a distance, I caught site of a tall figure wearing a long black coat, with a briefcase perched at his feet, standing alone near the obelisk in the center of the square. It took me a moment to realize it was Cardinal Christoph Schönborn of Vienna. At the time he was just fifty-four, the second-youngest cardinal in the world, and an ecclesiastical wunderkind.

Schönborn comes from a distinguished Bohemian family, with nineteen priests, bishops, and archbishops among his ancestors. A Dominican, Schönborn did his postgraduate work in theology under Joseph Ratzinger at the University of Regensburg in Germany. John Paul II tapped him in 1988 to serve as editor of the *Catechism of the Catholic Church*, published in 1992. He was named auxiliary bishop of Vienna in 1991, archbishop in 1995, and entered the College of Cardinals in 1998. Many Vatican watchers have treated Schönborn for years as Ratzinger's crown prince, the favorite to succeed him at the Congregation for the Doctrine of the Faith. Others think he may be destined for still higher office—the papacy itself.

Seeing Schönborn standing there alone, my first impulse was to try to wrest some insight from him about the synod. As we approached, I noticed he was staring up at the windows of the papal apartments. My cynical side prevailed, so I walked up and jokingly asked: "Thinking about what kind of drapes you want when you move in?"

Schönborn was startled, then, as he placed who we were, he had the good manners to fake a sort of quiet amusement. I broke the silence that followed by asking what he was doing.

"You want to know why I'm really here?" he asked, in his polished English. I waited.

"Because Peter is here," he said.

What?

"Peter is here," he repeated. "He was crucified alongside this obelisk when it was in the Neronian circus, just over there," he said, pointing beyond the Palazzo di Sant'Ufficio. "But Peter is also up there, in the papal apartment, watching over the Church, just as he has been doing for two thousand years. It's an awesome sensation, standing in the space that has been the focus of a tradition that goes back to Christ himself, and to the prince of the apostles. This is Peter's house."

Schönborn was not making a speech; he spoke softly, almost not caring if we heard. The words obviously came from deep within his personal spirituality, his devotion to the papacy and the person of the Pope. The journalistic side of me realized that some Catholics might find his piety troubling, since it has the potential to shade off into an uncritical approach to papal authority. Yet it was an emotional moment, because it brought home how deep the feeling for the papal office runs among those for whom Christ's words, "You are the rock and upon this rock I shall build my Church," remain the expression of a living spiritual ideal.

Schönborn is not, at least as of this writing, a member of the Roman Curia, but that moment of prayer before the successor of Peter, and his exposition of what it meant, offers an excellent window onto the theology of many Vatican officials. Serving the Holy Father in the Roman Curia is, through the eyes of those who do this work, in the end a spiritual experience, a *vocation*. This is not to say that Vatican officials float angelically through their days on wings of prayer. Office politics and the drudgery of the work get to them as much as anyone else. Still, when you press them on why they do it, what they get out of it, the bottom line is usually a theological response focusing on their share in the ministry of Peter.

Pope Paul VI, who served in the Secretariat of State for thirty-two years before becoming archbishop of Milan and eventually Pope, had a similarly exalted notion of curial service. He liked to refer to the Roman Curia as a "permanent cenacle," a reference to the "upper room" described in the gospels (Mark 14) where Jesus and the disciples celebrated the Passover seder, and where Christian tradition believes the sacrament of the Eucharist was instituted. It was a room "totally consecrated to the good of the Church," as John Paul II wrote during the Holy Year of 2000, when he announced a Jubilee of the Roman Curia on the occasion of the Feast of the Chair of Peter. Paul VI also described the Roman Curia as "an instrument of immediate adhesion and perfect obedience." He had in mind not the mindless obedience of a police state, but the heart-and-soul obedience of a group of people acting together on the basis of love.

Anyone seeking to know the mind of the Vatican cannot do so solely through the lens of political science, sociology, and the principles of organizational dynamics as worked out by Max Weber. Without appreciating the faith convictions held by the men and women of the Roman Curia about themselves, their work, and the role of the papacy in the universal Church, the picture would be seriously distorted. It would be like attempting to understand socialism without reference to Marx and *Das Kapital*, or insisting that one should analyze the Romantic poets exclusively from the perspective of linguistic theory. Of course, not everyone in curial service shares the same theological perspective. Nevertheless, the bulk of Vatican officials take quite seriously a few basic theological concepts about the papacy, its role of service to the universal Church, and the mission of the Roman Curia in supporting that role. Without a grasp of these concepts, observers of the Holy See are lost.

Church officials often complain that journalists try to understand the Catholic Church as if it were merely a corporation or a political society, using the models familiar to them from secular culture. In fact, these officials insist, the Church cannot be properly understood apart from a theological frame of reference. Journalists tend to be skeptical of these protests, sensing that they're designed to mask ecclesiastical power plays. Certainly the Church has a political dimension that is open to analysis and critique. There is, nevertheless, a degree of merit to the Church officals' point. Every organization deserves to be evaluated according to its own self-understanding. CEOs of major companies often lament that critics expect them to operate like a public trust when their mission is to maximize shareholder profit. Politicians likewise argue that their function is not to pursue a personal agenda, but to reflect the interests and desires of their constituents. If we accept such reasoning in the corporate and political realms, we ought to accept it for the Church as well.

THE PAPACY

Contemporary Roman Catholic theological discussion features a vast literature on the papacy, some of it stimulated by Pope John Paul II's 1995 encyclical *Ut Unum Sint* (That they may be one). The Pope invited other members of the Christian family to join him in considering how the papacy might be reshaped in order to make it more acceptable ecumenically, without losing its essentials. Catholic theology today reflects a wide range of views, from those who argue in favor of a strong papal office to those who prefer to situate the Pope within the College of Bishops, with much real authority elsewhere—in a Synod of Bishops or with the local churches. In this section, we cannot do justice to the complexity of this discussion. Instead, we will present a traditional vision that is most prominent within the Roman Curia, without any pretense that this is the only or even the best perspective on offer. The view described here must be seen as an ideal type that individual Vatican officials will be closer to or further away from depending upon their personal outlook, training, and dispositions.

The biblical basis for the office of the papacy, its powers and its role, comes in two New Testament texts, Matthew 16:17–19 and John 21:15–17.

• In Matthew, Jesus has asked the disciples who they believe he is, and Peter replies, "You are the Messiah, the Son of the living God." Jesus says: "Blessed are you, Simon son of Jonah. For flesh and blood has not revealed this to you, but my heavenly Father. And so I say to you, you are Peter, and upon this rock I will build my church, and the gates of the netherworld shall not prevail against it. I will give you the keys to the kingdom of heaven. Whatever you bind on earth shall be bound in heaven; and whatever you loose on earth shall be loosed in heaven." In St. Peter's Basilica, inside the cupola that rises above the tomb of St. Peter and the main altar, these words are written in Latin letters almost two yards high. It is the very heart of how Catholics have traditionally understood Peter's role.

• In the Gospel of John, the risen Jesus notes the other disciples and asks Peter: " 'Simon, son of John, do you love me more than these?' He said to him, 'Yes, Lord, you know that I love you.' He said to him, 'Feed my lambs.' He then said to him a second time, 'Simon, son of John, do you love me?' He said to him, 'Yes, Lord, you know that I love you.' He said to him, 'Tend my sheep.' He said to him the third time, 'Simon, son of John, do you love me?' Peter was distressed that he had said to him a third time, 'Do you love me?' and he said to him, 'Lord, you know everything; you know that I love you.' (Jesus) said to him, 'Feed my sheep.' " Several Church fathers argued that this text should always be bundled together with Matthew's in thinking about the papal office.

Over the years, in fact, this passage from John has sometimes been interpreted as the fulfillment of the promise in Matthew 16. Where the traditional interpretation of Matthew's text emphasized the *power* of the office, John presents its nature as one of *service*. This is why among the traditional titles of the Pope is "Servant of the Servants of God." Power in this understanding is real and absolute, but it is never an end in itself. It is ordered to the service of others.

Traditional theological reflection developed the image in Matthew's gospel of the papacy as the rock, finding three layers of significance. First, the papacy is intended to guarantee the *unity* of the Church, since the entire structure is erected on the basis of this one foundation. In the Creed recited each Sunday in the Catholic Mass all over the world, the marks, or distinguishing characteristics, of the Church are listed as being "one, holy, Catholic, and apostolic." The guarantor of the "oneness" of the Church is its center of authority in Rome, in the Pope. John Paul II has been keenly aware of this aspect of his role. In a rare interview on the papal plane in 1989, David Willey of the BBC asked the Pope to respond to criticism that he shouldn't travel so much. He replied: "The problem about the universal Church is how to make it more visible. There are tendencies in theology and above all in the Orthodox Church to reduce everything to the level of the local church. But the Church was born universal from the moment it began in Jerusalem. Saint Paul's travels, Saint Peter's coming to Rome, the Apostolic tradition, everything confirms the Petrine tradition of giving the Church its universal dimension, and making all the local churches feel this universal dimension. And it seems to me that my travels help to make it more visible."

The second sense of what it means to be the rock is that of ensuring the *endurance* of the Church, despite the historical storms that rage around it. This theological conviction is reinforced by the experience that a weak papacy has tended to correspond with times of crisis for the Catholic Church, while successful reforms generally unfold in periods of strong papal leadership. It has been the experience of local churches suffering persecution or harassment that a strong papal office is often the only force that sees them through. The experience of the Greek Catholics in Ukraine during the Soviet era, for example, or of underground Chinese Catholics today, is that the Pope's capacity to rally world opinion and to mobilize resources to assist them is vital in keeping their struggling communities afloat. Members of these communities often regard Western proposals to hem in the papacy as the luxury of theologians who do not have to worry about knocks on the door in the middle of the night.

Finally, tradition sees in the papacy a guarantee of *growth*, since the rock is intended to be the foundation for a much larger structure. It is the Pope who impels the Church to carry the gospel message to the world, fulfilling the mandate of Christ to "make disciples of all the nations." In a time when the Catholic Church is questioning the meaning of the very concept of mission, John Paul has attempted to revitalize this role of the papacy as well. He has repeatedly spoken of the need for a "new springtime of evangelization" and called Catholics to boldly "set out into the deep" (*duc in altum*). From this point of view, it is of the nature of the papal office to prevent the Church from closing in upon itself, to keep it directed toward ceaseless proposal of the Gospel.

Implied in this brief synthesis are two core values cherished by believers in a strong papacy. The first is *fidelity*, the notion that Christ entrusted his revelation to Peter and asked him to keep it safe. "Will the Son of Man find the faith upon the earth when he returns?" Jesus asked rhetorically. From the point of view of traditional Catholic theology, it is ultimately up to the successor of Peter to ensure that the answer to that question will be yes. This responsibility weighs heavily in the consciousness of Vatican officials and implies first of all a duty to integrity in the transmission and presentation of the doctrine of the Roman Catholic Church. Thus when the Vatican intervenes against a theologian, they see such action not in terms of a corporation protecting a copyright, or a police state exercising thought control, but a doctor protecting a patient from harm.

Cardinal Joseph Ratzinger has expressed this idea. "When a doctor errs and, instead of patiently accommodating himself to the laws of anatomy and life, risks a 'creative' idea, the consequences are readily apparent," Ratzinger said at a press conference in Menlo Park, California, in February 1999. "The patient suffers. Although the damage is not so immediately noticeable in the case of a theologian, in reality even here too much is at stake for him to trust himself simply to his momentary conviction. He is dealing with a matter which affects man and his future and in which every failed intervention has its consequences."

Many theologians would argue that the danger in this image is that of ignoring creative ideas that are not mere momentary convictions, but that emerge from decades of study and thought and discussion, ideas that can be fruitful for the whole Church—medical breakthroughs, if you like. As always, the question of whether a given new idea is a wonder cure or a dangerous toxin is a subjective one, and analysts will draw divergent conclusions. The point here is to understand the psychology involved when the Curia concludes that a given theological proposal has to be corrected. They understand themselves to be acting to preserve the health of the community, because ultimately the happiness of the human person is conditional upon knowing and accepting God's truth about human destiny. Anything that distorts or obscures that truth is ultimately harmful, so it is no act of kindness to simply let it go.

The second core value which arises from what has been said is *accountability*. Critics often complain about a lack of accountability in the Vatican, by which they mean that popes do not stand for reelection, are not subject to recall, and are not otherwise answerable to public opinion as expressed in modern democracies. This is correct so far as it goes, and it's a fair matter of debate whether the undemocratic character of the Holy See leaves it too far removed from the sensibilities of the people whose spiritual welfare it is intended to serve. Yet it is a terrible misconception to believe that Vatican officials do not regard themselves as accountable. In fact, the sense of the Petrine role as described above, focusing on Christ's mandate of fidelity, creates an almost overwhelming sense of accountability within those who take the tradition most seriously.

For Vatican officials, this accountability is first of all to Peter, in terms of how faithfully they collaborate in his threefold mission of teaching, sanctifying, and governing. Ultimately, accountability is to God. Vatican officials are accountable to the tradition, to the faith, to truth, and to Christ himself. Most of them sincerely believe they will stand before the bar of judgment someday to answer for their performance. This concept is hard for the modern mind to accept, because most of us believe with Lord John Acton that "power tends to corrupt, and absolute power corrupts absolutely," a remark Acton coined precisely in reference to the 1870 declaration of papal infallibility at Vatican I. Power without checks and balances is, from a democratic point of view, unaccountable, and unaccountable power is another expression for tyranny. But in the traditional Catholic theological framework being described here, power does not corrupt, it ennobles, because it flows from the sacramental grace of Holy Orders. Leaders in the Church thus do not represent the people; they represent Christ to the world. Some people will suspect that this is rhetoric designed to protect clerics from challenges to their authority, and that suspicion may sometimes have a foundation, but one will misunderstand the Holy See unless it's appreciated how deeply this understanding of accountability shapes its culture. To call the Church undemocratic is within the realm of fair debate, but to call Church leaders unaccountable does not do justice to their theology or their psychology.

Veteran *Newsweek* correspondent Robert Blair Kaiser challenged Belgian Cardinal Jan Schotte at a press conference in October 2001 about what Kaiser saw as the lack of accountability during a Synod of Bishops, which Schotte heads within the Vatican. The cardinal responded, as Kaiser records the exchange, that bishops are "accountable to no one but the Holy Father, and the Holy Father is accountable to no one but Jesus." The comment came across as arrogant, and anyone who knows Schotte realizes that despite his erudition and good humor, he can in fact be rather imperious. At the same time, if one assumes the remark was not flippant but intended to be in earnest, it is consistent with the theological principles described here. Accountability in this rather traditional understanding runs up, not down, and, ultimately, those who serve the Church are accountable to its founder. This does not mean they are insensitive to the concerns of the faithful, but rather that they believe the range of options to satisfy those concerns is circumscribed by the deposit of faith, which must always be their principal concern.

PRIMACY

The tool Vatican officials believe Christ gave the papacy to promote fidelity and accountability, thus understood, is known as *primacy*. This refers to the "supreme, full, immediate and universal ordinary power" that canon 331 of the *Code of Canon Law* says belongs to the Pope, and to the Pope alone. He has primacy over other bishops and the entire Catholic Church. In reality, as Catholic writer Russell Shaw has noted, it is not so much papal infallibility that creates controversy within the Catholic Church as primacy. Officially decreed at the First Vatican Council in 1870, papal infallibility is the doctrine that states that when popes make a solemn pronouncement on matters of revealed faith or morals and invoke full authority as the Successor of Peter, the Holy Spirit preserves them from error. Only rarely have popes formally exercised this teaching authority. Moreover, canon 749.3 of the *Code of Canon Law* states clearly that, "No doctrine is understood to be infallibly defined unless this is manifestly demonstrated."

Popes, however, make constant use of primacy. They establish dioceses, name bishops, promulgate laws, and perform numerous other acts of supreme and universal jurisdiction. This is the everyday business of the papacy, and it tends to be what gets the attention of Catholics for whom one or another decision rankles. In some sense, papal primacy goes back to the era of the primitive Christian communities. Writing to Christians in the Greek city of Corinth midway through the last decade of the first century, St. Clement, according to tradition Peter's third successor, wanted to bring the Corinthians in line. Clement complained about "impious and detestable sedition" and demanded that they obey the leaders of the local church. "But if some will not submit to them," Clement added, "let them learn what He [Christ] has spoke through us, that they will involve themselves in great sin and danger." Whether Clement was writing as a "proto-Pope" or a sort of "foreign minister" within a college of Roman Church leaders is a debated point, but the letter reflects an early exercise of primacy centered in the see of Rome.

In fits and starts over the centuries, men who would later be known as the first popes asserted their authority to intervene in the affairs of other churches, to settle doctrinal disputes, and to establish patterns of ritual and moral life. This was not a linear development, and theological reflection always tempered the growing power of the papacy with an emphasis on other centers of authority—ecumenical councils, local councils, synods, the bishops, and the local churches.

The ecumenical Council of Florence in the fifteenth century defined papal primacy as a dogma of the Catholic Church. The doctrine was elaborated by the First Vatican Council (1869–70) and reaffirmed by the Second Vatican Council (1962–65). Vatican I, in the same document that defined papal infallibility, *Pastor Aeternus* of July 18, 1870, provided a clear statement on primacy. It declared, "that the Roman Church, by the disposition of the Lord, holds the sovereignty of ordinary power over all others, and that this power of jurisdiction on the part of the Roman Pontiff, which is truly episcopal, is immediate; and with respect to this the pastors and the faithful of whatever rite and dignity, both as separate individuals and all together, are bound by the duty of hierarchical subordination and true obedience, not only in things which pertain to faith and morals, but also in those which pertain to the discipline and government of the Church spread over the whole world." Vatican I also taught that the primacy was instituted by Christ, with St. Peter; that the primacy is transmitted in perpetuity to Peter's successors, the popes; and that there can be no appeal from the Pope to some higher authority. This marked the end of a centuries-long debate as to whether the bishops in an ecumenical council constituted a power superior to the papacy.

At the same time, it is also important to understand what Vatican I did *not* teach. In the wake of the council, Chancellor Otto Bismarck of Germany attributed to it the view that the Pope had absorbed all episcopal jurisdiction. The German bishops insisted against Bismarck that the council did not in any way undermine the legitimate authority of the local bishop. The Pope's jurisdiction implied only that he had the responsibility to ensure the welfare of the churches, intervening only because of the incapacity of the local bishop or because the good of the church required it. Pius IX immediately applauded the German bishops for their response and officially confirmed the authenticity of their interpretation.

Vatican I's definition of primacy is nevertheless a sweeping assertion of power, and many critics of the Vatican would charge that it induces the Curia to pride, to the delusion that they in Rome know better than the local churches how things ought to be done. Once again, no doubt there's reality to this temptation. Yet at least on the level of personal spirituality, it can break the other way. Curial officials who take most seriously the powers of the Holy See tend to be the most conscious of their own unworthiness of such an immense responsibility. They tend to regard their share in the authority of the primacy as a lofty vocation, one of the most important responsibilities that can be entrusted to someone within the Church, and this can produce a kind of idealism about their work. This is often what gets Vatican officials through the long hours, the low pay, the anonymity, the slow pace of change, and the sometimes cold and impersonal atmosphere in their office. Seen from the outside papal primacy can appear to create an exaggerated sense of self-importance, but understood from the inside it can have precisely the opposite effect. Rather than an invitation to pride, it can be an occasion for humility and an acute sense of one's limits.

THE CASE FOR A STRONG POPE

Curial officials, by the nature of their global responsibility, have to think through the consequences of policy choices for every sector of the

worldwide 1-billion-strong Catholic Church. Speaking with these officials, what becomes clear is their perception of just how fragile this
global communion can be, how many centripetal forces are constantly
pushing the Church toward fragmentation. They include:

- Theological movements trumpeting "inculturation"
  threaten to produce a kind of weak Catholicism, in which
  the only thing really uniting Catholics is the name. The
  experience of the faith, its content and modes of expression, fragment to the point of being unrecognizable, especially in places such as Africa and Asia.
- Hostile governments in Cuba, China, Vietnam, and in
  parts of the Arab world are constantly trying to decouple
  their national Catholic communities from the rest of the
  Catholic world, especially Rome, in an attempt to minimize the capacity of those churches to threaten the regime.
- Hostile cultures, especially in the developed First World,
  that don't approve of the moral teaching of the Catholic
  Church encourage individual believers to "do their own
  thing," be Catholic on their own terms—so-called "cafe-
  teria Catholicism."

Against these forces, Vatican officials tend to believe, the only real
defense the Church has is its strong center of authority in Rome.

This conviction that it is a strong papacy that will see the Church
through times of crisis is deeply rooted in Catholic history. The battles
that have been waged by popes over the centuries to defend the prerogatives of their office are the stuff of legend. One thinks of Pope Gregory VII, for example, who in 1076 excommunicated the German king
Henry IV and deposed him during their bitter struggle over lay investi-
ture. This was the practice by which lay lords under the feudal system
symbolically conferred ecclesiastical office upon bishops and abbots,

reinforcing their claim to be superior to the ecclesiastical authorities and to have the power to decide who held ecclesiastical office. The underlying issue was the subjugation of church to state, which in some ways stretched all the way back to the fourth century and the declaration by Theodosius that Christianity was to be the official religion of the Roman Empire. The question was whether Christianity was to be subject to the secular power, in effect an instrument of state policy, or whether the Church would chart its own course. Secular powers in the West never forgave Pope Gregory for his victory. He was not canonized until 1606, and even then nearly another century and a quarter had to pass before Pope Benedict XIII extended his feast to the universal Church. When he did so, many of Europe's Catholic princes objected. In fact, the feast of Gregory VII, which falls on May 25, was banned in Catholic Austria until 1848.

Eventually the popes prevailed in Western Christianity, allowing the Church to function as a supranational "voice of conscience" and to remain united, juridically and theologically, across national boundaries. In the East, on the other hand, Caesaropapism, or domination by the state, took the upper hand. Eastern Orthodox churches have thus tended to be dependent upon, and thus uncritical of, the civil power. Even today, the bond between Orthodox Churches and the nation is sacral and quasi-absolute. Some critics would observe that the leaders of the fifteen autonomous churches across Eastern Europe and the Balkans are often identified with the most ultranationalist political elements within those countries, and this may be in part because there is no strong supranational authority in Orthodoxy as in Roman Catholicism. The argument runs that Catholicism's sense of universality has acted as an antidote to exaggerated nationalism in a way that Orthodoxy's loose, confederate structure has not.

In the 1937 encyclical *Mit brennender sorge*, Pope Pius XI laid out the argument for papal primacy in the face of a hostile regime that sought to subordinate the church to the state. The Pope said there are four reasons for defending the primacy of the Roman Pontiff as defined by Vatican I:

• The primacy is assigned to the Pope in Scripture. When Peter confessed Jesus as "the Messiah, the Son of the Living God" in Matthew 16, Jesus responded with the pledge that Peter was the rock upon which the Church would be built. This passage, Pius argued, shows the intimate bond that unites Christ, the Church, and the primacy of the Pope.

• The primacy of the Pope is a "guarantee against division and ruin."

• Only a world church, held together through the primacy of the Pope, is "qualified and competent for a universal evangelical mission."

• The primacy of the Pope assures that the Church retains its supranational character. National churches, Pius wrote, result in "paralysis, domestication and subjection to worldly powers."

The fact that these arguments were laid out with such clarity in response to the rise of the Nazi regime in Germany illustrates the close association in the Roman mind between papal primacy and the capacity of the Church to resist totalitarian, secular regimes.

Consider the experience of Eastern Europe in the twentieth century, when Communist regimes did everything in their power to break the ties that connected the Catholic communities with Rome. In Hungary, for example, the state-sponsored Free Church Council promoted an autonomous "Hungarian" Catholic Church. The theological arguments advanced were strikingly similar to some of those from today's left-leaning reformers in the West: that the Vatican is an authoritarian institution determined to foist its own cultural patterns upon local churches. The Hungarian government sponsored a "patriotic priests" organization, called Opus Pacis, that was intended to transfer the loyalty of the Catholic clergy from Rome to the socialist cause and, ultimately, to the Hungarian government. The policy had some success. Lutheran Bishop Zoltan Kaldy developed the so-called Theology of *Diakonia*, or service, which in essence identified Christianity with socialism and the Church with the socialist regime. Some Catholic priests in the Opus Pacis circle endorsed this theological perspective.

The pattern was replicated across the Communist block. In Czechoslovakia, a priest's association called Pacem in Terris, named cynically for Pope John XXIII's 1963 encyclical that marked an opening of the Catholic Church to the socialist world, encouraged Catholic clergy to distance themselves from Rome. Again, in some cases the strategy worked. Catholic priests such as Fr. Joseph Plojhar became leading figures in the regime, ending up defending policies that saw faithful Catholics tossed in prison. The Czech government's Office for Ecclesiastical Affairs approved clerical appointments, paid their wages, checked the budgets of Catholic organizations, and actually ran the seminaries in an attempt to control the ideological formation of future priests. Priests and nuns were required to take the following oath:

I promise on my honor and conscience that I shall be loyal to the Czechoslovak Republic and its People's Democracy and that I shall do nothing that is detrimental to its interests, its security and its integrity. As a citizen of the People's Democracy I shall honestly and sincerely carry out all duties which are incumbent upon me in the position which I occupy, and I shall support with all my strength the efforts towards reconstruction which are being made for the welfare of the people.

The unstated premise of the oath was that this loyalty to "people's democracy" trumped one's obligations to Rome or to papal authority. Between 1950 and 1955, the bishops of all fourteen Czech dioceses were removed by the government, and five were imprisoned. Administration of the dioceses was handed over to a mixed clerical/lay commission loyal to the government. In the 1960s, new bishops were approved who were chosen from the ranks of the Pacem in Terris movement, who could be counted upon to keep their distance from Rome. In the end, these bishops abandoned thousands of clergy and believers who did not wish to be assimilated to the gulags.

204 ALL THE POPE'S MEN

These historical episodes are still within the living memory of many Vatican officials, some of whom experienced them personally. The conclusion they usually draw is that fidelity to Rome, and the capacity of the papacy to withstand these sorts of pressures, made the difference between integrity and collaboration, between the survival of the faith and its co-option by a secular power for its own purposes.

Moreover, these officials would argue, the same sort of phenomenon is observable in China today, where the Communist government's Patriotic Association has long aimed at creating an indigenous Chinese Catholic Church independent of Rome, once again because it would pose less of a threat to the government's authority. In 1999 alone, five Chinese bishops who refused to register with the Patriotic Association were jailed, three of them men in their eighties who had already served twenty-year prison sentences. The suffering of Chinese Catholics for their fidelity to the Pope at times defies belief. Bishop Peter Joseph Fan Xue-Yan, for example, was arrested in 1958 and imprisoned for thirty-four years. In April 1992, security officers returned his frozen and broken body to his chancery in a plastic sack. It is precisely the power that Catholic tradition and the *Code of Canon Law* assigns to the Pope, defenders of a strong papacy argue, that allows faithful Chinese Catholics to withstand the pressures of the state. A system that put the premium on the local church would collapse under this kind of pressure.

Of course, one can make a theological argument for decentralization of the papacy without serving the interests of hostile regimes or being an enemy of the Church. The sense that the distribution of authority and responsibility is today out of balance is widespread, even among bishops, heads of religious orders, and mainstream theologians—the very bedrock of loyalty to the institution. Vatican officials are keenly aware, in fact, that some of the most forceful arguments for greater respect for local churches comes precisely from Eastern Rite Catholics who suffered terribly during the era of Soviet persecution and who now want their legitimate autonomy recognized. The point, however, is that from the perspective of many in curial service, the bitter experience of the twentieth century is that a strong papacy is the

Church's best guarantee of survival in times of crisis. That was what Christ had in mind, they believe, when he said that Peter would be the rock upon which the Church was built.

Nor is it the case, by the way, that the only threat to the Church in today's world comes in the form of overt government hostility as in China. The cultural hegemony of Western-style consumerism and secularism, fostered by liberal democratic governments, especially in the United States, may pose an even more serious danger to authentic Christianity. In the face of this challenge, many would argue that there is a much greater need today for Catholic counterculturalism than there is for inculturation. In other words, this argument runs, Catholics in this moment of history need to recover their capacity to be critical of the dominant culture rather than adapt themselves to it. This countercultural instinct is as the heart of the Communio school associated with Catholic thinkers such as David Schindler, Tracey Rowland, and Kenneth Schmitz. In this effort, a strong papacy is seen as an essential bully pulpit, able to break through the cultural noise to propose an alternative understanding of life.

THE ROMAN CURIA

Surprisingly, Catholic theology is relatively underdeveloped when it comes to the precise relationship between the primacy of the Pope and the Roman Curia, the administrative arm through which the Pope exercises the primacy. There is general agreement that the papacy cannot simply be collapsed into the Curia and that not every document that comes out of a Vatican office can be accorded the same authority as formal papal teachings such as encyclical letters. Beyond that, however, the precise nature of the authority exercised by the Roman Curia, and the extent to which it draws upon the personal authority of the Pope, is a disputed point. Noted Catholic theologian Richard Gaillardetz has put the question this way: "While it is generally recognized that in certain circumstances papal primatial authority extends to the activities of

Curial offices, the scope of this extension, its purpose and limits, and more importantly, the relationship of the activity of the Curia to the supreme power and authority exercised by the College of Bishops, has not been satisfactorily clarified with respect to sound canonical and ecclesiological principles."

In contemporary Catholic debate, generally speaking, doctrinal conservatives support a strong Curia and strong papacy, while liberals tend to support decentralization and the prerogatives of local bishops and churches. This may seem ironic to observers of secular politics where the normal tendency is the reverse—liberals support a strong central government, conservatives advocate local control. In Catholicism, however, conservatives tend to think of the Roman authorities as more sympathetic than many local bishops or ecclesiastical bureaucracies. Yet this should not obscure the point that in some circles on Catholicism's right wing there is also a fierce critique of the Roman Curia, not so much for having too much power, but for being feckless in how they exercise it. Indeed, perhaps the most widespread conservative criticism of Pope John Paul II is that his pontificate has failed to systematically root out the sources of alleged dissent from ecclesiastical institutions.

One point does appear settled, which is that the Roman Curia is not part of the divine mandate for the Church. In his 1988 apostolic constitution on the Curia, *Pastor Bonus*, John Paul II acknowledges that the Roman Curia does not belong "to the essential constitution of the Church as willed by God." In other words, while it is theologically impossible to imagine a Roman Catholic Church without the papacy, or the bishops, or the sacraments, it is possible to imagine Catholicism without the Roman Curia. In fact, as we saw in chapter 1, the Curia as currently structured dates only from the sixteenth century. Popes carried out their work in a variety of ways, and used a variety of instruments, in earlier centuries. While the Pope has to have some administrative support, in principle there is nothing sacrosanct about the structures and procedures of the Roman Curia as they now exist.

In traditional canonical language, the authority of the Roman

Curia is considered to be both *ordinary* and *vicarious*. It is ordinary in the sense that it depends upon the office and is not delegated to anyone individually. The authority of the Congregation for the Doctrine of the Faith thus comes from relevant Church law, especially *Pastor Bonus*, and not from the personal authority invested in Cardinal Joseph Ratzinger. This power is vicarious because it has been delegated to the Curia from the Pope, and in that sense the various dicasteries are the Pope's vicars. This ordinary and vicarious power extends to the entire Church. It is not extinguished with the death of the Pope, since John Paul's 1996 apostolic constitution, *Universi Dominici Gregis*, acknowledges that on urgent matters that cannot await the election of a new Pope the Curia will continue to make decisions also during the interregnum. This curial power, according to canon law, obliges all the faithful to obedience.

The fact that the Curia's power is derivative from that of the Pope is reflected in the fact that prior to the publication of their decrees, dicasteries must obtain the Pope's approval. This approval may come in one of two forms: *comune* or *specifica*. There are various Latin formulas used to signal the difference between the two, and canon lawyers and bishops are always attentive to this point. The essential difference is that documents approved in the *comune* form remain documents of the dicasteries that issue them, while documents issued in the *specifica* form become documents of the Pope himself. Ecclesial tradition recognizes that an inferior legislator, meaning a local bishop or the head of a religious community, has some discretion when it comes to the edicts of dicasteries. He or she can apply these decrees as seems best, and can even in some circumstances modify or abrogate them if serious circumstances warrant. With a document approved in the *specifica* form, however, its content becomes normative, and any evasion of its terms would be considered sinful. Canonical tradition holds that approval in the *specifica* form has the effect of giving even otherwise invalid decrees full legal force. In either case, curial decrees are considered to be officially promulgated once they are published in the *Acta Apostolicae Sedis*, the official bulletin of the Holy See.

Thus from a theological point of view, some texts are more authoritative than others depending on the content, the manner in which the text is presented, and under whose authority the text is given. Catholicism recognizes a series of gradations in Church teaching as described in the document *Lumen Gentium*, paragraph 25, at the Second Vatican Council. The idea is that not all doctrines are of the same importance or on the same level, and the authority a particular document carries is to some extent tied to how important the teaching it presents is in terms of human salvation. Generally theologians would recognize something like the following gradation in the importance of Roman documents.

- Definitive teaching solemnly proposed as infallible by the Pope and/or ecumenical councils.
- Teachings of ecumenical councils, which themselves have differing levels of authority, such as constitutions, decrees, and declarations. Vatican II, for example, did not intend to teach new doctrine, so the principles in documents such as *Gaudium et Spes* arguably enjoy a less binding status than the decrees of the Council of Trent.
- Papal encyclicals
- Apostolic constitutions, such as Pope John Paul's 1990 document on Catholic education, *Ex Corde Ecclesiae*
- Papal apostolic exhortations, such as those following the Synod of Bishops
- Apostolic letters (for example, a personal letter written by a Pope either to the whole church, a local church, or some particular group or body; or used to issue norms, establish a new institute, restructure various situations, etc.)
- Occasional papal allocutions, such as the Pope's catechesis at the Wednesday audience
- Documents of Roman dicasteries. These differ as to whether they come from a congregation, council, or tribunal, and what form they take—whether it is a declara-

tion, instruction, letter, notification, or response to a *dubium*, or formal question, submitted by a bishop.

The point is not that Catholics are free to ignore the documents of the Roman Curia, but rather that the evaluation of precisely what authority they enjoy, and exactly how much freedom local authorities may have to make adaptations for their own circumstances, is a debated point. Canon 18 of the *Code of Canon Law* says, "Laws which prescribe a penalty, or restrict the free exercise of rights, or contain an exception to the law, are to be interpreted strictly." Nevertheless, it is generally the case that in Vatican offices, there is a fairly maximalist stance on the binding force of curial decrees. Cardinal Joseph Ratzinger has said that the distinctions made above among different types of teaching concern the mode in which they oblige the conscience of the faith, not whether they do so.

To some extent, distinctions in the authority of Vatican pronouncements become especially relevant when observers suspect that a particular dicastery is actually working at cross-purposes from the Pope. The system is designed to make this impossible, and yet over the years it's been clear that sometimes the Roman Curia, or at least elements within it, have attempted to undercut particular papal initiatives. Resistance from within the Curia to Pope John XXIII's calling an ecumenical council, for example, and to the reform energies it unleashed, is well documented. It is to avoid this sort of conflict that *Pastor Bonus* in article 18 specifies that the Curia must do nothing of significance without the knowledge of the Pope, to ensure that orders being issued in his name genuinely reflect his will. It is for the same reason that Paul VI once said the Roman Curia must be "an instrument of immediate adhesion and perfect obedience," to avoid the impression that curial prefects are calling their own shots. The climate of submission to the will of the Pope is indeed very strong within the Holy See. Yet human nature being what it is, different officials will have different readings of the Pope's inclinations on any given issue. Inevitably, therefore, there is a tendency to attach less importance to the documents of a dicastery than to those of the Pope himself.

This tendency at times exists within the Curia itself. When *Dominus Iesus* appeared in September 2000 from the Congregation for the Doctrine of the Faith, for example, among the people it riled was Cardinal Edward Cassidy, an Australian who at the time was the head of the Council for Promoting Christian Unity. He felt the document's slighting attitude toward other Christians, refusing in many cases to call their denominations "churches," was unhelpful, an example of ill-considered "timing and tone." Questioned by reporters, he pointed them to the Pope's 1995 encyclical, *Ut Unum Sint*, saying, "I prefer to focus on the Pope's own words." Those opposed to a particular Vatican action or document will thus often attempt to soften the blow by suggesting that the document is inconsistent with the Pope's views. This is more a rhetorical than a juridical ploy, however, since curialists rightly point out that no document exits the Vatican without the Pope's approval. Whether that approval is always well considered is another matter.

Another debated point in Catholic theology surrounding the question of curial, and indeed papal, authority is that of "reception." Medieval theologians said that one test of the validity of a law is whether or not it is received—that is, whether communities actually order their lives by it and accept its wisdom, or whether practical experience shows the law is ill-conceived or inapplicable. Many Catholic theologians have argued, for example, that the 1968 teaching of Pope Paul VI on birth control, expressed in the encyclical *Humanae Vitae*, fails this test of reception. While not denying the principle, Vatican officials argue that reception cannot be measured using the gauges of opinion polls and secular incomprehension. It instead has to be measured against the patient experience of those faithful Catholics who are honestly trying to think with the Church. (In fairness, it should be pointed out that even some of those who argue for this more restrictive standard would support a revision in the teaching on birth control.) Vatican officials also insist that the need for community discernment does not release the individual believer from the obligation of obedience in the meantime. It is up to the universal Church, these officials insist, in communion with the Pope, not the theological faculty of the local Catholic college or the editorial page of the local newspaper, to decide what has been received.

This brief overview suggests that Catholic theological reflection on the Roman Curia rules out two extremes. One would invest every document and disciplinary decision of the Holy See with a patina of infallibility, blurring the proper distinction between different levels of authority. The other would draw too sharp a distinction between the Pope and the Curia, ignoring the reality that the Curia is the Pope's vicar. One extreme exaggerates the theological status of the Curia, while the other undervalues it. How exactly the relationship between the Pope and the Curia should be understood, and to what extent decisions of Vatican dicasteries in common form can be treated differently than papal teaching, remains an open question.

THE COLLEGE OF CARDINALS

As we saw in chapter 1, the Roman Curia developed out of the consistories, or gatherings of cardinals, that from roughly the eleventh century had become the most important body of advisors to the Pope. It was the reform of Sixtus V in 1588, in *Immensa aeterni Dei*, that established a set of congregations, conceived as subsets of cardinals, to deal with particular problems. That tradition survives today in the fact that heads of congregations are also cardinals. There is thus a sense in which the Roman Curia and the College of Cardinals are inextricably linked, and to understand the theological framework within which Vatican officials locate themselves, we need to understand something about the college.

The term *cardinal* originally referred to clergy who had been incardinated, or transferred, into a new position, as opposed to the one for which they were originally ordained. Generally when a cleric was incardinated, it meant he had been promoted, so the cardinals were thus the upper crust of the clerical ranks. The cardinals in Rome were, therefore, the most important clergy of the diocese. They were responsible for running important Roman parishes, administering diocesan programs, or advising the Pope in special capacities. All the cardinals together constitute what is known as the College of Cardinals. In 1179, this college acquired its most important prerogative when Pope Alexander III specified that the papal election was the prerogative of all, and only, the cardinals. In the thirteenth to fifteenth centuries, cardinals reached the zenith of their power, though their wealth and political clout meant they were not always universally popular. One popular Roman ditty of the era scrambled the Italian word *cardinali* into two other words: *cani*, meaning dogs, and *ladri*, meaning thieves.

If one thrust of the Second Vatican Council was to revitalize the College of Bishops, that by default implied some reduction in the importance of the College of Cardinals. Under Paul VI, this trend reached its high-water mark when the Pope contemplated a reform in papal elections that would have included some presidents of bishops' conferences in the electoral body. Yet Paul was dissauded from this change, and under John Paul II, the College of Cardinals has made something of a comeback. Six times to date, the Pope has called all the cardinals together in an extraordinary consistory to advise him on some topic of importance. The most recent was May 21–24, 2001, when he solicited ideas from the cardinals for taking the Church into the third millennium. The Pope has also often preferred to work with the cardinals rather than the bishops' conference when a nation or region has had an especially urgent problem. In April 2002, for example, John Paul called the American cardinals to Rome to discuss the sexual abuse crisis. In *Universi Domenici Gregis*, John Paul II gives two arguments for having the cardinals as the papal electors. They are Roman, the Pope says, because they are linked by tradition to the churches of Rome, but they also embody the universality of the Church because they come from every continent.

Some theologians, however, regard the College of Cardinals as problematic. Retired Archbishop John Quinn, for example, in *The Re-*

form of the Papacy: The Costly Call to Christian Unity, wrote that the College of Cardinals is difficult to locate with respect to the College of Bishops. Does it form a rival source of authority? Is it a "college within a college"? The observation builds on the longstanding complaint of many national bishops' conferences that the opinions of individual cardinals are sometimes taken more seriously in Rome than the collective judgments of the conference. This point is aggravated by the fact that while the office of bishop is clearly part of the divine constitution of the Church, the office of cardinal is not. Thus it is not obvious to many observers why an office that is a product of history should hold greater sway over governance than an office which was instituted by Christ. Further, the College of Cardinals is alien to the ecclesiology of the Eastern churches, whose top prelates are patriarchs. Indeed, when John Paul has occasionally named men from the Eastern churches as cardinals, it's always been awkward for them to decide whether to accept, and if so, how to express the office, since it's not part of their tradition.

During the second session of the Second Vatican Council, Melkite Patriarch Saigh Maximos IV made this point in a memorable speech (delivered in French rather than Latin in protest of the council's bias in favor of the Latin Rite). Historically, he pointed out, the College of Cardinals is an organization of the clergy of Rome. Born with this original sin, it can never be fully representative of the universal Church. Far better, he suggested, to have a council including patriarchs, some cardinals who happen to be residential bishops, and some bishops who are heads of bishops' conferences. Such a body, the patriarch concluded, would contribute substantially to universalizing the Church and promoting its adaptation to various situations and cultures.

In past centuries, laymen have been appointed cardinals. For example, Pope Pius IV appointed his young lay nephew Charles Borromeo a cardinal in 1560 and brought him to Rome, where he served as "cardinal-nephew," a forerunner of the secretary of state. It was not until 1563 that Borromeo was ordained a priest and transferred to Milan, taking up the duties of archbishop and leading the implementation of the decrees of the Council of Trent. Today, however, the link between the cardinal's office and sacramental ordination is clear. Canon 351§1 of the *Code of Canon Law* specifies that a cardinal must be at least a priest. In keeping with a policy adopted by Pope John XXIII in 1962, a cardinal who is not yet a bishop must first receive episcopal consecration. (Some cardinal appointees, especially those already over 80, ask to be excused from this provision.)

Given that the Roman Curia evolved from the College of Cardinals, and that the college grew out of the Roman clergy, there is a tendency inside the Vatican to regard the Curia as essentially *clerical*. From this point of view, the Curia is more than a bureaucratic structure analogous to the staff of a national bishops' conference. The Curia is an organic extension of the cardinal's office, and as such is linked to the sacrament of holy orders. In a positive sense, this encourages the view that service in the Roman Curia is a ministry and a vocation, not just a bureaucratic function; negatively, it can reinforce clerical elitism. Since the Second Vatican Council, there has been a growing presence of laypeople inside the Roman Curia, and *Pastor Bonus* welcomes this. The Curia, John Paul II writes, includes not just clergy but "lay men and women who by virtue of baptism and confirmation are fulfilling their own apostolic role. By this coalition of many forces, all ranks within the Church join in the ministry of the Supreme Pontiff." Yet there is no question that in the Vatican, clergy hold most of the cards. There are only four laity at the level of the superiors, and all four occupy the lowest level for a superior, undersecretary or its equivalent. Many Vatican officials believe it would actually be impossible for a noncleric to head a dicastery, because their share in the power of governance necessarily implies that they share the hierarchical authority imparted by the sacrament of holy orders. We'll return to this issue below. For now, the key point is that its connection to the College of Cardinals makes the Curia, for those steeped in the traditional theological outlook, something more than a papal civil service. If it is not expressly part of the divine constitution of the Church, it is nevertheless more than a mere accident of history.

CRITICISM

The aim in this chapter has been to present the theology of the papal office and of the Roman Curia as it is understood within the Vatican, as a key to understanding the cultural psychology of the institution. Readers should be aware, however, that several key elements of this view are contested within the field of Roman Catholic theology. Here we can provide only the briefest glimpse of that debate.

First, some theologians and Church historians would argue that the reading of the history of the papacy from the Vatican perspective often gives little evidence of historical consciousness. There sometimes seems to be little recognition that the papacy of the first millennium looked and functioned much differently than the papacy of the present. Current curial structures did not drop from Heaven, which means that if particular offices, institutions, or ways of doing business no longer serve the best interests of the Church, they may be reformed or eliminated.

Second, some theologians would argue that much Vatican thinking suffers from a defective theology of power. Ecclesial power emerges from baptism, these theologians insist, before it is reconfigured through Holy Orders. To be a member of the Christian community, to live in *communio*, is in itself to be "empowered" for daily Christian living and for service of the Church's mission. This is the exercise of ecclesial power in its most fundamental sense. The power received through baptism enables the faithful to fulfill their calling as disciples of Jesus. They are empowered to share the good news of Jesus Christ, to pursue holiness, to love their neighbor, to care for the least, to work for justice, and to build up the body of Christ through the exercise of their particular gifts in service of the Church. A more comprehensive theology of ecclesial empowerment, from this point of view, would not deny the unique sacramental power conferred upon the clergy, but it would insist that the source of all ecclesial power is the Spirit of Christ who empowers the whole Church. The power of the ordained cannot be appealed to as a kind of ecclesiastical trump card over the power of all disciples of Jesus to participate in the life and mission of the Church.

Third, many Catholic theologians today support an ecclesiology of communion that sees the universal Church as a communion of local churches. From that frame of reference, authority is not something that first pertains to the universal Church and then is conceded to the local churches. Rather, authority is always exercised within the communion of churches. The papacy, on this model, is understood as an office in service to communion. Local churches order their lives as they see fit, with the Pope intervening, based on the principle of subsidiarity, only when the local church is incapable of resolving a problem or when its own health demands it. In this sense, to even phrase the contemporary debate as over decentralization of power gets it wrong, since that term evokes a sense of concession—that the papacy ought to concede authority to the periphery, meaning the bishops and/or local churches. But in this version of the communion model, this authority is not the Pope's to concede. It belongs by right to the local church.

Finally, some theologians offer a criticism of the Roman Curia that has less to do with the content of its theology than the scope and depth of it. In some cases, they say, curial personnel do not have the appropriate theological training and expertise for the jobs they are called upon to do. In other cases personnel are perfectly qualified, but reflect a more narrow range of views than is reflected within the Catholic theological discussion. In both cases, what sometimes results is that documents are not subjected to the close scrutiny they should receive before they are issued, and thus critical discussion only takes place when the document is already out in the wider world. This puts theologians in the awkward position of being forced to criticize a Vatican document in the public forum, when many would have gladly offered reactions to the Holy See on a collaborative, nonconfrontational basis had they been called upon to do so before the fact. One ardent hope among theologians is that the Roman Curia will become more interested in tapping the theological expertise of the wider Catholic community.

REFORM

No topic in Catholic theological debate is more discussed these days than reform of the power structures within the Church. In part, this conversation is driven by forces in the Church who perceive an imbalance of power between Rome and the local churches. This overconcentration of power in the Pope, they would argue, is the product of complex historical evolution, beginning with the papacy's loss of temporal power in 1870 and its desire to compensate by asserting its control over the ecclesiastical realm. This campaign has culminated, they believe, in the pontificate of Pope John Paul II, whose omnipresence in the media because of his travels and his personal charisma has swamped other levels of authority in the Church. In part, too, this debate results from the progress of the ecumenical movement, and the recognition that no topic divides the Catholic Church from the other branches of the Christian family like the papacy. Both Pope Paul VI and Pope John Paul II have recognized that the price to pay for greater Christian unity will be some reconceptualization of the papacy that better respects the legitimate autonomy of local churches. Privately, many Eastern Orthodox prelates say they have an enormous admiration for the papacy and recognize that being part of a worldwide communion would better enable them to withstand pressures from their secular governments and cultures. They are often alienated, however, by what they see as the invasive and micromanaging tendencies of the papal bureaucracy.

The massive literature around these questions contains literally thousands of different proposals for reform. Some have to do with content-area limits on curial authority, such as restricting the ability of the Vatican to veto or amend the translations of liturgical texts made into the various vernacular languages. Some are procedural, such as Archbishop Quinn's idea that the Pope should establish a commission headed by three presidents (the president of an episcopal conference, a layperson, and a representative of the Curia) to come up with a plan for restructuring within three years. It would then be voted on by the presidents of episcopal conferences and presented to the Pope for approval.

It is impossible to examine all these ideas here, or even to enumerate them. Instead we'll consider two representative proposals that illustrate some of the tensions in contemporary theological discussion. The focus will be on the reaction that the two proposals often generate inside the Roman Curia, as a way of illustrating the theological attitudes often found there.

The first was presented in Fr. Thomas Reese's 1994 book *Inside the Vatican*, and echoed by Quinn and others. In a nutshell, the idea is that the number of bishops working in the Vatican should be radically reduced, if not eliminated altogether. For one thing, in a time of priest shortages and great pastoral need, it is an abuse of the sacrament of holy orders to have so many bishops performing essentially administrative tasks. Also, much confusion as to the authority of Vatican documents, including even routine correspondence, is created by the fact that they are signed by cardinals, archbishops, and bishops. It would clarify matters tremendously, and make the relationship between the Pope and the College of Bishops much more clear and direct, if curial functions were performed by lower clergy or by laity. A related form of this proposal argues that it would be wonderful symbolism for the Church if more laypeople, including women, were moved into top curial positions vacated by bishops.

Such a proposal assumes a basically instrumental view of the Curia, that it is a bureaucratic system the Pope is free to reshape at will and that its offices can be occupied by anyone, just as any qualified person can be a school administrator or accountant for the Church. Set against this view would be a more sacramental understanding of the Roman Curia, described above in the discussion of the College of Cardinals. While recognizing that the Curia is not part of the constitution of the Church as revealed by Christ, this model nevertheless holds that its intimate association with the ministry of the Pope implies an organic connection with the sacrament of holy orders. On that view, the power of governance exercised in the Roman Curia is bound up with the hierarchical power vested in Catholic priests by ordination and that reaches its fullness in ordination to the episcopacy. By that logic, it would seem appropriate and even essential that top offices in the Vatican be held by bishops.

One expression of the sacramental view came from Cardinal Jan Schotte, the Belgian who runs the Synod of Bishops, in response to a question I put to him in June 2003, in connection with the issuance of John Paul's apostolic letter *Ecclesia in Europa*. A working group at the 1999 European Synod had proposed that a woman be named to head an agency of the Curia, but the idea did not survive in the propositions presented to the Pope at the close of the synod, and neither was it in the letter. Does that mean, I asked, that the idea is off the table? "Right now the dicasteries have jurisdiction, and so they participate in episcopal authority," Schotte said. "We're a hierarchical organization and power comes from ordination. So for now, there cannot be a woman. If the job is redefined, you could have a woman, but then it would not be the same dicastery as we think of now when people say there should be a woman." As Schotte suggests, the sacramental view of the Curia limits the possibilities for lay participation at the leadership levels, especially by women.

A second proposed reform worth a brief examination is that the Curia should be balanced by, or even subservient to, an enhanced Synod of Bishops. From the creation of the synod in 1965, popes have been aware of a potential rivalry between this body and the Curia. It is for this reason, in fact, that Paul VI included in his constitution *Apostolica sollicitudo* of September 15, 1965, which erected the synod, a provision specifying that the cardinal-prefects of the various dicasteries are to be participants in all the meetings of the synod. Similarly, Pope John Paul II in a 1990 discourse to the College of Cardinals said: "An interpretation of the Curia that would present it as an antithetical subject with respect to the Synod is without foundation; neither would it be legitimate to hypothesize a competitive attitude between these two ecclesial entities." Yet the potential for rivalry exists. Indeed, every time a synod is held, complaints about the Curia are frequent. The refrain became so insistent at the Synod of Bishops in 2001, in fact, that on October 11 Secretary of State Cardinal Angelo Sodano actually pleaded for mercy. "To the brothers who work in the dioceses, allow me to ask that you not demand impossible things from us who work in the Curia," Sodano said. "We all have our limits. The Apostle told us counter-positions are not useful: *Alter alterius onera portate!*"

Advocates believe that a synod, especially one composed primarily of the elected presidents of national bishops conferences, and perhaps the elected heads of religious orders, would provide a more representative body to collaborate with the Pope, offering a better expression of the lived experience of Catholics around the world. In that sense, its most optimistic champions often see the synod as a kind of ongoing ecumenical council that would extend the role of the bishops witnessed at Vatican II into the daily experience of the Church. No less a figure than Joseph Ratzinger gave voice to this view in 1965: "If we may say that the synod is a permanent council in miniature—its composition as well as its name justifies this—then its institution under these circumstances guarantees that the council will continue after its official end; it will from now on be part of the everyday life of the Church."

Many Vatican officials argue, however, that synods simply are not capable of collaborating in the governance of the universal Church in the sense in which reformers intend. Either it would mean lifting bishops out of their dioceses for long periods of time in order to truly think through the issues—which would destroy the very pastoral closeness they are supposed to bring—or it would mean short synods with superficial and confused results. Some of these critics would add that the experience of many of the twenty synods held to date has made the point. Given that many Catholic conservatives are already suspicious of national bishops' conferences for being too dominated by staff (the syndrome of experts instead of common sense) and by questionable doctrinal positions, the idea of giving these conferences a greater say in the universal Church is for some an unappetizing option. Many curial personnel also suspect that behind the proposal to beef up the synod is a desire to water down the papacy, and for all the reasons noted above, they are deeply suspicious of such an agenda.

A SPIRITUALITY FOR THE CURIA

The argument of this chapter has been that the attitudes of the men and women of the Roman Curia toward themselves and their work cannot be understood apart from their faith convictions. We'll end with a look at a spirituality of the Roman Curia, developed by one of the men who knows this world best: Argentine Cardinal Jorge Mejia, the former prefect of the Vatican library, and a man who has done almost everything there is to do in Vatican service.

Mejia, eighty as of this writing, attended Vatican II as a *peritus*, or theological expert, from 1962–65, and was then the director of the Commission on Ecumenism of the Archdiocese of Buenos Aires in 1966. In 1967, he was named secretary of the Department of Ecumenism of CELAM, the prestigious assembly of Latin American bishops' conference, and then became president of the Executive Committee of the World Catholic Federation for the Biblical Apostolate from 1969–72. He entered Vatican service with his appointment as secretary of the Pontifical Commission for Religious Relations with the Jews in 1977. He was then appointed vice-president of the Pontifical Commission for Justice and Peace on March 8, 1986. He was consecrated in Rome on April 12, 1986, by Cardinal Roger Etchegaray, president of the same council. Among other things, the appointment was seen as John Paul's seal of approval on Mejia's role as architect of the Pope's visit to the Rome synagogue that same month. It marked the first time since the era of primitive Christianity that a pope had gone to a Jewish place of worship and was a special point of pride for Mejia, whose background is in Scripture. Mejia was made archbishop and secretary of the Congregation for Bishops on March 5, 1994, a job that has always foreshadowed an eventual cardinal's red hat. He was named archivist and librarian of the Holy Roman Church on March 7, 1998, and entered the College of Cardinals in February 2001.

In an interview for this book in the spring of 2003, Mejia said he had once come up with a list of virtues that he felt working in the Roman Curia fosters. This is not to say that everyone who works there develops them, he hastened to add, merely that the environment is conducive to eliciting these particular traits. He listed four:

• **Patience:** "Anyone who serves the Holy Father in the Roman Curia learns to wait," Mejia said. Attempts to rush the institution almost always backfire, he said. Moreover, there is a certain wisdom in learning to rely on God's time rather than one's own.

• **Anonymity:** "It is amazing what you can accomplish in the Vatican if you have absolutely no interest in claiming the credit," Mejia said. He suggested that the happiest people he has met over the years in the Vatican are those least interested in the consequences of their service for their own careers.

• **Humility:** "You start to think about the vastness of the responsibility the Holy Father carries, and it becomes overwhelming," Mejia said. There is of course a danger that this awareness could make someone drunk with power rather than humble, and Mejia quickly acknowledged that he'd seen examples of it. "At the same time, the vast majority of sane people around here come to understand very quickly how little they are measured against the size of the challenges."

• **Pleasure in the success of others:** "This is the most difficult of all," Mejia said. "It will happen in the course of one's career here that you will see other people receive appointments or favors that you might have regarded yourself as having earned. What do you do? Do you become bitter, or do you learn to take pleasure that something good has happened to another?" Curial service, he suggested, is a crucible in which this virtue can be forged.

In the end, my experience of knowing several dozen men and women at all levels and in all kinds of jobs inside the Holy See suggests that more people make a good faith effort to live by Mejia's virtues than not. Still, it would be naïve romanticism to pretend that this is universally the case. I'll tell one anecdote to make the point. In the fall of 2002, I took a longtime curial veteran out to lunch, a *monsignore* who had entered the Vatican during the pontificate of John XXIII. He had been exiled from the Holy See on the watch of Archbishop Giovanni Benelli, the tough-as-nails *sostituto* of Pope Paul VI. The *monsignore* described in graphic terms how much he had come to hate Benelli, how he bore resentment against him for many years, since he blamed Benelli for the fact he never became a bishop. He hung around Rome in various capacities, something of a lost soul. After many years, he heard about Benelli's death in 1982. By that time his old nemesis had been made the cardinal-archbishop of Florence, and the *monsignore* told me he rang up a friend who had been similarly tossed out by Benelli and proposed that the two of them go to Florence for the funeral.

"Do you know why?" the *monsignore* asked me. I expected that it had something to do with making peace, putting the ghosts of old resentments to rest.

"To make sure the bastard was really dead," he said, without a trace of irony.

He said he and his friend drank a champagne toast to Benelli's demise. All this by way of making the point that while the Roman Curia might invite its personnel to certain virtues, not everyone accepts the invitation.

6

THE VATICAN AND THE
AMERICAN SEXUAL ABUSE CRISIS

*A*merican Catholics have never been as angry with the leadership of their Church, and therefore as angry with Rome, as in the wake of the sexual abuse crisis that exploded in January 2002. This book is animated by the hope of putting English-speaking Catholicism and the Holy See in conversation with one another, and at the outset of this chapter it's important to offer some plain talk about what's at stake in the United States. Polling even before the crisis suggested that a substantial block of Catholics in the United States regarded the institutional dimension of their faith, especially the hierarchy, as increasingly irrelevant. The consequence had been a de facto loosening of ties with Rome. This tendency was given a turbocharge by the crisis. A May 2003 poll in the *Boston Globe* found that 39 percent of Catholics in the Boston area would support the creation of an American Catholic Church independent of the Vatican. The news is actually worse, because among American Catholics aged eighteen to thirty-nine, support for the proposal for cutting ties with Rome rises to 50.9 percent. Granted that attitudes in Boston are undoubtedly sharper than elsewhere, this finding nevertheless has to be alarming for anyone concerned with the communion that should exist between American Catholicism and the universal Church, as embodied by the Holy See.

To be clear, a schism in American Catholicism is improbable. Church history suggests that formal schisms are triggered by bishops, and there is no bishop prepared to lead American Catholics in rebellion against the Vatican. There is no Archbishop Marcel Lefebvre, who led traditionalist Catholics in a walkout over Vatican II's liberalizing changes, of the Catholic reform movement in the United States. But if present antagonisms fester, what may result is a body of American Catholics more and more hostile to any exercise of authority from Rome and an administration in Rome increasingly irritated with American exceptionalism and assertiveness. The ground is being prepared for a cycle of recrimination and misunderstanding that could last a generation, producing a sort of undeclared rupture such as the Catholic world has already seen in Holland, Germany, and Austria. Given that the United States is the leading political and commercial power in the world, and the Holy See the leading voice of conscience in public affairs, American Catholics and the Vatican should be collaborating on bringing a Catholic critique to current global injustices. Human dignity is not served by a breach between Rome and the American Catholic street.

The relationship between the Holy See and the United States thus stands at a crossroads. The two sides can decide to think outside the box, giving each other the benefit of the doubt and each striving to glimpse the other's point of view. They can become, in a wonderful phrase of former Dominican Master General Fr. Timothy Radcliffe, "mendicants for the truth," begging with outstretched hand for every scrap of genuine insight anyone is willing to offer, regardless of where it originates. Or the two parties can opt instead, as so many appear prepared to do, to go on vilifying and dismissing one another. The choices made in this regard will be consequential not just for the Catholic Church, but for the entire human family.

THE TOLL OF THE CRISIS

The sex abuse crisis has been the most painful episode in American Catholicism since its foundation. One can say this with confidence, despite the many ways the story of the Catholic Church in the United States was distorted during the *annus horribilis* of 2002. That distortion can be glimpsed from the following:

• The American press invested incalculable resources broadcasting the failures of the Catholic Church, but made no similar effort to publicize anything the Church did right. To provide just a bit of context, in the same year that the sex abuse scandals finished on the front page of the *New York Times* for forty-one days in a row, 2.7 million children were educated in Catholic schools in the United States, nearly 10 million persons were given assistance by Catholic Charities USA, and Catholic hospitals spent $2.8 billion in providing uncompensated health care to millions of poor and low-income Americans.

• The percentage of priests guilty of sexual abuse, whatever the final number, is almost certainly comparable to that of other clergy or other professions. Research in the field of mental health care, for example, shows that between 1 to 7 percent of female professionals and 2 to 17 percent of male professionals sexually exploit their patients. A 1998 study by *Education Week* found there are as many as nine cases of sexual abuse in the public education system in the United States each week. The mental health care and education professions, however, were not subjected to twelve months of witheringly negative media attention.

• While some Catholic bishops failed to protect the most vulnerable members of their flock, others dealt with the scourge of sexual abuse aggressively and effectively. Yet while American reporters wrote extensively about Bernard Law, Rembert Weakland, John McCormack, Thomas Daily, William Murphy, Anthony O'Connell, and other bishops tarred by the scandals, most never heard of Sean O'Malley until he was appointed to Boston, or Michael Sheehan until he took over in Phoenix—two bishops with a track record of outreach to victims and firm responses to allegations of abuse.

It's little wonder that some Catholics, inside the United States and out, concluded that the treatment of the Church during the course of the scandals was unfair.

Yet there is no evading the truth that this crisis produced an unparalleled hurt in the heart of the Church. After all the explanation and all the gloss, the bare facts remain: thousands of children were abused by priests, bishops who should have known better let it happen, and the Church too often attempted to protect itself rather than to accept its failings and make efforts to repair them. Compassion from Church officials was too little and too late. Images of the bishops engaging in hardball legal tactics and Nixonian damage control speak for themselves. As Archbishop Sean O'Malley of Boston said in his July 30, 2003, installation Mass, "The whole Catholic community is ashamed and anguished because of the pain and damage inflicted on so many young people, and because of our inability and unwillingness to deal with the crime of sexual abuse of minors."

The crisis has left many rank-and-file lay Catholics confused, weary, and dispirited. At its most profound, it has permanently alienated a group of sexual abuse victims, their families and friends and supporters, from the Catholic faith. Many of these people are psychologically and spiritually incapable of ever setting foot again in a Catholic place of worship. A much wider circle of Catholics, not personally caught up in the sex abuse issue, will continue to take part at least sporadically in Church life, but has nevertheless experienced its own crisis of confidence. They find themselves newly suspicious of priests and newly skeptical of bishops. The crisis has also deepened the ideological split in American Catholicism between a left that diagnoses the situation in terms of antiquated sexual teachings and a dysfunctional hierarchy, and a right that insists instead on doctrinal dissent and pervasive homosexuality as the principal causes. The recrimination, in a perverse cycle, makes the atmosphere of resignation and weariness that much worse.

Priests also have been hard hit, although too often in recent months the public climate in the United States has made any expression of sympathy for the clergy sound like complicity. Not only do priests second guess themselves about any gesture of intimacy with a young person, but they feel depressed about the priesthood itself, wondering how an institution to which they have devoted their lives could have gone so badly off the tracks. They also worry about a cultural climate in which any accusation of sexual abuse, however unfounded or ill-motivated, could be enough to ruin their lives. A 2002 report by the *Cleveland Plain Dealer* revealed that sixteen priests accused of sexual abuse had committed suicide since 1986, and in the almost two years since that time, a handful of others have followed suit. They are simply the most dramatic examples of widespread demoralization. This despite the fact that, as noted author and sociologist Fr. Andrew Greeley points out, American priests who like being priests are generally among the most satisfied professional classes in the country.

Catholic bishops in the United States have also been badly wounded. Those who should have been aware of the sexual misconduct of priests and yet allowed them to do harm have been disgraced. To date, a small number has resigned, but more face civil and potentially even criminal procedures that will forever mar their legacies, regardless of whether they survive in office. Bishops not personally culpable in the crisis nevertheless face criticism for their failure of leadership and of imagination in responding when it broke out. Many priests are angry for what they perceive as the bishops' collective decision to adopt punitive policies for priests, but to do little to address their own culpability. Priests thus feel hung out to dry by the men who should be their last line of defense, who according to the traditional Catholic theology are supposed to be their father and brother. Many laity, meanwhile, feel unable to trust the leadership of the Church. They want to respect and honor their bishops, but in too many cases recent experience has made that difficult. The bishops, who are overwhelmingly caring and pastoral men, realize this. One American bishop who sits on the Ad-Hoc Committee on Sexual Abuse of the United States Conference of Catholic Bishops said in 2002 that the last nine months of his life had been like "a nightmare from which I can't wake up." A further cost has been exacted in terms of the bishops' moral authority. They are less capable of bringing a critique to social questions because their moral standing has been compromised.

In times of crisis, Catholics instinctively turn to Rome for solace. Too often, however, a climate of mutual incomprehension and distrust between Rome and America has made the situation worse rather than better. During the early period of the crisis, from January 6 to March 21, 2002, the Vatican kept silent, feeding public perceptions in the United States that the Holy See and Pope John Paul II were out of touch. When the Pope did eventually speak, in his annual Holy Thursday letter to priests, the language was indirect, circumspect, and unsatisfying. At a Vatican press conference to present the Pope's letter, Colombian Cardinal Dario Castrillón Hoyos, head of the Congregation for Clergy, the Vatican office that supervises priests, seemed defensive and combative. From that point forward, an adversarial dynamic set in, with the American press and a large sector of public opinion accusing the Vatican and the Pope of being in denial, of regarding the crisis as an "American problem," of not caring enough to take the problem in hand. Such impressions were exacerbated by the Pope's physical condition, which led many Catholics to believe he was incapable of addressing an out-of-control situation, and by the rhetoric used by some foreign cardinals in complaining about media persecution of the Church, likening it to the worst of Hitler and Nero's oppression. Some pundits began to speak about a mar on the Pope's legacy. For average American Catholics, the impression of having been abandoned or misunderstood by Rome added to their dismay.

From Rome's point of view, meanwhile, the crisis deepened reservations that many in the Holy See already felt about American culture. Some saw the ferocious reaction in the press as an extension of the same puritanical hysteria about sexual misconduct that produced the Clinton/Lewinsky fiasco. Others saw it as an extension of the historical anti-Catholicism that has always percolated among American elites. Still others regarded it as a form of payback to the Church for her counter-cultural stands on abortion, birth control, women's ordination, and a host of other issues. The deepest thinkers in the Vatican have always harbored their doubts about the United States, seeing it as a culture forged by Calvinism and hostile to a genuinely Catholic ethos. The sexual abuse crisis compounded that impression. One archbishop put it this way: "Americans have a bad combination of youth, wealth, power, isolation and very little serious Catholic intellectual tradition. It's a recipe for a lot of mischief."

Observers in Rome watched as lay groups such as Voice of the Faithful arose to demand reform and interpreted such activism as another instance of Americans seeing the Church in terms of power and class struggle rather than as a communion. Many Vatican officials reacted with shock to the June 2002 meeting of the U.S. bishops in Dallas, and especially the norms for sexual abuse adopted there, which seemed a capitulation to a lynch-mob mentality. Aware of the drumbeat of criticism in the American press that the Vatican was wrong to put up roadblocks, these officials resented the apparent assumption that two thousand years of tradition should give way so the institution could be reshaped according to American exigencies. Despite being a mere 6 percent of the global Catholic population, American Catholics seemed convinced that their problems should trump everyone else's. From a Roman point of view, that could look like American narcissism. It did not help that the crisis was unfolding at a moment in which European stereotypes about American isolationism and arrogance were being revived by the foreign policy choices of the Bush administration, a point to be developed in the next chapter about the war in Iraq.

While it is flippant to say, "Americans are from Mars, the Vatican from Venus," there is nevertheless a cultural gap between the two worlds that was enormously consequential as the crisis unfolded. Quite often, American Catholics and the Holy See found themselves speaking two different languages, usually without realizing it. They thought they were talking to each other, but in many instances they were talking past each other, making deceptively similar statements that were in fact rooted in different psychological and sociological assumptions and that meant very different things to each of the two parties. There was a work of translation necessary to bring the two sides into genuine dialogue that too often was missing, so that statements intended to be helpful ended up making things worse, and policy choices designed to promote healing sometimes actually deepened the pain.

This chapter will review the various ways in which American Catholicism and the Holy See misunderstood one another during the sexual abuse crisis. Ultimately, the hope is to promote better communication between Rome and the English-speaking Catholic world. This is not to justify individual positions on either side, and no amount of improved communication will paper over the real differences in perspective and priorities that sometimes divide mainstream American Catholic sentiment from the Vatican's way of thinking. But perhaps some of the acrimony generated by mistaken assumptions can be reduced, so that at least conversations can unfold on the basis of clarity, and disagreements can be rooted in differing approaches to shared values.

THE STATUS QUO

Though the focus in this chapter is on the crisis triggered on January 6, 2002, with the first *Boston Globe* report about former Boston priest John Geoghan, it should be noted that the phenomenon of sexual abuse by clergy is not new. In the United States, the 1985 case of former priest Gilbert Gauthe in Louisiana, who is alleged to have had more than seventy victims, first brought attention to the issue, to a great extent through the pioneering reporting of the *National Catholic Reporter*. But the roots go much deeper. To take one example, St. Peter Damian (1007–1072) stated: "Vice against nature creeps in like a cancer and even touches the order of consecrated men . . . unless the strength of the (church leadership) intervenes as soon as possible, there is no doubt but that this unbridled wickedness, even though it should wish to be restrained, will be unable to stop on its headlong course." Even earlier, St.

Basil (330–379) had stated, "A cleric or monk who seduces youths or young boys . . . is to be publicly flogged. . . . For six months he will languish in prison-like confinement, . . . and he shall never again associate with youths in private conversation nor in counseling them."

The American bishops had commissioned a study from the John Jay College of Criminal Justice in New York as to the overall national dimensions of the crisis. The National Review Board instituted by the U.S. bishops noted in an interim report in July 2003: "A puzzling dimension of the scandal is that no accurate statistical snapshot had ever been taken over decades of the number of offending priests, the number of youthful victims and the financial cost to the Church. This led to mounting accusations of secrecy and stonewalling."

Issued on February 27, 2004, the John Jay report found a total of 4,392 priests faced allegations of sexual abuse that were not either withdrawn or known to be false, lodged by some 10,667 alleged victims during the period 1950 to 2002. This means that some 4.3 percent of diocesan priests and 2.5 percent of religious order priests faced at least one accusation of sexual abuse. The number of accusations peaked in 1970, and there were more accusations from the 1970s than any other decade. In some cases the alleged abuse extended over several years. Two-thirds of the accusations were reported after 1993, with one-third reported in 2002–2003 alone, suggesting that the total scope of the crisis has only recently become clear. The total amount of money paid by the church as a result of these accusations is $572,000,000. The majority of priests, 56 percent, were alleged to have abused one victim. The 149 priests (3.4 percent) who had more than ten allegations of abuse were allegedly responsible for abusing 2,960 victims, thus accounting for 26 percent of allegations. Therefore, a very small percentage of accused priests are responsible for a substantial percentage of allegations. The largest group of alleged victims, 50.9 percent, was between the ages of 11 and 14 at the time of the incident, while 27.3 percent were 15–17, 16 percent were 8–10, and nearly 6 percent were under age 7. Overall, 81 percent were male. Males tended to be older than females, with over 40 percent of alleged victims being males between the ages of 11 and 14.

Thomas Plante, a lay psychiatrist at the University of Santa Clara and a consultant to several Church review boards, concludes that "research suggests that less than 6 percent of Roman Catholic priests or other male Catholic clergy such as brothers have had a sexual experience with a minor." Plante also said, "When all of the current evidence is examined from police records, treatment facilities, and researchers who investigate these matters, no evidence suggests that Catholic priests are more likely to sexually abuse minors than other male clergy or men in general." The same point applies to other professions that enjoy positions of trust with vulnerable people. For example, Plante said, in mental health professions, a percentage of therapists analogous to rates among priests sexually abuse people entrusted to their care. In that regard, Plante offers one encouraging parallel. In the 1960s and 1970s, he said, studies indicated that up to 23 percent of male psychotherapists had sexual contact with their patients. Within a generation, Plante said, that number was cut to between 1 percent and 1.5 percent, through a combination of aggressive one-strike policies, better training, and changing sensitivities.

The norms adopted by the American bishops in Washington, D.C., in November 2002 envision that when a priest is credibly accused of sexual abuse of a minor, two procedures will be launched. First, the accusation will be referred to the police, which could lead to a criminal investigation and indictment. Second, the Church will initiate a canonical investigation that could lead to the imposition of penalties such as permanent removal from ministry, or laicization. The Church understands these procedures as parallel and complementary. At least in theory, the canon law process is intended to be in addition to, not instead of, full cooperation with civil authorities. In 2002, the *New York Times* story reported, 432 priests had resigned, retired, or been removed from ministry. Not all did so, however, because of the sexual abuse crisis. Conventional estimates are that some 325 of the current crop of roughly 46,000 American priests have been removed under the weight of allegations of sexual abuse. The initial determination of credibility is critical, and most bishops are relying upon lay review boards to make it.

Under the terms of a May 18 papal decree called *Sacramentorum Sanctitatis Tutela*, a bishop is obliged to report every credible allegation to the Congregation for the Doctrine of the Faith in Rome, which has exclusive canonical jurisdiction over cases of sexual abuse of a minor. As of the summer of 2003, some 199 American cases had been reported to the congregation, with most still awaiting action. When a case is submitted to the congregation, it may decide that insufficient evidence exists to proceed to trial, and direct that the priest be returned to ministry. If it decides that the allegation is credible, it can authorize one of three procedures:

- Canonical trial
- An extrajuridical procedure envisioned under canon 1720. This option allows the bishop, if he is morally certain the priest is guilty, to remove him from ministry without the time and expense of a trial. The canon requires that the accused be notified of the charges and given an opportunity for defense.
- Dismissal from the clerical state *ex officio et in poenam*, meaning an involuntary laicization approved personally by the Pope. This is a rare option because it short-circuits procedural guarantees. In most cases, however, the accused priest has already had several opportunities to mount a defense. Sometimes he may already have been convicted criminally.

In October 2002, the Vatican rejected the first set of norms approved by the U.S. bishops in Dallas. The reason was the need to protect due process rights of accused priests; the Vatican insisted that priests receive a full canonical trial, instead of being dismissed through the exercise of a bishop's administrative authority. The American bishops had opted for this administrative procedure on the basis of perceptions that the Holy See was reluctant to remove abuser priests, based in part on the case of a Pittsburgh priest named Anthony Cipolla. In 1988, Cipolla and the Pittsburgh diocese were sued by a thirty-three-year-old man who claimed that Cipolla had begun molesting him at age twelve and continued until he was seventeen. Bishop Donald Wuerl removed Cipolla from ministry in 1988 but allowed him to remain a priest, settling the civil lawsuit in 1993. In 1991, Cipolla filed a canonical appeal with the Vatican asking that he be returned to ministry. His first attempt failed, but a second appeal to the Apostolic Signatura succeeded. In March 1993, the Signatura ordered Cipolla reinstated. The basis was that by sending Cipolla to St. Luke Institute in Silver Spring, Maryland, for an assessment, Wuerl had denied Cipolla the right to a fair judgment. "St. Luke Institute, a clinic founded by a priest who is openly homosexual and based on a mixed doctrine of Freudian pan-sexualism and behaviorism, is surely not a suitable institution apt to judge rightly about the beliefs and the lifestyle of a Catholic priest," Cipolla's appeal read. Wuerl fought back, heading to Rome with the case files. In 1995 the Signatura reversed itself, and again ordered Cipolla barred from ministry. Despite the edict, Cipolla continued to act as a priest, leading to a 2002 decree expelling him from the priesthood signed by John Paul II. The experience taught many American bishops that trying to handle cases in Church courts could be long, cumbersome, and fraught with potential setbacks.

Despite the Holy See's initial insistence on canonical trials, Vatican sources say that as American case files arrive in Rome, in many instances the accused priest's guilt appears clear to the canonical tribunals in the Congregation for the Doctrine of the Faith. In such cases, the Vatican is opting for the swifter extrajudicial option, a solution not all that different from what the American bishops had originally intended. This stance is of concern to some American canonists, who worry that the due process rights of accused priests may be sacrificed.

A further reason for the extrajudicial route can be prescription, the statute of limitations in canon law, which for the sexual abuse of a minor is ten years from the victim's eighteenth birthday. When the American norms were debated, many victims' advocates worried that prescription would be used to shield accused priests. In fact, however,

Vatican sources say such an outcome is more likely in secular criminal law, where the statute of limitations is an absolute barrier to action against the accused. For example, the June 26, 2003, decision of the U.S. Supreme Court in *Stogner v. California*, which struck down a California law restricting the statute of limitations for some sex crimes, resulted in the dismissal of charges against some priests. Canon law's bias is that a rupture in the community has to be repaired even if penal action is barred, and hence the extrajudicial option remains.

On the other hand, the congregation may review the case file, and any accompanying submissions from the bishop, and conclude there isn't any warrant for proceeding. In that case, the congregation will direct that the priest should either be reinstated to his position or, in any event, returned to active ministry. In July 2003, Fr. Philip Feltman of the Toledo archdiocese became the first American priest to be reinstated following a finding of insufficient evidence. Most observers expect there will be other such cases, and it's an open question how public opinion in the United States will react. News reports suggest that Feltman's congregation cheered his return.

As of this writing, the Congregation for the Doctrine of the Faith was preparing a set of guidelines about the ongoing obligations of dioceses to former priests even after dismissal from the clerical state. The idea is that a diocese should not simply dump an abuser on the wider community. The Vatican is also preparing to take another look at the American norms after the two-year review called for by the U.S. bishops. Some officials believe that a quiet, case-by-case relaxation of the zero tolerance stance may result from that review. This is based in part on evidence from therapists. St. Luke Institute claims a 4 percent recidivism rate for priests it has treated and released. Although this figure reflects only instances of abuse reported either to the police or the Church, and the actual number of new acts of abuse could be higher, nevertheless it suggests that treatment and follow-up supervision can be successful in at least some cases. Other observers, however, believe that public pressure and the interests of the broader community will make any relaxation of the zero tolerance standard impossible, even if the Holy See should favor it.

In terms of civil litigation, the damage to the Catholic Church has been enormous. In terms of settlements that are a matter of public record, Catholic dioceses have paid out between $138 million and $173.5 million. This, however, is the tip of the iceberg, because only a couple dozen dioceses out of the 195 in the United States have disclosed how much their settlements have cost. *Forbes* magazine estimated in June 2003 that the Church in the United States has paid a total of $1 billion either in jury-awarded damages or settlements to end lawsuits, and projected that the eventual price tag would be $5 billion. In the Boston archdiocese, personnel have been laid off and fifteen properties are up for sale in an attempt to offset costs related to litigation.

A similar toll is being taken across the country. The Worcester, Massachusetts, diocese acknowledged in January 2003 that it had spent $2.1 million settling lawsuits related to sexual abuse by priests. In June 2003, the Louisville, Kentucky, archdiocese agreed to pay $27.5 million to 243 people who accused priests of child sexual abuse. In 1997 the Dallas diocese was hit with a $120 million jury verdict in the case of former priest Rudy Kos, which was eventually negotiated down to $30 million. To date no American diocese has declared bankruptcy as a result of sexual abuse litigation, but several, including Boston, Dallas, and Santa Fe, have seriously considered the option. They have held back in part in fear of the ripple effects for other dioceses, since insurers and credit agencies might be more reluctant to do business with Catholic dioceses once the precedent is set that they can default on their obligations. The millions of dollars being consumed by dioceses on litigation is obviously money that otherwise could be spent on building church facilities, educating students, or feeding the hungry.

The total number of lawsuits pending against Catholic dioceses in the United States as of this writing was estimated to be 1,500, representing thousands of alleged victims. Attorneys who specialize in this kind of litigation, such as Roderick MacLeish Jr. of Boston, Jeffrey Anderson of Minneapolis, and Raymond Boucher of Beverly Hills, themselves represent hundreds of clients. MacLeish alone has won some $30 million for more than one hundred clients in the past decade. Boucher has a website with a secure form for alleged victims to submit information as potential clients. Moreover, these attorneys predict that success in litigation against the Catholic Church will prompt victims of sexual abuse by agents of other social institutions to come forward, including schools, day-care centers, the entertainment industry, and even the Boy Scouts. Some legal experts believe the eventual impact of sex abuse litigation may be measured in the tens of billions of dollars.

Though this book is not the place to develop the point, it's important to note that while the dimensions of the sexual abuse crisis are perhaps greater in the United States, this is not an "American problem." To take just a few examples, Archbishop Juliusz Paetz of Poznan in Poland was accused in 2002 of sexually abusing seminarians, and stepped down from office on March 28. Cardinal Hans Hermann Gröer of Vienna was forced to resign in 1995 after similar accusations. The Roman Catholic Church in Ireland agreed in 2002 to pay the equivalent of $110 million to compensate thousands of victims of molestation in church-run schools and child-care centers over most of the last century. Thirty French priests have been convicted in recent years of pedophile activities and eleven are currently in prison. One French bishop, Pierre Pican of Bayeux, received a suspended three-month jail sentence for failing to report the conduct of a priest who was allegedly engaged in sexual abuse. In October, then-Archbishop George Pell of Sydney, Australia, now a cardinal, was cleared after suspending himself when faced with charges of sexual abuse. More than ninety priests and church employees have been convicted of sexual abuse in Australia over the last decade. A former Catholic brother in Australia, for example, was recently jailed for ten years for a series of sexual assaults against young children from 1975 to 1999. Examples could be taken from all over the world. My newspaper, National Catholic Reporter, broke a story two years ago concerning the sexual abuse of nuns by priests in Africa and elsewhere. No one whose eyes are open can pretend that the phenomenon of sexual abuse within the Catholic Church is restricted to American airspace.

The financial and legal dimensions of the American crisis, despite the difficulty of obtaining precise data, are in many ways far easier to establish than the human and spiritual costs. Few would argue the point, however, that the Catholic Church in the United States has been badly damaged and that it will likely be the work of a generation or more to recover. Many U.S. bishops had no doubt hoped that with the December 13, 2002, resignation of Cardinal Bernard Law, the dramatic arc of the sex abuse story had come to a close. Many signals gave them reasons for optimism, above all the fact that media interest in the story dropped off dramatically in the early months of 2003. As the year wore on, however, indicators suggested a much longer shelf life for the story. Chief among them were the burgeoning lawsuits in the Los Angeles archdiocese, bringing with them the potential for more explosive revelations of documents unsealed by court order, such as the ones that had originally triggered the crisis in Boston. The deal struck by Phoenix Bishop Thomas O'Brien with Maricopa County to avoid criminal prosecution, followed by his arrest on a hit-and-run charge and resignation from office, further sullied the public image of the Church at a critical moment. With the Church still facing hundreds of lawsuits, and new accusations continuing to emerge, it seems clear that the close of the sexual abuse crisis is not at hand.

Moreover, the Church in the United States does not appear to have reached anything like a consensus on the root causes of the crisis. Public debate seems polarized between leftists who blame a clerical culture of secrecy, a hierarchy that looks more to Rome than to the local community, and celibacy; and their right-wing counterparts who blame tolerance for doctrinal dissent, asleep-at-the-switch bishops, anything-goes sexual morality, and homosexuality. Not only do these perspectives seem to be moving further apart, but it is increasingly difficult to identify spaces in the public life of the Church in the United States where people who hold these views are engaged in conversation with one another. The drift seems to be a more fragmented and divided American Catholicism—sociologically, one could make the argument that there are in fact three or four American Catholic "churches."

The crisis has generated a new literary genre of insta-books devoted to the scandals, from George Weigel's *The Courage to Be Catholic:*

Crisis, Reform, and the Future of the Catholic Church (Basic Books, 2002) and Fr. Benedict Groschel's *From Scandal to Hope* (Our Sunday Visitor, 2002), representing the conservative view, to *Sacred Silence: Denial and the Crisis in the Church* by Fr. Donald Cozzens (The Liturgical Press, 2002) and *Toward a New Catholic Church: The Promise of Reform* by James Carroll (Houghton Mifflin, 2002), embodying the liberal perspective. Each book is well written, thoughtful, and contains useful insights. They should be read by anyone seeking to understand the situation facing the American Church. At the same time, however, each reads like it could have been written before the crisis began. In a sense, the books were written before the crisis, because they present familiar points of view from each of the authors. Weigel decried doctrinal dissent well before he knew who John Geoghan and Paul Shanley were; and likewise, Cozzens thought clericalism was a serious woe long before Boston's Cardinal Bernard Law ever gave a deposition. The books thus become a battleground for familiar ideological duels. Where Weigel exonerates celibacy, Cozzens challenges it. Cozzens allows that there is no "inherent relationship, in itself, between Catholic clergy abuse and celibacy," but goes on to say, "it may foster or reinforce, at least in some, the very psychosexual immaturity that leads to compulsive and diverse manifestations of destructive behavior." Where Weigel scoffs at the notion that an "authoritarian church" played any role, Cozzens is sure of it. Cozzens condemns the "sacred silence" imposed by church leaders and laments the "feudal, clerical culture of secrecy."

The status quo in American Catholicism, therefore, seems to be an ongoing crisis that is exacting massive financial, legal, human, and spiritual costs, and a Catholic community badly divided as to how to analyze what has happened. In this context, the frequent misunderstandings between the American street and the Holy See have been an important factor in aggravating and prolonging the crisis. It is to that story we now turn.

THE VATICAN RESPONSE TO THE AMERICAN CRISIS: A CHRONOLOGY

This section provides a chronological review of events involving the exchange between the United States and the Holy See connected to the American sex abuse crisis. In certain cases the items below summarize interviews given by foreign prelates to the respected Italian Catholic magazine *30 Giorni*, to the *National Catholic Reporter*, or other news outlets. While some of these prelates are not Vatican officials, they are included because these interviews were widely read and discussed in the Vatican, and they often gave voice to views held by many in the Holy See.

December 2001 The Catholic News Service and the *National Catholic Reporter* reported that under a papal *motu proprio* entitled *Sacramentorum Sanctitatis Tutela* and dated May 18, 2001, but not previously disclosed, John Paul had assigned exclusive canonical authority over cases of sexual abuse of a minor by a priest, along with five other grave crimes, to the Congregation for the Doctrine of the Faith. This action predated the eruption of the current American scandals, but was in part motivated by a desire to bring the handling of these cases in other countries in line with procedures established in the United States. Under the rules, bishops were required to report probable sexual abuse of minors by priests to the congregation, which can decide to let a local tribunal handle the case or to take it up in Rome. The rules imposed strict secrecy, extended the canonical statute of limitations for this crime to ten years from the accuser's eighteenth birthday, and specified that such cases must be handled by priest-staffed courts. In addition to sexual abuse of minors, the new rules assigned several other matters to the doctrinal office, including sacrilege of the Eucharist, forbidden concelebration with Protestant ministers, and abuse of the sacrament of penance, including cases in which a priest uses the pretext of confession to solicit sexual favors.

February 2002 In an interview with *30 Giorni,* then-secretary of the Congregation for the Doctrine of the Faith, Italian Archbishop Tarcisio Bertone commented on the new Vatican norms. (Bertone has since become the Cardinal of Genoa.) Among other points, he suggested that the desire for financial payoffs was fueling the American litigation. "Even though the absolutely negative judgment on this behavior remains even if the acts happened 30 or 40 years ago, there is a well-founded suspicion that some of these charges, that arise well after the fact, serve only for making money in civil litigation," he said. Bertone called it a "strange fact" that in the United States the Church is forced under civil law to pay for the misdeeds of single individuals. "This ordinarily doesn't happen, and shouldn't happen," he said. Bertone criticized proposals to make bishops "automatic reporters" of abuse allegations, arguing that a priest should be able to confide in his bishop without fear of being denounced to the police or other civil authorities. "In my opinion, the demand that a bishop be obligated to contact the police in order to denounce a priest who has admitted the offense of pedophilia is unfounded," Bertone said. "Naturally civil society has the obligation to defend its citizens. But it must also respect the 'professional secrecy' of priests, as it respects the professional secrecy of other categories, a respect that cannot be reduced simply to the inviolable seal of the confessional. If a priest cannot confide in his bishop for fear of being denounced," Bertone said, "then it would mean that there is no more liberty of conscience."

March 3, 2002 In an interview on the sexual abuse crisis published in the *New York Times,* Vatican spokesman Joaquin Navarro-Valls cited canon law on homosexuality and said, "People with these inclinations just cannot be ordained" as priests. Navarro-Valls compared the situation of a man with homosexual inclinations who becomes a priest to that of a man with the same affliction who marries. Just as such a marriage can be annulled, he said, the ordination might similarly be invalid. (Canon lawyers later said that this argument is incorrect since sexual orientation is not one of the conditions for a valid ordination.) Navarro-Valls also insisted that the Vatican was not out of touch with regard to the American crisis. "We're very well aware of the dimension and implications of the problem," Navarro said, "very well aware." He said the Pope was distressed by the scandals. "He has shown tremendous sadness, a very physical sadness that affected his whole body and said, 'How can this happen?' "

March 13, 2002 Archbishop John Foley, president of the Vatican's Pontifical Council for Social Communications, suggested that "the best defense against the crisis is virtue, and in the absence of virtue, candor." Foley spoke at St. Charles Borromeo Seminary in Philadelphia. "The real tragedy of the present crisis, apart from the undermining of confidence in the Church and her clergy from such terrible actions and such revelations, is not embarrassment for the Church. It is the fact of a grave offense against God and a grave offense against God's children," he said. Foley added: "We truly need holy priests, priests who are pure in thought, word and deed; priests who are men of prayer; priests who are generous in service; priests who are self-giving, self-sacrificing; priests who are dedicated to making known the saving knowledge and love of Jesus."

March 21, 2002 John Paul II made his first public comment since the crisis broke on January 6 in his annual Holy Thursday letter to the priests of the world. "As priests, we are personally and profoundly afflicted by the sins of some of our brothers who have betrayed the grace of ordination in succumbing even to the most grievous forms of the *mysterium inquitatis* [mystery of evil] at work in the world," the Pope wrote. "Grave scandal is caused, with the result that a dark shadow is cast over all the other fine priests who perform their ministry with honesty and integrity and often with heroic self-sacrifice. . . . As the church shows her concern for the victims and strives to respond in truth and justice to each of these painful situations, all of us . . . are called to commit ourselves more fully to the search for holiness."

The Pope's letter was presented at a news conference by Colombian Cardinal Dario Castrillón Hoyos, head of the Congregation for Clergy, the Vatican office that supervises priests. Castrillón Hoyos and his top aide, Archbishop Csaba Ternyák, read statements commenting on the Pope's letter, which was mostly about the sacrament of reconciliation. When they finished, Navarro-Valls invited a large group of reporters, including many Americans, to ask questions. My questions were:

- Will the Vatican support a zero tolerance policy, under which any credible allegation of sexual misconduct against a priest means he is automatically removed from ministry?
- Will the Vatican support an automatic reporter policy, under which any credible allegation of sexual misconduct against a priest is automatically reported to the civic authorities?
- What is the status of proposals, widely circulated and debated within the Vatican in recent months, to ban the admission of homosexuals to Catholic seminaries?
- Does the Vatican still have full confidence in Cardinal Bernard Law of Boston or is there consideration of asking him to resign?

Robert Mickens of *The Tablet*, an English Catholic journal, wanted to know why the language in the papal letter about the sexual abuse problem was indirect. Stephen Weeke of NBC asked why the Pope wasn't speaking himself, rather than signing a letter and having someone else talk about it.

Castrillón Hoyos took notes, jotting down each question as it was asked. After the reporters had finished, he then declined to answer the questions. "I don't want to take more risks than are necessary," he said, and instead produced a two-page prepared statement which he said was the only response he could offer. The statement made two points: few priests are guilty of this sort of misconduct, and the Catholic Church has long had strong policies against sexual abuse by clergy. He cited the 1917 *Code of Canon Law* as evidence.

Castrillón Hoyos added to his prepared statement several times, however, in the course of reading it aloud. First, when Castrillón Hoyos started to speak, he observed that most of the questions had been put to him in English. "That in itself is an X ray of the problem," he said. The comment was taken as an indirect way of presenting the sexual abuse issue as an American or Anglo-Saxon problem. Then, in arguing that the Catholic Church has never ignored the problem of sexual abuse, Castrillón Hoyos added that this was true "even before it ended up on the front page of newspapers." Citing provisions of the *Code of Canon Law* that fix penalties for sexual misconduct with minors, Castrillón Hoyos issued a challenge: "For the non-Catholic world, I want to know what other institutions have laws like this for defending children from the behavior of officials? What other great institution?" In noting that the Church had recently adopted a statute of limitations of ten years from the date when an alleged victim turns eighteen for prosecuting sexual misconduct cases against priests, Castrillón Hoyos asked: "I would like to know, has this been legislated elsewhere?" Still later, in describing new Vatican norms that insist priests should have a right of reply to charges of abuse, Castrillón Hoyos said: "We live in an era of human rights, not totalitarianism. This is an era of law." At the end, Castrillón Hoyos defended the Church's preference for "keeping things within the family," which does not, he said, mean that the Church refuses to cooperate with the state, except when it comes to its sacramental secret. He then expressed the Pope's solidarity with the priests and bishops of the United States, but said nothing about victims.

April 8–13, 2002 Bishop Wilton Gregory, president of the U.S. bishops' conference, Vice-President Bishop William Skylstad, and Secretary-General Monsignor William Fay attended a week-long series of meetings in the Vatican. This regular biannual visit had been scheduled before the sexual abuse crisis erupted, but conversations were dominated by the scandals. "The Holy Father is an extraordinary pastor of souls," Gregory said afterward to the media. "Given the level of anxiety and anguish, this has touched him deeply." Gregory insisted that the

Vatican was engaged in the crisis. "We came away from these conversations with a strong sense of the Holy See's desire to listen and to support our efforts," he said. The Pope communicated a desire to help the American church "at this difficult moment," Gregory said. "He extended his hand in support to the bishops of the United States. The Holy See has demonstrated an extraordinary openness in understanding the particular situation that we face in the United States."

April 15, 2002 The Vatican announced that Pope John Paul II had called the American cardinals to Rome, along with Gregory and Skylstad, for an extraordinary two-day summit on the sexual abuse crisis, April 23–24. The news triggered a flood of speculation in the U.S. press about likely Vatican concerns and American responses. The eight residential American cardinals who attended were: William Keeler of Baltimore; Bernard Law of Boston; Francis George of Chicago; Adam Maida of Detroit; Roger Mahony of Los Angeles; Edward Egan of New York; Anthony Bevilacqua of Philadelphia; and Theodore McCarrick of Washington, D.C. The American cardinals had been called to Rome as a group previously in 1989 to discuss the situation of divorced and civilly remarried Catholics, and in December 1996 the seven American cardinals active at the time went to the Vatican en masse to try to resolve a liturgical dispute. Also to take part in the summit were the three American cardinals resident in Rome: James Francis Stafford, president of the Pontifical Council for the Laity; Edmund Szoka, president of the government of the Vatican City-State; and William Baum, retired.

April 23–24, 2002 The forty-eight-hour Vatican summit took place. On the Vatican side, eight officials took part. Cardinals Angelo Sodano, secretary of state; Joseph Ratzinger, head of the Congregation for the Doctrine of the Faith; Giovanni Battista Re, head of the Congregation for Bishops; Jorge Medina Estévez, of the Congregation for Divine Worship; Castrillón Hoyos; Archbishops Julian Herranz, head of the Pontifical Council for the Interpretation of Legislative

Texts; Tarcisio Bertone, secretary of the doctrinal congregation; and Francesco Monterisi, secretary of the Congregation for Bishops. Media interest from the United States was intense, with one portion of the large piazza in front of St. Peter's Square cordoned off for all the satellite trucks dispatched by American networks.

The Pope received the participants in an audience the first day and lunched with them the second day. He spoke to the American bishops April 23, and the key phrase from his address for policy purposes was the following: "People need to know that there is no place in the priesthood and religious life for those who would harm the young." The sentence was widely taken by the American bishops and in the press as a green light for a zero tolerance stance.

The full text of the Pope's remarks:

1. Let me assure you first of all that I greatly appreciate the effort you are making to keep the Holy See, and me personally, informed regarding the complex and difficult situation which has arisen in your country in recent months. I am confident that your discussions here will bear much fruit for the good of the Catholic people of the United States. You have come to the house of the Successor of Peter, whose task it is to confirm his brother Bishops in faith and love, and to unite them around Christ in the service of God's People. The door of this house is always open to you. All the more so when your communities are in distress. I too have been deeply grieved by the fact that priests and religious, whose vocation it is to help people live holy lives in the sight of God, have themselves caused such suffering and scandal to the young. Because of the great harm done by some priests and religious, the Church herself is viewed with distrust, and many are offended at the way in which the Church's leaders are perceived to have acted in this matter. The abuse which has caused this crisis is by every standard wrong and rightly considered a crime by society; it is also an

appalling sin in the eyes of God. To the victims and their families, wherever they may be, I express my profound sense of solidarity and concern.

2. It is true that a generalized lack of knowledge of the nature of the problem and also at times the advice of clinical experts led bishops to make decisions which subsequent events showed to be wrong. You are now working to establish more reliable criteria to ensure that such mistakes are not repeated. At the same time, even while recognizing how indispensable these criteria are, we cannot forget the power of Christian conversion, that radical decision to turn away from sin and back to God, which reaches to the depths of a person's soul and can work extraordinary change. Neither should we forget the immense spiritual, human and social good that the vast majority of priests and religious in the United States have done and are still doing. The Catholic Church in your country has always promoted human and Christian values with great vigor and generosity, in a way that has helped to consolidate all that is noble in the American people. A great work of art may be blemished, but its beauty remains; and this is a truth which any intellectually honest critic will recognize. To the Catholic communities in the United States, to their Pastors and members, to the men and women religious, to teachers in Catholic universities and schools, to American missionaries in all parts of the world, go the wholehearted thanks of the entire Catholic Church and the personal thanks of the Bishop of Rome.

3. The abuse of the young is a grave symptom of a crisis affecting not only the Church but society as a whole. It is a deep-seated crisis of sexual morality, even of human relationships, and its prime victims are the family and the young. In addressing the problem of abuse with clarity and determination, the Church will help society to understand and deal with the crisis in its midst. It must be absolutely clear to the

Catholic faithful, and to the wider community, that bishops and superiors are concerned, above all else, with the spiritual good of souls. People need to know that there is no place in the priesthood and religious life for those who would harm the young. They must know that Bishops and priests are totally committed to the fullness of Catholic truth on matters of sexual morality, a truth as essential to the renewal of the priesthood and the episcopate as it is to the renewal of marriage and family life.

4. We must be confident that this time of trial will bring a purification of the entire Catholic community, a purification that is urgently needed if the Church is to preach more effectively the Gospel of Jesus Christ in all its liberating force. Now you must ensure that where sin increased, grace will all the more abound (cf. Rom 5:20). So much pain, so much sorrow must lead to a holier priesthood, a holier episcopate and a holier Church. God alone is the source of holiness, and it is to him above all that we must turn for forgiveness, for healing and for the grace to meet this challenge with uncompromising courage and harmony of purpose. Like the Good Shepherd of last Sunday's Gospel, Pastors must go among their priests and people as men who inspire deep trust and lead them to restful waters (cf. Ps 22:2). I beg the Lord to give the Bishops of the United States the strength to build their response to the present crisis upon the solid foundations of faith and upon genuine pastoral charity for the victims, as well as for the priests and the entire Catholic community in your country. And I ask Catholics to stay close to their priests and Bishops, and to support them with their prayers at this difficult time. The peace of the Risen Christ be with you!

Sodano also made a statement to the American prelates at the opening of the two-day session. Sodano said:

I wish to open this meeting with the words of Psalm 133, which we often sing: "*Ecce quam bonum et quam iucundum habitare fratres in unum,*" "How good and how pleasant it is when brothers live in unity" (v. 1). This is a distressing time for the Church and for all of us. Still, the joy of Easter must be the disposition of our heart and the source of our confidence in addressing the present difficulties. It is true that the immediate reason for this fraternal meeting of the Pastors of various particular Churches in the United States of America with the Holy Father and some of his collaborators is our common concern about what has emerged so forcefully in the last three months. It is a sign of charity to "rejoice with those who rejoice and weep with those who weep," "*gaudere cum gaudentibus et fiere cum flentibus,*" as Saint Paul wrote to the Romans (Rom 12: 15).

As we begin this meeting, the Holy Father has asked me to convey greetings to you, the Cardinals and Bishops from the United States. He has urged me to assure you of the importance he attaches to this meeting, in which we will study the many issues involved and share our pastoral experience. As you are well aware, this meeting has come about for two purposes. On the one hand, a number of American Bishops expressed a desire to inform the Holy See of the difficulties in which they have found themselves in these last months. On the other, the various Roman Dicasteries also wish to hear at first hand from the American Cardinals and the leading officials of the United States Conference of Catholic Bishops an overall evaluation of the situation.

We have come together today, conscious of the great responsibility which Christ has laid upon us for the good of God's People. Let us not be disheartened by the difficulties involved; let us seek the way forward in fidelity to the great tradition of the Church, Mother and Teacher, instrument of justice, mercy, and redemption. Our task is to reflect on the problems of the present moment with great openness of spirit, knowing that the Church should be transparent. The Church loves the truth, and must always put it into practice in charity, following what St Paul taught nearly two thousand years ago: "*veritatem facientes in caritatem*" (Eph 4:15).

The summit produced two documents: a letter from the American bishops to U.S. priests, and a final communiqué outlining areas of agreement between the American cardinals and the officials of the Roman Curia.

The letter read:

We, the Cardinals of the United States and the Presidency of the National Conference of Catholic Bishops, gathered with our brother Cardinals of the Roman Curia around the Successor of Peter, wish to speak a special word to you, our brother priests who give yourselves so generously from day to day in service of God's people. At our meeting, you have been very much in our minds and hearts, for we know the heavy burden of sorrow and shame that you are bearing because some have betrayed the grace of Ordination by abusing those entrusted to their care.

We regret that episcopal oversight has not been able to preserve the Church from this scandal. The entire Church, the Bride of Christ, is afflicted by this wound—the victims and their families first of all, but also you who have dedicated your lives to "the priestly service of the Gospel of God" (Rom 15:16). To all of you we express our deep gratitude for all that you do to build up the Body of Christ in holiness and love. We pledge to support you in every possible way through these troubled times, and we ask that you stay close to us in the bond of the priesthood as we make every effort to bring the healing grace of Christ to the people whom we serve.

We are in complete harmony with the Holy Father when he said in his address yesterday: "Neither should we forget the immense spiritual, human and social good that the vast majority of priests and religious in the United States have done and are still doing. . . . To the Catholic communities in the United States, to their Pastors and members, to the men and women religious, to teachers in Catholic universities and schools, to American missionaries in all parts of the world, go the wholehearted thanks of the entire Catholic Church and the personal thanks of the Bishop of Rome."

As we look to the future, let us together beg the eternal High Priest for the grace to live this time of trial with courage and confidence in the Crucified Lord. This echoes the summons of our Ordination: "Imitate the mystery you celebrate; model your life on the mystery of the Lord's Cross" (Rite of Ordination); and it is a vital part of what we now offer the Church as she passes through this time of painful purification. From the house of the Successor of Peter, who has confirmed us in our faith, we wish in turn to confirm you in the humble and exalted service of the Catholic priesthood to which we have been called. Peace be with you!

The final communiqué read:

On April 23–24, 2002, an extraordinary meeting was held in the Vatican between the Cardinals of the United States and the leadership of the United States Catholic Conference of Bishops and the heads of several offices of the Holy See on the subject of the sexual abuse of minors.

The meeting was called with three goals in mind:

• On the part of the American Bishops, to inform the

Holy See about the difficulties which they have faced in recent months,

- On the part of the Roman Dicasteries, to hear directly from the American Cardinals and the chief officials of the United States Conference of Catholic Bishops a general evaluation of the situation,
- And together to develop ways to move forward in addressing these issues.

As is known, the Holy Father received the working group in his private library late in the morning of Tuesday, April 23, and gave a programmatic address. Today, at the end of the morning session, His Holiness invited the American cardinals and bishops to lunch, to continue their discussion of some of the themes raised at the meeting. The participants first of all wish to express their unanimous gratitude to the Holy Father for his clear indications of direction and commitment for the future. In communion with the Pope they reaffirm certain basic principles:

1) The sexual abuse of minors is rightly considered a crime by society and is an appalling sin in the eyes of God, above all when it is perpetrated by priests and religious whose vocation is to help persons to lead holy lives before God and men.

2) There is a need to convey to the victims and their families a profound sense of solidarity and to provide appropriate assistance in recovering faith and receiving pastoral care.

3) Even if the cases of true pedophilia on the part of priests and religious are few, all the participants recognized the gravity of the problem. In the meeting, the quantitative terms of the problem were discussed, since the statistics are not very clear in this regard. Attention was drawn to the fact

that almost all the cases involved adolescents and therefore were not cases of true pedophilia.

4) Together with the fact that a link between celibacy and pedophilia cannot be scientifically maintained, the meeting reaffirmed the value of priestly celibacy as a gift of God to the Church.

5) Given the doctrinal issues underlying the deplorable behavior in question, certain lines of response have been proposed:

> a) the Pastors of the Church need clearly to promote the correct moral teaching of the Church and publicly to reprimand individuals who spread dissent and groups which advance ambiguous approaches to pastoral care;
>
> b) a new and serious Apostolic Visitation of seminaries and other institutes of formation must be made without delay, with particular emphasis on the need for fidelity to the Church's teaching, especially in the area of morality, and the need for a deeper study of the criteria of suitability of candidates to the priesthood;
>
> c) it would be fitting for the Bishops of the United States Conference of Catholic Bishops to ask the faithful to join them in observing a national day of prayer and penance, in reparation for the offenses perpetrated and in prayer to God for the conversion of sinners and the reconciliation of victims.

6) All the participants have seen this time as a call to a greater fidelity to the mystery of the Church. Consequently they see the present time as a moment of grace. While recognizing that practical criteria of conduct are indispensable

and urgently needed, we cannot underestimate, in the words of the Holy Father, "the power of Christian conversion, that radical decision to turn away from sin and back to God, which reaches the depths of a person's soul and can work extraordinary change." At the same time, as His Holiness also stated, "People need to know that there is no place in the priesthood and religious life for those who would harm the young. They must know that bishops and priests are totally committed to the fullness of Catholic truth on matters of sexual morality, a truth as essential to the renewal of the priesthood and the episcopate as it is to the renewal of marriage and family life." Again in the Holy Father's words, "Neither should we forget the immense spiritual, human and social good that the vast majority of priests and religious in the United States have done and are still doing. The Catholic Church in your country has always promoted human and Christian values with great vigor and generosity, in a way that has helped to consolidate all that is noble in the American people. A great work of art may be blemished, but its beauty remains; and this is a truth which any intellectually honest critic will recognize. To the Catholic communities in the United States, to their pastors and members, to the men and women religious, to teachers in Catholic universities and schools, to American missionaries in all parts of the world, go the wholehearted thanks of the entire Catholic Church and the personal thanks of the Bishop of Rome."

For this reason, the cardinals and bishops present at the meeting today sent a message to all the priests of the United States, their coworkers in the pastoral ministry.

As part of the preparation for the June meeting of the American bishops, the United States participants in the Rome meeting presented to the Prefects of the Roman Congregations the following proposals:

1) We propose to send the respective congregations of the Holy See a set of national standards which the Holy See will properly review (*recognitio*), in which essential elements for policies dealing with the sexual abuse of minors in dioceses and religious institutes in the United States are set forth.

2) We will propose that the United States Conference of Catholic Bishops recommend a special process for the dismissal from the clerical state of a priest who has become notorious and is guilty of the serial, predatory, sexual abuse of minors.

3) While recognizing that the *Code of Canon Law* already contains a judicial process for the dismissal of priests guilty of sexually abusing minors, we will also propose a special process for cases which are not notorious but where the diocesan bishop considers the priest a threat for the protection of children and young people, in order to avoid grave scandal in the future and to safeguard the common good of the Church.

4) We will propose an Apostolic Visitation of seminaries and religious houses of formation, giving special attention to their admission requirements and the need for them to teach Catholic moral doctrine in its integrity.

5) We will propose that the bishops of the United States make every effort to implement the challenge of the Holy Father that the present crisis "must lead to a holier priesthood, a holier episcopate, and a holier Church" by calling for deeper holiness in the Church in the United States, including ourselves as bishops, the clergy, the religious, and the faithful.

6) We propose that the bishops of the United States set aside a day for prayer and penance throughout the Church in the United States, in order to implore reconciliation and the renewal of ecclesial life.

Though neither document mentioned an expanded role for laypeople in reviewing and implementing policies on sexual abuse, McCarrick said in response to an *NCR* question at a concluding press conference that this was an editing oversight. Stafford said there were "constant references" inside the summit to the need to bring laity into the process, "both from the Curia and from the U.S." The news conference was broadcast live on CNN and other press outlets in the United States.

April 29, 2002 Spanish Archbishop Julian Herranz, president of the Pontifical Council for the Interpretation of Legislative Texts and a participant in the summit, addressed the American crisis in a speech in Milan. Herranz called large Church payouts for clerical misconduct "unwarranted," and criticized a climate of "exaggeration, financial exploitation and nervousness" in the United States. Herranz also complained of a "tenacious scandalistic style" in the American press. Certain media outlets, he suggested, seek to "sully the image of the Church and the Catholic priesthood, and to weaken the moral credibility of the magisterium." Herranz referred to pedophilia as a "concrete form of homosexuality." He underscored the need to protect the due process rights of all parties, including the accused priest, referring both to canon law and to the 2001 *motu proprio* centralizing juridical responsibility for sexual abuse of a minor in the Congregation for the Doctrine of the Faith. "To ignore these processes," Herranz said, "or other penal or disciplinary measures that must be taken in order to prohibit or limit the pastoral activity of those priests about whom there are serious indications of behaviors of this sort, would denote a lack of the most fundamental sense of justice." He called the demand for bishops to report priests to civil authorities an "unwarranted simplification." He said, "When ecclesiastical authorities deal with these delicate problems, they not only must respect the presumption of innocence, they also have to honor the rapport of trust, and the consequent secrecy of the office, inherent in relations between a bishop and his priest collaborators. Not to honor these exigencies would bring damages of great seriousness for the Church."

May 1, 2002 In an interview with the Italian Catholic magazine *30 Giorni*, Cardinal Oscar Rodriguez Maradiaga of Honduras, widely seen as a leading candidate to be the next Pope, addressed the American crisis. He blamed the American press for "persecution" of the Church. "We all know that Ted Turner is openly anti-Catholic, and he is the owner not just of CNN but also Time-Warner," Rodriguez said. "This is to say nothing of dailies such as the *New York Times,* the *Washington Post* and the *Boston Globe,* protagonists of what I do not hesitate to call a persecution against the Church." Rodriguez suggested this persecution served political ends. "In a moment in which the attention of the mass media was focused on what was happening in the Middle East, the injustices directed against the Palestinian people, the TV and the newspapers in the United States became obsessed with sexual scandals that happened forty years ago, thirty years ago. Why? I think it has to do with these motives: What Church has received Arafat the most and has called for the creation of a Palestinian state the most? What Church has never accepted that Jerusalem should be the indivisible capital of the state of Israel, but must be the capital of the three great monotheistic religions? What Church opposes abortion, euthanasia, and the death penalty? What Church does not accept projects for the family that are not in keeping with God's plan? It's the Catholic Church," Rodriguez said. "It is the only one, to put it this way, that stands in the way of a dehumanizing political program. Only in this fashion can I explain the ferocity that reminds me of the times of Nero and Diocletian, and more recently, of Stalin and Hitler."

Rodriguez called for a tempered approach to sexual abuse. "If there are priests, or also bishops, who are stained by grave sins they must be punished with the appropriate canonical penalties, and if necessary, must also face civil justice," Rodriguez said. But this must happen, he said, without a "witch hunt" inside the Church. "We bishops must not forget that we are merciful pastors and not agents of the FBI or CIA. We must always ask how Jesus would conduct himself. Pedophilia is an illness, and it is just that whoever has it should leave the priesthood. But the accusations must always be proved with a just process, and without persecution from the civil authorities, which is what is actually happening."

In this context, Rodriguez came to the defense of Cardinal Bernard Law. "I know him well," Rodriguez said. "He is a man who has done much good for us in Latin America, and now we suffer for him and we suffer for the injustice of what is defined as justice. I heard that the judge who is conducting the case is one who supports all the feminist movements," Rodriguez said, in an apparent reference to Judge Constance M. Sweeney of the Massachusetts Superior Court, who had been assigned responsibility for the sex abuse complaints filed against the Boston archdiocese. "Thus it happened," Rodriguez said, "that despite the fact that cases in the United States take a long time, Cardinal Law was quickly subjected to interrogation using methods that recall the most dark times of Stalinist processes against churchmen in Eastern Europe. Then transcripts from these interrogations were put into circulation on the Internet and published with great emphasis by all the big dailies. I don't agree with this theatrical form of justice. This is not justice, I repeat, this is persecution."

May 2, 2002 Ratzinger called on the American bishops to perform a public day of penance connected to the sexual abuse scandal. Ratzinger had not been available to the press during the April 23–24 summit. He spoke on this occasion at a May 2 Vatican news conference concerning a new apostolic letter on the sacrament of reconciliation. In his prepared remarks, Ratzinger spoke of the need for "purification and pardon." He was asked by reporters if that idea might apply to the American bishops committing a public act of penance for their mishandling of cases of sexual abuse by priests. Vatican press officer Joaquin Navarro-Valls attempted to deflect the question, saying that there were two press sessions dedicated to the American situation last week. Ratzinger, however, said he would respond.

"The American bishops have already decided on a day of expiation, which will probably be the feast of the Sacred Heart of Jesus," Ratzinger said. The feast fell on Friday, June 7. "It will be an act of purification which can promote the idea of expiation in the daily life of Christians. Such a public act takes note of the reality of sin and invites us to think about sin and mercy. Above all, it can promote a praxis of penitence, focusing on both education and prevention against these human failings. It can renew our sense of the sacrament [of reconciliation] that the Lord offers us." Later in the news conference, Ratzinger described the two-day summit with the Americans as "very opportune, very fraternal." He said it offered an opportunity for "understanding points of view that are somewhat diverse. We understand the situation better, the roots of the situation, and the responses to give to it. The American bishops are now working on a national standard which will have to receive the formal approval of the Holy See."

May 16, 2002 Rodriguez was in Rome to receive an honorary doctorate from the Pontifical Salesian University (he is a member of the Salesian religious order). Rodriguez, fifty-nine, appeared at a May 16 press conference and spoke again about the crisis.

"I have my doubts about the motivation behind some of these scandals," said Rodriguez, who has lived and studied in the United States. "Obviously, someone who has the sickness of pedophilia should not be in the priesthood. But why bring up these things now from 40 or 30 years ago? [The U.S.] is a society that has such compartmentalized information, such closed information. Often when you watch TV news, so many of the themes are local, there's very little international coverage. Why in this moment of terrible conflict in the Middle East do these scandals surface, creating a polarization in the media that is almost obsessive? I have said in other places, and I'm not afraid to say it, that obsession is a mental illness that causes us to get blocked on one theme and to keep moving around it forever. Why is it that they bring these skeletons out of the closet?

"We know well that every time money mixes with justice it becomes unjust," Rodriguez said. "When I was in the United States in the 1970s, there was a fashion when one slipped on a sidewalk to sue the owner of the house for millions. This became a kind of industry. I remember that people used to put on a neck brace and go find a lawyer. Eventually this was prevented by putting up signs saying, 'Sidewalk is wet.' So why now is there such interest in taking up these cases from the past? Because there is money in play. But we know that money doesn't heal any wound. Only psychological and spiritual accompaniment can help. If it were up to me, I would give the money neither to the lawyers nor even to the victims, but to a fund to help accompany people in a spiritual and psychological way, to help to heal them. This would be a real healing. That's the reality.

"Pedophilia is a sickness, and those with this sickness must leave the priesthood," Rodriguez said. "But we must not move from this to remedies that are non-Christian. I think the world should reflect. We must ask, where is Jesus in all this? For me it would be a tragedy to reduce the role of a pastor to that of a cop. We are totally different, and I'd be prepared to go to jail rather than harm one of my priests. I say this with great clarity." Rodriguez added that he feels the Church will exit from the crisis "more humble and more strong," with "a new pastoral approach" that is "closer to the people, which always does us good."

Speaking of calls for bishops to report accusations against priests to the civil authorities, Rodriguez said, "We must not forget that we are pastors, not agents of the FBI or CIA. Our attitude must be that people can change, that this can happen every day of our life, and that to the very end our goal is to save people. I don't know the situation of 40 years ago, but we can imagine what was the basic level of sexual education in the seminaries when they could not talk about this because it was perceived as something wrong. Today there is a different type of education, and we can speak about it with much greater clarity. Many of the psychological implications were not known at that time. At times they even thought the seminary was a kind of tube where you enter on one side and exit ordained. This kind of thinking no longer exists. Some of these priests, and I say it with much respect, did not have the opportunity of psychological consultation, and therefore they can also be victims. As far as judging is concerned, that is very difficult. We can judge the exterior facts, but not the interior life of the person. We must always have a pastoral, Christian attitude."

May 18, 2002 Fr. Gianfranco Ghirlanda, dean of the canon law department at Rome's Gregorian University, published an article in *Civiltà Cattolica* on the issue of sex abuse by clergy. *Civiltà Cattolica* is a twice-monthly Jesuit-edited journal considered a semiofficial Vatican organ because it is reviewed by the Secretariat of State prior to publication. Ghirlanda wrote that if bishops decide to reassign a priest who had previously committed an act of sex abuse but who the bishop believes will not reoffend, the bishop should not tell the priest's new congregation about his past. He argued that a priest whose abuse was revealed "would be totally discredited in front of his parochial community and in fact would be blocked from any effective pastoral action." Ghirlanda also denied that bishops or religious superiors are responsible for abuse by priests. "From a canon law perspective, the bishop and the superior are neither morally nor judicially responsible for the acts committed by one of their clergy," he wrote. In an apparent reference to civil suits, Ghirlanda wrote that the relationship between bishops or superiors and priests is not comparable to that of an employer and employee. "The cleric doesn't 'work' for the bishop or for the superior, but is at the service of God," Ghirlanda wrote. He also said Church leaders confronted with accusations of abuse should first attempt to resolve the problem informally. "Only if these methods prove useless, the bishop and the superior may move ahead with the judicial process," Ghirlanda said. He added, "The cleric's right of good name must be protected by the bishop and superior. Therefore any act that has public repercussions, undertaken by the bishop or superior in dealing with one of his clerics, is legitimate only if the good of the community requires it and if the bishop and superior have reached moral certainty." Ghirlanda also wrote that priests should not be forced to take psychological tests to assess the likelihood of their committing abuse. "To our thinking, it's not admissible that the incriminated cleric be forced to undergo a psychological investigation to determine if his personality is inclined to commit the crimes in question," the article said.

June 1, 2002 Cardinal Norberto Rivera Carrera of Mexico City, in an interview with *30 Giorni,* echoed Rodriguez's comments on the American crisis. "Not only in the United States but also in other parts of the world, one can see underway an orchestrated plan for striking at the prestige of the Church. Not a few journalists have confirmed for me the existence of this organized campaign," he said. "Cardinal Rodriguez expresses well the common sentiment of many of us, cardinals and bishops, in Latin America, in the context of what appears to us to be a generalized and ungenerous attack on the U.S. Church." Rivera Carrera said that he is a "great friend" of Cardinal Bernard Law and that as a Latin American he feels a special responsibility to defend the U.S. Church when under fire. Rivera Carrera added that up to now there has been no "documented denunciation" alleging priestly sexual abuse of minors in Mexico. "Certainly the men of the Church have their defects, their sins, like everyone," Rivera Carrera said. "If necessary, and after a regular process, they must suffer the eventual canonical censures and the civil penalties that they deserve. But this does not authorize anyone to put into effect a generalized program of ferocious persecution against the U.S. Church. Reviewing church history, one can see that many persecutions started precisely with the moral delegitimization of its members and of its hierarchy, with the aim of disqualifying the Church and dismantling its prestige. This is what happened in the early centuries of Christian history, with Nero for example. This is what happened in the past century with the persecutions in Mexico, in Spain, in Nazi Germany, and in Communist countries. It is this that seems to be happening today in the United States." Asked to respond to American journalists such as E. J. Dionne of the *Washington Post* and Tom Fox of the *National Catholic Reporter* who had written that Rodriguez could no longer be considered a papal candidate because of his comments, Rivera Carrera said: "Archbishop Rodriguez Maradiaga, as a cardinal, is always *papabile,* as are naturally all the members of the

Sacred College. . . . Fortunately, in a conclave, which I hope will not happen for a long time, only the cardinals will participate, and not those gentlemen whose overly aggressive opinion in this regard I firmly believe will not be taken into consideration."

June 1, 2002 *Civiltà Cattolica* carried an unsigned editorial complaining of "morbid and scandalous curiosity" in the American media with respect to the priest sex abuse crisis. Noting the large number of satellite trucks American TV networks parked outside the Vatican during the April 23–24 summit meeting, the article warned of an "anti-Catholic" and "antipapal" spirit in the United States. "For many newspapers and television stations," *Civiltà Cattolica* said, "it seemed too good to be true to be able to slap the 'monster' of the day on the front page, this time identified in the Catholic clergy." The article said it was not seeking to minimize the problem, which it called a "tragedy" for the Church in the United States. But it asked why the American Church is subject to a "cross fire of suspicions, violent accusations, recriminations, and demands for million-dollar settlements, as if the phenomenon of pedophilia was restricted to the Catholic clergy."

June 8, 2002 Cardinal Jan Schotte of Belgium, head of the Synod of Bishops, told the *National Catholic Reporter* ahead of the U.S. bishops' meeting in Dallas that he was concerned about their response to the crisis. Schotte's main fear was that under the weight of intense media criticism, lawsuits, and public pressure, the bishops might adopt ad-hoc solutions, thereby "forgetting general principles." Those principles, Schotte said, were laid out by Ghirlanda in his *Civiltà Cattolica* article of May 18. Schotte expressed reservations about calls for quasi–automatic cooperation with the police and the courts. He said that in Belgium the bishops had successfully resisted demands to turn over their records about priests accused of misconduct, on the grounds that these are confidential Church documents. (A Belgian Church spokesperson later said, however, that Schotte had been confused, because in five cases in Belgium involving priests accused of sexual abuse of a minor, the

Church had to turn over its files each time. What Schotte may have been thinking, the spokesperson said, is that the Church resisted demands to pay damages to victims of sexual abuse on the grounds that the bishop is not a parish priest's "employer.")

June 14, 2002 The U.S. bishops in Dallas adopted a Charter for the Protection of Children and Young People and a set of Essential Norms for Diocesan/Eparchial Policies Dealing with Allegations of Sexual Abuse of Minors by Priests or Deacons. The norms envision bishops removing priests from ministry on the basis of their administrative authority. That penalty would apply for even one act of sexual abuse of a minor, the so-called zero tolerance standard. The *National Catholic Reporter* posted a news article the same day quoting Vatican officials with reservations about the policy. " 'One strike and you're out' assumes that it's a complete swing," one official said. "But let's face it, there are cases in which someone makes an accusation and later retracts it. Are you going to defrock every priest against whom there is even one allegation?" Another said, "They're being forced into a conclusion rather than sorting things out in a dispassionate way. The Church is about reconciliation. Its highest priority can't be driving out the pedophiles." One canon lawyer who works with several Vatican offices said that he picked up a "cautiousness," a "reserve," in the Curia about the policies under consideration by the U.S. bishops. "There is a real sense that all this may not pass muster," the canon lawyer said. Another Vatican official said one frustration is the apparent desire of the American bishops to create new policies and procedures rather than follow the steps outlined in canon law for imposing discipline upon a priest who commits sexual abuse. "The bishops may say it's too complicated," the official said. "But how many of them have actually tried it? My guess would be it's a small number."

July 1, 2002 Cardinal Juan Sandoval Íñiguez, sixty-nine, of Guadalajara, Mexico, addressed the American crisis with *30 Giorni*. "First of all, I want to say that every crime committed against children is abhorrent, and an ecclesiastic who stains himself with this sin must be ready, after a regular procedure, to suffer the canonical penalties, and if necessary the civil penalties, that he deserves," Sandoval said. "What is happening in the United States, however, apart from very rare cases, regards not pedophilia but homosexuality. I have to say it is surprising that present-day society, which is pleased enough with homosexuality to organize 'gay pride' events in all the great cities of the world, becomes enraged against priests accused of this vice.

"Priests must be saints. That's what the Lord wants and what his Church desires. In fact, it's what everyone wants, even those who don't believe. Thus today's world does not apply to priests the same Christian mercy and human understanding it concedes to others. However, it's necessary to remember that there have always been scandals in the Church, and there always will be, and not just regarding the sixth commandment. The men of the Church also have original sin. The Lord Jesus himself was betrayed, denied, and abandoned by his apostles. . . . I agree fully with what has been said by these two brother cardinals [Rodriguez and Rivera Carrera]. It's a matter of a persecution unleashed by the powerful of the world. The motives? The powerful don't like what the Church affirms and testifies to regarding the defense of life and of the family. For the powerful of the world, the positions of the Church against the financial strangulation of the countries of the Third World and in favor of the millions and millions of robbed and exploited poor don't go down well. The powerful also won't tolerate the balanced position of the Church regarding the dramatic situation in the Holy Land."

July 19, 2002 In my Word from Rome column, I quoted unidentified Vatican officials who had suggested that Jewish bias against the Catholic Church may play a role in American media coverage of the scandals. "In part, the hypothesis reflects the pro-Palestinian slant of much European public opinion, which has long vilified America's 'Jewish lobby.' In part, it reflects the strained Catholic/Jewish relationship in the wake of the beatification of Pius IX, the acrimonious debate over Pius XII and his alleged 'silence' during the Holocaust, and the collapse of a Jewish-Catholic scholarly commission empanelled by the Vatican to investigate its World War II archives. In such an atmosphere, it's easy for some around the Vatican to imagine that influential Jews in the American press might want to wound the church," I wrote.

July 28, 2002 Before a crowd of some 1 million young people gathered at Toronto's Downsview Park for the concluding Mass of World Youth Day, John Paul II again addressed the sexual abuse scandals. The relevant passage from his homily was: "If you love Jesus, love the Church! Do not be discouraged by the sins and failings of some of her members. The harm done by some priests and religious to the young and vulnerable fills us all with a deep sense of sadness and shame. But think of the vast majority of dedicated and generous priests and religious whose only wish is to serve and do good! There are many priests, seminarians and consecrated persons here today; be close to them and support them! And if, in the depths of your hearts, you feel the same call to the priesthood or consecrated life, do not be afraid to follow Christ on the royal road of the Cross! At difficult moments in the Church's life, the pursuit of holiness becomes even more urgent." When the Pope pronounced the word *but,* signaling a shift from contrition to defense of the Church, he drew it out for emphasis, eliciting strong cheers from the crowd.

September 1, 2002 In an interview with *30 Giorni,* Cardinal Miguel Obando Bravo of Nicaragua spoke on the American crisis. "It's as if the Church in the United States is being rocked by a hurricane," Obando Bravo said. "The winds have knocked down the spotted apples, but have also caused the good fruit to come up early. My brothers in the episcopate in the United States are singled out as those who covered up the presumed malfeasance of priests accused of the crime of sexual abuse. Their situation can be understood by reference to exemplary cases recounted in the Bible itself. Let's take the example of Potiphar's wife as told in chapter 39 of Genesis, when Joseph is imprisoned by the Egyptians because he's unjustly accused by the woman of having seduced her. The reasons that drive Potiphar's wife to lie are pleasure, spite, and unrequited love. I don't want to deny the drama of the authentic victims of sexual abuse, and in this case the ecclesiastics who are marred with these horrible crimes must suffer the appropriate canonical censures, and, if it's the case, must also confront civil justice. But one can't hide the fact that in some cases we're dealing with presumed victims who want to gain large payoffs on the basis of calumnious accusations.

"It seems to me that in this moment the Church in the United States is living through a heroic moment, of bloodless martyrdom. Of persecution. The Church swims against the current when it comes to the protection of life, sexual morality, conjugal morality, and bioethics. These are all fields in which the magisterium of the Church is not popular in certain environments. This does not mean that the Church is wrong in these areas. Rather it means that in its proclamation in these areas the Church is up against huge economic interests that see in it a mortal enemy. The cardinal of Washington, [D.C.,] Theodore McCarrick, recently offered an analysis of why the theme of the sexual abuse by priests has occupied the front pages of the newspapers for so long and has had such a notable impact in society. For McCarrick, there are two reasons, one good and one bad. He explained that the good one is, 'that the people expect much of priests.' The bad one is, 'there are many, in our society, and among them some powerful people, who see in the Catholic Church an enemy in questions connected to life, such as abortion, euthanasia, and assisted suicide. They think that by attacking the Church they reduce its credibility, and in this way the words of the bishops will be ignored,' " Obando Bravo said.

"Cardinal Law is a pastor who certainly participates in the pain of the victims of sexual abuse. We in Nicaragua know him very well. We know well his generosity. It's also thanks to his help that we were able to build the cathedral in Managua where we can glorify the Creator. And when Hurricane Mitch devastated our lands, he came personally to visit the affected families and contributed amply to feeding the population and rebuilding in the damaged zones. Those who attack him today don't recognize the value of his commitment, the weight of his burden, and the coherence of his life. Despite everything, I believe that the Catholics of Boston know that however much a nugget of gold may be buried in mud, when the mud is washed away, the gold continues to shine."

October 14, 2002 As news outlets had anticipated, the Vatican indicated that changes would be necessary before Rome could approve the U.S. bishops' norms on sexual abuse adopted in Dallas. The rejection came in a letter from Cardinal Giovanni Battista Re, prefect of the Congregation for Bishops, to Bishop Wilton Gregory, president of the U.S. bishops' conference. Re's letter expressed "full solidarity with the bishops of the United States in their firm condemnation of sexual misdeeds against minors." It went on, however, to cite "confusion and ambiguity" in the norms, to assert that the Dallas texts "contain provisions which in some aspects are difficult to reconcile with the universal law of the Church," and "vague or imprecise" terminology that is "difficult to interpret." In an October 18 news briefing, Gregory listed the three key issues: the role and powers of lay review boards, the definition of sexual abuse, and due process guarantees for accused priests. A unique mixed commission, composed of four representatives from the Vatican and four American bishops, was formed to hammer out a resolution of the issues before the full meeting of the U.S. bishops in Washington, D.C., November 11–14. The men chosen to represent the Vatican on the commission were Herranz, Bertone, Castrillón Hoyos, and Monterisi. U.S. prelates chosen were: Chicago Cardinal Francis George; San Francisco Archbishop William Levada; Rockford, Illinois, Bishop Thomas Doran; and Bridgeport, Connecticut, Bishop William Lori. Gregory said in his comments to the press that Re had proposed the commission and he had accepted.

October 30, 2002 Vatican spokesperson Navarro-Valls released a statement indicating that the commission had completed its work, but he revealed nothing in terms of how it had resolved differences between the Dallas norms and the *Code of Canon Law.* "On the days of October 28 and 29, the mixed commission of the Holy See and the bishops' conference of the United States of America met in the Vatican for the revision of the 'norms,' " Navarro's statement read.

November 4, 2002 The mixed commission released the results of its work. Those results included:

1. A more restrictive standard for what constitutes "sexual abuse." The move followed complaints that the definition in Dallas was so broad as to include a wide range of behaviors that, while inappropriate, do not necessarily justify permanent removal from ministry. In place of the "physical and non–physical interactions" definition in the Dallas charter borrowed from the Canadian bishops' document *From Pain to Hope* of 1992, the commission reverted to the language currently in the *Code of Canon Law*: "An external, objectively grave violation of the Sixth Commandment." By way of explanation, the commission added that, "a canonical offense against the Sixth Commandment need not be a complete act of intercourse. Nor, to be objectively grave, does an act need to involve force, physical contact, or a discernible harmful outcome."

2. A clarification of the powers and status of lay review boards. Norm 4 from Dallas had read: "To assist the diocesan/eparchial bishop in his work, each diocese/eparchy will have a review board." The revised norms read: "Each diocese/eparchy will also have a review board that will function as a confidential consultative body to the bishop/eparch in discharging his responsibilities." The change in wording emphasizes that these boards are consultative only and that it is the diocesan bishop who has responsibility for priestly discipline. The revised document also drops norm 6 from Dallas, which called for the creation of appellate boards at a regional level. The mixed commission felt these boards would conflict with the role of existing appellate courts under the *Code of Canon Law.*

3. Insistence on canonical trials. Instead of automatic removal from ministry as soon as an accusation of sexual abuse surfaces, the re-

vised norms call on the bishop to conduct a "preliminary investigation in harmony with canon law." If the accusation appears credible, the priest is to be suspended from ministry, and even prohibited from celebrating Mass in public. The bishop is also to report the case to the Congregation for the Doctrine of the Faith, in keeping with the papal *motu proprio* of May 18, *Sacramentorum Sanctitatis Tutela*. That document gives the congregation the authority to take up the case itself or to remand it to a local church court. The assumption was that local ecclesiastical tribunals would generally handle American cases, although experience in 2003 suggested there may be fewer trials than originally anticipated because in many concrete instances of clear guilt the congregation seemed inclined to authorize an extrajudicial solution.

November 11–14, 2002 The U.S. bishops met in Washington and adopted the Essential Norms for Diocesan/Eparchial Policies Dealing with Allegations of Sexual Abuse of Minors by Priests or Deacons as revised by the mixed commission.

November 21, 2002 *The National Catholic Reporter* published the full text of the norms governing "grave delicts" including sexual abuse of minors decreed by Pope John Paul II's May 18, 2001 *motu proprio* titled *Sacramentorum Sanctitatis Tutela*. Previously these norms had been released by the Vatican only on a confidential, case-by-case basis. Canon lawyers able to examine the document for the first time concluded that it generally did not create conflicts with the norms adopted by the American bishops.

November 25, 2002 Cardinal Julio Terrazas Sandoval of Bolivia, a Redemptorist, was in Rome for the plenary assembly of the Pontifical Council for the Laity and spoke at a press conference. He was asked if he agreed with what his fellow Latin American cardinals had said about the American crisis. "I have of course heard the opinions of my fellow cardinals," Terrazas Sandoval replied. "I don't know the situation well, but it does seem there is an institution in [U.S.] society that has as its goal to speak ill of the Church. In Bolivia, we hear there is a tendency [in the United States] to overgeneralize about the Church. There seems to be a morbid focus on bad news. I don't know if this is an accurate impression, but some news reports certainly create doubts in those who read them. There seems to be an effort to demonize situations and movements."

November 30, 2002 Cardinal Joseph Ratzinger, prefect of the Congregation for the Doctrine of the Faith, addressed the American crisis during an appearance in Murcia, Spain. The occasion was the congress "Christ: Way, Truth and Life," over which the cardinal presided, at the Catholic University of St. Anthony. The cardinal was asked, "This past year has been difficult for Catholics, given the space dedicated by the media to scandals attributed to priests. There is talk of a campaign against the Church. What do you think?" His response: "In the Church, priests also are sinners. But I am personally convinced that the constant presence in the press of the sins of Catholic priests, especially in the United States, is a planned campaign, as the percentage of these offenses among priests is not higher than in other categories, and perhaps it is even lower. In the United States, there is constant news on this topic, but less than 1 percent of priests are guilty of acts of this type. The constant presence of these news items does not correspond to the objectivity of the information or to the statistical objectivity of the facts. Therefore, one comes to the conclusion that it is intentional, manipulated, that there is a desire to discredit the Church." Ratzinger's assertion concerning "less than 1 percent of priests" appears to have been based on an analysis by Philip Jenkins, which concluded that 3 percent of priests have engaged in sexual abuse and 0.3 percent are pedophiles. As noted above, other analysts have suggested slightly higher percentages on both points.

November 31, 2002 Representatives of the Conference of Major Superiors of Men, the American federation of men's orders, voiced concern in Rome that the revised U.S. norms may compromise the autonomy traditionally enjoyed by religious communities. The objections came at an assembly of the Union of Superiors General, the worldwide umbrella group for men's orders, and in Vatican meetings in early December. On December 1, the USG voted to give full backing to the position taken by the Conference of Major Superiors of Men. The top officers of the American federation, Conventual Franciscan Fr. Canice Connors, president, and Marist Fr. Ted Keating, executive director, came to Rome to present their objections. Worries included that diocesan bishops might try to compel superiors to divulge confidential information on priests, might seek to block even an internal assignment with the order, or try to revoke a priest's authorization to say Mass within the community. Some bishops may also seek to prevent international members from entering the United States. In addition, since religious communities generally do not have canonical tribunals as dioceses do, it was not entirely clear how religious superiors were to proceed. Religious order priests were not covered by the norms adopted by the U.S. bishops in Dallas in June. However, when the norms were revised by the mixed commission, religious priests were included through a little-noticed change in the document's first footnote. Leaders in religious life discovered the switch only on November 5, prompting urgent requests for dialogue with the U.S. bishops and an appeal to the Vatican. Meanwhile, Connors and Keating drew an appreciative response at the USG meeting for the general way religious orders had approached the problem. One superior general said he had been contacted by U.S. diocesan priests to express gratitude for the stand taken by the Conference of Major Superiors of Men in Philadelphia in August, when it was decided that priest abusers would be removed from public ministry but not necessarily from their communities.

December 4, 2002 Respected Vatican affairs writer Orazio Petrosillo addressed the conference of the International Catholic Union of the Press (UCIP). During a roundtable discussion, Petrosillo, who writes for the Rome daily *Il Messagero* and who teaches journalism at the Center for Interdisciplinary Communication Studies at the Gregorian University, responded to the question, "Why has the mass media mounted this campaign against the Church?" Though Petrosillo is Italian, he spoke in French. Petrosillo indicated three groups in the United States that may have inspired such a campaign: "Masonic lodges," "Jewish lobbies," and "groups of free thought and free morals" such as gays. As for the Jews, Petrosillo specified that their motive would be "to punish the Catholic Church for its defense of the right of the Palestinians to have a country." Petrosillo said he was only giving voice to what "everyone thinks," while acknowledging that one can't make conclusive judgments on the basis of circumstantial evidence.

December 13, 2002 Cardinal Bernard Law resigned in Rome. He remains, however, a member of the College of Cardinals in good standing. As a cardinal, Law continues to be a member of several congregations, the key decision-making organs of the Vatican, which handle matters related to the sexual abuse crisis. They include: the Congregation for Bishops, which recommends new bishops to the Pope and oversees the performance of bishops and bishops' conferences; the Congregation for Clergy, which handles clerical discipline and oversees the financial management of dioceses, including the prospect of bankruptcy; the Congregation for Consecrated Life, which has the same responsibility for religious orders; the Congregation for Catholic Education, which oversees seminaries and priestly formation; and the Congregation for Divine Worship, which handles cases of laicization of priests. Law's membership means that, at least theoretically, he could still be involved in setting Vatican policy on these issues. Law also remains the Holy See's ecclesiastical delegate, overseeing the pastoral provision in the United States for priests and laity from the Episcopal Church seeking communion with the Roman Catholic Church. In this capacity he oversees the ordination of married Episcopal priests as Roman Catholic priests, and the establishment of personal parishes for faithful who wish to maintain Episcopalian liturgical traditions. This function is under the jurisdiction of the Congregation for the Doctrine of the Faith.

December 16, 2002 The Congregation for Bishops granted the *recognitio,* or formal legal approval, to the American sexual abuse norms as approved by the November meeting of the U.S. bishops in Washington, D.C. The decree is published in Latin and dated December 8. Because the U.S. bishops established that after two years of application the norms would be reexamined, the Vatican *recognitio* is valid for a period of two years. The clock started running from the effective date of March 2003, meaning the norms expire in March 2005. The decision is announced in the form of a letter from Re to Gregory. The text of the letter:

> With your letter dated November 15, 2002, you requested the *recognitio* for the *Essential Norms for Diocesan/Eparchial Policies Dealing with Allegations of Sexual Abuse of Minors by Priests or Deacons,* approved by the Episcopal Conference at the Plenary Assembly of the United States Conference of Catholic Bishops which took place in Dallas on June 13–15, and revised in the recent General Meeting held in Washington on November 11–14. I am pleased now to send you the Decree of *recognitio* for the "Essential Norms" and wish to express renewed and sincere appreciation for the pastoral concern and resolve with which the bishops of the United States have addressed the distressing situation caused by such aberrant crimes.
>
> The Holy See is fully supportive of the bishops' efforts to combat and to prevent such evil. The universal law of the Church has always recognized this crime as one of the most serious offenses which sacred ministers can commit, and has determined that they be punished with the most severe penalties, not excluding—if the case so requires—dismissal from the clerical state (cf. Canon 1395 § 2). Moreover, the Holy Father in the year 2001 already had determined that this crime should be included among the most serious delicts (*graviora delicta*) of clerics, to underscore the Holy See's aver-

sion to this betrayal of the trust which the faithful rightly place in Christ's ministers, and to ensure that the guilty will be appropriately punished. He therefore gave to the Congregation for the Doctrine of the Faith a special competence in this matter, applicable for the whole Church, establishing a particular procedure to be followed (cfr. *Motu proprio Sacramentorum sanctitatis tutela* of May 18, 2001).

As the Holy Father has affirmed on various occasions, the Holy See is spiritually united to the victims of abuse and to their families, and encourages particular concern for them on the part of the bishops, priests, and the whole Catholic community. This closeness is now once again confirmed through the approval of the present "Essential Norms," which will help to restore, wherever necessary, the trust of the faithful in their pastors, assuring at the same time the defense of the innocent and the just punishment of the guilty. The "Essential Norms" in their present formulation are intended to give effective protection to minors and to establish a rigorous and precise procedure to punish in a just way those who are guilty of such abominable offenses because, as the Holy Father has said, "there is no place in the priesthood and religious life for those who would harm the young." At the same time, by ensuring that the true facts are ascertained, the approved Norms protect inviolable human rights—including the right to defend oneself—and guarantee respect for the dignity of all those involved, beginning with the victims. Moreover, they uphold the principle, fundamental in all just systems of law, that a person is considered innocent until either a regular process or his own spontaneous admission proves him guilty.

The genuine ecclesial communion between the Episcopal Conference and the Apostolic See, demonstrated once again in these painful circumstances, prompts us all to pray earnestly to God that from the present crisis might emerge, as the Holy Father has stated: "a holier priesthood, a holier episcopate, and a holier Church" (cf. *L'Osservatore Romano*, 24 April 2002). In this way, the bonds of communion which unite the bishops with their priests and deacons, and the faithful with their pastors, will be further strengthened. The Holy See, moreover, together with the bishops of the United States, feels duty-bound in justice and in gratitude to reaffirm and defend the good name of the overwhelming majority of priests and deacons who are and have always been exemplary in their fidelity to the demands of their vocation but have been offended or unjustly slandered by association. As the Holy Father has said, we cannot forget "the immense spiritual, human and social good that the vast majority of priests and religious in the United States have done and are still doing." Indeed, it appears necessary to devote every available resource to restoring the public image of the Catholic priesthood as a worthy and noble vocation of generous and often sacrificial service to the People of God.

As regards religious priests and deacons I would ask the representatives of the Episcopal Conference to continue to meet with the representatives of the Conference of Major Superiors of Men to examine more closely the various aspects of their particular situation, and to forward to the Holy See whatever agreements they may reach.

February 7, 2003 John Paul II signed a set of revisions to *Sacramentorum Sanctitatis Tutela* designed to speed up trials of accused priests and to make it easier to remove guilty priests from the clerical state. The changes allow deacons and laypeople to serve on criminal tribunals in the Catholic Church, even as judges. The changes cite canon 1421, which stipulates that on a three-judge panel, one judge may be a layperson. Under the May 18 *motu proprio,* those roles had been restricted to priests. The changes also drop the requirement that tribunal members must have a doctorate in canon law, insisting only that they hold the lesser degree of a licentiate and have worked in tribunals for "a reasonable time." Both moves should expand the pool of judges and lawyers and make it easier to form tribunals. The changes also give the Congregation for the Doctrine of the Faith the power in "clear and grave" situations to dismiss someone from the priesthood without a trial. That administrative power had belonged only to the Pope himself. The congregation also acquired the power to "sanate," meaning clean up, procedural irregularities in the acts of a local tribunal. That means that if a case comes to Rome on appeal on procedural grounds, the problem can be resolved without remanding the case for a new trial. The changes permit a recourse, or appeal, against decisions of the congregation only to the regular Wednesday assembly of cardinal members of the congregation. All other appeals are excluded, meaning that the congregation's decisions are final.

March 26, 2003 In a personal message to three Boston-area men who said they are victims of sexual abuse by Catholic priests, John Paul II vowed that he "realizes the seriousness of the problem" and "will see that this doesn't happen again." Monsignor James Green, a senior official in the Secretariat of State, carried the Pope's message to the men, who had arrived in Rome on March 23 seeking a meeting with John Paul. The three were Gary Bergeron and Bernie McDade, who claim to have been abused by the same priest, and Joseph Bergeron, Gary's father, who said he was abused as an altar boy by another priest. Green visited the men at their hotel ten minutes from the Vatican at 6:30 P.M. Green opened the meeting by praying an Our Father. He then presented the Pope's message. "The Holy Father realizes the seriousness of this problem, and is doing all he can," Bergeron said Green told them, saying they were free to share the message with other victims. "[The Pope] will continue to do all he can to heal the Church and to pray for the victims. He will see that this doesn't happen again."

Bergeron said Green then said that John Paul had instructed him to ask if the men had any message for the Pope. Joseph Bergeron spoke first. "The Holy Father needs to make sure that this never, ever, ever happens to another child," he said. McDade followed. "The Holy Father needs to heal the Church, not just the survivors but the Church itself. He needs to realize how the Church in the United States is hurting." Gary Bergeron concluded. "The Holy Father needs to put a face with the problem, meaning he needs to meet with us," he said. "If not me, meet with my father. If not him, then some victim he can associate with the problem. Only then will he understand the depth of the wound." Bergeron said the session was "very intense, very emotional," but that he would continue to press for a personal meeting with John Paul.

April 2–5, 2003 The Holy See sponsored a unique four-day, closed-door symposium on pedophilia. An April 5 Vatican statement said the meeting featured eight of "the most qualified experts on the theme." There were four Germans, three Canadians, and an American. All eight, in what planners described as a coincidence, were non-Catholic. The chief organizer of the symposium was Dr. Manfred Lütz, a member of the Pontifical Council for the Laity and a psychiatrist from Germany. The idea, according to participants, was to expose Vatican officials to "state-of-the-art information" from a scientific point of view. Participants included officials from the Congregation for the Doctrine of the Faith and Secretariat of State, as well as from the Vatican congregations for clergy, religious, and Catholic education. The lone American expert was Dr. Martin P. Kafka of the Harvard Medical School, whose field is sexual impulsivity disorders.

During question and answer periods, discussion touched upon not merely pedophilia but the broader phenomenon of sexual abuse. On the question of a possible connection between homosexuality and the abuse of adolescent males, Vatican officials were told that homosexuality is a risk factor, but not the cause, of this behavior. In other words, while homosexuality is statistically associated with a higher incidence of sexual contact with teenage boys, so are other factors, such as being within five years of having been ordained. The experts asserted that there is no causal link between being homosexual and abuse. One Vatican official said that this message came through "loud and clear" and predicted that it might help delay, or even derail, a document on the admission of homosexuals to Catholic seminaries. Vatican observers were also struck by criticism of zero tolerance policies, suggesting that it may lead to guidelines about support of priests after they are removed from ministry.

Kafka told the *National Catholic Reporter* afterward that homosexuality was not the main focus of the meeting, though there was interest in the subject. "A risk factor is not a cause," he said. "The great predominance of homosexual males are in no way sexual abusers," Kafka said. "We don't really know in a scientific way what the factors are" that cause abuse, Kafka said. "We don't have the evidence." Other topics, Kafka said, included whether more effective screening could filter out potential abusers, and what promise rehabilitation programs might hold. Kafka said the experts were not optimistic about a "magic bullet" screening program. Presenters also stressed the need for open discussion of sexuality among young priests, and improving the ongoing supervision of priests. "As a non-Catholic, I was impressed with the deep, genuine concern about the issue, the willingness to be open and listen, and the proactive approach to doing the right thing," Kafka said. "I was very encouraged by this meeting."

June 18, 2003 Bishop Thomas J. O'Brien resigns in Phoenix after being arrested on charges of fleeing the scene of an auto accident. O'Brien was taken into custody two days after the car he had been driving was involved in an incident in which a forty-three-year-old pedestrian died. The news came just two weeks after O'Brien made a deal with county prosecutors to avoid criminal charges for his handling of sex abuse charges against Phoenix priests. Though the Vatican did not make any formal comment, one source told *NCR* that this O'Brien affair "weighed heavily" upon the Holy See.

June 19–21, 2003 The U.S. bishops met in St. Louis amid controversy over the resignation of former Oklahoma governor Frank Keating as head of the National Review Board. Apostolic nuncio Archbishop Gabriel Montalvo gave the meeting's opening address. "We all know that we are going through difficult times and that some real problems within the Church have been magnified to discredit the moral authority of the Church," said Montalvo, a Colombian. Montalvo referenced the Book of Wisdom to advise the bishops: "As gold in the furnace he proved them!" Fire, said Montalvo, "can quickly reduce to ashes what was built in years," though it also has "the power to purify and to draw out from the earth that which is precious and rich." Montalvo urged the bishops to look to examples of those in the Church who had dealt with crisis. He pointed to Pope John XXIII's determination to continue to support the Second Vatican Council despite "criticisms that were expressed by bishops and cardinals who felt that this initiative would disrupt the Church and prove to be a fiasco." Likewise, said Montalvo, Pope Paul VI, through his encyclical *Humanae Vitae,* "never shrunk from proclaiming and teaching the truth about the dignity of human life" even "in the face of vocal opposition and awful dissent." And Pope John Paul II, said Montalvo, though "visibly weakened and limited by his physical condition, continues to press forward on the mission to which he has been called by almighty God."

July 1, 2003 The Holy See announces the appointment of Bishop Sean O'Malley of Palm Beach, Florida, as the new archbishop of Boston. Vatican sources cited O'Malley's experience in dealing with the sexual abuse crisis in Palm Beach and also in Fall River, Massachusetts, his positive public image in the Boston area, and his Capuchin Franciscan spirituality in explaining the appointment.

July 7, 2003 Rodriguez revisited his comments on the American crisis in an interview in Rome with the *National Catholic Reporter.* "I don't repent," Rodriguez said. "Maybe I was a little strong, but sometimes it's necessary to shake things up." Rodriguez said that he did not question the suffering of victims of sexual abuse, or deny the failures of some bishops to intervene. What he wanted to raise, he said, is a question of emphasis. In the context of massive global poverty and injustice, does sexual abuse by Catholic priests merit the extensive coverage it received in the American press? "Many people said that I am against the media, but this isn't true," Rodriguez said. "Sexual abuse is heartbreaking and victims deserve compassion. What I'm against is the lack of global perspective." Rodriguez also said he hopes the crisis is teaching the American bishops a new style of leadership. "Bishops of the First World sometimes saw themselves as related to wealth, power, and privilege," Rodriguez said. "I've even seen that in the Vatican, where First World bishops are sometimes treated with more respect than bishops from the Third World, because they are seen as VIPs. . . . Perhaps this is calling the bishops to become servants, closer to the people," he said.

July 29, 2003 The *Worcester Telegram and Gazette* reported on a 1962 Vatican document titled *Crimen Sollicitationis,* which decreed that canonical investigations of various sorts of sexual misconduct by priests, especially as it pertained to the confessional, were to be covered by pontifical secrecy. Excommunication was the penalty for violations. CBS gave the story national exposure on August 6 with a segment that began: "For decades, priests in this country have abused children in parish after parish while their superiors covered it all up. Now it turns out the orders for this coverup were written in Rome at the highest levels of the Vatican." Canon lawyers and Church spokespersons, however, said that the document imposed secrecy only on canonical procedures, and did not prohibit anyone from reporting criminal acts by priests to the police. Moreover, the document's relative obscurity and short duration in force meant, these sources said, that it did not set the pattern in the Church for the handling of sex abuse cases. The Vatican had no official comment, but on background spokespersons echoed the analysis of canon lawyers and the U.S. bishops' conference.

August 23, 2003 John Geoghan was murdered by an inmate at a prison in Shirley, Massachusetts. Geoghan had been held in protective custody, but still had some limited contact with other inmates. The Vatican had no official comment, but Herranz gave an interview to the

Roman daily *La Repubblica* on August 25 in which he referred to the death as a "painful" incident. "As soon as I heard, I prayed for his soul and for his aggressor," Herranz said. Asked what lesson the Church might draw from the episode, Herranz replied, "That there is always the reality of sin in the world, in this case the sin of homicide. What caused this we don't know. We can't judge. Now all is in the hands of God, the Supreme Judge: only he knows how to judge because he knows that even the most persistent sinner in the end can repent. Maybe Geoghan in prison had already begun to repent for the evil he did." Asked if the Holy See was succeeding in crushing the problem of pedophilia in the Church, Herranz said, "The drama of pedophilia is a problem that doesn't regard just priests of the Catholic Church, but the entire society. It's enough to look on the Internet. I don't understand why it's talked about only with the Church, as if somebody wants to sully its image in order to take away its moral force." The reporter then said that priestly pedophilia in the American Church was a reality that couldn't be ignored. Herranz responded, "That's true. But pedophilia is only minimally identified with the Church, touching scarcely 1 percent of priests. Meanwhile for other categories of persons, the percentages are much higher. In any event, this is a very painful question for the Church, because the Church is the first to condemn pedophilia as an abominable crime and for this reason has launched a very severe discipline with tough disciplinary measures, which are difficult to equal in other civil societies."

SPANNING THE CULTURAL GAP
BETWEEN ROME AND AMERICA

As is clear from the above chronology, the Holy See responded to the American sexual abuse crisis at times with deep doubts about the cultural forces in the United States driving the scandals, as well as reservations about some responses from the American bishops. At the same time, discussion in the American press and on the American Catholic street was often fueled by assumptions about why the Vatican was acting, or not acting, that inflamed passions. Often, neither side trusted the other.

At the outset, it should be said that both formulas used here—the Vatican and the American Catholic street—are ideal types to which no actual person or community perfectly corresponds. As discussed in chapter 2 and throughout this book, not everyone in the Vatican thinks the same way, and this has been true of the American situation as well. At critical junctures, such as what response to give to the Dallas norms or what policy to adopt on the admission of homosexuals to the priesthood, there have been serious internal disagreements within the Holy See. At the same time, as noted above, American Catholics are also divided on what caused the crisis and what to do about it. In contrasting Roman and American attitudes, it should be understood that we are talking about clusters of ideas rather than specific persons or institutions. Many Americans are sympathetic to elements of the Roman diagnosis, and many Vatican officials are open to much of what America would regard as essential to addressing the crisis.

The aim of this section is to engage in an act of translation, so that both the Holy See and the American Catholic community can understand what the other party is trying to say. One may not agree with any given sentiment that comes from the American Church, or any given decision from the Holy See, but these matters cannot be discussed constructively until the values that motivate the proposals and decisions are properly understood. The objective is thus one of clearing the air, making conversation possible.

How America Misunderstood Rome

1. **Power.** Many Americans take it as axiomatic that the Vatican's top concern is the preservation of its own power. Reading the crisis through this prism, observers in the United States often presumed that the Holy See was primarily concerned that the already-rambunctious American Catholic Church would slip further from its control. Its decisions were assumed to be driven by the desire to preserve an ancien

régime in which American bishops are subservient to the Pope, and thus not to the people or communities they serve. Many American Catholics believe that the Holy See tries to keep the local church in the United States on an especially short leash, because anything that happens in the United States will be studied and imitated elsewhere.

This bias in favor of seeing power as the driving force in Vatican psychology led to serious misunderstandings. The best illustration came in mid-October, when, as reviewed above, the Holy See turned down the norms adopted by the American bishops at Dallas and proposed a mixed commission to resolve the differences. Those norms had envisioned that bishops would remove priests from ministry on the basis of their administrative authority, without a canonical trial. Many commentators in the United States, and a broad swath of the American public, assumed this was a Vatican power play intended to assert control over the American Church, especially to thwart the zero tolerance stance that had become the cornerstone of the American approach. It took time for the real issues to emerge, that the Vatican's primary concern was a clear definition of the offense and due process for the accused. The objection was never to zero tolerance, but zero tolerance *for what* and *after what process*. Far from being a heavy-handed Vatican intervention, the revisions were actually welcomed by many American bishops and canon lawyers—including, ironically, many of the more liberal bishops who normally complain about Rome telling America what to do. In this case, they shared many of the same reservations, especially in terms of restorative justice. The American press largely missed this story, especially in the crucial early stages, because it was stuck with the power model through which every Vatican action is understood.

Insistence that the Vatican should leave the American Church alone was at times voiced in the same breath with the demand that the Pope take personal charge of the situation and crack heads. The fact that the Pope did not "fire" bishops responsible for allowing abuse to continue was a constant source of outrage. It was in some sense a case of damned if you do, damned if you don't. In fact, the Vatican's tendency to leave bishops' conferences to solve their own problems outside the doctrinal realm was never more clear than in the American crisis. Early on, officials in Rome concluded that the American cultural and legal situation with respect to sexual misconduct was unique and that the proper response had to come from the local Church. Whatever one makes of this stance, and it is obviously open to critique, it does not seem the behavior of a power-obsessed cabal concerned only with potential threats to its own control.

2. **Fear.** In the American press, the issues within the Catholic world most commonly linked to the abuse crisis are those involving sexuality and gender—women's ordination, clerical celibacy, and homosexuality. Given that the positions upheld by the Holy See on those issues face terrific pressure in much of the developed world, it is sometimes assumed that the Vatican is afraid that things are slipping out of hand. Some believe this fear is compounded by the fact that celibate males who lack a mature personal understanding of the issues under consideration set Vatican policy on sexuality. (Whether that is a fair assumption is beside the point.) Connecting these dots, many Americans have assumed that the Vatican is afraid that the abuse crisis might unleash new pressures for doctrinal change on matters of sexuality, or, in the case of celibacy, change in this discipline.

This assumption is a misreading. It is true that most Vatican officials, especially those at the highest decision-making levels, tend to hold conservative views on sexual morality and are resistant to pressures for change. But they are not making policy on the sexual abuse crisis on that basis, because they take it for granted that there will be no such change, at least under the present Pope. Many Americans assume that most Vatican moves are calculated with respect to these issues, as if they represent top institutional priorities. In reality, Vatican officials do not spend much time thinking about these questions, largely because they regard them as settled. It would not occur to Cardinal Joseph Ratzinger of the Congregation for the Doctrine of the Faith to evaluate the proposed norms from the American bishops or calls for a plenary council from the perspective of their potential impact on the debate surrounding women's ordination or the discipline of celibacy. It would be like suggesting that the U.S. Defense Department is crafting strategy in the Middle East in order to defend the presidential veto over acts of the legislative branch. Whatever most officials in the Pentagon might make of that bit of constitutional law, it would never have occurred to them to think it was in jeopardy, and hence it's not part of their calculations. One needs to search for their motives elsewhere, and it's much the same for the Vatican with respect to the American crisis.

Moreover, psychologically, Vatican officials understood themselves to be reacting with relative calm in comparison to the American bishops, who many in the Vatican felt were driven by fear of adverse financial impact, negative publicity, and "damage control" into adopting measures not in the long-term best interests of the Church. This is why, some Vatican officials believed, a number of American bishops were hesitant to defend the Church in the public discussion, or were too eager to surrender chunks of their episcopal authority either to civil prosecutors or to lay review boards. By way of contrast, many Vatican officials regarded themselves as capable of applying a more rational and thoughtful approach because of their distance and objectivity. Whether that is accurate or not is for the moment beside the point. What is relevant is that "fear" was not a driving force in the policy calculations of the Holy See, at least in the sense in which critics intended it.

3. Denial. Many American Catholics feel that officials in the Vatican "don't get it," that they are "in denial" about the seriousness of the American situation. This accusation hung in the air especially in the early stages from January to March 2002, when the Pope had not yet spoken. In fact, Vatican officials had their own reasons for not putting the Pope on record about the American crisis sooner. For one thing, despite repeated references to a papal silence, John Paul had already spoken several times on the issue of sexual abuse by priests, including in the United States. In June 1993, the Pope sent a four-page letter to American bishops in which he referred to "shocked moral sensibilities." Later that year, in August, before a crowd of eighteen thousand in Denver's McNichols Arena, the Pope condemned the "suffering and scandal caused by the sins of some ministers of the altar." Then, in an address to the Roman Curia in December 1993, John Paul said, "Among those that are particularly painful are sexual (deviations) which sometimes have involved, I say it crying, members of the clergy." Most recently, in the November 2001 document *Ecclesia in Oceania*, John Paul wrote, "Sexual abuse within the Church is a profound contradiction of the teaching and witness of Jesus Christ."

That Vatican officials did not rush out new statements in the early stages of the crisis perhaps illustrates an underestimation of its serious-ness, since the Pope often repeats points that he wishes to emphasize. But it has to be remembered that the Holy See was taking its cues on the issue to a significant extent from the American bishops, some of whom were advising Rome that premature papal statements might backfire, keeping the story alive artificially or even providing fodder for civil litigation. Further, the Pope no doubt felt caught between express-ing his pastoral concern for the American situation, but also backing up his senior managers in the United States.

At no stage did anyone from the Holy See express anything other than revulsion at the sexual abuse of children by priests. What Ameri-cans sometimes interpreted as denial was more like ambiguity, born of the widespread sense within the Vatican that factors other than the crime of sexual abuse were contributing to the crisis. From a Roman point of view, those factors included: anti-Catholicism, opposition to the Church's countercultural stands on abortion and sexuality, the desire to cash in with large financial payouts, and the exploitation of the crisis by activist groups of both left and right to advance their pet causes. The hesitance of some Vatican officials to engage in public acts of contrition was, to some extent, a hesitance to fuel these forces perceived as hostile to the Church. In other words, these Vatican officials may have be-lieved that by not being more contrite or self-critical, they were help-ing the American Church defend itself. This belief may have been in error, but in any event it is not denial.

There was a further layer of ambiguity in the Holy See, having to do with international perspective. During much of 2002, the Catholic sex abuse crisis received saturation coverage in the American press, so that it became the top item on the agenda, in some cases the only item on the agenda, for the American bishops. They were constrained by the force of overwhelming public attention. When the Vatican did not exhibit the same level of engagement, many Americans took this as evidence of willful denial. In fact, however, public opinion and the media overseas simply did not replicate the environment in the United States. During the spring of 2002, the major religion story in the Italian press was not the American crisis, which drew relatively little attention, but the thirty-nine-day standoff between Israelis and Palestinians at Bethlehem's Basilica of the Nativity. It was this drama that was on the front pages of the newspapers every day, and the lead item on the evening news. While Americans were frustrated that the Holy See did not have a laser-beam focus on their crisis, some in the Vatican were equally annoyed that the fate of the holy sites did not seem important to the American Catholic community. In other words, what Americans sometimes read as denial, some officials in the Holy See regarded as a matter of perspective.

In terms of whether or not the Vatican "gets it," it should also be noted that the Holy See's mode of responding to the American crisis shifted significantly from 2002 to 2003, suggesting an institution that was learning from experience. The changes to norms governing sex abuse cases signed by John Paul II in February 2003 were based on feedback from American canon lawyers, showing a willingness to be flexible in order to make the system work. The scientific symposium on pedophilia held in the Vatican, April 2–5, 2003, was an extraordinary event, both because all the experts enlisted were non-Catholics with no theological ax to grind and because Vatican officials took what they had to say with extraordinary seriousness. Among other things, their input seems to have stalled, at least temporarily, the move to issue a document banning the admission of homosexuals to Catholic seminaries. Finally, the Vatican's response when a group of three sex abuse victims from Boston arrived in Rome, dispatching a senior official from the Secretariat of State with a personal message from the Pope, also suggests a higher level of sensitivity than had once been the case.

4. An American Problem. It was widely asserted that Vatican officials regarded the sexual abuse crisis as an "American problem," meaning the result of some special defect in American culture that could be left to the Americans to resolve. This impression, however, turned on a critical ambiguity. It is true that there are unique features shaping the cultural reaction to the sexual abuse problem in the United States. Aspects of Anglo-Saxon tort law, for example, provide one such factor. In the United States, it is much easier to hold the Church corporately responsible for damages caused by priests than in most other parts of the world.

Other cultural differences also came into play, such as differing conceptions of what constitutes "sexual abuse." In Italy, which is the cultural matrix for many Vatican policy-makers, the age of consent for sexual relations is fourteen. In Spain, where Herranz is from, it's thirteen; in Honduras, where Rodriguez is from, it's fourteen; and in Mexico, where Rivera Carrera and Sandoval are from, the age of consent in some states is twelve. Canon law sets the age of consent for marriage at sixteen for a man and fourteen for a woman. Many Vatican officials and Catholic prelates in other parts of the world are thus culturally inclined to believe that adolescents are capable of adult decisions about sex. Since so many cases in the American crisis involved a priest and an adolescent male— this tempted many Vatican officials to construe the crisis as one of homosexuality, not abuse. They saw it through the lens of a supposed homosexual subculture in the United States and among American clergy, and in that sense saw an "American problem."

It's also true that over the past twenty years, Americans have developed a heightened awareness of the prevalence of child sexual abuse within society and a deeper appreciation of the long-term consequences for the victim, especially if there is no therapeutic intervention. Public anger was exacerbated in the United States by a greater understanding of the trauma experienced by victims. This is a cultural development that many officials in the Holy See have not experienced, and it too tended to distance the "gut reactions" in the Vatican from those on the American street.

All that can be granted, and yet few officials in the Holy See are under the illusion that sexual abuse by clergy is a uniquely American phenomenon. The evidence that it is a problem affecting the universal Church, as discussed above, is simply too obvious. Nor did the conviction that some aspects of the problem are uniquely American lead anyone in the Vatican to believe it is therefore unimportant. For better or worse, everyone in the Vatican realizes that if America sneezes, the rest of the Catholic Church will eventually catch a cold. In fact, the concern that the U.S. bishops were setting a precedent that would be widely studied and imitated around the world is one of the reasons the Holy See took such an interest in the American norms. Once again, it is ironic that the same people who derided the Vatican for regarding sex abuse by priests as an American problem also got upset when the Holy See took an interest in the American norms.

The bottom line is that the accusations reviewed here were for the most part false, unfair, and unhelpful. Taking such a polemical stance as the premise for conversation led nowhere. This is not to defend the Vatican's stance on any particular dimension of the crisis. It may well be that the Pope should have spoken out sooner, that he should have moved against Law and other bishops more forcefully, and so on down the list of complaints. The point, however, is that American Catholicism and the American press can never have a serious discussion with the Holy See about these issues so long as they rely on a set of assumptions about Vatican thinking that in effect renders dialogue impossible. A much more effective strategy would be to grasp which values are really motivating the Holy See's response and attempt to show how proposed American solutions in the long run will better satisfy those concerns. That's the stuff of conversation.

How Rome Misunderstood America

Conversation is of course a two-way street. It is equally true that when the Holy See gazes across the Atlantic Ocean, its analysis is often impaired by a bundle of stereotypes about the United States and the American Church. Four are most relevant to the sexual abuse crisis.

1. Sexual Hysteria. Recall what we said in chapter 4 about the European sociology of the Holy See. Many Vatican officials tend to carry around a rather typical set of European prejudices about the United States, including a kind of live-and-let-live sophistication when it comes to sexual misconduct, as opposed to what is often construed as America's puritanical hysteria. The Clinton/Lewinsky scandal was cited repeatedly by Vatican officials in background interviews in explaining why they found the overwhelmingly negative coverage of the sexual abuse crisis by the American press exaggerated. In the end, they said, it is obviously repugnant that a small number of Catholic priests engaged in the sexual abuse of minors. But being human, some priests will fail, even in these terrible ways. It has always been thus. Are Americans just discovering original sin?

The Vatican's mistake in this regard was interpreting the American reaction as having to do primarily with sex. In fact, it was not really the sexual misconduct by priests that fueled the explosion in January 2002, but the managerial misconduct by bishops. It was not John Geoghan who ignited the blaze, since his story was already well known in the Boston press. It was Cardinal Bernard Law, and the pattern that began to emerge of his failure to intervene against Geoghan and others when the evidence gave him a clear basis to do so. To the extent Vatican officials construed the crisis as driven by shock over the moral failings of priests, they were bound to misdiagnose the situation. Certainly, many Americans have high expectations of priests, and when priests fall from their pedestals, it generates more trauma than it probably should. Still, most American Catholics were primarily concerned with the bishops and what they perceived as a collective failure by the Church to protect its children, to admit the truth, and to take the proper steps to restore confidence.

2. Anti-Catholicism. Some officials in the Holy See were predisposed by their cultural background and experience to interpret the hostile reaction of the American press and of elite segments of American

culture through the lens of anti-Catholicism. Not only did Vatican officials and sympathetic prelates around the world sound the alarm about
anti-Catholicism, but they did so in language that could not help but
fuel the sense among many Americans that they were out of touch.
Rodriguez compared what he saw as the American press's "persecution" of Catholics with Hitler, Stalin, Nero, and Diocletian. Obando
Bravo called it a kind of bloodless martyrdom. Americans took this as
an example of Church leaders wanting to "blame the messenger" rather
than confront their own responsibility for the crisis.

Yet it must be understood by American readers how difficult it is
to explain to non-Americans how the sexual abuse story in the United
States became a story about the Catholic Church. Since most sexual
abuse of minors happens in the family, since priests are no more likely
to abuse than other clergy or professional groups, and since the vast majority of priests are innocent, how did the Catholic Church become the
primary focus for this story? This is a reasonable question, and Americans must be prepared to give a response. Perhaps there is some truth to
the suspicion that anti-Catholicism played a role. Philip Jenkins in *The
New Anti-Catholicism: The Last Acceptable Prejudice* (Oxford University
Press, 2003) argues that whereas conservative nativist sentiment was the
carrier for anti-Catholicism in America in the nineteenth century, secular political liberalism has become its incubator today, and it had a field
day with the sex abuse crisis.

In the end, however, Vatican officials misplaced the emphasis
in construing the American reaction primarily in terms of anti-
Catholicism. Some of the reporters who led the charge on the sex abuse
story were in fact practicing Catholics, shocked and pained by what
they learned about their Church. Most reporters, however, are not so
much hostile to organized religion as indifferent to it. If there was a bias
at work, it was not against the Catholic Church, or even religion, but
institutions generally. This reflects the culture of American journalism,
which holds up the investigative reporter as the highest realization of
the profession's ideals. European journalism idolizes the essayist who
pens pithy philosophical essays; American journalism lionizes the gritty

street reporter who meets sources in parking garages at 3:00 A.M. to get the dirt. The working assumption is that institutions tend to corruption, and the less accountable an institution perceives itself to be, the more ripe it is for an exposé. Once the Catholic Church began to appear an institution under siege, attempting to suppress the release of documents, ducking the press, using hardball legal tactics to try to discourage claims, reporters smelled blood. The article of faith underlying such coverage is that exposure brings reform. For the most part the American reaction was thus not about anti-Catholicism, and interpreting it in that light missed the passion for bringing injustice to light that actually drove most of the public discussion.

As a footnote, it may be that Boston was a special case. It may be that the long history of antagonism between Cardinal Bernard Law and the press, especially the *Boston Globe* but by no means limited just to the *Globe*, generated a particularly adversarial climate. This in turn helped shape a regional difference in the way American Catholics experienced the scandals, since the media coverage at several critical moments was far more intense on the East Coast than in other parts of the country. Midwestern Catholics, for example, may not have had the same experience as Catholics in the epicenter on the Eastern seaboard.

A variant of the anti-Catholicism thesis, as the chronology above notes, is that Jewish hostility to the Catholic Church, perhaps in combination with Masons and others, helps account for the persecution related to the sex abuse scandals. Is it true that in the United States, Jews are overrepresented in the media? Perhaps. In his book *Jewish Power: Inside the American Jewish Establishment*, J. J. Goldberg found that while jews are 5 percent of the working press nationwide, they represent one fourth or more of the writers, editors, and producers in America's "elite media." This includes network news divisions, the top newsweeklies, and the four leading daily papers (the *New York Times, Los Angeles Times, Washington Post*, and *Wall Street Journal*). Yet even if this reality biases the American media against the Catholic Church, a debatable proposition in itself, it would be a serious distortion to imagine that American Jewish reporters went after the sexual scandals on this basis. I can offer personal testimony. I worked extensively with American broadcast and print reporters throughout the most intense periods of the crisis, sometimes as an interview subject, sometimes as a journalistic colleague. Not once did I ever have the impression that Jewish animus for the Church had anything to do with their coverage. Most of the re- porters associated with this story, as a point of fact, are not Jewish. Moreover, it's unlikely that most American Jews are even aware of the Vatican's position on the Middle East conflict, let alone that they would desire to exact revenge for it.

3. Greed. Some Vatican officials have suggested that the desire to cash in at the expense of the Catholic Church was at the root of the American crisis, especially since in many cases the lawsuits being filed today brought against the Church are decades old. Bertone, for exam- ple, hinted at this in his *30 Giorni* interview of February 2002, saying there is a "well-founded suspicion" that the scandals are all about money. This is largely a misperception, although one not without its grain of truth.

In accounting for why the Catholic sexual abuse crisis has been so much deeper in the Anglo-Saxon world, probably the single most im- portant factor is the unique nature of Anglo-Saxon, and especially American, tort law. To put it simply—no lawsuits, no crisis. Tort law in the United States makes it possible to sue the Catholic Church as a legal person and force it to pay up for the acts of abuse committed by indi- vidual priests. In most other parts of the world, this is much more diffi- cult, if not impossible. Without the lawsuits and the inherent drama they created, it's difficult to imagine that the sex abuse story would have generated the same media interest, or attracted the same corps of legal specialists dedicated to uncovering what had been concealed.

The concept of corporate liability began to develop in earnest in the United States in the 1950s, when companies began to be sued for faulty products or the incompetence of their employees. Ralph Nader's famous 1965 book *Unsafe at Any Speed*, about his successful lawsuit against General Motors over the dangers of the Chevrolet Corvair, made corporate liability seem a noble area of the law, a way for the little guy to even the score with vast corporate conglomerations. Since the late 1950s, the annual cost of settling tort lawsuits in the United States has outstripped the gross domestic product every year. This trend was accelerated in the 1970s, with development of class action lawsuits, growing reliance on expert testimony, and procedural reforms regarding evidence that combined to make it much easier to sue corporations and obtain large settlements. Today the average American company spends between three and eight times more defending itself from tort actions than comparable firms in other parts of the world. Beginning in the 1980s, these concepts of legal personality, corporate liability, and negligent hiring and retention began to be extended by courts to church groups, and the Catholic Church is easily the most lucrative target for such litigation.

In Europe, accusations of sexual abuse against Catholic priests tend to be one-day stories, except in the rare instances where the law permits a criminal trial. Generally speaking, there is no one to sue. In the United States and other parts of the Anglo-Saxon world, however, lawsuits keep the story alive for months, if not years. Legal recourse also gives victims, lawyers, and journalists procedural tools to extract information from the institution, such as the right to depose Church officials and to subpoena records. In many cases, it has been the public unsealing of Church records under court order that has fueled the most significant and explosive media attention. The potential for large financial settlements or jury verdicts sustains public interest and gives journalists some quantitative way to measure the impact of the scandals. That potential also, obviously, attracts lawyers.

None of this means, however, that the crisis amounts to a shakedown of the Catholic Church. It is true that attorneys would probably not pursue this litigation unless there were a payoff, and there have been a few cases where money was an obvious factor in triggering apparently false accusations. A fifty-one-year-old Fresno, California, woman, for example, accused Cardinal Roger Mahony of Los Angeles of having sexually abused her at a Catholic high school thirty-two years ago. Mahony denied the charges and Fresno police concluded there was no evidence upon which to pursue a case. The woman, who has a history of mental illness, later said she was motivated to come forward in part because the state was cutting her disability payments and she needed a cash settlement from the Church. Yet attorneys, investigators, therapists, and review board members all report that false allegations, while possible, are rare. The vast majority of people who come forward do so with integrity.

Moreover, the size of individual payouts in clerical sex abuse cases is often not that great. The Louisville, Kentucky, archdiocese, for example, agree to pay $27.5 million to settle outstanding litigation. That sounds likes a lot of money, but it's spread over 243 plaintiffs, representing an individual total of $113,168.72. That amount will likely be cut in half for the attorney's share, so each victim will see a payout of something like $57,000. Compare that figure to industry standards in other cases. In 2001, for example, the Insurance Information Institute reports that the average settlement of a medical malpractice claim was $3.9 million. It's clear that suing the Catholic Church is not the best way to get rich in the United States. McDonald's and General Motors both have deeper pockets and better insurance (if also better lawyers). Men and women who come forward to allege sexual abuse by Catholic priests are not normally doing so for the sake of financial gain, and to the extent that Vatican officials saw the crisis in this light, they misread it.

Patrick Schiltz, a lawyer who has represented Catholic dioceses and other denominations in over five hundred clergy sex abuse cases, put it this way in *America* magazine in August 2003: "What distinguishes those who choose to sue from those who choose not to sue is not the seriousness of their abuse or the extent of their injuries, nor is it greed or lack of greed. Rather, it is the extent to which they trust the Church to do the right thing—to take them seriously, to give them help finding emotional and spiritual healing, to deal effectively with the priests."

4. Exaggerated Individualism. Finally, there is a not-so-subtle critique of American culture that is widely held in the Holy See that regards the Catholic Church in the United States as infected with radical individualism. Americans tend to be, in a celebrated phrase of Cardinal Francis George of Chicago, "Catholic in faith, Protestant in culture." Americans are at heart congregationalists, according to this analysis, accustomed to thinking of parishes as quasi-autonomous local bodies with at best a quid pro quo relationship with the bishop, the diocese, and the broader universal Church. American Catholics have little sense of their organic incorporation into the Church understood as an image of the Body of Christ. They construe governance inside the Church on the model of the social contract, meaning that one structure is essentially as good as another as long as it passes the test of common consent. They construe relationships within the Church on the corporate model— managers and employees are useful so long as they achieve their objectives, but expendable if that changes. All this, many in the Holy See believe, is a distortion of a genuinely Roman Catholic ecclesiology and reflects the imprint of Calvinism and its individualistic theology. In analyzing the crisis, therefore, some in the Holy See would regard the ferocious public response and vocal demands for reform as indicators of a brash but essentially superficial American Catholic sensibility.

Once again, it is possible to find elements of truth to this critique. But what drops from view is that American anger about the sexual abuse crisis pivots on the point that the most vulnerable members of the Church community, its children, were violated and then placed at risk of further violation. In fact, the argument could be made that in privileging the welfare of individual priests above children and the broader Church, it is the bishops and, at least indirectly, the Holy See who most egregiously failed the community throughout the course of this crisis. It is true that Americans are shaped in a thousand ways by economic and political liberalism and its exaltation of individual freedom, which often means they do not have a sufficient appreciation for the importance of community. That is perhaps the fundamental challenge to Catholic catechesis in the United States. Yet it would be an analytical mistake to regard American Catholics as cavalier or rootless when it comes to the Church. If American Catholics felt no investment in the community, there would be no crisis.

SPEAKING THE SAME LANGUAGE

Philosopher Alasdair MacIntyre has described the difficulties these days of staging rational debate across cultural and political differences:

> *It is easy to understand why protest becomes a distinctive moral feature of the modern age and why indignation is a predominant modern emotion. . . . Protest is now almost entirely that negative phenomenon which characteristically occurs as a reaction to the alleged invasion of someone's rights in the name of someone else's utility. The self-assertive shrillness of protest arises because . . . protestors can never win an argument: the indignant self-righteousness of protest arises because . . . the protestors can never lose an argument either. Hence the utterance of protest is characteristically addressed to those who already share the protestors' premises. . . . Protestors rarely have anyone else to talk to but themselves. This is not to say that protest cannot be effective; it is to say that it cannot be rationally effective.*

MacIntyre believes protest is futile because the protestors and those against whom their protest is lodged do not share a common set of philosophical assumptions, and hence in a literal sense neither understands what the other is talking about. In this final section, the aim will be to bring the Holy See and the American Catholic street into conversation, rather than the sterile exercise of protest as MacIntyre has described it. The device we'll use is to identify a set of values that both Rome and the American street strove to assert and defend during the sexual abuse crisis, albeit with different ideas of what those values mean in practice. The hope is to indicate places where thoughtful conversation might lead to deeper understanding.

Justice
As the scandals unfolded in 2002, American Catholics and the Vatican accused each other of injustice. Many Americans believed the Vatican

was more interested in covering up for priests and bishops than in taking decisive action to ensure justice for victims. This reaction exemplified the larger problem of clericalism presumed to explain, at least in part, why bishops looked the other way rather than dealing more firmly with abuser priests. Hardball legal tactics and evasion with the press, critics charged, reflected a choice to bolster the institution at the expense of victims and the broader community. These charges were amplified in the press because the Church is supposed to set a moral standard, so its failures seem all the more spectacular.

On the other hand, Vatican officials accused the American Church and even the American bishops of caving in to a lynch-mob mentality, rushing to punish accused priests without adequate protection of their natural law rights to defend their good name. They also felt the American bishops were too feckless in defending the public reputation of the Church, an impression that also reached its zenith at the June meeting of the bishops' conference in Dallas and its extraordinary "listening session" with victims of sexual abuse and other lay commentators. This too, some Vatican officials felt, was unjust, since it amounted to defamation of the Catholic Church. Finally, some Vatican officials believed that the real injustice at the heart of the American crisis was that too many American bishops had lacked the courage to combat moral and doctrinal laxity in the ranks of their clergy, and the American Church was reaping the bitter fruits of that failure. Failure to preach, teach, and enforce the truth is, from this point of view, the height of injustice.

In the end, a balanced analysis would probably find that both critiques are onto something. In their concern to support priests and to protect the institution, some bishops did fail to do justice to victims. The lengths to which some bishops went to keep struggling members of the clerical club afloat, so transparent in Cardinal Law's letters to Paul Shanley, a Boston priest accused of multiple acts of sexual abuse, was a vice born of an excess of virtue. Bishops such as Law saw these priests as fellow members of the clerical fraternity and wanted to give them every last benefit of the doubt. They were also acting out of the theology inherent in the rite of ordination, in which a new priest pledges loyalty to the bishop, and the bishop in turn annoints the priest's hands with oil, signifying his share in the sacrificial ministry of Christ. This creates a sacred bond of reciprocal obligation and support, and most clergy take it quite seriously.

In itself, that's a noble enough instinct. The problem is that it tends to define those not in the clerical club as of lesser importance, which is the inherent weakness in every tribal morality. One Vatican official told me that many American priests certainly knew about the misdeeds of their brother priests, but were too hesitant in denouncing them. They will have to learn, he said, the practice of fraternal correction based on Matthew 18:15–17: "If your brother sins, go and tell him his fault between you and him alone. If he listens to you, you have won over your brother. If he does not listen, take one or two others along with you, so that every fact may be established on the testimony of two or three witnesses. If he refuses to listen to them, tell the Church. If he refuses to listen even to the Church, then treat him as you would a Gentile or a tax collector." The bottom line is that the clerical club was too often fatally soft on wayward members.

At the same time, however, a class of zealots in the American press and in the Church arguably pushed the bishops toward a harshly punitive stance that was not consistent with the gospel. Certainly it seemed ironic that the American bishops had often criticized "three strikes and you're out" policies in the criminal justice system, while implementing what amounted to a "one strike" policy for their own priests. In his typically tart, but not wholly inaccurate, fashion, Fr. Andrew Greeley wrote that some victims' leaders "probably would not be satisfied if the Vatican had mandated castration for every priest in the nation."

Underlying this divergence between Rome and the American street, however, is a common concern for justice. Both sides agree that the Church's response to the scandals must be more than a pragmatic exercise in damage control. If necessary, even overwhelming public pressure and normal corporate logic must give way to doing the right thing. If bishops have to defy their lawyers and insurance companies to

meet with victims, they should, and if the bishops have to defy Bill
O'Reilly and the *Boston Globe* to uphold due process for accused priests,
again, so be it. This common passion for justice could have created, and
still could create, the basis for much constructive conversation about
what the demands of justice are in the American situation. This conversation struggled for traction, however, because it was often obscured by
suspicions from one party that the other was merely feigning concern
for justice and was really acting on the basis of more craven motives.

Accountability
Perhaps no aspect of the sex abuse saga so angered American Catholics
as the perception that the bishops, especially Law, were "getting away
with it," that no one was holding them accountable. As long as Cardinal
Law remained in office, the sense grew that the system was broken.
This reaction was drawn from American corporate and political life,
where poor performance or scandals are always followed by the resignation or firing of key personnel. Football coaches lose their jobs if their
teams don't win; corporate CEOs are sacked if their companies don't
perform. Americans often accuse the Vatican of being "the last absolute
monarchy on earth," with accountability being to no one but the Pope.
If he's not cracking the whip, then his deputies can get away with murder, and many Americans felt that has largely described the response
from the Holy See to the crisis in the United States.

From the Vatican's point of view, as we saw in chapter 3, accountability has a very different ring. A bishop's accountability is not to
shareholders, fans, or electoral constituencies, but to God and to the
Roman Catholic faith. A bishop is not judged on the basis of performance, but fidelity. This is not a job, but a sacramental bond between
bishop and diocese that is more akin to a marriage. In the early centuries of the Church, it was considered almost heretical for a bishop to
move from one diocese to another on exactly this basis. It wasn't until
Pope Marinus I in 882 that a bishop of Rome was named who had previously been the bishop of another diocese, and it caused a furor.
Among other things, it was a violation of canon 15 of the Council of

Nicea: "Bishops, priests, and deacons are not to pass from one church to another." (In 897, the deceased Pope Formosus was the subject of the infamous "Cadaver Synod." Eight months after his death, his successor, Pope Stephen IV, ordered Formosus exhumed and placed on trial for a variety of offenses, including the charge of having deserted his original diocese. Formosus was found guilty and his body was mutilated before being tossed into the Tiber River.)

Under sacramental logic, a diocese does not have a right to a superstar bishop, just as a family does not have the right to a perfect father. One's continuance in office is not calculated on the basis of the bottom line. What counts is the faithful determination to soldier on when things get tough. For this reason, in the institutional culture of the Holy See, the bias is strongly in favor of a bishop remaining in place during times of crisis. To walk away would seem a failure in fidelity, and a kind of behavior that is itself unaccountable. It is not that a bishop is not accountable to his people, but rather precisely that his bond with his people is sacramental, not contractual, and he doesn't have the right to walk away even if they're angry or disappointed in him. It is precisely in such a moment when he must buckle down and repair the harm.

The Holy See also tends not to remove problem bishops because, politically, retirement is seen as a reward for a job well done. A retired bishop, and a fortiori a retired cardinal, has all of the privileges of rank with few of the burdens. The tendency is not to let a man retire until he has cleaned up any obvious mess. The case of Cardinal Michele Giordano of Naples offers an illustration. Italian prosecutors began investigating Giordano in January 1997 when his brother Mario Lucio was indicted for running a loan-sharking ring. Investigators found that most of the cash had come from the cardinal, an amount equivalent to roughly $800,000. The case went to trial, making Giordano, seventy-one, the highest-ranking Church official ever to stand in the dock. Judge Vincenzo Starita, who heard the case without a jury, eventually found Giordano innocent on December 22, 2000. Giordano's alibi was that the money came out of personal funds he had saved over fifty years as a priest. Giordano acknowledged that he was guilty of poor record keeping. In essence, the defense boiled down to Giordano being guilty of naïveté, not fraud.

At every stage—when the investigation was first announced, when the charges were filed, when the trial began, and right up to the day the verdict was announced—rumors abounded that Giordano would be removed by the Vatican. One version had him heading off to a monastery, another that he would be brought to the Vatican City-State and given a job where the Italian civil authorities could not reach him. As was the case with Law, local newspapers were full of stories about how Giordano had lost the confidence of his people, how he could not govern, how embarrassed and angry the Vatican was, and how it was only a matter of time until the ax fell. Yet Giordano is still the cardinal of Naples as of this writing. Officials in the Secretariat of State said after the fact that they never had any intention of coming to Giordano's aid. That was how the system held him accountable: he was forced to stay and fix his problems.

Americans complain that this model fails to account for a situation in which a bishop is simply unsuited to lead. Vatican officials reply that Americans are too quick to cry "off with their heads," and do not appreciate that a bishop is not a CEO but a spiritual father. Both points undoubtedly have merit, and both can be pushed too far. It's true, for example, that the Vatican often struggles to appreciate even elementary notions of accountability that could be helpful from the point of view of good government. For example, one cardinal has been pushing the Holy See for years to hire an outside accounting firm to perform a certified annual audit of its accounts. To date, Vatican powers-that-be have not responded favorably, in part because they resist building Anglo-Saxon cynicism about abuse of power into the system. That leaves the Holy See vulnerable to corruption and incompetence. At the same time, it is also true that America is a disposable society where relationships are too often, and too easily, discarded. Americans are sometimes too quick to let themselves off the hook, as witnessed by the divorce rate. Americans sometimes lack a sense of accountability to their commitments and should welcome the Vatican's insistence that bishops live up to theirs.

What is not helpful is for one party to assert that the other lacks respect for the very idea of accountability. Expressions such as, "Rome couldn't care less what the people think," or "Americans think two thousand years of Church tradition don't apply to them," are both unfair and counterproductive. Both parties seek a more accountable Church, and that provides a basis for common cause.

Compassion

Both Rome and the American street accused one another of failures of compassion at key moments during the crisis. Many in the Holy See have been shocked at the punitive character of American reaction to the crisis, the mania to drive out guilty priests. At its worst, this impulse can be evocative of other American purges of alleged sinners—witch burnings, for example, or the McCarthyite "red scare." Such a mentality seems far removed from the redemption and forgiveness described in the gospels and incarnated in the Roman Catholic sacrament of reconciliation. On the other hand, Americans accused the bishops and the Vatican of lacking compassion in their treatment of the victims of sexual abuse. This perceived insensitivity runs all the way to the top, since Pope John Paul II, at least as of this writing, has not responded to requests to meet with victims.

Both sides would perhaps reassure the other if there were more evidence of compassion in their own positions. American Catholics would assuage much Roman anxiety if they toned down attacks on bishops and on clerical culture, and spoke more of recovery as a project of the entire community, clergy and laity together. This is one reason that movements such as Voice of the Faithful make Roman sensibilities nervous, since it can look like an interest group inside the Church, pitting the laity against the hierarchy. This is not to say Voice of the Faithful is unhelpful, but that the vocabulary and strategies used can sometimes raise apprehensions. Vatican officials, meanwhile, would strike a much more positive chord if they were to visibly meet with victims and offer in a personal way the compassion of the gospel to which they so often refer in statements. The bold appointment of Archbishop Sean O'Malley to Boston, whose record on outreach to victims is exemplary, shows that someone in the Holy See gets the point. It would be far more effective, however, if the Pope himself were to offer consolation in his own name and through his own presence.

Truth

American Catholics accuse the Vatican of dishonesty on sexuality. It preaches sexual chastity, but does not seem willing to address in a forthright way notorious violations of chastity among its own clergy. The Holy See, on the other hand, often suspects that Americans come from a culture of political compromise in which the very notion of objective truth is alien. Americans, they worry, have a pragmatist view of doctrine and discipline that reflects the imprint of American philosophers such as William James, John Dewey, and Charles Sanders Peirce—if it's not working, get rid of it. When Americans press the Vatican to be more flexible, to be more willing to compromise on matters such as celibacy and the role of laity, officials in Rome often conclude that the hidden message is the age-old response of Pilate before Christ: "Truth? What is that?" Thus Vatican officials believe that across a whole range of issues, from celibacy to the authority of the hierarchy, the already-tenuous American commitment to Catholic tradition may crack under the strain of the crisis.

Americans would reassure Roman anxieties by making their acceptance of the doctrinal tradition in the *Catechism* more explicit. This does not have to mean a slavish or uncritical assent to every jot and tittle, but rather an unabashed acceptance of the broad parameters for debate marked out by orthodoxy. Voice of the Faithful's motto is "Keep the Faith, Change the Church." Such slogans would seem more credible if their proponents talked as much about the faith to keep as the Church to change. The Holy See, meanwhile, would help the healing process in the United States by more clearly recognizing that there is no clerical monopoly on truth and that the experience of the lay faithful has much to contribute in terms of practical wisdom on issues such as finance, administration, and personnel. One positive step would be a public signal from the Pope that he intends the already-existing instruments of consultation, such as parish councils and finance councils, to be taken seriously. If the Pope were to receive a delegation of American laity to discuss the crisis, perhaps alongside the executive officers of the U.S. bishops' conference to demonstrate that this is not an either/or proposition, that too would be powerful symbolism.

Role of the Bishop

Both the American street and the Holy See agree that at the heart of the American crisis is the bishop. For Americans, the negligence of certain bishops in not stopping abuser priests when they should have known better is the single most galling aspect of the crisis. A core concern for the Holy See, meanwhile, has been a kind of gradual chipping away at episcopal authority that could end up with the bishop as a sort of facilitator rather than the teacher, sanctifier, and governor of his flock. Thus Vatican officials worried about the National Review Board, to the extent that it could exercise an ill-defined supervisory role over the bishops. They worried when Bishop Thomas O'Brien in Phoenix bargained away portions of his canonical authority in order to avoid criminal prosecution by Maricopa County. They have been concerned by mandatory reporter policies that obligate bishops to report accusations against priests to the civil authorities. All seem fraught with the potential to reduce the discretion and authority of the bishop, undercutting his role in canon law as the final authority in the local church.

Both the American and the Roman response, it should be noted, build on longstanding concerns that predate the sexual abuse crisis. Many Americans have long complained about imperious and arrogant bishops who did not perceive themselves to be answerable to their own communities. In fact, the response of the American Catholic community to the crisis of 2002 cannot be understood without appreciating that it provided a focus for a great tide of anger that had its origins elsewhere, in resentments that had been gathering for decades. The Holy See, on the other hand, has long been alarmed by various forces it sees undercutting the authority of the local bishop, rooted in the theological conviction that a bishop by virtue of ordination is personally responsible for his diocese and should live up to that obligation. The 1998 document *Apostolos Suos*, which many commentators took as an attack on the authority of bishops' conferences, was from the Holy See's point of view intended to emancipate individual bishops from domination by ecclesiastical bureaucracies.

What both sides share, beneath their various ways of expressing the point, is a profound conviction that bishops matter. The quality of life in a local church depends on little else like it rests on the quality of episcopal leadership. This realization clears a space for fruitful discussion between the Vatican and American Catholics about how bishops might best be selected, how they might be trained and formed, and how they might best be supported in their ministry by the collaboration of the Catholic laity. Psychologically, American bishops and their colleagues in Rome are probably more ready to have this conversation in a serious way, after the shock of the crisis, than at any time since the Second Vatican Council. Such a discussion, if it could succeed in avoiding adversarial dynamics, might find surprising areas of common ground.

Reform

Both the Holy See and the American Catholic street regard reform as essential to healing the crisis of sexual abuse, and both sometimes charge the other with stifling that reform. Voice of the Faithful has proposed reforms such as financial transparency and greater lay participation. While the group would assign primary responsibility for the failure to implement these reforms to the American bishops, many also point to a culture of closure and defensiveness from Rome as another key to the problem. The Holy See certainly could insist that American bishops adopt the Voice of the Faithful program. By failing to do so, critics argue, the Vatican at least passively endorses business as usual.

But governance and consultation hardly exhaust the areas of reform floated by various forces in the American Church. Some Catholics from the left would like to see clerical celibacy made optional, power decentralized from Rome to the local churches, bishops elected rather than appointed by the Holy Father, and perhaps even the ordination of women as priests. Catholics from the right would prefer a campaign of weeding dissenting theologians out of Catholic colleges and seminaries, eliminating homosexual candidates from programs of priestly formation, jettisoning ecclesiastical bureaucracies that have caved into the magisterium of the so-called experts, and boldly proclaiming Catholic doctrine in season and out. Both sides often blame Rome for its failure to approve, and insist upon, these proposed reforms.

Meanwhile, the Holy See believes in a program of reform too, but in the classically Catholic sense of the term—a movement that is primarily spiritual rather than ideological, doctrinal, or managerial. This is the sense in which one refers to the Cistercian reform of the Benedictines, for example, or the Capuchin reform of the Franciscans. Such reform begins with a desire to live the gospel and the tradition more fully. As the French Dominican Yves Congar wrote in *True and False Reform in the Church*, "The great law of a Catholic reformism will be to begin with a return to the principles of Catholicism." Any reform that does not feature immersion in the sacraments and in prayer will be suspect. Authentic reform always stresses the need to *sentire cum ecclesia*— "to think with the Church." It is a project to be carried out in cooperation with the pastors of the Church, never in struggle against them.

Cardinal Avery Dulles, in an August/September 2003 essay in the journal *First Things*, has offered eight principles for assessing reform proposals:

- Genuine reform is always a return to Sacred Scripture and tradition.
- Any reform conducted in the Catholic spirit will respect the Church's styles of worship and pastoral life. It will be content to operate within the Church's spiritual and de-

votional heritage, with due regard for her Marian piety, her devotion to the saints, her high regard for the monastic life and the vows of religion, her penitential practices, and her eucharistic worship.

- A genuinely Catholic reform will adhere to the fullness of Catholic doctrine, including not only the dogmatic definitions of Popes and councils, but doctrines constantly and universally held as matters pertaining to the faith.
- True reform will respect the divinely given structures of the Church.
- A reform that is Catholic in spirit will seek to maintain communion with the whole body of the Church, and will avoid anything savoring of schism or factionalism. . . . To be Catholic is precisely to see oneself as part of a larger whole, to be inserted in the Church universal.
- Reformers will have to exercise the virtue of patience, often accepting delays.
- A valid reform must not yield to the tendencies of our fallen nature, but must rather resist them.
- We must be on guard against purported reforms that are aligned with the prevailing tendencies in secular society. . . . We must energetically oppose reformers who contend that the Church must abandon her claims to absolute truth, must allow dissent from her own doctrines, and must be governed according to the principles of liberal democracy.

I suspect both sides in this conversation would feel more at ease if they could somehow assuage the worries of the other. Americans often suspect that when Rome talks about reform, they spiritualize the concept in order to avoid any substantive changes in structures. In truth, the Holy See, at least in the person of John Paul II and the best and brightest around him, are not closed to the possibility of structural changes in the Church. The point of the Pope's 1995 encyclical *Ut*

Unum Sint was to invite the Church's ecumenical partners into a "patient dialogue" about precisely such reforms of the papacy that might be needed to further the cause of Christian unity. If that conversation is proceeding slowly, it is at least proceeding. Perhaps what is called for in this historical moment is a similar papal invitation directed to Catholics themselves, calling them to a similar "patient dialogue" on renewal of the Church and laying out some parameters for that discussion. What Roman Catholicism may need, in other words, is an *Ut Unum Sint* addressed to Catholics, a charter document from the Pope focused on dialogue inside the Catholic Church, on how to foster communion without papering over differences or ducking problems. The document could build upon Paul VI's 1965 encyclical *Ecclesiam Suam*, in which the Pope called for a dialogue within the Church that would be "open and responsive to all truth, every virtue, every spiritual value." Such a gesture from the Holy Father, followed by efforts to foster the dialogue it describes, would help to reassure the vast majority of reasonable Roman Catholics in the United States of the goodwill of Rome.

In the Vatican, meanwhile, the suspicion is often that Americans know only the language of political power, and their reform agenda is more akin to a putsch than a purification. American Catholics would reduce anxiety levels in Rome if they would learn to speak in a more spiritual argot. For example, since forgiveness and healing are essential elements of resolution to the sex abuse crisis, perhaps the various groups and movements in the United States could promote a nationwide return to the Sacrament of Reconciliation. If the Vatican were to see churches across the United States filled with Catholics desiring to make confessions, imploring God's grace on themselves and this wounded church, it would speak volumes about the underlying ecclesiology of the reform movement. Further, it would help to avoid phrasing public activism in antagonistic terms, as if it's "the laity versus the clergy," or "the left versus the right." Obviously, no one is pretending that pious exercises by themselves can solve the sexual abuse crisis; it will take more than prayer to address the underlying political, legal, and cultural problems. It may also seem perverse to suggest that American

Catholics seek reconciliation, when those who are principally in need of confession are the priests who abused children and the bishops who failed to stop them. Yet the whole Church in the United States has been hurt, not just by the crisis, but by the anger and division it has generated. To heal, an examination of conscience by all parties is essential. Prayers for forgiveness and grace are never wasted. The more the reform movement can be visibly rooted in committed, faithful Catholicism, the better.

In the end, the Vatican and the American street will continue to clash on many issues, and that tension can be healthy. One of the factors that has given Catholicism a kind of sane, moderate balance over the centuries is that no one faction in the Church, including Rome, ever dominates for very long. History always steps in and restores equilibrium, one sign that the Holy Spirit is faithful to Christ's promise never to desert the Church. Still, exchanges between Rome and America would be more constructive if both sides were to drop the pretense that they know the real motives of the other, and consider instead their actual aims and fears. Each has much to learn, and this mutual exchange could foster the communion that is at the heart of what it means to be a *Catholic* Church.

7

THE VATICAN AND THE WAR IN IRAQ

lthough President George Bush declared from the deck of the USS *Abraham Lincoln* on May 1, 2003, that major combat operations were finished in Iraq, the war of words between Washington and the Holy See over the moral legitimacy of the conflict did not let up. For example, a lead editorial in the May 17, 2003, issue of the Jesuit-edited journal *Civiltà Cattolica*, reviewed by the Secretariat of State prior to publication, asserted that "the United States has put international law in crisis." The editorial said the U.S.-declared war on terrorism had generated strong anti-American sentiment in Europe. Especially repugnant, it said, had been the decision to hold six hundred Taliban, including five teenagers between thirteen and sixteen, and five men over eighty, at Guantanamo Bay in Cuba without recognizing them as prisoners of war. In another explosive charge, the editorial said the rebuilding of Iraq is "chancy" because "the Western countries that should make it happen seem more interested in exploiting Iraqi oil than in the reconstruction of the country."

The editorial bluntly said the U.S.-led war had been unjustified. Noting that Iraq's army was weak and that weapons of mass destruction had not been found, the editorial said these facts "have clearly shown that there were not sufficient reasons for moving against Iraq, because the country did not constitute a true threat for the United States and its allies." The editorial said the most urgent task now is to "reestablish international legality, wounded by the 'unilateralism' of the United States." It called for the United Nations, not the United States, to direct the postwar work in Iraq. "It's a matter of relaunching the spirit of the United Nations charter, based on cooperation, rather than on competition among enemy states and on domination of an imperialistic sort by the hegemonic superpower."

Many Americans, especially American Catholics, have been surprised to hear this sort of rhetoric from the Vatican, which can call to mind the harsh anti-American broadsides of the secular European left. Indeed, key officials in the Bush administration were initially taken off guard by the depth of Vatican opposition to the war when public discussion first began in earnest in late 2002. Many on the Bush team had expected support, at least implicitly, from John Paul II, given what they perceived as his blessing for the American-led strikes in Afghanistan after the terrorist attacks of September 11, 2001. Moreover, the Bush team had become accustomed to thinking it enjoyed an unusually warm relationship with the Holy See, born of common interests on issues such as cloning, abortion, and the role of religion in public life. Condoleezza Rice was not being disingenuous when she told the Italian weekly *Panorama* in the fall of 2002 that she "didn't understand" the Vatican's argument against the war. That incomprehension was widely shared among American personnel, both in Washington and in Rome.

The surprise reflects the fact that the political psychology of many Americans, including Bush administration officials, took shape in the Reagan years. During the Cold War there was a clear intersection of interests between the United States and the Holy See in support of anti-Soviet resistance in Eastern Europe, above all Solidarity in Poland. Some American Catholic thinkers, most eminently the so-called Whig Thomists George Weigel and Michael Novak, saw this "holy alliance" as a harbinger of a broader global partnership between America and the Catholic Church, based on shared values (pro-life, pro-family) and on shared political objectives (human rights, economic freedom, and democracy). The project, on this theory, was delayed by eight years of Clinton liberalism, but the election of Bush put things back on track. And indeed, there was a Catholic honeymoon in the early days of the Bush administration, as the president's elimination of public funding for abortion, his restrictive decision on stem cell research, and his two visits to the Pope during his first year in office all played to positive Vatican reviews.

From the perspective of many conservative Catholic Americans, the rift over the Iraq war was thus a temporary disruption of a natural alliance; the needle would eventually swing back into place. In fact, however, a careful reading of recent history suggests another hypothesis—that Cold War politics made temporary bedfellows out of the Vatican and the United States, and what is reemerging now is the caution and reluctance that have always characterized Vatican attitudes about America. In other words, perhaps it is the alliance that was the aberration and the rift that is the natural state of affairs. From this point of view, the clash of cultures most exacerbated by the Iraq war may not be between Christianity and Islam, but between the Holy See and the United States.

Both the Iraq war and the sex abuse crisis suggested to Vatican observers that the ghost of John Calvin is alive and well in American culture. These reservations are well documented, from Pope Leo XIII's 1899 apostolic letter *Testem Benevolentiae*, condemning the supposed heresy of "Americanism," to Pius XII's opposition to Italy's entrance into NATO based on fears that the alliance was a Trojan horse for Protestant domination of Catholic Europe. Key Vatican officials, especially Europeans from traditional Catholic cultures, have long worried about aspects of American society—its exaggerated individualism, its hyperconsumer spirit, its relegation of religion to the private sphere, its Calvinist ethos. A fortiori, they worry about a world in which America is in an unfettered position to impose this set of cultural values on everyone else.

The Calvinist concepts of the total depravity of the damned, the unconditional election of God's favored, and the manifestation of election through earthly success, all seem to them to play a powerful role in shaping American cultural psychology. The Iraq episode confirmed Vatican officials in these convictions. When Vatican officials hear Bush talk about the evil of terrorism and the American mission to destroy that evil, they sometimes perceive a worrying kind of dualism. The language can suggest a sense of election, combined with the perversity of America's enemies, that appears to justify unrelenting conflict. After Cardinal Pio Laghi returned to Rome from his last-minute appeal to Bush just before the Iraq war began, he told John Paul II that he sensed "something Calvinistic" in the president's iron determination to battle the forces of international terrorism.

In the aftermath of the war I once found myself in the Vatican and struck up a conversation with an official eager to hear an American perspective on the war. He told me he sees a "clash of civilizations" between the United States and the Holy See, between a worldview that is essentially Calvinistic and one that is shaped by Catholicism. "We have a concept of sin and evil too," he said, "but we also believe in grace and redemption." Vatican officials, it should be noted, are not the only ones to detect a strong Calvinist influence in American culture. Cardinal Francis George of Chicago made a similar statement during the Synod of Bishops for the Americas in November 1997. George said that U.S. citizens "are culturally Calvinist, even those who profess the Catholic faith." American society, he said, "is the civil counterpart of a faith based on private interpretation of Scripture and private experience of God." He contrasted this kind of society with one based on the Catholic Church's teaching of community and a vision of life greater than the individual.

This does not mean relations between the United States and the Vatican are destined for crisis. The Vatican is realistic enough to understand that if it wishes to exert influence on world affairs it needs to work with the Americans, and the Bush team continues to desire the moral legitimacy it believes Vatican support can lend its policies. What seems increasingly clear, however, is that this is not destined to be the special relationship enjoyed by America and Britain, allies linked by a common history, language, and worldview. This is a dialogue between two institutions with common interests, but also divergent cultures that will from time to time flare up into sharp policy differences.

No one should be shocked, in other words, the next time *Civiltà Cattolica* takes America to task.

THE VATICAN RESPONSE TO THE WAR IN IRAQ: A CHRONOLOGY

In the classic style of Vatican diplomacy, the Pope avoids committing himself to specific positions in political debates, since he is supposed to be *super partes*, that is, above the parties. He will state general principles, leaving it to his aides and to the global media to fill in the blanks in terms of the practical implications of his words. On his various trips to Poland prior to the collapse of the Communist system, John Paul would avoid direct conflicts with the regime, but would carefully employ the word *solidarity* at key moments in his addresses, leaving no doubt as to his sympathy for the opposition movement. Similarly, during the public discussion of the Iraq conflict, John Paul would cite the suffering of the Iraqi people and implore peace, leaving it to other Vatican voices to comment in more direct terms on the proposed, and then actual, American-led "preventive war."

Vatican officials began speaking out against a possible war in early August 2002, while the Pope himself did not begin to mention Iraq by name until January 2003. The Pope never did directly condemn the war, and some commentators have taken this as evidence that his opposition was less absolute than media reports suggested. In fact, however, John Paul was clear as to where he stood. His closest and most authoritative aides told reporters at critical moments that the Pope was convinced the war was a mistake, and that he was aware of and approved the aggressive vocabulary with which they were stating the case against it. At no time did John Paul offer any public utterance that distanced him from the antiwar declarations of Vatican personnel. The only possible reading of the record is that John Paul II was strongly opposed to the Iraq war.

This does not mean that in opposing the war the Pope intended to bind the consciences of Catholics. The distinction was laid out by Cardinal Joseph Ratzinger, in an interview with *30 Giorni*, an Italian Catholic publication: "The Pope," Ratzinger said, "has not proposed the [antiwar] position as the doctrine of the Church, but as the appeal of a conscience illuminated by the faith. . . . This is a position of Christian realism which, without dogmatism, considers the facts of the situation while focusing on the dignity of the human person as a value worthy of great respect."

August 6, 2002 Jesuit Fr. Pasquale Borgomeo, the general director of Vatican Radio, asserted in a live broadcast that instead of trying to get inspectors into Iraq to see if the country has weapons of mass destruction, the United States seems determined to launch a war. The Bush administration seems to have decided to ignore the opportunity for inspection and continues to focus on "the military option," he said. "Experience should have taught us something about the recurrence of certain wars, including those considered won, which are undertaken to resolve one crisis but are destined to create others, sometimes even more serious. To many, including not a few Americans, this policy appears to be wavering—its tactical aspects uncertain—and, even more, lacking the strategy one would expect of a superpower called to exercise global leadership," he said. "The United States is trying to combat terrorism, but it deals with the Israeli-Palestinian conflict—even after September 11—as if it has no relation to the growing tide of resentment against the United States and the West on the part of large segments of the planet's Arab and Muslim populations," Borgomeo said.

September 1–3, 2002 The Community of Sant'Egidio sponsored its annual interreligious gathering, this year held in Palermo. Several

Vatican officials used the occasion to address the possible war in Iraq. They included Cardinals Roger Etchegaray (French), Ignatius Moussa I Daoud (Syrian), and Walter Kasper (German), along with Archbishop Diarmuid Martin (Irish).

Etchegaray, former president of the Pontifical Council for Justice and Peace who now functions as an informal papal diplomatic troubleshooter, had long been critical of United Nations sanctions against Iraq. At Palermo, he said he was "happy to see growing opposition" in the international community to a war in Iraq. "The threat coming from Washington is something that is simply unthinkable. There is no war, least of all today and least of all in the Middle East, that can resolve something," Etchegaray said. Kasper, meanwhile, said there are neither "the motives nor the proof" to justify a war. Both men spoke in response to questions from reporters. Kasper's comments were taken as an indication of shifting winds in the Holy See, since he had been publicly sympathetic to the U.S.-led strikes against the Taliban in Afghanistan following September 11, 2001.

The criticism from Martin and Daoud was more indirect, coming in the context of prepared remarks on other topics. Commenting on the response of the United States to the attacks of September 11, Daoud said: "Every part of the earth suspected of complicity in terrorism has fallen under threat. Iraq now finds itself on the waiting list. Where will this campaign finish? Will it succeed in stabilizing an order of peace, preventing war with war, violence with violence, demanding the arms of the enemy through the use of arms?" Daoud's conclusion seemed negative. "In the end, the arms remain in the hands of a part of the world, and their presence expresses in itself an explosive situation."

Martin, who at the time was the Pope's representative to the United Nations in Geneva, argued that a successful "war against terrorism" has to be focused on development and social justice. He made no direct reference to Iraq. "The great weapon of the war will have to be that of trust and respect towards other people. The war against terrorism will not be won with some 'quick fix' that resolves tensions for the moment, disregarding a sustainable future for all," said Martin, who subsequently was named the coadjustor bishop of Dublin.

September 3, 2002 Borgomeo devoted his weekly commentary to the buildup to war in Iraq. "A year after September 11, we feel like disappointed friends of the United States—but still friends. We believe in the cultural and moral potential of this great country more than in its technological and military might," he said. "What is most worrisome is that the United States continues to consider military action as the most effective means to combat terrorism and an attack on Iraq as a priority. Beyond Arab and Muslim countries, isn't there enough resentment in the world against the United States and the West? We in the West all considered ourselves Americans [after September 11]," Borgomeo said. "Afterward, that resource of solidarity crumbled away."

September 10, 2002 Then-Archbishop Jean-Louis Tauran, a Frenchman who was at the time the secretary for Relations with States, in effect the Pope's foreign minister, gave an interview on the possible war in Iraq to the Italian Catholic daily *L'Avvenire*. Tauran insisted that any action against Iraq "should happen within the framework of the United Nations." He added that consideration must be given to the consequences for the civilian population of Iraq, as well as the repercussions for the countries of the region and for world stability. Tauran's bottom line seemed negative. "One can legitimately ask if the type of operation that is being considered is an adequate means for bringing true peace to maturity," he said.

September 15, 2002 Cardinal Camillo Ruini, president of the Italian bishops' conference, criticized the idea of a preventive war in Iraq. "That vast net of international solidarity that rapidly took shape after September 11 now seems marked by growing tears, especially in its primary and traditional strong point, which is the close rapport between the United States of America and Western Europe," Ruini said.

"Differences with an economic origin, or on matters of international law, add up to a very dangerous divergence as to the way to guarantee security and combat terrorism. In this regard, and with special attention to the attitude to be held on Iraq, without doubt the most rigorous vigilance is necessary in order to prevent the risk of new and greater tragedies, whose development would be quite difficult to control. But this does not mean that the path of a preventive war can be undertaken, which would have unacceptable human costs and extremely grave destabilizing effects on the entire Middle East region, and probably on all international relations. The weapon of dissuasion, exercised in the ambit of the United Nations with the strongest determination and with the sincere and engaged commitment of all countries capable of exercising a concrete influence, can represent, also in this difficult situation, an alternative able to guarantee security and peace. For its part, the Iraqi government obviously will have to give proof of realism and a willingness to find and respect agreements."

Like Kasper, Ruini's antiwar comments marked a turnaround in Vatican opinion. He was among the European Catholic leaders most sympathetic to the U.S. campaign in Afghanistan in the immediate aftermath of September 11. On October 24, 2001, at a press conference during the Synod of Bishops, Ruini answered questions about the morality of the American incursion in Afghanistan by referring to the "necessity of the fight against terrorism."

September 21, 2002 *L'Avvenire* published the text of an address given by Cardinal Joseph Ratzinger, prefect of the Congregation for the Doctrine of the Faith, at a conference in Trieste in which he criticized the idea of a war in Iraq. Asked if such a war could be justified, Ratzinger said: "In this situation, certainly not. There is the United Nations. It is the authority that should make the decisive choice. It's necessary that the choice be made by the community of peoples, not a single power. The fact that the United Nations is seeking a way to avoid the war seems to me to demonstrate with sufficient proof that the damages which would result [from the war] are greater than the values it would seek to save." Ratzinger criticized the new doctrine of preventive war. "The concept of preventive war does not appear in the *Catechism*," Ratzinger said. "One cannot simply say that the *Catechism* does not legitimate war, but it's true that the *Catechism* has developed a doctrine such that, on the one hand, there may be values and populations to defend in certain circumstances, but on the other, it proposes a very precise doctrine on the limits of these possibilities."

September 24, 2002 In an interview with the *National Catholic Reporter,* then-Archbishop Stephen Hamao, president of the Pontifical Council for the Pastoral Care of Migrants and Itinerant Peoples, and now a cardinal, said, "I'm very worried by what the U.S. is doing. I hope they don't attack. We don't need to excite more violence and hate." Hamao, who as archbishop of Yokohama, Japan, took part in protests at a U.S. naval base, said that U.S. policy makers need to do a better job of understanding how their choices look from other global vantage points. "A war between the United States and Iraq could not help but seem to many of the world's people a war between white Westerners and Arabs," Hamao said. "It would complicate relationships everywhere. It must be avoided." Asked about the suffering of the Kurds at the hands of Saddam Hussein's government, Hamao responded: "I feel very much for the Kurds. As a Japanese, I live with the memory of the atomic bomb," Hamao said. "We too have experienced the terrible reality of weapons of mass destruction, in our case at the hands of the United States. A war will not solve the problem of these weapons. Negotiations through the United Nations must be pursued. If all else fails, then leave it up to the United Nations to intervene, not just a single country."

October 1, 2002 Then-Archbishop Renato Martino, an Italian who heads the Pontifical Council for Justice and Peace, and now a cardinal, criticized the idea of a war in Iraq in an interview with Italy's *Famiglia Cristiana* magazine. He said the idea of a preemptive U.S. strike against Iraq, carried out as part of the war on terrorism, was based on a hypothetical right of a single country to decide when and where to intervene across the globe. "It presumes that it is up to the United States to decide between peace and war. In short, it is pure unilateralism," he said.

Borgomeo said on Vatican Radio that the doctrine of preventive attack would represent a "harsh blow to international law, which the West has recognized since 1945. International law certainly can be reformulated, but not in a unilateral manner. The doctrine of preventive attack not only represents a real wound to international law, and not only another setback for the credibility of the United Nations, but also, if put into action, a dangerous precedent for future imitators." He also questioned the political wisdom of a U.S. attack on Iraq, saying it went against Bush's post–September 11 efforts to garner a global consensus against terrorism. The plan to attack Iraq has instead caused deep divisions, even among U.S. allies. One certain effect of such an attack would be a "deepening of the gulf between the Islamic and Western world" and an increase in the anti-American resentment that fuels terrorism, he said.

November 2, 2002 A rare exception to the quasi-pacifist Vatican line came in a November 2 editorial in the semiofficial journal *Civiltà Cattolica*. It suggested that an American attack on Iraq, even without authorization from the United Nations, could be justified if there were an imminent danger of aggression from Hussein. Still, the journal insisted that a preventive war in the absence of a specific threat would be immoral. "The 'preventive war' does not serve peace, but places humanity in a state of permanent war, in addition to the very grave fact that the theory of 'preventive war' lies beyond the most ethically secure rules and those most universally accepted by international law," it read.

November 14, 2002 The Pope addressed the Italian parliament. While he did not mention Iraq, he spoke about the need for peaceful solutions to conflicts. "The new century just begun brings with it a growing need for concord, solidarity, and peace between the nations: for this is the inescapable requirement of an increasingly interdependent world, held together by a global network of exchanges and communications, in which nonetheless deplorable inequalities continue to exist," he said. "Tragically our hopes for peace are brutally contradicted by the flaring up of chronic conflicts, beginning with the one which has caused so much bloodshed in the Holy Land. There is also international terrorism, which has taken on a new and fearful dimension, involving in a completely distorted way the great religions. . . . Italy and the other nations historically rooted in the Christian faith are in a sense inherently prepared to open up for humanity new pathways of peace, not by ignoring the danger of present threats, yet not allowing themselves to be imprisoned by a 'logic' of conflict incapable of offering real solutions."

December 3, 2002 Borgomeo again criticized the U.S. buildup to war. Speaking on Vatican Radio, he said the United States holds a "preconceived attitude that disqualifies the inspection campaign as useless and reduces it to a sort of farce. In reality, the desire to use force appears increasingly evident: to rely on military mega-power to fill the holes and failures of politics." He said U.S. allies are "more justified than ever" in having reservations about being asked by America to participate "in the fight against terrorism while precipitating unilaterally toward military adventures with unforeseeable consequences." Borgomeo said that "bankrupt policies cannot be compensated by multiplying military commitment." War on Iraq, he asserted, would backfire as an attempt to clamp down on terrorism. "The war on Iraq, which in U.S. public opinion is being sought with every means to be made to seem unavoidable, is in fact an incentive for terrorism itself."

December 17, 2002 Martino spoke at a press conference to present the Pope's message for the World Day of Peace. Martino was blunt in his application of these principles to Iraq. "A preventive war is a war of aggression," Martino said. "There is no doubt. This is not part of the definition of a just war. There has to be an offense, an invasion, and then there can be a legitimate defense." Asked about the need to disarm aggressors, Martino stressed anew the need to work through the United Nations. "This disarming of belligerents must be done through the organs at our disposition, which is the United Nations," Martino said, recalling that Paul VI had referred to the UN as "the obligatory path for humanity in modern times."

December 23, 2002 Tauran used his strongest language to date to criticize a possible Iraq war in an interview with the Roman newspaper *La Repubblica*. He cited one Arab minister who said an attack on Iraq would "open the gates of hell." The warning concerned a possible clash of cultures between Christianity and Islam. "We need to think about the consequences for the civilian population and about the repercussions in the Islamic world. A type of anti-Christian, anti-Western crusade could be incited because some ignorant masses mix everything together," Tauran said. The French prelate was critical of what he called an American tendency toward unilateral action. "A single member of the international community cannot decide: 'I'm doing this and you others can either help me or stay home.' If that were the case, the entire system of international rules would collapse. We'd risk the jungle," he said.

Archbishop Martino, frustrated that the world's media did not pick up on Pope John Paul's call for "individual gestures of peace" as part of his message for the World Day of Peace, goes on Vatican Radio to relaunch the idea.

December 24, 2002 John Paul delivered his Christmas Eve homily. The Pope said: "The Child laid in a lowly manger: this is God's sign. The centuries and the millennia pass, but the sign remains, and it remains valid for us too—the men and women of the third millennium. It is a sign of hope for the whole human family; a sign of peace for those suffering from conflicts of every kind; a sign of freedom for the poor and oppressed; a sign of mercy for those caught up in the vicious circle of sin; a sign of love and consolation for those who feel lonely and abandoned."

December 25, 2002 The Pope delivered his Christmas Day meditation. It contained his first clear reference, albeit indirect, to the possibility of war in Iraq. He said: "Christmas is a mystery of peace! From the cave of Bethlehem there rises today an urgent appeal to the world not to yield to mistrust, suspicion and discouragement, even though the tragic reality of terrorism feeds uncertainties and fears. Believers of all religions, together with men and women of goodwill, by outlawing all forms of intolerance and discrimination, are called to build peace: in the Holy Land, above all, to put an end once and for all to the senseless spiral of blind violence, and in the Middle East, to extinguish the ominous smoldering of a conflict which, with the joint efforts of all, can be avoided."

January 1, 2003 John Paul II formally issued his annual message for the World Day of Peace, building upon the fortieth anniversary of Pope John XXIII's famed encyclical *Pacem in Terris*. John Paul wrote: "With the profound intuition that characterized him, John XXIII identified the essential conditions for peace in four precise requirements of the human spirit: truth, justice, love and freedom. Truth will build peace if every individual sincerely acknowledges not only his rights, but also his own duties toward others. Justice will build peace if in practice everyone respects the rights of others and actually fulfills his duties toward them. Love will build peace if people feel the needs of others as their own and share what they have with others, especially the values of mind and spirit that they possess. Freedom will build peace and make it thrive if, in the choice of the means to that end, people act according to reason and assume responsibility for their own actions."

The Pope delivered his New Year's Day homily. He said: "In the face of the events that unsettle the planet, it is very clear that only God can touch the depths of the human soul; his peace alone can restore hope to humanity. We need him to turn his face toward us, to bless us, to protect us and give us his peace. . . . Today despite the serious, repeated attacks on the peaceful harmony of peoples, peace is possible and necessary. Indeed, peace is the most precious good to ask of God and to build with every effort, by means of concrete gestures of peace on the part of every man and woman of goodwill. . . . Faced with today's conflicts and the threatening tensions of the moment, once again I ask you to pray to find the 'peaceful means' for a solution inspired by 'a desire for genuine and constructive dialogue,' in harmony with the principles of international law."

In his Angelus address for New Year's Day the Pope said: "Today I ask each person to make his/her contribution to foster and bring about peace, through generous choices of reciprocal understanding, reconciliation, forgiveness and concrete attention to those in need. Concrete 'gestures of peace' are necessary in families, in the workplace, in communities, in civil life as a whole, in national and international public gatherings. Above all, we must never stop praying for peace. . . . How can we not express once more the wish that world leaders do everything in their power to find peaceful solutions to the many tensions present in the world, especially in the Middle East, avoiding further suffering for those peoples who have been so sorely tried? May human solidarity and law prevail!"

January 4, 2003 Martino gave an interview to Rome's *La Repubblica* in which he once again criticized America's apparent willingness to go to war in Iraq without United Nations support. "Evidently, unilateralism is unacceptable," Martino said. "We cannot think that there is a universal policeman who takes it upon himself to punish those who act badly. . . . The United States, being part of the international assembly, has to adapt to the exigencies of others."

January 7, 2003 John Paul's forceful language about peace, widely interpreted as criticism of American policy in Iraq, brought an unusual rebuke from conservative Italian political analyst Ernesto Galli della

Loggia, in a front-page opinion piece in Italy's most read daily newspaper, *Corriere della Sera*. Della Loggia is normally a booster of the Wojtyla pontificate. "Does anyone remember papal pronouncements comparable to those of recent weeks on the occasion of that terrible decade-long war unleashed by Saddam Hussein against Iraq in 1980? And the roughly 200,000 Kurds massacred with Saddam's gas in the mid-1980s; how many protests were raised by the Holy See commensurate with the enormity of the crime? To speak frankly," Della Loggia wrote, "the impression is that it's only when the issue is the West, and more specifically the United States, that the Pope's voice becomes a tuning fork and the Catholic world expresses its maximum mobilization 'in favor of peace.' "

January 8, 2003 In an interview with the *National Catholic Reporter,* Auxiliary Bishop Andraos Abouna of Baghdad expressed gratitude for the papal peace initiative. "When the Pope speaks about Baghdad, he does so from the heart, because this is the land of Abraham, the first believer in God. For us it is the Holy Land," said Abouna, who was ordained a bishop by John Paul in a January 6 ceremony in St. Peter's Basilica, along with eleven other new bishops from seven countries. Abouna—who helped pull charred bodies out of the Amiriya bomb shelter in Baghdad, which was obliterated by U.S. stealth bombers on February 13, 1991, killing six hundred to one thousand civilians—was also realistic about the likely impact of the Vatican interventions. "Politicians act in their own interest, often for economic reasons," he said. "They don't so much care what religious leaders say."

January 13, 2003 The Pope delivered his annual address to the diplomatic corps accredited to the Holy See. John Paul offered, for the first time, a direct public statement of opposition to a war in Iraq: "War is not always inevitable. It is always a defeat for humanity. International law, honest dialogue, solidarity between States, the noble exercise of diplomacy: these are methods worthy of individuals and nations in resolving their differences. I say this as I think of those who still place their trust in nuclear weapons and of the all-too-numerous conflicts which continue to hold hostage our brothers and sisters in humanity. . . . The solution will never be imposed by recourse to terrorism or armed conflict, as if military victories could be the solution. And what are we to say of the threat of a war which could strike the people of Iraq, the land of the Prophets, a people already sorely tried by more than twelve years of embargo? War is never just another means that one can choose to employ for settling differences between nations. As the Charter of the United Nations Organization and international law itself remind us, war cannot be decided upon, even when it is a matter of ensuring the common good, except as the very last option and in accordance with very strict conditions, without ignoring the consequences for the civilian population both during and after the military operations." The Pope also called on all nations to respect international agreements. "Today political leaders have at hand highly relevant texts and institutions. It is enough simply to put them into practice," he said. "The world would be totally different if people began to apply in a straightforward manner the agreements already signed!"

U.S. Ambassador to the Holy See James Nicholson was interviewed on Vatican Radio following the Pope's address to the diplomats. Nicholson was asked by the host how he squared the Pope's language on international agreements with the U.S. track record of refusing to join the Kyoto Accord, pulling out of the Antiballistic Missile Treaty, and declining to recognize the new International Criminal Court. Nicholson's response was that the Pope was speaking not of these matters, but of Iraq and North Korea and their refusal to live up to international agreements. In that sense, Nicholson argued, the Pope and Bush were saying the same thing.

January 15, 2003 Nicholson announced that he had invited conservative American Catholic intellectual Michael Novak, known as a supporter of the Bush administration's approach to the war on terrorism, to lecture in Rome and meet with Vatican officials. The purpose of his visit was to discuss the moral issues surrounding application of the "just war" theory to the conflict in Iraq. Novak's arrival was expected in early February.

January 16, 2003 The Congregation for the Doctrine of the Faith released a "doctrinal note" entitled "On Some Questions Regarding the Participation of Catholics in Political Life." While it did not address the Iraq issue, it did distance the Church from certain forms of antiwar protest. "Finally, the question of peace must be mentioned," the document says. "Certain pacifistic and ideological visions tend at times to secularize the value of peace, while, in other cases, there is the problem of summary ethical judgments which forget the complexity of the issues involved. Peace is always 'the work of justice and the effect of charity.' It demands the absolute and radical rejection of violence and terrorism and requires a constant and vigilant commitment on the part of all political leaders."

January 18, 2003 Antiwar demonstrations dominated news reports from various parts of the world, including the United States. On the occasion, Martino told reporters in Rome that he hoped "governments will take into consideration the sentiments of their citizens" as expressed in the demonstrations. To defeat terrorism, Martino said, "it's necessary to address the political, economic and cultural causes that determine it," and he invited the West to an "examination of conscience." A final decision on war in Iraq, Martino said, "depends upon the United Nations and the international community."

January 24, 2003 Cardinal Kasper, in remarks to the *National Catholic Reporter* after a lecture in Perugia, predicted that Novak's effort to persuade Rome of the morality of a possible preventive war in Iraq would fail. "I am of the opinion of the Pope himself, and of the Secretariat of State, of the Roman Curia," Kasper said. "I do not think all the methods of peaceful negotiations, of diplomatic relations, have been exhausted." With respect to a possible U.S.-led attack on Iraq, Kasper said, "I do not see how the requirements for a just war can be met at this time. A war would touch the poorest of the poor, not Saddam Hussein," Kasper said. "Women and children and sick people would have to suffer, and we should consider the destiny of such people." Kasper echoed concern about Muslim reaction. "Very often the Muslims make an identification, which is wrong but they do it, between Christianity and the West," Kasper said. "I think this war could become a very heavy problem and could destabilize the entire region of the Middle East. . . . I don't think I have all the information about Iraq, it is impossible, but as much as I have, I am not in favor of this war. . . . I think we should use other means to solve these questions. I do not defend Saddam Hussein, nobody would. But there are also other means to resolve the questions of peace and justice in the world," he said.

January 29, 2003 Secretary of State Cardinal Angelo Sodano held a lunch for Italian journalists in which he spoke against the war in sharp terms. "I said to an old American friend: didn't the lesson of Vietnam teach you anything?" Sodano said, as quoted in Italian press reports. "The Holy See is against the war, it's a moral position," Sodano said. "There's not much to discuss, whether it's a preventive war or nonpreventive, because this is an ambiguous term. It's certainly not a defensive war. The keys in this moment are in the hands of the United States and Great Britain, and we're trying to provoke reflection not so much on whether it's just or unjust, moral or immoral, but whether it's worth it. From the outside we can appear idealists, and we are, but we are also realists. Is it really a good idea to irritate a billion Muslims? Not even in Afghanistan are things going well," Sodano said. "For this reason we have to insist on asking the question if it's a good idea to go to war."

January 30, 2003 Tauran criticized a preventive war in response to reporters' questions at a conference sponsored by the Association of Volunteers for International Service in Rome. "People are talking about a preventive war, but the question we must put before ourselves is how to prevent the war," Tauran said. "We are not pacifists, we are realists," Tauran said, but added that in this case a strike against Iraq does not pass the "just war" test. He mentioned the traditional criteria of proportionality and protection of civilian populations. "Specifically, a war would exacerbate extremism and threaten to inflame the situation in the Middle East. These are two obvious concerns," Tauran said. Asked if the Vatican's position would change should the United Nations approve a strike, he seemed to suggest it would not. "A UN resolution would be a different track," he said. "It would address the legality of the action. But humanitarian and moral concerns would remain." Tauran denied that the U.S. embassy to the Holy See was applying extraordinary pressure. "We are having conversations, but they are calm and serene," Tauran said. "I would say they are persevering in making their argument." Finally, Tauran was asked if the Pope might try some gesture of peace in the near future, such as sending emissaries to Baghdad and Washington. "We're thinking about it," Tauran said. "Something might happen in the coming days. But for now there is no concrete plan of action."

February 1, 2003 The Vatican's official newspaper, *L'Osservatore Romano,* said American policy in Iraq lacked intelligence. "To define a preventive war as a sensible act means not to have, or not to know how to exercise, the intelligence necessary at certain levels," *L'Osservatore* stated in its February 1 Italian edition. In another article, the official Vatican newspaper wrote that "the international media, determined to understand in the nuances of diplomatic statements the possible development of the Iraqi situation, often forget to concentrate attention on the principal victim of the crisis: the civilian population. Tested by a long embargo and vexed by a dictatorial regime, the Iraqi people [have] lived for months under the exhausting threat of a conflict."

February 3, 2003 American Cardinal Francis Stafford, at the time the president of the Pontifical Council for Laity, put out a statement asserting that "the American government has not offered conclusive evidence of imminent danger to its national security" sufficient to justify a war. Stafford had been contacted by *Inside the Vatican* magazine and released a written statement to several press outlets in Rome. "The concept of a 'preventive' war is ambiguous," Stafford wrote. " 'Prevention' does not have a limit; it is a relative term and is subject to self-serving interpretations. Objective criteria must be applied with intellectual rigor. The threat must be clear, active and present, not future. Nor has the American administration shown that all other options before going to war have proven 'impractical or ineffective,' " he wrote. Stafford contrasted the call to arms coming from the political leadership of America, Britain, and Iraq with John Paul II's call to youth to be agents of peace and hope.

February 4, 2003 Martino gave an interview to the *National Catholic Reporter* in which he discussed the Iraq war, arguing that Catholic "just war" doctrine is undergoing an evolution similar to that on capital punishment, from grudging acceptance to a quasi-abolitionist stance. In both cases, he said, modern society has the means to resolve problems without the use of lethal force. Thus the Catholic response to a preventive war in Iraq is negative. "I would draw a parallel with the death penalty," Martino said. "In the *Catechism of the Catholic Church,* there is an admission that the death penalty could be needed in extreme cases. But Pope John Paul II in *Evangelium Vitae* said that society has all the means now to render a criminal harmless, who before might have been sent to the gallows. This could well apply to the case of war. Modern society has to have, and I think it has, the means to avoid war," Martino said.

Martino argued that nonviolent alternatives exist to a preventive war in Iraq. "Resolution 1441 provides all the elements in order to solve the problem without going to war," he said. "If there is indeed any proof [that Iraq has weapons of mass destruction], the inspectors are ready to receive them, and to proceed to either destroy them or render them harmless. Let's try this first." Martino allowed for the "extreme possibility" of war, if convincing proof is offered and Iraq refuses to disarm, but said even then the means of the war would have to be just, meaning protecting civilian populations, and the potential consequences of conflict would have to be weighed. "There will be an increase in terrorist acts, I'm sure," Martino said. "There will be fire, tumult, all over the Middle East. The oil supplies could suffer. The environment could be endangered, as happened in the Gulf War, and in an even worse manner this time.

"Another element to take into account is world public opinion," Martino said. "Everybody is against the war." Pointing to the Israeli-Palestinian conflict, Martino challenged Bush and the West to resolve it before striking Iraq. "There is a double standard. We already have a war. Why don't you stop that one instead of starting another one?" Martino expressed strong skepticism about the motives of the Bush administration for seeking conflict. Asked if, like the semiofficial Vatican journal *Civiltà Cattolica*, he believed oil was a factor, he was indirect but clear. "I don't have the list of the advantages that those who want the conflict are seeking," he said. "But I can say that it's not excluded that this is on the list of advantages." So when Donald Rumsfeld says oil has nothing to do with it, Martino finds that hard to believe? "I'm not the only one," he said.

Martino said that Western policy makers should examine their own responsibility for global conflicts. "Why do we impose our cultural patterns, of consumption, of corruption, of sex, of whatever, on the other parts of the world? They get fed up with that," he said. "When developing nations have been given promises of help, of debt forgiveness, and they are not kept, this causes frustration," Martino said. "That frustration can translate into terrorism. When a young man doesn't foresee anything for his future, being dead or alive is about equal. I always say that terrorism can be eradicated not only by rendering harmless one or two thousand terrorists, but by searching for the causes of terrorism," Martino said. "Those causes are three kinds: political, economic and cultural. If we examine our conscience, we can say that there has been, and there is, oppression on these three fronts." Martino stopped short of counseling Catholic men and women in the U.S. armed forces to refuse to cooperate in the event of war. "The responsibility is not theirs, it is of those who send them," he said.

A letter of protest signed by more than sixty American Catholics, including prominent laity and men and women religious, challenged Ambassador James Nicholson's decision to bring Michael Novak to Rome to argue for the morality of war in Iraq. The letter was faxed to the U.S. embassy to the Holy See.

"As leaders of Catholic organizations, religious orders, theologians, educators, and pastoral workers, we have dialogued and reflected on the current situation in light of our rich tradition of Catholic Social Teaching and our practical experiences," the letter stated. "Our reflection, guided also by the clear and consistent statements from our Church leaders, including Pope John Paul II, have led us to conclude that any military action against Iraq at this time is not morally justifiable. We are very concerned that you have selected one theologian to represent the U.S. Catholic community's position on the morality of this war without any consultation with recognized Catholic leaders in the U.S. who have helped many of us craft our clear and consistent message against the administration's actions."

Signatories included the president of the Conference of Major Superiors of Men, the chief umbrella group for men's religious communities in the United States; the national coordinator of Pax Cristi USA, a Catholic peace group; the executive director of the U.S. Catholic Mission Association; and leadership figures in a variety of men's and women's religious orders. In a cover sheet accompanying the fax to Nicholson, Trinitarian Fr. Stan DeBoe of the Conference of Major Superiors of Men said Novak represents "a thread of Catholic teaching that is dissenting from current statements from our recognized teaching office in the Church. . . . In his book *Tell Me Why*," DeBoe wrote, "Mr. Novak explains to his daughter that to be 'fully Catholic' one must hold to the teachings of the Church, and if one holds 'x when the Church teaches non-x, are you fully Catholic? The obvious answer is no' (page 149). I hope that you and he will not be presenting this as a

Catholic analysis of a war on Iraq, since it is not in keeping with current statements and teachings, it is a dissident voice. While dissent is always welcome, it should not be confused with the clear statements made by Church leaders and theologians regarding preemptive strikes, use of nuclear weapons, and the current situation," De Boe wrote.

Nicholson told the *National Catholic Reporter*, however, that the letter was based "on a misunderstanding of the nature of Novak's visit to Rome. Novak is coming to Rome as a private citizen to present his own views on the relation of the current crisis to traditional notions of just war theory, which have been the focus of considerable discussion in Europe and the United States," Nicholson said. "He is not coming here to represent Catholic teaching or the Conference of U.S. Bishops; he is also not representing the U.S. government. He is participating in the Department of State's International Speaker program, which seeks to bring leading American scholars and experts from many walks of life to address foreign audiences on issues of priority concern to the United States."

February 5, 2003 Stafford spoke with the *National Catholic Reporter* and was asked if he could envision any circumstances under which a war in Iraq might pass moral muster. "I come at this as a Christian and religious leader who celebrates the Eucharist every day," Stafford said. "It's not possible for me to celebrate that Eucharist and at the same time to envision or encourage the prospect of war." Asked about whether Catholics in the Armed Forces should comply with orders to fight, Stafford said: "I can't make the decision for them. As mature, baptized Christians, each layperson has to decide if their being in Christ Jesus, whose peace extends to all persons, allows them to proceed to the destruction of some persons. Each person has to weigh what is being said by the country's leaders . . . and come to their own conclusion." Stafford added that the Church has always supported a right to conscientious objection, and he hoped that such a right would be available this time as well if it came to armed conflict.

February 7, 2003 German Foreign Minister Joschka Fischer met the Pope in the Vatican. Fischer also held talks with Sodano and Tauran. "The visit of Minister Fischer was a fitting occasion for an exchange of opinions on the problems of the present moment, in particular, on the well-known crisis of Iraq and on the theme of the future European constitution," a Vatican statement said afterward.

February 8, 2003 The Pope received members of the Community of Sant'Egidio in audience. He said to them: "These days you have gathered to reflect on the theme, 'The Gospel of Peace,' a theme that is very important and deeply felt as we pass through the present time marked by tensions and the winds of war. It is therefore ever more urgent to proclaim the Gospel of peace to a humanity strongly tempted by hatred and violence. It is necessary to multiply all the efforts for peace. We cannot be hindered by acts of terrorism or by the threats that are gathering on the horizon. We must not be resigned as if war were inevitable."

Novak met with officials in the Pontifical Council for Justice and Peace and in the Secretariat of State. At the Secretariat of State, Novak was received by Tauran. At the Pontifical Council for Justice and Peace, however, Martino delegated the session with Novak to his staff. Novak gave an interview to Vatican Radio after his meetings. He defended America's willingness to act even without unanimous international support. "It would absolutely be best if there is complete agreement, but the moral principle stands whether there is complete international agreement or not. That is, that it is wrong to allow this violation of the international order we want, when there is a whole group trying to promote international disorder and willing to use the most dramatic acts of terrorism to destabilize existing democracies."

Novak criticized some Vatican commentary on the U.S. stance. "Some of the comments that have come from some Vatican sources have been, they've been a little bit emotionally anti-American. Somebody said Americans are inebriated with power, well that's pretty much of an interpretation, and I don't see that at all. . . . I just wish people would mind their rhetoric a little bit more. I've also seen a number of sources, in Europe generally, but even in *Civiltà Cattolica*, saying that the real motive of the Americans was imperialism or oil. Well I think, if we wanted oil, why didn't we just take it ten years ago, twelve years ago, when Hussein's army was broken, the Republican Guard was broken, and the way to Baghdad was straight, the way to the oilfields was straight? That's not what we want."

Novak argued that focus on preventive war was a red herring, since the conflict with Iraq was a matter of self-defense. "I think we're in the war, the war is already here, and we can't prevent it. We didn't ask Saddam to invade Kuwait, and we didn't ask him to disobey what he promised to do in the peace negotiations, and we certainly didn't ask Osama bin Laden to attack us everywhere, to look for Americans all over the world and declare *jihad* on us. So we're in war with a traditional argument of self-defense."

February 9, 2003 The Pope delivered his Sunday Angelus address. He said: "At this time of international concern, we all feel the need to turn to the Lord to implore the great gift of peace. As I pointed out in the Apostolic Letter, *On the Most Holy Rosary,* 'the grave challenges confronting the world at the start of this new millennium lead us to think that only an intervention from on high . . . can give reason to hope for a brighter future' (n. 40). Many prayer initiatives are taking place these days all over the world. While I endorse them wholeheartedly, I invite all to take up the Rosary to ask the intercession of the Blessed Virgin Mary: 'One cannot recite the Rosary without feeling caught up in a clear commitment to advancing peace' (same place, n. 6)."

The Vatican announced that the Pope had dispatched Cardinal Roger Etchegaray, eighty, to Baghdad as his special emissary to Saddam Hussein. Etchegaray would also bring the Pope's support to the Christian community in Iraq. Though the wording of the announcement was vague, it seemed that Etchegaray's mission was twofold: To plead with Hussein to cooperate with the weapons inspectors and United Nations resolutions in an attempt to stave off conflict and to signal to the Muslim world the Vatican's opposition to war. Media reports also confirmed that Hussein's best-known deputy, Tarik Aziz, would be visiting the Holy See and the birthplace of St. Francis in Assisi in coming days.

February 10, 2003 The Iraqi ambassador to the Vatican, Amir Alanbari, told the Reuters news agency on February 10 that a papal visit to Iraq would be welcome, and that Tarik Aziz might invite the Pope when he visited the Holy See later in the week. "For the Pope to visit a country that is really about to be victimized by a superpower, to be destroyed I would say . . . would be viewed by the rest of the world as expressing sympathy, even if he does not say a word," Alanbari said.

Famiglia Cristiana published the results of a much-discussed survey asking readers if they supported the Pope's position on Iraq or that of George Bush. Results splashed across the front cover indicated that 95 percent of readers of the popular Italian weekly backed the Pope's antiwar stance.

February 11, 2003 John Paul issued his annual message for the World Day of the Sick. He wrote: "In this year, troubled by such great anxiety for the future of humanity, I wished the prayer of the Rosary to have as specific intentions the cause of peace and of the family. Dear sick brothers and sisters, you are 'on the front line' to intercede for these two great designs. May your life, marked by trial, instill in everyone that hope and serenity which can only be experienced in meeting Christ."

Novak delivered his lecture before an invitation-only crowd at Rome's Center of American Studies. He went out of his way to avoid any impression of disagreement with John Paul II, stressing that he has publicly termed this Pope "John Paul the Great." Novak argued that Saddam Hussein presents a clear and present danger to the security of the United States, especially in a post-9/11 world in which nonstate terrorist groups have the means to inflict serious damage. Even if a clear connection between Hussein and the Al Qaeda network cannot presently be established, Novak argued, "only an imprudent, foolhardy statesman would trust that these two forces will stay apart forever."

In that sense, Novak said, a war in Iraq falls under the traditional standards of self-defense, not some speculative new category of preventive war. Under certain circumstances, Novak said, it is not only possible to go to war, but morally obligatory. "For the public authorities to fail to conduct such a war would be to put their trust imprudently in the sanity and good will of Saddam Hussein," Novak said. He also underscored that according to the *Catechism of the Catholic Church*, it is the "public authorities"—in this case, the Bush administration—which have the right and duty to decide whether to use force.

Novak was asked how he squared his position on the war with that of the American bishops. Their November 13 statement had said, "Based on the facts that are known to us, we continue to find it difficult to justify the resort to war against Iraq, lacking clear and adequate evidence of an imminent attack of a grave nature." In response, Novak told a story related to the U.S. bishops' 1983 pastoral letter on the threat of nuclear war, called *The Challenge of Peace*. In 1981 and 1982, Novak said, there was alarm in some American Catholic circles about early drafts of that letter, which seemed to some conservative critics to lean too strongly toward disarmament. Leading conservative Catholic laypersons such as Zbigniew Brzezinski, Henry Hyde, and Clare Boothe Luce approached him with similar concerns, and together they drafted their own letter. Novak said the main difference between the two documents is that the bishops focused on weapons systems, while Novak's group centered on Communism. Weapons don't kill, they argued, ideologies do, and if they could change attitudes in the Soviet Union, disarmament would follow. Twenty years later, Novak argued, his group's letter holds up better than that of the bishops. "This is the lay role in the church," Novak said, "to argue about matters of prudence rather than doctrine."

February 12, 2003 Fr. Vincenzo Coli, custodian of the Franciscan convent in Assisi, rejected suggestions of a political subtext to Tarik Aziz's impending visit in an interview with *Corriere della Sera*. "Here we follow the teachings of Francis," Coli said. "We never put ourselves in the position of asking a pilgrim, 'Who are you? What is your program?' " He compared the reception for Aziz to St. Francis's taming of the wolf of Gubbio.

February 13, 2003 John Paul received Rabbi Riccardo di Segni, chief rabbi of Rome, in a Vatican audience. He said: "In these days we can hear resounding in the world dangerous shouts of war. We, Jews and Catholics, perceive the urgent mission of imploring peace from God, the Creator and Eternal One, and of being ourselves peacemakers."

February 14, 2003 Tarik Aziz, deputy Prime Minister of Iraq, visited the Pope in the Vatican, and held talks with Sodano and Tauran. "The meetings furnished the opportunity for an ample exchange of views on the well-known danger of an armed intervention in Iraq, which would add further grave sources of suffering to those populations already tried by long years of embargo," the Vatican statement afterward read. "Mr. Aziz wanted to give assurances concerning the will of the Iraqi government to cooperate with the international community, in particular in terms of disarmament, while on the part of the Holy See the necessity of faithfully respecting, with concrete undertakings, the resolutions of the Security Council of the United Nations, guaranteed by international law, was reaffirmed. Further, it was confirmed that the Catholic Church will continue its work of education for peace and co-existence among peoples, so that in every circumstance they may find solutions of peace."

The Vatican summoned all the ambassadors to the Holy See from countries represented on the United Nations Security Council and from the European Union for a briefing by Tauran about the Pope's session with Aziz. Tauran used the occasion to reiterate the Holy See's opposition to war in Iraq.

Aziz attended an evening press conference at Rome's Foreign Press Club. At Aziz's right hand was Fr. Jean-Marie Benjamin, a fifty-six-year-old French priest living in Italy who has long been a fierce critic of the UN-imposed sanctions in Iraq. "Why this initiative?" Benjamin asked rhetorically, introducing Aziz. "To remind the world that Iraq is a lay republic, with a Christian minister," he said. "Cooperation between Christians and Muslims is exemplary." Bin Laden, Benjamin said, would never allow one of his men to go pray at the tomb of St. Francis.

Aziz spoke positively about the Pope's stance on the war. "I came first and foremost to meet the Pope, and to deliver a message for His Holiness from Saddam Hussein," Aziz said. "The president and people of Iraq appreciate the clear position of the Holy See in rejecting the logic of war and in saying straightforwardly that this war is immoral. I can add, illegal," Aziz said. He warned European nations to stay out of a U.S.-led war. "If the Christian countries of Europe participate in a war of aggression, it will be interpreted as a crusade against the Arab world and Islam," he said. "It will poison relations between the Arab world and the Christian world." Aziz was also asked about the possibility of a papal trip to Baghdad. "We have excellent diplomatic relations with the Holy See," Aziz replied. "A visit to Iraq by the Holy Father or any Vatican official is a matter of principle. It is a normal thing. Right now there is a high-ranking official in Baghdad, Cardinal Etchegaray. But in the present crisis, such a visit would not be a good idea, for security reasons, as you know."

Asked by CNN in a separate interview for his reaction to John Paul's insistence on complying with the weapons inspectors and United Nations resolutions, Aziz was gracious. "I am not annoyed by that, you see," Aziz said. "There is a different motive when a good-hearted, impartial person like the Holy Father says that. When an American says it, with a different motive, it's different. It looks like the same thing, but it's different."

The dramatic peak of the press conference came when Menachem Gantz, the Rome correspondent for the Israeli newspaper *Maariv*, asked

Aziz if Iraq had any plans to attack Israel, and what Aziz thought about Arab states such as Qatar and Kuwait, which supported the U.S. position. "When I came to this press conference, it was not my intention to answer questions from the Israeli media," Aziz said. "I'm sorry." The president of the Foreign Press Club insisted that Gantz was an accredited journalist and member of the society and asked Aziz to respond. Again, Aziz refused. Some journalists booed and whistled and a few walked out, but the press conference continued. Benjamin told the *National Catholic Reporter* on February 17 that while Aziz's refusal to respond to Gantz was a mistake looked at through the lens of Western politics, it had to be understood from Iraq's point of view. "Israel has defied thirty-one United Nations resolutions, and no one is threatening to bomb them," Benjamin said. Anyway, he said, refusing to respond to the Israeli media is official Iraqi policy.

February 15, 2003 Cardinal Roger Etchegaray, John Paul's special envoy, met with Saddam Hussein in Baghdad. He released this statement to journalists, in French: "I understand that you have been awaiting the present moment with great interest, given the importance of the meeting I have just left. For your part, you understand that the spiritual nature of my mission gives my words a special tone to which you are doubtless not accustomed. The Church indeed has her own way of speaking of peace, making peace, among those who, for diverse reasons, employ themselves with such great tenacity. The Church, according to words by Pope John Paul II, is the spokesman of the 'moral conscience of mankind in its purest state, of a mankind that desires peace, that needs peace.'

"It is in this sense that my meeting with President Saddam Hussein touched upon concrete questions that I cannot mention through respect for the person who sent me, as well as for the person who received me. It is a matter of seeing if everything has been done to safeguard peace, while establishing a climate of confidence that allows Iraq to rediscover its place in the international community. At the heart of our meeting were the Iraqi people who, I have noted from Baghdad to

Mossoul, aspire so much to a just and lasting peace after years of suffering, for which the Pope and the universal Church have always expressed their solidarity. In the name of the Pope, I dare to appeal to the conscience of all those who, in these decisive days, shoulder the future of peace. For, in the end, it is one's conscience which will have the final word, which is stronger than all strategies, all ideologies and even all religions."

Aziz, a Chaldean Catholic, visited Assisi. He prayed in front of the Porziuncola, the small church built by Francis, which is now contained within the massive basilica of Santa Maria degli Angeli. Then Aziz moved to the lower basilica and the tomb of St. Francis. The Franciscans gave Aziz a replica of the perpetual lamp John Paul II lit during the January 24, 2002, gathering of world religious leaders in Assisi to pray for peace. They also showed Aziz the ivory horn that Sultan Kamil of Egypt gave Francis in 1219 at the height of the crusades. It is a symbol of Christian/Muslim understanding. The congregation of some twenty-five people then read a prayer the Pope wrote for the January 24 event: "Violence never again. War never again. Terrorism never again. In God's name, may all religions bring upon the earth justice and peace, forgiveness, life and love."

Some argued that the warm welcome for Aziz was inappropriate, given the human rights record of the Hussein government. Others objected to the presence of Archbishop Hilarion Cappucci, an auxiliary bishop of the Greek Melkite church in communion with Rome. Cappucci, who led a tiny Melkite community in Jerusalem in the 1960s and 1970s, carries the personal title of patriarch. He first came to public attention when he was arrested on August 18, 1974, by Israeli security forces after returning to Jerusalem from a trip to Lebanon. His car was found stuffed with TNT and guns headed for the Palestinian Liberation Organization. In October 2002, Cappucci and Benjamin held a press conference during a trip to Baghdad to oppose a U.S.-led war. "If Bush attacks Iraq, the resentment and hatred of the Arab-Islamic world will be accentuated against him personally and against the interests of the American people," Cappucci warned. In Assisi, Cappucci was ubiquitous alongside Aziz. He spoke freely to the press. "I said to Aziz that he must not give anyone an excuse for attacking Iraq, and hence resolution 1441 must be scrupulously observed. The Iraqis, he assured me, will respect these norms. . . . I pray that the angels may return to sing in heaven of peace on earth." Cappucci then added a critical remark about Israel. "Israel is like a spoiled child that has ended up living a double standard," he said.

February 16, 2003 Etchegaray released a statement prior to his departure from Baghdad. He said: "I have just experienced in Iraq an extraordinary intensity of communion with the person who sent me there, Pope John Paul II. Seldom have I felt so strongly that I was not only the bearer of his message of peace, but that he himself was present. I only followed him among the Christian communities, among all the Iraqi people, to President Saddam Hussein who showed a profound willingness to listen to a living word that comes from God, and that every believer, as descendant of Abraham, welcomes as the surest leaven of peace. As I leave this land, unjustly cut off from all others, I want to be more than the simple echo and amplifier of the aspiration of a country that has an urgent need of peace. Among the dark clouds that recently have gathered, here is a small glimmer of light. But let no one stop praying. The new and brief respite that has been granted must be used by all in a spirit of reciprocal confidence to respond to the demands of the international community. The least step in these days will have the value of a great leap towards peace. Yes, peace is still possible in Iraq and for Iraq. I depart for Rome crying this out more strongly than ever."

A full-length interview with Etchegaray is published in *L'Avvenire*, the official newspaper of the Italian bishops. He said of Hussein, "He appeared to me to be in good health, and seriously aware of the responsibility he must face before his people. I was convinced that Saddam Hussein now wishes to avoid war." Etchegaray was asked if his emphasis on the suffering of the Iraqi people could end up providing an alibi to the regime. "It could, but faced with a people that has suffered for so many years just to survive, you can't speak of alibis, there are no alibis," he said. Asked if he saw a new global openness to peace, Etchegaray said: "The world needs gestures that express the desire for peace. I believe it's necessary for public opinion to influence the decisions of leaders, but this must be a well-formed and well-informed opinion, because—I'm speaking generally—there is the possibility for manipulation. . . . The Iraqi people have a natural goodness of heart, but after two wars and the embargo they have been stricken in every aspect of their lives and cannot inform themselves."

February 18, 2003 United Nations Secretary General Kofi Annan met with the Pope in the Vatican, followed by talks with Sodano, who in this case was accompanied by Etchegaray. "In a cordial and detailed colloquium, the Pope and Mr. Annan were able to examine the diverse aspects of the critical situation currently regarding Iraq. Underlining the essential role of the United Nations, it was hoped that just and effective solutions may be found to the challenges of the moment with respect to international law, of which the United Nations is guarantee. May these solutions avoid additional grave sources of suffering for those populations already tried by long years of embargo," the Vatican statement read.

Respected Italian journalist Sandro Magister voiced the discomfort some conservative Catholics, including some Vatican officials, felt over Etchegaray's peace mission to Baghdad in his www.chiesa online column. Reflecting on Etchegaray's interview with *L'Avvenire*, Magister complained of an "incomprehensible" and "deafening" silence on Hussein's brutality to his own people. "The cardinal does not devote a single word to the horrible sufferings endured for decades by the Iraqi people, not at the hands of external agents, but at those of its tyrant and those who surround him," Magister wrote. Noting the Etchegaray interview and the February 12 interview in *Corriere della Sera* with Coli about the Aziz visit to Assisi, Magister sounded a warning about moral fuzziness. Both suggest "a certain confusion between true and false, between good and evil, between just and unjust," Magister wrote. "On a question like that of Iraq, so critical for the destiny of the world, the danger is . . . that same indiscriminate relativism, in the dressings of peace, that the Church itself is the first to identify as the great temptation of today's Christians."

February 19, 2003 Archbishop Celestino Migliore, the Holy See's observer at the United Nations, spoke before the Security Council on the Iraq issue. Migliore said: "The Holy See is convinced that in the efforts to draw strength from the wealth of peaceful tools provided by the international law, to resort to force would not be a just one. To the grave consequences for a civilian population that has already been tested long enough, are added the dark prospects of tensions and conflicts between peoples and cultures and the deprecated reintroduction of war as a way to resolve untenable situations. . . . The Holy See is convinced that even though the process of inspections appears somewhat slow, it still remains an effective path that could lead to the building of a consensus which, if widely shared by nations, would make it almost impossible for any government to act otherwise, without risking international isolation. The Holy See is therefore of the view that it is also the proper path that would lead to an agreed and honorable resolution to the problem, which, in turn, could provide the basis for a real and lasting peace. . . . On the issue of Iraq, the vast majority of the international community is calling for a diplomatic resolution of the dispute and for exploring all avenues for a peaceful settlement. That call should not be ignored. The Holy See encourages the parties concerned to keep the dialogue open that could bring about solutions in preventing a possible war and urges the international community to assume its responsibility in dealing with any failings by Iraq."

February 20, 2003 The Pope received an interreligious delegation from Indonesia that had come to Rome to express opposition to the war in Iraq. He said: "At this time of great tension for the world, you have come to Rome, and I am grateful to have this occasion to speak to you. With the real possibility of war looming on the horizon, we must not permit politics to become a source of further division among the world's religions. In fact, neither the threat of war nor war itself should be allowed to alienate Christians, Muslims, Buddhists, Hindus and members of other religions. As religious leaders committed to peace, we should work together with our own people, with those of other religious beliefs and with all men and women of good will to ensure understanding, cooperation and solidarity. Earlier this year, I said: 'War is always a defeat for humanity' (*Address to the Diplomatic Corps accredited to the Holy See,* 13 January 2003, 4). It is also a tragedy for religion. My fervent prayer is that our efforts to promote mutual understanding and trust will bear abundant fruit and help the world to avoid conflict. For it is through commitment and continuing cooperation that cultures and religions 'will be able to break through the barriers which divide them, to understand one another and to pardon those who have done them wrong' (*Pacem in Terris,* V). This is the way that leads to true peace on earth. Together, let us work and pray for this peace."

February 22, 2003 British Prime Minister Tony Blair visited John Paul II in the Vatican, and then held talks with Sodano and Tauran. "The Holy Father expressed the hope that in resolving the grave situation in Iraq, every effort will be made to avoid new divisions in the world," the Vatican statement afterward read. "In the meetings in the Vatican this morning the necessity was reconfirmed for all interested parties in the well-known Iraqi crisis to be able to collaborate with the United Nations, and to make use of the resources offered by international law, for dispelling the tragedy of a war that is still regarded in many quarters as avoidable. Special consideration was given to the humanitarian situation of the Iraqi people, already so harshly tried by long years of embargo."

February 23, 2003 The Pope delivered his Sunday Angelus address. In it, he called for a day of prayer and fasting to implore peace on Ash Wednesday, March 5. He said: "For months the international community has been living in great apprehension on account of the danger of a war that might upset the whole Middle East region and aggravate the tensions that, unfortunately, are already present at the beginning of the third millennium. It is a duty for believers, regardless of the religion they belong to, to proclaim that we can never be happy if we are against one another, the future of humanity can never be assured by terrorism and the logic of war. We Christians, especially, are called to be sentinels of peace wherever we live and work. We are asked to watch out so that consciences may not yield to the temptation to egoism, lying and violence. Therefore, I invite all Catholics to dedicate with special intensity next 5 March, Ash Wednesday, to prayer and fasting for the cause of peace, especially in the Middle East. Above all, let us ask God for the conversion of hearts and the farsightedness of just decisions to resolve with adequate and peaceful means the conflicts that impede the pilgrimage of humanity in our time."

February 23–24, 2003 The annual meeting of a joint committee between the Vatican and Cairo's prestigious al-Azhar institute, widely considered the Vatican of the Islamic world, took place in Cairo. The Vatican was represented by Archbishop Michael Fitzgerald, head of the Pontifical Council for Interreligious Dialogue. "War is a proof that humanity has failed," its concluding statement read. "It brings about enormous loss of human life, great damage to the basic structures of human livelihood and the environment, displacement of large populations, and further political instability. . . . In the present circumstances there is the added factor of increased tension between Muslims and Christians on account of the mistaken identification of some Western powers with Christianity, and of Iraq with Islam. . . . The Muslim members of the committee welcomed the clear policy and strenuous efforts of His Holiness Pope John Paul II in favor of peace," it said.

February 24, 2003 Tauran spoke at a conference on peace held at a Roman hospital, warning that "a war of aggression would be a crime against peace." He said the conflict would be illegal without UN warrant, especially if it were launched "by one or more states" outside the framework of the United Nations. "For us, everything must be undertaken and decided in the context of the United Nations," Tauran said. "No rule of international law authorizes one or more states to have unilateral recourse to the use of force for changing the regime or form of government of another state, because for example they may possess weapons of mass destruction. Only the Security Council could, on the basis of particular circumstances, decide that those facts constitute a threat to peace." He warned of the likely response to a war from countries in the region, which "in solidarity with Iraq could assume extreme attitudes."

Tauran appeared to downplay one of the key motives advanced by the Americans for this conflict, Saddam's arsenal. "Weapons of mass destruction are present not only in the Middle East, but also elsewhere," Tauran said. "Their destruction is certainly a pressing necessity, but it can be achieved with the inspections now underway." A war would lead to "disproportionate damages in relation to the objectives to be reached and would violate the fundamental rules of international humanitarian law," Tauran said, in language widely taken as a reference to the Geneva Convention. Tauran indicated that Iraq must act in ways consistent with its membership in international organizations, and that Bush should opt for "the force of law instead of the law of force."

Borgomeo used his Vatican Radio broadcast to again assert that the United States was acting in Iraq on the basis of its oil interests. Borgomeo took his cue from signs reading "no blood for oil" that many American antiwar protestors had been carrying, and suggested that they had a point. He noted that in late November representatives of American oil companies met with Iraqi opposition groups in London to open talks about the disposition of oil rights in a postwar Iraq. Despite the fact that Blair called the suggestion a "conspiracy theory," Borgomeo said it is "difficult" not to believe that Iraq's vast resources, estimated at some 112 billion barrels, has something to do with the military buildup.

February 27, 2003 John Paul II received Prime Minister José María Aznar of Spain, who also held talks with Sodano and Tauran. "In the cordial conversation, which lasted a half-hour, it was agreed that the situation created in Iraq is grave and that there is a need for a solution. The Holy Father hopes that all the parties involved—without exceptions—will adopt just decisions and will take up effective peaceful initiatives which conform to justice, inspired by international law and ethical principles," the Vatican statement read. "The head of the Spanish government explained the line of action followed by the Spanish government up to this point on the Iraqi crisis, illustrating, in particular, the danger of terrorism, and hence the necessity of a common action on the part of the United Nations. On these points was noted a convergence of views with the Holy See."

John Paul II received Seyyed Mohammad Reza Khatami, vice-president of Iran's parliament and the brother-in-law of the country's reformer president, who then held talks with Sodano and Tauran. "The meetings permitted an exchange of opinions on the necessity of protecting the peace in the area of the Middle East," the Vatican statement read. "On this very serious subject, the vice-president was the carrier of a message from President Mohammad Khatami for the Holy Father."

In a rare session, the ambassadors from all the nations accredited to the Holy See had a briefing session with Tauran, in which he outlined the Holy See's reasons for opposing a war in Iraq. In brief, Tauran argued that all decisions about the use of force on Iraq should be made in and through the United Nations. A war, he insisted, would have unacceptable consequences for the civilian population and would inflame extremist sentiments in the other countries of the area. It would inflict damages disproportionate to the good to be achieved and would violate international law, including the Geneva Convention. The Holy See acknowledged, Tauran said, the urgency of disarmament, but believed that the process of inspections could be effective.

March 2, 2003 The Pope delivered his Sunday Angelus address. He returned to the call for prayer and fasting to avoid the war in Iraq. He said: "This year we will undertake the penitential journey toward Easter with a greater commitment to prayer and fasting for peace, that is put at risk by the growing threat of war. Last Sunday, I already announced this initiative whose purpose is to involve the faithful in fervent prayer to Christ, Prince of Peace. Indeed, peace is a gift of God to be invoked with humble and insistent confidence. Without surrendering before difficulties, it is also necessary to seek and pursue every possible avenue to avoid war, which always brings mourning and serious consequences for all.

"The liturgy of Ash Wednesday invites us to add fasting to prayer, a penitential practice that calls for a more profound spiritual effort, the conversion of the heart, with the firm decision to turn away from evil and sin, to be better disposed to fulfill the will of God. With physical fasting, and, even more so with interior fasting, the Christian prepares himself to follow Christ and to be his faithful witness in every circumstance. Moreover, fasting helps us to understand better the difficulties and sufferings of so many of our brothers and sisters who are oppressed by hunger, severe poverty and war. In addition, it prompts us to a concrete solidarity and sharing with those who are in need. Dear Brothers and Sisters, let us dispose ourselves to participate intensely in the Day of Prayer and Fasting for Peace, which we will observe next Wednesday. We will pray for peace in the world, in particular, for Iraq and the Holy Land, especially through the recitation of the Rosary, which will involve shrines, parishes, communities, and families. From every part of the earth may this collective prayer rise through the intercession of Mary, Mother of Mercy and Queen of Peace."

March 5, 2003 In his general audience on Ash Wednesday, the Pope repeated his call for prayer and conversion aimed at avoiding war. He said: "As we enter the Lenten season, we need to be aware of today's international situation, troubled by the tensions and threats of war. It is necessary that everyone consciously assume responsibility and engage in a common effort to spare humanity another tragic conflict. This is why I wanted this Ash Wednesday to be a Day of Prayer and Fasting to implore peace for the world. We must ask God, first of all, for conversion of heart, for it is in the heart that every form of evil, every impulse to sin is rooted; we must pray and fast for the peaceful coexistence of peoples and nations."

John Paul performed the annual Ash Wednesday liturgy, as is papal custom, at the Dominican basilica of Santa Sabina on the Aventine Hill. He said: "This prospect of joy obliges believers to do everything possible to anticipate at the present time something of the future peace. This calls for the purification of heart and reinforcing of communion with God and with the brethren. This is the aim of the prayer and fasting to which, in the face of the threats of war looming on the horizon, I have invited the faithful. With prayer, we abandon ourselves totally into God's hands, and from him alone we await true peace. With fasting, we prepare our hearts to receive peace from the Lord, his greatest gift and the privileged sign of the coming of his Kingdom. Prayer and fasting, however, must be accompanied by works of justice; conversion must be translated into welcome and solidarity. The ancient Prophet warns: 'Is not this the fast that I choose; to loose the bonds of wickedness, / to undo the thongs of the yoke, / to let the oppressed go free, / and to break every yoke?' (Is 58,6). There will be no peace on earth while the oppression of peoples, social injustices and existing economic imbalances continue. Yet for the great and hoped for structural changes, extrinsic initiatives and mediations are not enough; above all, we need the unanimous conversion of hearts to love."

Cardinal Pio Laghi, former papal nuncio to the United States and John Paul's special peace envoy, met with President George Bush in the White House to plead that war be avoided. Afterward he released this statement: "I was privileged to have been sent by the Holy Father as his Special Envoy to President George Bush. I assured him of the Holy Father's great esteem and affection for the American people and the United States of America. The purpose of my visit was to deliver a personal message of the Holy Father to the President regarding the Iraqi crisis, to expound upon the Holy See's position and to report on the various initiatives undertaken by the Holy See to contribute to disarmament and peace in the Middle East. Out of respect for the President and because of the importance of this moment, I am not in a position to discuss the substance of our conversation, nor am I able to release the text of the personal letter of the Holy Father to the President.

"The Holy See is urging those in positions of civil authority to take fully into account all aspects of this crisis. In that regard, the Holy See's position has been twofold. First, the Iraqi government is obliged to fulfill completely and fully its international obligations regarding human rights and disarmament under the UN resolutions with respect for international norms. Second, these obligations and their fulfillment must continue to be pursued within the framework of the United Nations. The Holy See maintains that there are still peaceful avenues within the context of the vast patrimony of international law and institutions which exist for that purpose. A decision regarding the use of military force can only be taken within the framework of the United Nations, but always taking into account the grave consequences of such an armed conflict: the suffering of the people of Iraq and those involved in the military operation, a further instability in the region and a new gulf between Islam and Christianity.

"I want to emphasize that there is great unity on this grave matter on the part of the Holy See, the Bishops in the United States, and the Church throughout the world. I told the President that today, on Ash Wednesday, Catholics around the world are following the Pope's request to pray and fast for peace this day. The Holy Father himself continues to pray and hope that all leaders who face difficult decisions will be inspired in their search for peace."

Laghi presided over the Ash Wednesday liturgy at the Shrine of the Immaculate Conception in Washington, D.C. He delivered a homily, in which he said: "The Holy Father has worked untiringly for peace. He has not spared any effort in these last weeks to use every means available to him to ask those entrusted with the highest political authority 'to make just decisions in order to resolve with adequate and pacific means the strife that hinders mankind on its journey in our times.' He and his closest collaborators have received numerous leaders in the Vatican reminding them of the noble cause that is theirs when they build a world of peace. He sent a Special Envoy to the President of Iraq, and today he has sent me to the President of the United States. . . . The Church's solicitude for peace has been a constant one and that is why she never tires in her work for the cause of peace. She believes that peace can always be constructed even in the darkest moments. She believes in the power of the human mind and the courage of the human heart to find peaceful solutions to disagreements, using the vast and rich patrimony of international law and institutions created for that very purpose. Oh, yes, they may be incomplete; they may act too slowly at times; they may not have yet even caught up to deal with realities of our times that threaten world order. But they are based on principles that are true and relative for all times: honest and patient dialogue between and among disagreeing parties and the absolute duty of each member of the family of nations to comply fully with all its obligations."

March 8, 2003 Martino gave an interview to the Misna missionary news agency in which he warned that war in Iraq would deliver a near-fatal blow to the United Nations. "If, notwithstanding the lack of sufficient votes or the veto, war were to come all the same, the UN would suffer such a humiliating defeat that I don't know if it would be able to recover," Martino said. "In fact, it would end the scope for which the United Nations was created: the maintenance of peace and development."

March 9, 2003 The Pope delivered his Sunday Angelus address. He said: "In the present international context, there is a much stronger need to purify the conscience and convert the heart to true peace. In this regard, how much more eloquent is the image of Christ who exposes and overcomes the lies of Satan with the force of truth contained in the Word of God. In the inner heart of every person the voice of God and the insidious voice of the Evil One can be heard. The latter seeks to deceive the human person, seducing him with the prospect of false goods, to lead him away from the real good that consists precisely in fulfilling the divine will. But humble and confident prayer, reinforced by fasting, allows one to overcome even the harshest trials, and instills the necessary courage to combat evil with good. Thus Lent becomes a profitable time of spiritual training."

March 16, 2003 The Pope delivered his Sunday Angelus address, at one point departing from his prepared text to add personal comments about his experience of the Second World War. He spoke in unusually animated tones, waving his finger and raising his voice. He said: "I wish to renew an urgent appeal to intensify the commitment to prayer and penance, to invoke from Christ the gift of his peace. There is no peace without conversion of heart. The next few days will be decisive for the outcome of the Iraqi crisis. Let us pray, then, that the Lord inspire in all sides of the dispute courage and farsightedness.

"The political leaders of Baghdad certainly have the urgent duty to collaborate fully with the international community to eliminate every reason for armed intervention. To them I direct my urgent appeal: the fate of your fellow-citizens should always have priority. But I would also like to remind the member countries of the United Nations, and especially those who make up the Security Council, that the use of force represents the last recourse, after having exhausted every other peaceful solution, in keeping with the well-known principles of the UN Charter. That is why, in the face of the tremendous consequences that an international military operation would have for the population of Iraq and for the balance of the Middle East region, already sorely tried, and for the extremisms that could stem from it, I say to all: There is still time to negotiate; there is still room for peace, it is never too late to come to an understanding and to continue discussions. To reflect on one's duties, to engage in energetic negotiations does not mean to be humiliated, but to work with responsibility for peace. Moreover, we Christians are convinced that real and lasting peace is not only the fruit of necessary political agreements and understandings between individuals and peoples, but is the gift of God to all those who submit themselves to him and accept with humility and gratitude the light of his love.

"I belong to that generation that lived through World War II and, thanks be to God, survived it. I have the duty to say to all young people, to those who are younger than I, who have not had this experience: 'No more war' as Paul VI said during his first visit to the United Nations. We must do everything possible. We know well that peace is not possible at any price. But we all know how great is this responsibility. Therefore prayer and penance! Let us go forward confidently, dear Brothers and Sisters, in our Lenten journey. May the Blessed Virgin Mary obtain for us that this Lent may not be remembered as a sad time of war, but as a period of courageous effort for conversion and peace. We entrust this intention to the special intercession of St. Joseph whose Solemnity we will celebrate next Wednesday."

March 18, 2003 President George Bush set a final ultimatum for Saddam Hussein to go into exile, signaling abandonment of any hope of securing United Nations backing for the war. Vatican spokesperson Joaquin Navarro-Valls released the following statement: "Whoever decides that all peaceful means that international law has put at our disposition have been exhausted assumes a serious responsibility before God, his conscience and history."

March 19, 2003 The Pope spoke at his general audience on the Feast of St. Joseph. He said: "May St. Joseph, the Patron of the universal Church, watch over the entire ecclesial community and, as the man of peace that he was, may he obtain for all humanity, especially for the peoples threatened at this time by war, the precious gift of harmony and peace."

March 20, 2003 Hostilities broke out in Iraq. Navarro-Valls issued a statement from the Vatican: "The Holy See has noted with profound sadness the unfolding of recent events in Iraq. On the one hand, it regrets that the Iraqi government did not welcome the resolutions of the United Nations and the appeal of the Pope that requested a disarmament of the country. On the other hand, the Holy See deplores that the path of negotiations was interrupted, according to international law, towards a peaceful solution of the Iraqi crisis. In such a situation, it is noted with satisfaction that the various Catholic institutions in Iraq continue to carry out their activity of assistance to those populations. In order to contribute to this work of solidarity, the Apostolic Nunciatura, directed by Archbishop Fernando Filoni, will remain open in this period in its location in Baghdad."

March 22, 2003 John Paul II received in audience a delegation from the Italian Catholic television channel Telepace. He said: "Telepace! Its name expresses the objective that the transmitter wants to realize. Telepace wants to be the television of peace, of that peace which is the gift of God and a humble and constant human achievement. When war threatens humanity's destiny, as it does today in Iraq, it is even more urgent for us to proclaim with a loud and decisive voice that peace is the only way to build a more just and caring society. Violence and arms can never solve human problems."

Rumors appeared in the Italian press that the United States had asked governments, including the Holy See, to sever diplomatic relations with Iraq. French Cardinal Paul Poupard, head of the Pontifical Council for Culture, gave an interview on the subject to *Corriere della Sera*. "I'm not aware of a request and it's not in my competence to deal with it, but certainly the Holy See will not withdraw its own nuncios and will not break any diplomatic relations," Poupard said. "[The Vatican] will always take the opportunity to maintain every possible channel of communication, above all at times of conflict. It is not wise to leave the talking to missiles." Officials at the U.S. embassy to the Holy See later told the *National Catholic Reporter* that they had made no such direct request.

March 23, 2003 The Pope delivered his Sunday Angelus address. He said: "We now turn to the Blessed Virgin Mary. . . . Above all at this time we ask her for the gift of peace. To her especially, we entrust the victims of these hours of war and their families who are suffering. I feel spiritually close to them with my affection and my prayer."

March 24, 2003 John Paul received a delegation from the Evangelical Lutheran Church of America in audience at the Vatican. He said: "In a world situation filled with danger and insecurity, all Christians are called to stand together in proclaiming the values of the Kingdom of God. The events of recent days make this duty all the more urgent."

John Paul II received a group of military chaplains taking part in a study course in Rome. His language this day is perhaps his most blunt in rejecting the moral legitimacy of war. He also appeared to endorse the massive street protests in Europe and elsewhere in opposition to the conflict, referring positively to a "vast contemporary movement in favor of peace." The Pope said: "Your course is taking place at a difficult moment in history, when the world once again is hearing the clash of arms. The thought of the victims and the destruction and suffering caused by armed conflict brings ever-deeper anxiety and great sorrow. By now, it should be clear to all that the use of war as a means of resolving disputes between States was rejected, even before the UN Charter, by the consciences of the majority of humanity, except in the case of legitimate defense against an aggressor. The vast contemporary movement in favor of peace—which, according to the teaching of the Second Vatican Council, is more than 'the simple absence of war' (*Gaudium et spes*, n. 78)—demonstrates this conviction of people of every continent and culture. In this context, the influence of the different religions in sustaining the quest for peace is a reason for comfort and hope. In our view of faith, peace, even if it is the fruit of political agreements and understanding between individuals and peoples, is the gift of God, whom we should insistently invoke with prayer and penance. Without conversion of heart there is no peace! Peace can only be achieved through love! Right now we are all asked to work and pray so that war may disappear from the horizon of humanity."

In an address to the Italian bishops, Ruini expresses reservations about the pacifist movements in response to the Iraq crisis. He called for "constant discernment . . . in order that the commitment to peace not be confused with markedly different objectives and interests, or polluted by arguments that are really based upon conflict." Ruini then made an explicit plea for solidarity with the United States. "The reasons for solidarity that bind together the nations of the West retain their profound validity even after the fading of the threat of the 'Cold War,' as their roots are planted in a heritage of values that they still have in common, even amid undeniable differences," he said. "This solidarity finds new motivation in the great changes that are dawning on the world's horizon and which will require constructive and harmonious responses from the West."

In a comment to the *National Catholic Reporter*, Bishop Rino Fisichella, rector of the Lateran University and a powerful Vatican advisor, expressed concern that the antiwar movement in Europe was making a mistake by setting up America as the enemy. "This direction we are moving in, of isolating the United States, is terrible," he said. Fisichella said that in Italy there are forces "manipulating" the antiwar humor of the moment to grind old ideological axes against the United States and against the West.

March 26, 2003 The Pope spoke at his regular Wednesday General Audience. He said: "Dear friends, yesterday we celebrated the Solemnity of the Annunciation, the first of the 'joyful mysteries' that celebrates the Incarnation of the Son of God, Prince of Peace. As we prayed the Rosary, we meditated on this mystery, with our hearts oppressed by the news we are receiving from Iraq which is at war, without forgetting the other conflicts that rage around the globe. How important it is, during this Year of the Rosary, that we persevere in reciting the Rosary to ask for peace! I ask that it be continually recited, especially at the Marian shrines. To Mary, Queen of the Rosary, I now entrust my resolution to make a pilgrimage to her shrine at Pompeii, next

7 October, for the Feast of Our Lady of the Rosary. May Mary's maternal intercession obtain justice and peace for the whole world!"

A Roman newspaper reported that the Vatican was planning to offer exile to four Iraqi diplomats who had been expelled from Italy. Spokesperson Navarro-Valls told the *National Catholic Reporter* that this was "rubbish," that no request had reached the Holy See, and that the Vatican had no plans to take in the expelled diplomats. "It would be very strange," Navarro said.

March 28, 2003 A twenty-six-year-old Austrian named Andreas Siebenhoer took off from Rome's Villa Pamphili park in a flying seat borne aloft with a parachute and a small blower. He sailed across the skies of the city for fifteen minutes, violating Vatican airspace and landing at the edge of St. Peter's Square. Siebenhoer wanted to deliver a petition to John Paul II with more than two thousand signatures supporting the Pope's position on the war. He was part of a group of eight young Austrians and Germans who had been making flights for peace across Europe, accompanied by a seventy-three-year-old Franciscan named Fr. Pascal Shou. In the case of the drop-in at the Vatican, however, Siebenhoer said he acted on his own. Siebenhoer was taken into custody by Italian police, then released. The group had spent the previous night at Sant' Anselmo, the Benedictine monastery on the Aventine hill.

March 29, 2003 John Paul spoke before a group of bishops from Indonesia in Rome for their *ad limina* visit. He said: "I wish to assure you of my deep concern for the beloved Indonesian people at this moment of heightened tension in the entire world community. War must never be allowed to divide world religions. I encourage you to take this unsettling moment as an occasion to work together, as brothers committed to peace, with your own people, with those of other religious beliefs and with all men and women of good will in order to ensure understanding, cooperation and solidarity. Let us not permit a human tragedy also to become a religious catastrophe."

March 30, 2003 The Pope delivered his regular Sunday Angelus address. He said: "Today, the Fourth Sunday of Lent, the Gospel reminds us that God 'so loved the world that he gave his only Son, so that everyone who believes in him might not perish but might have eternal life' (Jn 3,16). We hear this comforting proclamation at a time when painful armed confrontation threatens the hope of humanity for a better future. Jesus affirmed 'God so loved the world.' So then, the Father's love reaches every human being who lives in the world. How can one not see the obligation that springs from such an initiative of God? Conscious of such great love, the human being can only open himself to an attitude of fraternal welcome towards his fellow human beings."

April 2, 2003 John Paul II spoke at his regular Wednesday General Audience, meditating on the theme of how to make sense of God's failure to prevent evil. He said: "The divine silence is often a cause of perplexity to the just, and even scandalous, as Job's long lamentation attests (cf. Jb 3: 1–26). However, it is not a silence that suggests absence, as if history had been left in the hands of the perverse, or the Lord were indifferent and impassive. In fact, that silence gives vent to a reaction similar to a woman in labor who gasps and pants and screams with pain. It is the divine judgement on evil, presented with images of aridity, destruction, desert, which has a living and fruitful result as its goal. In fact, the Lord brings forth a new world, an age of freedom and salvation. The eyes of the blind will be opened so that they may enjoy the brilliant light. The path will be leveled and hope will blossom, making it possible to continue to trust in God and in his future of peace and happiness. Every day the believer must be able to discern the signs of divine action even when they are hidden by the apparently monotonous, aimless flow of time. . . . Discovering this divine presence, with the eyes of faith, in space and time but also within ourselves, is a source of hope and confidence, even when our hearts are agitated and shaken 'as the trees of the forest shake before the wind' (Is 7:2)." As is customary, the Pope was greeted by a number of people and groups at the end of the audience, among them some Italian students preparing for careers in the hotel business. They brought the Pope a huge cake, which he received with a smile. It was decorated in the rainbow colors of the peace flag, with a large dove made of white glaze in the middle.

April 4, 2003 Two weeks into the war, the *National Catholic Reporter* carried a story reporting that the feared anti-Christian backlash in the Muslim world had not materialized. The newspaper contacted Christian and Muslim leaders in places where relations between the two faiths were strained: Pakistan, Nigeria, Egypt, Indonesia, Lebanon, Palestine, as well as Iraq. Based on reporting from March 29 to April 2, there had not been a single case recorded of harassment or violence against Christians related to the war. In fact, sources in several traditional hotspots said Christian/Muslim relations were better than ever. All sources concurred that a principal factor had been the strong anti-war line of John Paul II, which had received extensive coverage in the Arab press and praise from Islamic leaders.

April 6, 2003 The Pope delivered his Sunday Angelus address. He said: "My thoughts go in particular to Iraq and to all those involved in the war that is being waged there. I am thinking in a special way of the defenseless civilian population in various cities which is subjected to a harsh trial. Please God that this conflict ends soon in order to make way for a new era of forgiveness, love and peace."

April 9, 2003 John Paul spoke at his regular Wednesday General Audience. He linked the war in Iraq to other conflicts in Africa. He said: "While fighting with destruction and death continues in Baghdad and other urban centers in Iraq, equally disturbing news is arriving from the African continent. In the past few days we have received information about massacres and summary executions. The scene of these crimes was the tortured Great Lakes region and, especially, an area of the Democratic Republic of the Congo. As I raise to God a fervent prayer for the repose of the victims' souls, I address a heartfelt appeal to political leaders and to all people of good will to do their utmost to put an end to the violence and abuses, setting aside selfish personal and group interests, with the effective collaboration of the international community."

U.S. undersecretary of state for Arms Control and International Security, John Bolton, was in Rome for meetings with Vatican officials. Bolton met separately with Stafford, Ruini, and Tauran. Each meeting lasted for approximately one hour. Bolton then held a press conference before an invited group of Italian and American journalists at the U.S. embassy to the Holy See. Bolton was asked if he had detected any softening in the Vatican's position on the war, given that the Holy See had been a leading center of opposition. Bolton replied that he rejected that characterization of the Vatican's position. The Holy See expressed concerns, he said, but they recognized that it is up to the civil authority to make the decision. Vatican officials respect, Bolton said, the sense of conscience with which President Bush made this decision.

The common American interest with the Vatican now, Bolton said, is to look to the future. Concretely, that means installing a government that respects the will of the Iraqi people, making sure that a humanitarian disaster is avoided in Iraq, eliminating weapons of mass destruction, and moving forward toward a comprehensive peace settlement in the Middle East. On the humanitarian front, Bolton said the Vatican had offered some concrete suggestions as to how aid might be delivered. This was a pressing problem, since the destruction of the Ba'ath Party meant the destruction of the only instrument Iraq had for getting supplies from the Food-for-Oil program to its people. Churches and mosques in Iraq, Bolton said, may have a role to play in creating a substitute delivery system. He vowed to relay the suggestions to Washington, so that people on the ground could make the decision.

April 10, 2003 Fighting appeared to end in Iraq. Sodano issued the following statement: "The Secretariat of State, having been informed of the latest developments in Baghdad, which mark an important turning point in the Iraqi conflict and a significant opportunity for the future of the people, hopes that the military operations underway in the rest of the country will soon end, with the aim of sparing further victims, civilian or military, and further suffering for those populations. Given that the material, political and social reconstruction of the country are on the horizon, the Catholic Church is ready, through her social and charitable institutions, to lend the necessary assistance. The dioceses of Iraq are likewise available to offer their structures to contribute to an equitable distribution of humanitarian aid. The Secretariat of State hopes once again that, with the silencing of weapons, the Iraqis and the international community will know how to meet the compelling present challenge which is to definitively bring an era of peace to the Middle East."

John Paul spoke before an assembly of young people from Rome on the occasion of World Youth Day, giving special emphasis to Mary and the rosary. He said: "Responding to this invitation and taking Mary into your home will also mean working for peace. Mary, *Regina Pacis* (Queen of Peace), is indeed a Mother, and like every mother all she wants for her children is to see them living peacefully and in agreement with one another. In this tormented time in history, while terrorism and wars are threatening peace between men and women and religions, I would like to entrust you to Mary so that you may become champions of the culture of peace, today more necessary than ever."

April 13, 2003 The Pope delivered his Palm Sunday homily in Rome. Speaking to the youth present, he said: "And how could we fail to express our fraternal solidarity to your peers who are so sorely tried by war and violence in Iraq, in the Holy Land and in various other regions of the world?"

April 16, 2003 The Pope spoke on the occasion of the Easter Triduum, the final three days of Holy Week. He said: "Commemorating this central mystery of the faith also involves the commitment to put it into practice in the concrete reality of our lives. It means recognizing that Christ's passion is continued in the dramatic events which, unfortunately, still in our time afflict so many men and women in every part of the earth. The mystery of the Cross and of the Resurrection, however, assures us that hatred, violence, blood and death do not have the last word in human lives. The definitive victory is Christ's, and we must set out anew with him if we want to build a future of authentic peace, justice and solidarity for everyone."

April 17, 2003 The Pope celebrated the Holy Thursday liturgy. In his homily, he said: "I would like the collection taken during this Celebration to go to alleviate the urgent needs of all those in Iraq who are suffering the consequences of the war. A heart that has known the love of the Lord opens spontaneously to charity for his brethren."

April 18, 2003 The Pope celebrated the traditional Good Friday Way of the Cross liturgy at the Colosseum. Since he no longer is physically capable of carrying the cross for the fourteen stations, John Paul has adopted the custom of asking individuals to carry it for one or two stations to symbolize particular concerns. This year, the cross was borne for the twelfth and thirteenth stations by an Iraqi family. John Paul said: "Mystery of the faith! Man could not imagine this mystery, this reality. God alone could reveal it. Man does not have the possibility of giving life after death. The death of death. In the human order, death is the last word. The subsequent word, the word of the Resurrection, is a word that comes only from God, and this is why we celebrate this 'Sacred Triduum' with such profound feeling."

During a Rome press conference with three Catholic news outlets, Tommy Thompson, the secretary of Health and Human Services under President George Bush and himself a Catholic, discussed the standoff between Rome and Washington over the Iraq war. "If I had my druthers, I would rather have had the Pope on my side," Thompson said. "But we have much better information than the Pope about what's going on inside Iraq and what would happen in the rest of the Middle East. . . . The Pope is concerned about innocent children and citizens, and so are we," Thompson said. "We can show with empirical evidence and data that we have saved men, women and children from torture, from rapes and murders, in Afghanistan and Iraq," he said.

In an interview with the *National Catholic Reporter*, renowned Italian editorialist Ernesto Gallia della Loggia criticized the Vatican's handling of the Iraq crisis. He said he was surprised not by the Holy See's position on the war, but by the tone of its opposition, and especially by what he saw as its uncritical commentary about Iraq. Galli della Loggia noted that in John Paul's United Nations speeches on peace, the Pope had always placed his message in the context of human rights, yet the Pope did not use human rights language much during the Iraq crisis. Galli della Loggia suggested this may be because references to human rights would have invited awkward questions about the brutal character of the Saddam Hussein government. Galli della Loggia also speculated that the Holy See had gambled that it could afford to antagonize the Americans more than Islamic nations. "They probably think that no matter what the Pope says, American Catholics will be okay and the American administration will still see the Vatican as a great global institution. In that sense, there's nothing to lose by coming out against the Americans, and everything to gain by siding with Islam," he said.

Galli della Loggia observed that it was the most Catholic countries of Europe—Spain, Italy, and Poland—whose governments backed the United States on the war, while it was France and Germany, the birthplaces of Revolution and Reformation respectively, that sided with the Pope. Galli della Loggia said this is a sign of the political weakness of the Catholic Church in Europe. It does not have the throw-weight to determine policy, even in nations where ostensibly friendly governments are in power.

Galli della Loggia said that the Iraq crisis exposed a fundamental weakness in Vatican foreign policy—hesitation to confront corrupt regimes in the developing world. "The Vatican wants to be a global voice of conscience, supporting developing nations," Galli della Loggia said. "Often they express this support by spouting the same economic formula they always recycle, blaming rich nations for poverty. . . . But the principal obstacle to social and economic development is not the West, but dictatorial and corrupt regimes that strangle their own people. Catholic missionaries and even the Vatican polemicize against the West, hiding local responsibility. They're afraid of being tossed into the 'Western' mix if they make problems for these governments. Ironically, the only governments the Church criticizes are in the West, where it knows it won't have to pay any price because those governments respect human rights," Galli della Loggia said.

April 20, 2003 In remarks on Easter Day, the Pope seemed to support calls for the Americans to turn over responsibility for postwar Iraq as quickly as possible to the United Nations and to the Iraqis themselves. He said: "Peace in Iraq! With the support of the international community, may the Iraqi people become the protagonists of the collective rebuilding of their country. . . . Let there be an end to the chain of hatred and terrorism, which threatens the orderly development of the human family. May God grant that we be free from the peril of a tragic clash between cultures and religions. May faith and love of God make the followers of every religion courageous builders of understanding and forgiveness, patient weavers of a fruitful interreligious dialogue, capable of inaugurating a new era of justice and peace." The address was delivered live to fifty-three countries. The crowd in St. Peter's Square spontaneously burst into applause. From that point forward, every reference to peace brought cheers. In the end the Pope was interrupted by applause a campaign-style fifteen times.

April 22, 2003 Cardinal Achille Silvestrini, who served as the Vatican's foreign minister for ten years under John Paul II, gave an interview to *La Repubblica* in which he reflected on the Pope's peace initiative over the past few months. "In the entire Christian world, there was a spontaneous consensus around the Pope never before seen," Silvestrini said. "I don't recall any epoch in which the Pope had such attention from Christians of the various confessions, from patriarchs and

bishops. It was as if all had said: 'You are our spiritual guide in this reflection on peace.' " Silvestrini said the pan-Christian support for the
Pope elicited a dream. "I'm thinking about an ecumenical convocation
in which the exponents of the Christian churches together with the
Pope could carry out a grand reflection on the responsibility of Christians with respect to war," he said. A new ecumenical consensus in favor
of peace, Silvestrini argued, could be the "good" to come from the
"evil" of the Iraq conflict. "The sensation is spreading that we are arriving at a maturation in the history of humanity," Silvestrini said. "Just as
at a certain point slavery was abolished, and torture and the death
penalty were condemned, we are now dissolving the notion that war
can ever be justified. Apart from defense against aggression, but certainly not a preventive war."

April 30, 2003 Outgoing Israeli Ambassador to the Holy See
Neville Lamdan, in an interview with the *National Catholic Reporter,*
voiced concern that under the pressure of recent world events, including 9/11 and the Iraq war, the Catholic Church's primary interreligious
relationship is increasingly no longer Judaism but Islam. It is a situation,
he said, that could pose dangers both for Israel and for the broader
Catholic/Jewish dialogue.

June 2, 2003 U.S. Secretary of State Colin Powell met John Paul
II in the Vatican, followed by talks with Sodano and Tauran. U.S. officials presented the meeting as a sign that Vatican/American relations
were "back on track" following the dispute over the war. "Among
the themes discussed was the material and political reconstruction of
Iraq," the Vatican statement afterward read, "which must be able to
count on the cooperation of the international community and pay particular attention to fundamental rights, such as the right to religious
liberty."

FLASHPOINTS

Despite the positive spin on the Powell visit, it is clear from this review of the Holy See's activism on the Iraq war that fundamental differences exist between the foreign policy vision of the United States under the Bush administration and that of John Paul's Vatican. Absent a change of philosophy on either side, it is reasonable to assume that the following four disputes will be recurrent flashpoints in the Rome/Washington relationship.

Preventive War

The Roman Catholic tradition of moral reflection on the characteristics of a "just war" distinguishes between legitimacy *ad bellum*, meaning the reasons for waging the war, and *in bello*, meaning the manner in which the war is conducted.

For justice *ad bellum*, the tradition offers six tests:

- *Legitimate authority.* Private individuals and groups are not permitted to take up arms against others, however justified their cause may appear. Only governments—those who have been entrusted with the public good—may wage war, and they must do it openly and legally.
- *Just cause.* A government may wage war in self-defense, in defense of another nation, to protect innocents, or to regain something wrongfully taken. The desire for personal glory or revenge, or to impose tyrannical rule, is never an acceptable cause for waging war.
- *Right intention.* The ultimate end of a government in waging war must be to establish peace, rather than to use a "just war" as a pretext for its own gain.
- *Last resort.* A governing authority must reasonably exhaust all other diplomatic and nonmilitary options for securing peace before resorting to force.
- *Reasonable chance of success.* A government may not resort to war unless its prospects for success are good. In this way,

lives will not be needlessly wasted in the pursuit of a hopeless cause.

- *Proportionality*. A government must respond to aggression with force only when the effects of its defensive actions do not exceed the damage done by the aggression itself.

For determining justice *in bello*, two values are key:

- *Noncombatant immunity*. An authority waging war is morally obligated to seek to discriminate between combatants and noncombatants. While civilians may sometimes come in harm's way, a government may never deliberately target them.
- *Proportionate means*. This criterion pertains to specific tactics of warfare and seeks to restrict unnecessary use of force. It is intended to ensure that the military means used to achieve certain goals and goods are commensurate with their value, particularly when compared to the loss of life and destruction that could also occur.

Under the pressure of world events since the first Gulf War, the Holy See has been forced to clarify how it applies these principles to a new international situation in which nonstate actors such as terrorist networks have become threats and the role of old security alliances is not clear. Four moments have been key:

- In 1991, the Holy See opposed the Gulf War.
- In 1999, The Holy See supported an international intervention in Kosovo to stop the violence against the civilian population in that former Yugoslav province, although it expressed reservations *in bello*, especially with respect to the NATO bombing of Serbia.
- In 2001, the Vatican gave basic support to the U.S.-led strikes against the Taliban regime in Afghanistan.

- In 2003, the Holy See opposed the U.S.-led war in Iraq
  with a ferocity that few issues in the recent past have
  aroused.

In all of this diplomatic activity, the Holy See has worked out a
new understanding of when the use of force is morally legitimate. A
single state, in its view, has the right to use force only in self-defense,
meaning in response to a direct attack. A group of states, such as
NATO or the ad-hoc coalitions cobbled together by U.S. administra-
tions in recent conflicts, may have the right, even the duty, to engage in
"humanitarian intervention" to end a crisis in which civilians are being
persecuted by an unjust aggressor. In all other situations, the only legitimate use of force—such as a preventive war to disarm a potential aggressor—is that sanctioned by the international community working
through the United Nations. In all cases, morally legitimate use of force
is a response to violence that is already in act. The Holy See's bottom
line is that no state is ever justified in striking first.

This view is contested by the Bush administration, which argues
that sometimes rogue states are determined to skirt the will of the international community on disarmament, and their stockpiles of weapons
pose a threat to the security of the United States and the rest of the
world. The possible links between such governments and international
terrorism make that threat all the more serious. When the United States
has intelligence that an attack against American interests is imminent, it
reserves the right to strike first, even without the approval of the
United Nations—a process whose potential political complications
make it too cumbersome to be feasible in some real-life situations. It
would be irresponsible of any American administration, the Bush team
argues, to ignore credible information regarding possible hostile activity
and thereby put American lives and interests at risk. Moreover, this is
not just a matter of defending America, but the West and, for that matter, global civilization.

In many ways, this is less a dispute over principles than over prudential judgment. No one in the Holy See would deny that a man fac-

ing someone pointing a gun in his face has the right to use force to disarm him. One does not have to wait for the assailant to shoot. Nor would anyone in the Bush White House seriously argue that the United States has the right, or for that matter the desire, to invade any country whatsoever that might one day pose a threat to its security interests. The question is, where on this continuum does a particular case fit? The clash over Iraq seems to suggest that the Holy See sets the bar much higher than the White House in terms of how much evidence there must be, and how convincing that evidence must appear, before force can be considered.

International Law

As outlined in chapter 1, the Holy See has long been a supporter of the construction of a strong system of international law. Beginning with Pope John XXIII in *Pacem et Terris*, every pope of the late twentieth century has called for a strengthened United Nations with real enforcement powers to make international law stick. The argument is that the international community must be governed by the force of law, not the law of force.

In July 2002, as a concrete expression of this attitude, the Holy See gave a symbolic contribution of $3,000 to a trust fund established by UN Secretary General Kofi Annan to support the new International Criminal Court. The Vatican had long been a proponent of the court. In 1998, John Paul II said that the international court "could contribute to ensure the effective protection of human rights on the worldwide scale." The Pope's statement included a caution that the new court should be firmly based on the rule of international law. He added that, "Crimes against humanity should not be considered as the internal affair of one nation." This backing came despite the fact that conservative Catholic critics of the court complained that it is "permeated with feminist ideology" and warned that it could force through legal recognition of a "right" to abortion, or even put the Pope himself on trial.

The Holy See believes in the rule of international law in part as an antidote to a unilateral world in which strong nations impose their will on the weak. An additional, more realpolitik motive for the stance is the conviction that the growth of international law, and especially the concept of universal human rights, offers the best prospect for protection of the religious freedom of Christians where they are a minority, such as India and the Islamic world. This Vatican conviction leads to resentment of the United States when it is perceived to be obstructing the construction of an international legal order. As noted above, a May 17 editorial in *Civiltà Cattolica* excoriated the United States for holding prisoners of war at Guantanamo Bay in Cuba without guaranteeing them the procedural rights specified in the Geneva Convention or other relevant international agreements. Under the same logic, the Vatican has strongly supported recent international treaties on a host of other matters, from the Kyoto Accords on the environment to the agreement banning land mines and the UN treaty on the rights of the child.

Given the Bush administration's well-known reluctance to subject Americans to the jurisdiction of international courts out of a fear of politicized indictments, and its generally lukewarm attitude toward the concept of a binding international legal order, this is a difference that seems destined to endure. As the United States prosecutes its war against terrorism, it is increasingly likely to adopt strategies that sometimes place it outside commonly recognized international standards in terms of how a state is supposed to conduct intelligence, treat the citizens of other nations, and so on. Since much of the terrorist threat currently preoccupying the United States emanates from the Islamic world, this may exacerbate anti-American sentiment in the Islamic street. The Holy See is deeply concerned that anti-American Islamic anger not become anti-Western and anti-Christian. It will feel increasing pressure to be critical of the United States, in order to put public distance between itself and measures deemed to violate international law. In other words, it will be increasingly difficult for the Holy See to look the other way when the United States takes action in contravention of international standards and agreements.

United Nations

While some Americans, including the key tacticians in the Bush administration, are leery of surrendering power to the United Nations, the Vatican believes strongly in a reformed UN with real decision-making authority. John Paul II, in his message for the 2003 World Day of Peace, put it this way: "Is this not the time for all to work together for a new constitutional organization of the human family, truly capable of ensuring peace and harmony between peoples, as well as their integral development?" In a statement on the role of the United Nations in July 2003, Cardinal Renato Martino expanded on this point, calling the UN the only forum "that, by its representativeness, can offer a platform of dialogue at the world level. The Holy See is convinced, and this is not something recent, that the worldwide common good must be pursued with adequate structures of universal competence," he added. Martino advocated reform in at least two areas: the first would aim to "empower the functioning of the Security Council." The second would aim to ensure that the international body could "guarantee order and security better, not only from the political and military point of view, but also in the economic and social field. For example, the new problems relating to protection of the environment and health require urgent measures that are respected by all."

This position strikes some observers as curious, since in other contexts the Holy See has been an ardent critic of the United Nations, especially on issues of the family, sexuality, and reproductive health policies. In September 2000, for example, Cardinal Joseph Ratzinger writing in *L'Avvenire* rejected UN proposals for a New World Order targeting for special criticism the UN's goal of depopulation. Ratzinger wrote that the philosophy coming from recent UN conferences and the Millennium Summit "proposes strategies to reduce the number of guests at the table of humanity, so that the presumed happiness [we] have attained will not be affected." He criticized this philosophy for "not being concerned with the care of those who are no longer productive or who can no longer hope for a determined quality of life."

376 ALL THE POPE'S MEN

Ratzinger argued that "at the base of this New World Order" is the ideology of "women's empowerment," which erroneously sees "the principal obstacles to [a woman's] fulfillment [as] the family and maternity." The cardinal advised that "at this stage of the development of the new image of the new world, Christians—and not just them but in any case they even more than others—have the duty to protest."

Pressed to explain this seeming contradiction, Vatican officials generally say that in itself the United Nations is merely a tool, and as such may be applied for ends that are either morally legitimate or morally destructive. In order to build a more just world, however, they see it as an essential tool, and support augmenting its powers and responsibilities. They offer three arguments in support of this position. First, a strong United Nations would have a unique capacity to promote the common good on the global level, ensuring that global economic structures do not simply enrich elites at the expense of the rest of the world. The UN would be able to promote the "globalization of solidarity" that has been a cornerstone of Pope John Paul's international vision since the collapse of the old Cold War system. Second, a reformed UN would help ensure that strong nations do not simply impose their will on the weak. Third, Vatican officials believe that a UN committed to multilateral decision-making, in which small and medium-sized states have real possibilities to shape policy, would be less open to manipulation by powerful nonstate actors such as corporations and NGOs (think Planned Parenthood, for example). The Vatican learned from the battles at the Cairo and Bejing conferences in the mid-1990s that sometimes its most serious opposition in the UN system comes not from states, but from representatives of civil society. Vatican officials argue that a UN in which states counted more and these special interests counted less would actually be more democratic and less susceptible to the imposition of values such as those described by Ratzinger above.

The Bush administration and mainstream political sentiment in the United States find it hard to reconcile with this vision of the United Nations. From the dominant American view, the United Nations is a forum for international cooperation, useful when states can agree to a common effort to address some problem, but inessential to the legitimacy of the actions any individual state might take. While the Holy See would understand the United Nations in terms of sovereignty, the United States would see it rather as a means of cooperation among individually sovereign states, each of which retains complete liberty of action. Given that the post–September 11 world situation is witnessing a highly activist and interventionist approach from the United States, this difference with the Holy See and much of the rest of the international community would appear set to become steadily more serious.

The American Role in the World

In the end, the Holy See might be less concerned about unilateralism if it had more faith in the world's lone superpower to foster a world order conducive to the realization of Christian virtue. In fact, however, at the deepest level of analysis, there is serious doubt in many quarters in the Vatican that American culture is an apt carrier for a Christian vision of the human person and therefore of the just society. Many of the more reflective minds in the Vatican would agree with theologian David Schindler of the Communio school that "the religion of Americans contains within it a largely unconscious logical framework consisting of notions of the self, of human being and action, drawn mostly from Post-Enlightenment, democratic-capitalist institutions." The core values of this culture would include liberty in the form of individual autonomy; economic, social, and political liberalism; utility and modern progress; pragmatic morality and the work ethic. All have fueled America's spectacular success on the world stage, but from the point of view of Roman Catholic anthropology and social ethics, which stress being over doing, all these values are at least potentially dangerous.

Though no Pope and no Vatican diplomat will ever come out and say so, the bottom line is that despite great respect for the American people and their democratic traditions, the Holy See simply does not think the United States is fit to run the world. As a country it is too rich, too narcissistic, too shortsighted and voluble, too young, to be entrusted with the quasi-unfettered power that twentieth-century history entrusted to it. To be sure, there aren't many countries around that the Holy See would approve for such a role. It should be said, too, that if the Vatican had to choose between a world run from Washington, D.C., and one run from Islamabad, or Bejing, there's little doubt they would opt for Washington. Yet that doesn't strike most Vatican thinkers as an especially appetizing choice. Thus the Holy See's diplomatic energy in coming years will have as a central aim the construction of a multilateral, multipolar world, which will necessarily imply a limitation on the power and influence of the United States. For that reason, and despite strong agreement on a host of issues, the relationship between Rome and Washington seems destined to be complex and sometimes strained.

APPENDIX

Resources for Understanding the Vatican

For readers seeking to follow Vatican news, there are a number of good resources both online and in print. This appendix will list several. Some represent a rather conservative view, some are institutional and moderate, a few rather liberal. The principle of selection here, however, is not ideology but utility. Whether you agree with the point of view or not, you will learn things from these resources that you didn't previously know.

ONLINE RESOURCES

The Word from Rome, John L. Allen Jr. (American):
www.nationalcatholicreporter.org/word/

Daily news bulletin of the Holy See (official Vatican site, in multiple languages):
www.vatican.va/news_services/bulletin/bollettino.php?lang=en

Catholic News Service (sponsored by the United States Conference of Catholic Bishops, a subscription service): www.catholicnews.com

WWW.Chiesa: News, Analyses, Documents, Sandro Magister (Italian, but also available in English): http://213.92.16.98/ESW_lista_chiesa/english/

Settimo Cielo, Sandro Magister, a blog service on Church affairs (Italian):
http://blog.espressonline.it/weblog/stories.php?topic=03/04/09/3080386

Union of Catholic Asian News (sponsored by the Federation of Asian Bishops
    Conferences, a subscription service):
    www.ucanews.com/html/uca/main.asp
Catholic World News (American, a subscription service):   •
    www.cwnews.com
Zenit (Italian): http://zenit.org/english/english.phtml
Noticias Eclesiales (Spanish): www.eclesiales.org/index.html
Katholische Nachrichten-Agentur (sponsored by the German bishops, a
    subscription service): www.kna.de
Independent Catholic News (English):
    www.indcatholicnews.com/headline.html
Katholischer Nachrichtendienst (sponsored by the Austrian bishops, in
    German): www.kath.net
CathNews (Australian): www.cathtelecom.com
Ansa (leading Italian news wire, a subscription service): www.ansa.it
Servizio Informazione Religiosa, SIR (Italian):
    www.agensir.it/sirs2/s2magazine/index.jsp?idPagina=1
Fides (official news agency of the Congregation for the Evangelization of
    Peoples, in multiple languages): www.fides.org/eng/index.html

PUBLICATIONS
English
Catholic World Report (American, monthly):
    www.ignatius.com/Magazines/CWRCurrentIssue.asp
First Things (American, monthly): www.firstthings.com
Inside the Vatican (American, monthly): www.insidethevatican.com
The National Catholic Reporter (American, weekly): www.natcath.org
The Tablet (English, weekly): www.thetablet.co.uk/index.shtml

Italian
Adista (twice-weekly news bulletin): www.adista.it
Corriere della Sera (leading daily in Italy): www.corriere.it
Jesus (monthly): www.stpauls.it/jesus
L'Avvenire (official daily newspaper of the Italian bishops' conference):
    www.avvenire.it

L'Osservatore Romano (daily Vatican newspaper):
   www.vatican.va/news_services/or/home_eng.html
La Repubblica (daily): www.repubblica.it
Il Messaggero (daily): http://ilmessaggero.caltanet.it/

F r e n c h
La Croix (daily): www.la-croix.com/index.jsp

G e r m a n
Stimmen der Zeit (monthly): www.stimmen-der-zeit.de/c_aktuell.htm

INDEX

Thomas Aquinas, St., 76
Thompson, Tommy, 366–67
Thoolen, Fr. Frans, 10
Time as Vatican value, 103–4, 130–36
Tonini, Cardinal Ersilio, 171
Toward a New Catholic Church (Carroll),
    240
Tradition as Vatican value, 136–40
Tribunals, 34–35
True and False Reform in the Church
    (Congar), 309
Turner, Ted, 258

Union of Superiors General (USG), 273
United Nations
    High Commission for Refugees, 148
    Human Rights Commission, 183
    Iraq war and, 314, 325, 332, 349–50,
        356, 368
    Vatican support for, 186–87, 373,
        375–77
United States
    flashpoints in U.S.-Vatican relationship,
        370–78
    Vatican attitude toward U.S. culture,
        315–17, 377–78
    See also American sexual abuse crisis;
        Iraq war
Universi Dominici Gregis (Church
    document), 207, 212
Urban II, Pope, 40
Urquhart, Gordon, 162
U.S. Catholic Mission Association, 335
Ut Unum Sint (Church document), 191,
    210, 310–11

Values of the Vatican. *See* Psychology of
    the Vatican
Vanunu, Mordechai, 183
Vatican, the
    artistic treasures owned by, 81–82
    authorship of documents, policy
        regarding, 119
    careerism within, 83–89, 158–59
    central administrative system, Church's
        need for, 16–17
    communications operation, 6, 48–49
    decentralized decision making, 64–70
    diplomatic service, 24, 45–48
    diversity within, 57–64

employees of, 27
finances of, 56, 78–83
Holy See, 23–24, 27
income sources, 80
mail, handling of, 122–23, 136
parishes (informal networks), 114
personnel policy, 141–44
political influence, 169–72
"scandal" as understood by, 101–2
secrecy within, 70–78, 119–20
Synod of Bishops, 50–52, 71–72,
    219–20
United Nations, support for, 186–87,
    373, 375–77
U.S. culture, attitude toward, 315–17,
    377–78
U.S.-Vatican relationship, flashpoints
    in, 370–78
Vatican City-State, 24–27
See also American sexual abuse crisis;
    Iraq war; Myths about the Vatican;
    Papacy; Psychology of the Vatican;
    Roman Curia; Sociology of the
    Vatican; Theology of the Vatican
Vatican Bank, 78, 81
Vatican Radio, 48, 169, 170
Vatican TV Center, 48
Vienna Convention on Diplomatic
    Relations, 24
Vittorio Emmanuel, King, 25
Voice of the Faithful, 230, 305, 306, 308

Waldenfels, Hans, 107
Weakland, Archbishop Rembert, 65, 66,
    226
Website of the Vatican, 48–49
Weeke, Stephen, 244
Weigel, George, 10, 239–40, 314
Whelan, Fr. Barry, 129
Wildenstein, Daniel, 81
Willey, David, 193
Women
    ordination issue, 109
    Roman Curia, participation in, 219
World Youth Day of 2000, 166, 167–68
Wuerl, Bishop Donald, 130, 235

Xaverian Missionaries, 125

Yallop, David, 78